In Search of Equality

In Search of Equality

The Chinese Struggle against Discrimination in Nineteenth-Century America

CHARLES J. McCLAIN

University of California Press

BERKELEY LOS ANGELES LONDON

University of California Press
Berkeley and Los Angeles, California

University of California Press, Ltd.
London, England

Library of Congress Cataloging-in-Publication Data

McClain, Charles J.
In Search of equality : the Chinese struggle against discrimination in nineteenth-century America / by Charles J. McClain.
p. cm.
Includes bibliographical references and index.
ISBN 0-520-08337-7 (alk. paper)
1. Chinese Americans—Legal status, laws, etc.—History.
I. Title.
KF4757.5.C47M37 1994
346.7301'3—dc20
[347.30613] 93-4942
CIP

Printed in the United States of America
9 8 7 6 5 4 3 2 1

The paper used in this publication meets the minimum requirements of American National Standard for Information Sciences—Permanence of Paper for Printed Library Materials, ANSI Z39.48-1984. ♾

To my father,
Charles J. McClain,
and the memory of my mother,
Loretta Cahill McClain,
and to my wife, Laurene,
and son, Christopher

Contents

Acknowledgments

I have been at work on this project, off and on, for a good number of years and have incurred a good number of debts along the way. Several friends and colleagues have read all or parts of this manuscript and have given me the benefit of their comments and criticisms: Patty Blum, Robert Berring, Sucheng Chan, Robert Kagan, Him Mark Lai, Kristin Luker, Paul Mishkin, Harry N. Scheiber, Aviam Soifer, and Ling-chi Wang. I received valuable research assistance at the beginning of this project from Maureen Young and at the end from Torrey Shanks. I have been blessed with the services of two excellent translators cum research assistants, Winnie Wong and Kit Chui. Henry So, associate librarian at Boalt Hall, has also come to my assistance repeatedly with translations. Michael Griffith, historian/archivist of the U.S. District Court for the Northern District of California, has been an invaluable source of advice on tracking down court records. At various times I have been greatly assisted by the reference staffs of the Bancroft Library, Boalt Hall Library, and Asian American Studies Library, University of California at Berkeley, the law library, University of California at Davis, the National Archives, San Francisco Branch, the California State Library, the California State Archives, and the Library of the San Francisco Theological Seminary, San Anselmo, California. Thanks are due also to my editors at the University of California Press, Naomi Schneider and Dore Brown, for their patience and skill in shepherding this work through to publication and to Steve Gilmartin, my copyeditor, for the many valuable suggestions he made for its improvement.

I am greatly indebted to the National Endowment for the Humanities for a grant that allowed me to take a year off from administrative and teaching duties to do research on this project. For the support and encouragement they have given me over the years I wish to thank Sanford Kadish and Jesse Choper, former deans of the law school at Berkeley, the present dean, Herma Hill Kay, and the several chairs of the Jurisprudence and Social Policy Program with whom I have worked: Harry N. Scheiber, Sheldon Messinger, and Daniel Rubinfeld. I would like too to acknowledge the administrative assistance of Rod Watanabe and the help that Margo Rodriguez, Leslie Farrer, and Celia Ronis have given me in preparing parts of the manuscript.

The last and most important debt of gratitude I wish to acknowledge is to my wife, Laurene Wu McClain. She has assisted me with some of the research, has carefully read and commented on much of the text, and has given me her unstinting support and the benefit of her wise counsel throughout the project's duration.

I am grateful to the editors of the relevant journals for permission to use in revised form all or portions of the following previously published articles: "The Chinese Struggle for Civil Rights in 19th Century America: The First Phase, 1850–1870," *California Law Review* 72 (1984): 529–68, copyright 1984, California Law Review Inc.; "The Chinese Struggle for Civil Rights in Nineteenth-Century America: The Unusual Case of *Baldwin v. Franks,*" *Law and History Review* 3, no. 2 (Fall 1985): 349–73; "*In Re Lee Sing:* The First Residential Segregation Case," *Western Legal History* 3, no. 2 (Summer/Fall, 1990): 179–96, copyright the Ninth Judicial Circuit Historical Society; "Of Medicine, Race and American Law: The Bubonic Plague Outbreak of 1900," *Law and Social Inquiry: Journal of the American Bar Foundation* 3, no. 3 (1988): 447–513, copyright 1988, American Bar Association.

Introduction

I came to work on the subject of this book in a somewhat roundabout fashion. I teach constitutional history and have long had a special interest in the constitutional history of the United States in the period immediately following the Civil War. Some years ago I set about to do a short piece on the Supreme Court's treatment of the equal protection clause of the Fourteenth Amendment during this period. That provision of the amendment provides that "no State shall deny to any person within its jurisdiction the equal protection of the laws." The project led me to the well-known 1886 United States Supreme Court case of *Yick Wo v. Hopkins,* still one of the leading cases on the meaning and purport of that provision. There the Supreme Court had under consideration a challenge by a group of Chinese laundrymen to a San Francisco ordinance that required all operators of laundries in wooden buildings to obtain permits from the city's board of supervisors. The laundrymen alleged that the ordinance was being used routinely to deny Chinese applicants laundry permits and that its passage was a mere pretext for driving all Chinese out of the laundry business. The Supreme Court found merit in the laundrymen's contentions and held that the ordinance as applied violated the equal protection clause of the Fourteenth Amendment. As I reflected on the case, it occurred to me that it was as interesting for its socio-historical as for its legal-historical import. It certainly called into question the conventional image of the Chinese that one encountered in the history books.

The Chinese, I think it is safe to say, occupy at best an obscure niche in the historical consciousness of the average educated American. Most know that thousands of Chinese immigrants came to the West Coast in the second half of the nineteenth century—initially to work California's newly opened gold fields, later to labor on the construction of the transcontinental railroad and in other trades. Most know as well that their presence came to arouse hostility in the white population and that this hostility was eventually translated into discriminatory local and national legislation. But there general familiarity ends. This is not at all surprising. Most accounts of the great Chinese immigration to the United States in the nineteenth century have concentrated almost exclusively on the reaction it provoked in the white population.[1] They have tended to ignore the Chinese and their perception of their experience in this country. As one of the leading historians of anti-Orientalism in California, Roger Daniels, has put it, "Other immigrant groups were celebrated for what they had accomplished; Orientals were important for what was done to them."[2]

Those relatively few scholarly writings that have focused on the Chinese community, until very recently at any rate, have tended to be deprecatory, emphasizing what is usually described as the authoritarian structure of Chinese-American society; the corruption or ineptitude of the leadership; and the passivity, docility, and otherworldliness of the Chinese masses. These writings make much of what they see as the unique character of the Chinese immigration. The Chinese who came to this country, so the argument goes, had no desire to settle or assimilate, wishing only to accumulate a quick fortune and return home.[3] One historian, Gunther Barth, even suggests that it was this feature of their immigration that was most responsible for the misfortunes that were visited upon them. According to this thesis—one which, I hasten to add, I view as untenable—white Californians offered the hand of welcome to the newcomers from Asia but saw their overtures of goodwill rebuffed. They then turned on the Chinese and determined to exclude them from the privileges and obligations they extended to other immigrants.[4]

Two related views are that the nineteenth-century Chinese immigrants were utterly unacquainted with American political institutions and that they passively submitted to discrimination. U.S. Supreme Court Justice Stephen Field, who, as we shall see, should have known better, observed in 1884, "Our institutions have made no impression on [the Chinese] during the more than thirty years they have been in this country."[5] And Barth argues that the Chinese community failed to appreciate the severity of the legal restrictions under which it operated or to respond to them in any significant way.[6] On this view the Chinese were, in the words of the early twentieth-century historian of California, Robert Glass Cleland, a group of people "who suffered with helpless stoicism whatever indignities were thrust upon [them]."[7]

But *Yick Wo* could hardly be seen as an instance of a people suffering indignities with helpless stoicism. It was clearly an example of resistance to perceived discrimination. Furthermore, it took little rummaging around in the federal and state case reports to realize that it was but one of many cases brought by the Chinese during the nineteenth century. Indeed between 1880 and 1900 Chinese litigants carried some twenty appeals to the Supreme Court of the United States. Furthermore, I discovered, one could find examples of the Chinese protesting discriminatory treatment dating back to the very infancy of the immigration. Knowing that the Presbyterians had been active in the San Francisco Chinese community, I visited the San Francisco Theological Seminary, a Presbyterian institution in San Anselmo, California. There I found an extraordinary series of letters, indicating that the leaders of the Chinese community had in 1860 asked a churchman to help them find a lobbyist to speak on their behalf against anti-Chinese legislation then being considered by the state legislature. (I discuss this incident in detail in chapter 1.) *Yick Wo*, in fine, was but the small tip of a very large iceberg.

The thesis of this book is that the conventional wisdom concerning the Chinese and their supposed political backwardness needs to be stood on its head. The nineteenth-century Chinese-American community may, because of language, have been more isolated from mainstream society than other immigrant groups in certain respects, but lack of political consciousness was not one of its distinguishing characteristics. As this account will demonstrate, there is abundant evidence that the leaders of the nineteenth-century Chinese community—and many other Chinese as well—were thoroughly familiar with American governmental institutions, the courts in particular, and knew how to use those institutions to protect themselves. Far from being passive or docile in the face of official mistreatment, they reacted with indignation to it and more often than not sought redress in the courts. Indeed during the second half of the nineteenth century, the Chinese mounted court challenges to virtually every governmentally imposed disability under which they labored. Why a fact so obvious and so important as this should have been so largely ignored by American historiography shall always remain to me something of a mystery. The Chinese readiness to resort to the courts to remedy perceived wrongs is an aspect of their experience in the United States barely touched on in the published literature. Yet it is surely one of the most salient and defining features of that experience. To ignore it would be comparable to ignoring the many legal contests of black Americans. It would be as if an historian of African America should, after surveying the long, shameful treatment of blacks, ask why, in the midst of so much persecution did these people never think of going to court to defend themselves.

To ignore Chinese legal initiatives is, as well, to ignore an important facet of U.S. constitutional history in general. The cases brought by the Chinese raised immensely interesting questions of constitutional and statutory interpretation. Many of them contributed significantly to the molding of American constitutional jurisprudence. The general neglect of this important episode in American legal history has, thankfully, begun to change in the last few years, during which time a number of articles devoted to the Chinese decisions of the federal courts in the American West have appeared in print. Among them are Linda C. A. Przybyszewski's "Judge Lorenzo Sawyer and the Chinese Civil Rights Decisions in the Ninth Circuit" and Lucy Salyer's "Captives of Law: Judicial Enforcement of the Chinese Exclusion Laws, 1891–1905." These are welcome additions to the literature, and one hopes more will follow.[8]

This book seeks to chronicle the nineteenth-century Chinese conflicts with Caucasian officialdom and to provide an interpretative framework for understanding them. To the extent the sources allow, it tries to keep the Chinese in the foreground of the account and to document their view of events. It conversely pays comparatively little attention to their opponents, the Sinophobes. That subject, I think, has been adequately dealt with by others.[9] The book may be seen then, in this respect, as part of a movement in the historiography of the Chinese immigration that has taken hold in recent years, one that tries to break free of stereotypes and to see the Chinese more as subjects and shapers than as objects of history. Much good work along these lines has been produced in recent years. I might make particular mention of *This Bittersweet Soil,* Sucheng Chan's exhaustively researched and richly textured study of the Chinese in California agriculture; *Chinese Gold,* Sandy Lydon's sensitive, evocative portrayal of the Chinese community in Monterey Bay; and finally the numerous scholarly writings of Him Mark Lai, one of the true pioneers of Chinese American historical studies.[10]

Scholars working on a project of this sort must confront the fact that much of the primary source material they would expect to consult seems irretrievably lost to history. The earthquake that struck San Francisco, the state's most important city, on April 18, 1906, and the fires that followed it destroyed all of Chinatown, virtually all of the city's business district, and many of the city's principal government buildings. Numerous relevant documentary materials were lost in the conflagration. These include important government documents, the records of the principal organizations of nineteenth-century Chinese America, and, it appears, essentially all of the personal papers, correspondence, and business records of the lawyers and other Caucasians who dealt with the Chinese. Because of the absence of these records we will never be able to have as complete a picture as we would like. However, we do have complete runs of all major California newspapers published during the period and virtually all relevant federal and state court files. As the reader will see, I have relied on these sources extensively. We also have scattered issues of nineteenth-century Chinese-language newspapers. In an effort to get at the Chinese viewpoint, I have had these issues scanned and relevant items translated. Though they are far fewer in number than one might wish, I have found many extraordinarily revealing items in them. How much more complete our understanding of the dynamics and diversity of the Chinese-American community would be if we had more primary sources is made clear in the last chapter. For the episode chronicled there—an outbreak of bubonic plague in Chinatown and the court cases it gave rise to—we have available a complete run of one Chinese-language paper and are consequently able to provide a much fuller account of the Chinese perspective on the events (or perhaps better put the Chinese "perspectives," for as the sources clearly show here this was not a monolithic community) than in the book's other chapters. Because of the incomplete state of the archival record I have from time to time had to fall back on what is probably best called informed speculation. I have, however, always tried to keep that speculation tethered in the sources, and I remain confident that the picture I have painted here is correct in its essential details.

This is the first book to appear in print on the topic of the Chinese and their struggles in the courts, but it is preceded by Hudson Janisch's solid doctoral dissertation on the subject, "The Chinese, the Courts and the Constitution."[11] This work, lengthy and comprehensive, gives proportionately greater emphasis to the Chinese battles with the federal government arising out of the exclusion laws than it does to their battles with state and local government—the mirror image of this work's emphasis. It does not make use of court files, other archival material or Chinese-language materials to the extent this book does. Nor does it offer the same conceptual framework for understanding the events in question. It is, however, a valuable and illuminating work.

I wish to make two general remarks in conclusion. First, as the reader will quickly notice, this work focuses almost entirely on California. California was of course not the only place where nineteenth-century Chinese immigrants settled. As the century wore on, Chinese could be found living in increasing numbers in other western states and indeed, toward the end of the century, outside the West entirely. I do not mean to suggest that their story is unimportant. In these places too the Chinese encountered hostile treatment and there too one can find examples of resistance to racial oppression. The story of the Chinese outside of California is itself an interesting story, some of which in recent years has begun to be told by scholars.[12] But California was throughout the nineteenth century the place where the vast majority of Chinese lived. It was also the great epicenter of Sinophobia and the place where virtually all of the great Chinese cases originated.

Second, the Chinese names used in this book are taken from court records and reports in English-language papers. They are in almost all instances reprinted here exactly as they appear in those sources. Since, with a few exceptions, we do not have the Chinese characters to compare them with, we cannot say whether the English transliterations that were used are accurate. It is possible—indeed likely—that in some instances the names that appear in the court cases discussed in this book are not the names of persons at all but fictitious business names. The evidence at hand, however, is fragmentary and not absolutely dispositive. Rather than going to the trouble of trying to reach a determination in each case, I have adopted the convention of treating all of the names that appear in the cases as if they were the names of individuals.

I

THE BEGINNINGS OF DISCRIMINATION AND THE FIRST CHINESE RESPONSES

1 California's First Anti-Chinese Laws

The Rise of Anti-Chinese Resentment

The first Chinese to arrive in California were greeted with a mixture of enthusiasm and curiosity. They were few in number and seemed a harmless and exotic addition to the cosmopolitan mass of humanity that was gathering in Northern California in the wake of the discovery of gold at Sutter's Mill. In August 1850, for example, on the occasion of the ceremonies held in San Francisco to observe the death of Zachary Taylor, the city fathers invited the local Chinese to send a contingent to participate in the rites and assigned it a prominent place in the funeral cortege.[1] Many local observers noted with great satisfaction the large Chinese presence two months later at the San Francisco celebrations of California's admission to the Union.[2] And in a January 1852 address to the California legislature, Governor John McDougal endorsed the importation of Chinese for the purpose of draining California's immense swamplands, describing them as "one of the most worthy classes of our newly adopted citizens—to whom the climate and the character of these lands are peculiarly suited."[3]

This spirit of hospitality lasted but a brief time, however. As the number of Chinese grew, their presence came to be deeply resented, especially in the state's mining districts where they concentrated. (As early as 1852 a San Francisco newspaper reported that leaders of the Chinese community in California were sending circulars to their countrymen in China, urging them not to come to California because of the growing anti-Chinese hostility in the state.)[4] Many explanations have been offered for the hostility, and no doubt there is a grain of truth in each of them. But a principal reason for the resentment was nicely stated in a most revealing passage from Theodore Hittell's *History of California*, published in 1898:

> As a class, [the Chinese] were harmless, peaceful and exceedingly industrious; but, as they were remarkably economical and spent little or none of their earnings except for the necessaries of life and this chiefly to merchants of their own nationality, they soon began to provoke the prejudice and ill-will of those who could not see any value in their labor to the country.[5]

In short, they worked too hard (often for less pay than others were willing to accept), saved too much, and spent too little. In addition, they looked and behaved differently from the majority population. Beneath all the surface rationalizations, this was to be the gravamen of the complaint against the Chinese through the many phases of the anti-Chinese movement in California.

Calls for Legislation

As early as 1852, agitation commenced in some of the mining regions to stem the inflow of Chinese workers and to expel those who were already settled. The agitation first bore fruit in a report issued in April 1852 by a California assembly committee.[6] The report identified as the preeminent evil threatening the well-being of the mining districts "the concentration, within our State limits, of vast numbers of the Asiatic races, and of the inhabitants of the Pacific Islands, and of many others dissimilar from ourselves in customs, language and education."[7] Most of these persons, the report stated, had not come to California voluntarily but rather had been imported as servile labor by foreign capitalists and were held to labor under contracts not recognized by American law.[8] They had no desire to become U.S. citizens (or if they did it was not wise to encourage them in this wish), and their presence demeaned American laborers already in California and deterred the immigration of additional (white) citizens. The report urged legislative action at the national and state levels to deal with the problem. Specifically it suggested that California might revive a tax it had once imposed on all alien miners in the state—the Foreign Miners' License Tax[9]—but might now differentiate between those who had declared their intention of becoming American citizens and those who had not.[10]

Governor Bigler's Message and the Chinese Reaction

Governor John Bigler, California's third chief executive, gave a much more powerful impetus to the anti-Chinese movement when, one week after the publication of the report, he delivered a special message to the legislature on the evils of the immigration from Asia.[11] Extraordinary measures were needed, the governor said, to "check [the] tide of Asiatic immigration"[12] which he saw threatening to inundate the state, especially the mining districts. He called particular attention to the widely held belief that the mass of the Chinese immigrants were bound to long contracts of indentured servitude ("coolie labor") and that in some cases their families in China were held hostage to the faithful performance of these contracts.[13]

The legislative program he recommended to stop immigration from Asia contained two main elements: a request to the Congress to enact a bill making contracts for "coolie labor" unenforceable and the enactment of a state taxation program that would fall heavily on the Chinese and thus tend to discourage their continued presence. He also suggested—though he did not push the point quite as hard—that the state had the right to use its police power to prohibit completely Chinese immigration into California or at the very least to bar the Chinese from working in the state's mines.[14] Most ominously, though he did not include such a proposal in the recommended legislative agenda, Bigler suggested that California's Asian immigrants, since they were indifferent to the solemn obligations of an oath, ought not to be allowed to serve as jurors or to testify in court.[15]

Though Bigler doubtless spoke for a large segment of the population,[16] his harangue did not go without opposition. For example, the state's leading newspaper, San Francisco's *Daily Alta California*, reacted quite coolly to the governor's proposals. In a lengthy commentary published the day after Bigler's message, the paper, while allowing that a vastly increased Chinese population might at some point pose problems for the state, refused to see the existing situation as troublesome or one that required urgent legislative attention.[17] It described the Chinese as being "as industrious, as moral, and as orderly as any other class of our population" and saw them as a net benefit to the state's economy. Finally, it expressed grave reservations about the wisdom and constitutionality of Bigler's legislative proposals.[18]

Significantly, a few days later the paper published an open letter to Bigler from one Norman Asing, a San Francisco Chinese merchant and self-described naturalized citizen and Christian.[19] Asing came right to the point:

> [T]he effects of your late message has been thus far to prejudice the public mind against my people, to enable those who wait the opportunity to hunt them down, and rob them of the rewards of their toil. You may not have meant that this should be the case, but you can see what will be the result of your propositions.[20]

He flatly denied that California had any right under the Constitution to restrict immigration and took strong issue with Bigler's assertion that the Chinese were ineligible to become American citizens. "The declaration of your independence, and all the acts of your government, your people, and your history, are against you," he wrote.[21] He expressed contempt for Bigler's characterization of the Chinese as a degraded and inferior race. The Chinese could be considered degraded, he said, only if the desire to work hard in an honest trade was degraded. And on the question of ethnic inferiority, Asing begged to remind the governor "that when your nation was a wilderness, and the nation from whom you sprung barbarous, we exercised most of the arts and virtues of civilized life."[22]

The First Discriminatory Taxes

No doubt partially in response to Bigler's message and the agitation in the mining districts against the Chinese and other foreign miners, the legislature passed a bill in May 1852 reenacting the Foreign Miners' License Tax.[23] The new measure—captioned, interestingly, "An Act to Provide for the Protection of Foreigners, and to define their liabilities and privileges"—set the license fee at $3 per month and directed that revenues be split equally between the state and the counties where the mines were located.[24] It denied access to the courts to anyone who did not have a license[25] and authorized the sheriffs or affected counties to appoint deputies to assist them in collecting the tax.[26]

In the same month the legislature enacted another measure that became known as the "commutation tax."[27] It is clear from the context of the times that this tax was aimed primarily at the Chinese, though like the miners' tax it did not mention them by name. But where the Foreign Miners' License Tax was implemented to burden the pursuit of the mining trade by the Chinese who were already in California (and thereby to give them incentive to leave), the commutation tax was designed to discourage their coming in the first place. The act, as amended the following year, required the masters of all vessels arriving at California ports to prepare a list of all foreign passengers, and the owners of the vessels to post a $500 bond for each of these passengers. The bond could be commuted by the payment of $5 to $50 per passenger.[28] Other provisions required the master to specify further whether any of the incoming passengers were mentally ill or disabled and empowered the mayor to require an additional bond in these cases.[29] In practice, the bond was routinely commuted by the payment of the $5 fee, the sum having been simply added as a surcharge to the basic price of passage. The Chinese passengers, in other words, bore the full burden of the act.

The Chinese District Associations Complain to the Legislature

At first, there was no notable opposition in the Chinese community to either the 1852 license legislation or the commutation tax. The Chinese were apparently willing to bear the taxes, which seemed relatively modest in amount and appeared to offer the prospect of defusing some of the animosity felt towards them by the state's majority population.[30] It was a mistaken calculation on their part. The anti-Chinese agitation continued unabated, especially in the gold-mining districts, and in the next session of the legislature several bills were introduced in the assembly to increase radically the amount of the license or to exclude foreigners completely from the mines. The bills were referred for consideration to the Committee on Mines and Mining Interests, which was also charged with the more general task of gathering information on the state's Chinese population. In what doubtless was an effort to head off the threat of draconian legislation, the heads of the Chinese community's four major district associations contacted the committee through their attorney and requested an interview.[31] The committee acceded to the request and scheduled a series of interviews with these representatives in San Francisco. The district associations were unquestionably the most important organizations in nineteenth-century Chinese America. We shall encounter them time and again in this book, and we must pause at this point to say a word by way of background about them.

Chinese immigrants to the United States came overwhelmingly from several discrete geographic districts in Kwangtung province in southeastern China. Though these districts were contiguous to one another, the inhabitants spoke different dialects of Cantonese and in one case—that of the people known as the *Hakka*—a different tongue entirely. They identified strongly with their places of origin and often harbored rather strong antagonisms toward residents of the other districts. Early in the history of the California settlement Chinese merchants from the various districts took the lead in establishing associations, known in Chinese as *hui-kuan* (literally "meeting halls") composed of their regional and linguistic compatriots. (During the nineteenth century, smaller village, surname, and subregional organizations developed under the umbrella of the *hui-kuan*.) The American *hui-kuan* appear to have been adaptations of ancient Chinese models. For centuries merchants, officials and others from the same cities or regions, brought by business or official duties to other parts of the country, had been in the habit of forming associations (known also in China as *hui-kuan*) for mutual aid and support. These organizations, it is significant to note, in addition to discharging some of the traditional functions of a benevolent association (offering a common place for socializing, providing for the burial of dead members) also had as a main purpose, as one of the first Western scholars to study them put it, the protection of their members against "the hostility of the natives" and "harsh dealing and oppression by the authorities of the place."[32]

Though the American *hui-kuan* differed from their counterparts in China in that they eventually came to be made up predominantly of laborers, they resembled them in most other respects. They were first and foremost mutual and benevolent associations, in the early years of the immigration providing temporary shelter and accommodation to the newly arrived, escorting them to the mining districts, and assisting them to find work. They would offer rewards when their members were killed and would arbitrate disputes among them, including disputes concerning mining claims. They also saw to it that the remains of the deceased were returned to China for proper burial in their home villages. The *hui-kuan* leaders eventually came to claim that every Chinese in California was, simply by virtue of geographic provenance, a member of some district association, and they came to insist that everyone pay an assessment, ranging from $4 to $10, to his *hui-kuan* before returning to China. (These departure fees appear to have been their principal source of income.) They enforced this requirement through an arrangement they had with the Pacific Mail Steamship Company under which Chinese returning to China had first to obtain exit permits from their district associations before being able to purchase tickets. It is worth mentioning, finally, that under their bylaws the *hui-kuan* could be called upon by creditors to prevent debtors from leaving the United States before they had paid their debts. It is unclear to what extent the *hui-kuan* used the exit permit arrangement as a means of enforcing debt repayment.

Although relations among the various *hui-kuan* were at times quite strained, the organizations did at an early date in the immigration form the habit of meeting and working together on matters of common concern, especially when it came to dealings with the Caucasian world. By the early 1860s an informal coordinating council consisting of officers of the individual *hui-kuan* had emerged. Since *hui-kuan* was usually rendered into English as "company," and since eventually there came to be six constituent district associations, this coordinating council came to be referred to by the Caucasian world as the Six Chinese Companies or the Chinese Six Companies.[33] Throughout the nineteenth century Caucasians accused the *hui-kuan* of importing Chinese laborers as indentured servants and renting them out to American capitalists, a charge which in my view is supported by no reliable evidence.

The early leaders of the *hui-kuan* were invariably merchants (later on they were usually titled scholars recruited from China), and one may legitimately ask whether these men always sought to represent the interests of the community as a whole.[34] They would, however, on more than a few occasions during the nineteenth century prove themselves capable of acting vigorously to assert community rights when confronted with threats from the Caucasian world. The meeting in 1853 with the Committee on Mines and Mining Interests was the first such occasion.

The committee's report of its interviews with the *hui-kuan* leaders[35] offers compelling evidence of the well-developed political sensitivity of the Chinese community leadership even at this early date. (The very fact that the men had retained counsel bears witness to this fact itself, of course.) The representatives of the district associations came well prepared for these meetings.[36] They supplied copious information on the size, makeup, and social organization of the Chinese community in California. They vigorously disputed the charge (one that would be made repeatedly during the nineteenth century) that they were importing laborers and holding them in a condition of indentured servitude. They painted a very roseate picture (no doubt too roseate) of the democratic character of Chinese-American society and the benevolence of its leadership.[37] Referring to the committee's legislative agenda, the association leaders offered a proposal which they averred might persuade the people of the mining counties that the Chinese presence among them was a benefit rather than a burden. They expressed no opposition to an increase in the miners' tax if the legislature felt it was necessary, but they did suggest that the revenue so generated be left entirely with the counties where it was collected rather than be split with the state.[38]

They also laid boldly and frankly before the committee a list of grievances of which they said their countrymen complained. Chief among them was the increasing violence to which they were being subjected in the mining districts. The several association houses had kept records of the numerous instances of violent attacks on Chinese by white miners, and the committee, based on its own observations, attested to the correctness of these reports.[39] The association leaders complained, too, of a large number of instances in which courts of justice had not accepted the testimony and statements of Chinese witnesses because of the color of their skin. It was wrong, they declared, for the state to tax them and at the same time to withhold "that protection which is implied in the payment of taxes."[40] A point on which they were quite insistent was, in the committee's words, "that some settled and certain policy should be pursued towards their people [so] their persons and property may in *fact* [emphasis in original] as well as in law, occupy that same position as the persons and property of other foreigners."[41] It was a point that they would make time and again and that they would eventually see embodied both in statute and in court decision.

If the *hui-kuan* leaders' appeal to the committee's sense of justice and equity was not enough, the men also sought to appeal to the committee members' more worldly concerns. They assured the committee that if the Chinese grievances were addressed, "trade and commerce between the two countries [would] increase, . . . capital now lying dormant in China . . . [would] here seek investment in private trade and public improvements, and in fact [in] everything in the State that gives fair promise of its safe and profitable employment."[42]

The intervention of the heads of the *hui-kuan* was to good—albeit temporary—effect. The committee urged rejection of the proposals for radical change in the license laws. The tone and thrust of the report contrasted markedly with the committee's report of the previous year. The majority considered groundless the apprehension felt by some that the Chinese would soon inundate the state and crowd out the white population.[43] Moreover, the legislators thought it a libel on the national character to suggest that Americans could not compete with Asian immigrants.[44] The report also spoke of the detrimental effects that anti-Chinese legislation might have on trade with China which both the state and national governments were interested in promoting.[45] Ultimately, the committee recommended only that the monthly license fee be increased by $1,[46] a recommendation that the full legislature duly enacted into law.[47]

New Hostility and New Responses

The Chinese were not long able to savor this modest legislative success. Anti-Chinese hostility was—at this phase of its history—like a stubborn brushfire, whose flames could be dampened but never quite put out. And manifestations of hostility were not limited to the mining districts. One finds, for example, in an issue of the *Golden Hills News*, one of the few issues of a San Francisco Chinese-language newspaper from this early period that have survived, an advertisement announcing formation of a translation service for the purpose of communicating complaints about Caucasian mistreatment to the government. "Americans in this city," the notice reads, "have abused and humiliated Chinese unreasonably." It then goes on to urge Chinese who have been "teased, injured or deceived" by Americans to report the incident to the service so that a translation may be made and sent on to the government. "Hopefully," the notice says, "this will prevent mistreatment from being repeated."[48] In its very next session the legislature amended the original mining laws to exempt from the licensing requirement those who had declared their intention to become American citizens (as noted earlier, the general understanding at the time was that the Chinese were ineligible for naturalization).[49] On the same day, May 13, 1854, it passed a concurrent resolution, requesting California's congressional delegation to seek congressional authorization for a California statute that would impose a direct capitation tax on all natives of China and Japan entering the state.[50]

The following year brought further legislative action. Furious, ugly agitation in the mining regions, especially Shasta County, prompted both houses of the legislature in 1855 to empanel select committees to examine again the question of Chinese miners. The assembly committee recommended that the Chinese be flatly barred from working in the mines of California.[51] This unsubtle proposal proved too extreme to win the assent of either house, but the measure enacted was only slightly less severe. It provided for an increase in the license fee to $6 per month for foreigners ineligible to become citizens, effective October 1, 1855, and a ratcheting up an additional $2 per month on October 1 of each succeeding year ad infinitum.[52] If a sudden expulsion of the Chinese from the mines offended the scruples of too many legislators, the use of confiscatory taxation to gradually squeeze them out over time apparently did not.

The legislature also moved to discourage further immigration of new Chinese miners. On April 28, 1855, Governor Bigler approved a bill captioned "An Act to Discourage the Immigration to this State of Persons Who Cannot Become Citizens Thereof," which imposed on the master or owner of each vessel landing passengers "incompetent by the laws of the United States or the laws and constitution of this State to become citizens thereof" a tax of $50 for each such passenger.[53] As noted, less than a year earlier the legislature, doubtless aware of the serious constitutional questions raised by a direct state tax on immigration,[54] had urged California's representatives in Congress to solicit the national government's approval for the enactment of such a law.[55] However, it apparently was in no mood to wait very long for a reply and decided to take direct action itself. The 1855 session was perhaps the high-water mark of anti-Chinese sentiment in the legislature for the entire decade.[56]

The 1855 anti-Chinese measures were enacted impetuously, in response to the impassioned pleadings of a rather small, but very vocal, sector of the population. Others were not long in voicing their displeasure. Edward McGowan, the state's commissioner of immigrants, informed the legislature that some provisions of the capitation tax were unconstitutional and that he had no intention of enforcing them.[57] And in February 1856 some one hundred San Francisco merchants sent the legislature a memorial supporting the commissioner and decrying the policy of discouraging Chinese immigration as detrimental to the interests of the state.[58] Finally, the shipping companies which stood to sustain enormous financial losses if the act were enforced[59] determined to challenge the measure in court. The outcome was hardly in doubt, and in 1857, when *People v. Downer*[60] came before the California Supreme Court, it took the justices less than half a page of the reports to void the measure as an impermissible interference with the national government's exclusive power to regulate foreign commerce.

The *Downer* decision did not prevent the legislature from taking up the very next year a bill to flatly prohibit the immigration of any more Chinese into the state through any of its ports. The Committee on Federal Relations, to which the measure was referred for consideration, reported back that it saw nothing standing in the way of enactment. The states had the right to exclude persons they thought detrimental to their welfare, and the Chinese fit this description. Their "habits, manners, and appearance are disgusting in the extreme," it said, and it compared their influx into the mining districts to a visitation by the locusts of Egypt. The committee was convinced, it said, "that California is peculiarly the country of the white man and that we should exclude the inferior races." It recommended passage of the bill without amendment as the most effective way to stem any further Chinese immigration. Chinese already here could be forced to leave, it said, by "the enactment of stringent laws."[61] The bill was duly enacted into law[62] but was struck down by the California Supreme Court in an unpublished opinion when the first attempt to enforce it was made.[63]

A Successful Effort to Lower the Miners' Tax

The drastic increase in the miners' tax also provoked considerable disquiet after the public realized its full effects. Since enactment of the first foreign miners' license legislation the Chinese had been faithfully and punctually paying their license fees and, not incidentally, had been enriching the treasuries of both the state and many of its counties.[64] Many people, even in the mining counties, began to wonder whether it was altogether wise for state and local governments to drive the Chinese out through excessive taxes, thereby depriving themselves of a steady, reliable source of revenue. The legislature soon began receiving calls from the mining districts asking for reconsideration of the harsh mining license legislation. Representatives of the state's business classes, convinced that the immigration represented the opening phase of a potentially limitless commercial intercourse with the Chinese Empire, began to urge reconsideration as well. And for the first time Protestant missionaries began to speak out on behalf of the Chinese. Chief among these was the Reverend William Speer.

Speer was a Presbyterian missionary who had labored in China for several years before voyaging to San Francisco in 1852 to open a mission. He was fluent in Cantonese and quickly became a friend and confidant of the leaders of the local Chinese community. Like many Protestant missionaries of the era, he harbored hopes of Christianizing the immigrant masses and seeing them return to China to spread the good word among their fellow countrymen. Like many as well, he was capable of being quite patronizing toward the Chinese, but, unlike most, he counterbalanced this with a thorough understanding of Chinese history and an appreciation for the grand cultural attainments of Chinese civilization.[65] He was deeply conservative in his political values, and one of the things that attracted him most in the Chinese was their thrift and willingness to work hard.[66] He was, above all, genuinely repelled by the coarse racial demagoguery of the anti-Chinese movement and spoke out against it repeatedly during his four-year sojourn in California. He appears on the whole to have been a thoroughly decent man and proved a cogent, eloquent, and effective advocate on behalf of the Chinese.[67]

In January 1855, Speer began to publish a newspaper, the *Oriental* (*Tung-ngai san-luk*), which appeared thrice weekly in a bilingual edition and on a daily basis in Chinese for the next two years. The paper contained its share of moral uplift literature and unvarnished sectarian propaganda, but it considered as equally important missions the refinement of American feeling toward the Chinese and the overturning of hostile legislation. It campaigned actively in these causes as well. Speer spoke out against the mining legislation of 1855 both in the *Oriental* and in a special pamphlet which he prepared and had circulated in Sacramento.[68] He offered testimony from certain miners' license fee collectors that the fees were already oppressing many Chinese miners[69] and pleaded that they be reduced again to $4 per month.[70] Any policy aimed at excluding or debasing Chinese immigration, he argued, was detrimental to the interests of the state and unworthy of the people of a great nation.[71]

In response to lobbying of this sort, bills were introduced in the 1856 session of the legislature to repeal the 1855 law and to reduce the Foreign

Miners' License Tax to $4 per month. The standing mining committees of both houses took up the measures and issued separate reports recommending reduction of the tax.[72] In tone the two reports, however, were as night and day, and they stand again as testimony to the divided, fluid, and changeable character of political opinion on the Chinese question at the time.[73] The senate document breathed a spirit of openness and sympathy for the Chinese. It spoke of "the presence of this unfortunate people in our midst,"[74] reminded the legislature that the Chinese had come to California by implied invitation at least, and commented that it ill became "a proud, powerful, and magnanimous nation to oppress any one, least of all a class of defenseless strangers." It pointed out as well that it was especially mean-spirited to begrudge the Chinese miners their gains since they worked generally in marginal diggings that had been abandoned by other miners.[75]

The assembly report, by contrast, while it endorsed a lowering of the tax, was thoroughly hostile to the Chinese. Their presence, it said, was "neither beneficial nor desirable: but on the contrary, highly detrimental to the welfare, safety and happiness of the State."[76] Elsewhere, the report described them as a "distinct and inferior race,"[77] "horribly depraved," and "verily a nation of liars . . . unworthy of credit."[78] The report even foreshadowed the soon-to-become familiar charge that the Chinese dishonored and degraded labor.[79] On April 19, 1856, the legislature repealed the act of 1855 and reset the foreign miners' license fee at its former level of $4 per month.[80]

People v. Hall

If increases in the miners' tax increase threatened the ability of Chinese to earn a living, a decision that came down from the California Supreme Court in December 1854 represented a threat, quite literally, to life and limb. As noted, Chinese leaders as early as 1853 had complained to the legislature about the refusal of certain state courts to hear the testimony of Chinese witnesses. Concern heightened as the number of crimes committed against Chinese in the mining districts increased and as the conviction deepened that potential perpetrators were being emboldened by the likelihood that their victims would be forever unable to testify against them.

In August 1853, the grand jury of Nevada County returned an indictment against George W. Hall and two others for the murder of one Ling Sing.[81] In October, a four-day trial was held, during which three Chinese and one Caucasian testified on behalf of the state, with the Reverend Speer, especially recruited for the purpose, acting as interpreter.[82] The prosecutor was county District Attorney William M. Stewart, a man who would later be elected one of Nevada's first two senators and become a dominant figure in the state's politics for half a century. The jury returned a verdict of guilty, and Hall was sentenced to be hanged. Even though no exceptions were taken during the trial to hearing the Chinese witnesses, counsel for the defendant appealed the verdict on the grounds that their testimony was prohibited under Section 14 of the state's Criminal Proceedings Act, which provided: "No black or mulatto person, or Indian, shall be permitted to give evidence in favor of, or against, any white person."[83] For the first time the question of the testimonial capacity of Chinese immigrants was presented to the state's highest court for authoritative adjudication.

Chief Justice Hugh C. Murray, in an opinion containing some of the most offensive racial rhetoric to be found in the annals of California appellate jurisprudence, held that the Chinese testimony had been improperly received and the conviction must be reversed.[84] The decision rested on three grounds: on canons of statutory construction, as the court purported to understand them; on a kind of amateur foray into history and ethnography; and on what the court called a public policy consideration.

The court first purported to construe the meaning of the terms in the Criminal Proceedings Act. Relying on its understanding of history, the court reasoned that upon touching ground at San Salvador, Columbus thought that he had found "an island in the Chinese Sea," lying near the extremity of India. Acting on this supposition, he had given the islanders the name "Indians." "From that time, down to a very recent period," wrote the court, "the American Indians and the Mongolian, or Asiatic, were regarded as the same type of the human species."[85] Scientists, the court continued, had until quite recently believed that Indians and Asians came from the same ethnic stock.[86] While granting that most scientists no longer believed that North America had originally been populated by immigrants from Asia, the court said that California law was based on earlier enacted legislation from other states that had clearly treated Chinese and Indians as being of the same stock.[87] Further, even assuming that Asians were not the same as Indians, the word "black" in the statute, said the court, must be understood in the generic sense as excluding all races other than Caucasians.[88]

Finally, quite apart from reasons of statutory construction, Murray stated that he felt compelled to reach his decision on public policy grounds. If the Chinese were admitted to the witness stand, he wrote, we would "soon see them at the polls, in the jury box, upon the bench, and in our legislative halls,"[89] a prospect that must have filled him with something bordering on horror since he considered the Chinese "[a people] whose mendacity is proverbial; a race . . . nature has marked as inferior, and . . . incapable of progress or intellectual development beyond a certain point."[90] The court, confronted with an odious law, had chosen to expand rather than restrict its application.[91]

Reaction to the Decision

The Chinese reacted quickly and vocally to the *Hall* decision. Lai Chun-chuen, a prominent San Francisco merchant, attacked the decision in an open letter to Governor Bigler prepared in January 1855, primarily in response to an anti-Chinese speech by the governor.[92] On *Hall* the letter was indignant and characteristically ethnocentric:

> [O]f late days, your honorable people have established a new practice. They have come to the conclusion that we Chinese are the same as Indians and Negroes, and your courts will not allow us to bear witness. And yet these Indians know nothing about the relations of society; they know no mutual respect; they wear neither clothes nor shoes; they live in wild places and in caves.[93]

The Chinese, by contrast, had a record of thousands of years of civilization.[94] The decision to bar Chinese testimony by equating them with blacks and Indians, said Lai, could not have been the result of "enlightened intelligence and enlarged liberality."[95] Nor was reaction confined to the merchant strata of Chinese-American society. The minority report of a state senate committee noted, for example, that there was widespread resentment in the Chinese community at the refusal of courts to allow them to testify.[96]

As was to be expected, Speer's *Oriental* editorialized vigorously against the supreme court decision in *Hall*. "The principles of Magna Charta, the prerogatives of juries, the rights of judges and advocates, Republicanism, Christianity, and common humanity are all outraged by this iniquitous decision of the Supreme Court of California," thundered Speer.[97] But Speer's was not the only Caucasian voice to be heard speaking on behalf of the Chinese. In fact the ban on Chinese testimony was a source of deep embarrassment to the more civilized elements of white society, and some of the leading organs of Caucasian opinion, to their credit, spoke out forthrightly against it.[98] Protests, however, were to no avail, and in 1863 the legislature added insult to injury by codifying the *Hall* decision[99] and extending the principle to civil cases as well.[100]

Of all the wrongs visited upon the Chinese in the period from 1850 to 1870, the ban on their testimony in the state's courts—not surprisingly, given its fateful implications—rankled most deeply, and the removal of this disability was consistently the chief item on the agenda of the community leadership. (The ban, it should be stressed, applied only to the state courts. The United States District Court for the Northern District of California had begun to receive Chinese testimony on an unrestricted basis as early as 1851 and continued to do so throughout the period.)[101] Speer informed the California legislature in 1857, in a pamphlet aimed at overturning *Hall,* that the testimony ban was "a rock of offence" to the Chinese population and the "greatest stumbling block" preventing them from fully enjoying California's prosperity.[102]

The Chinese Hire a Lobbyist

Particularly interesting evidence not only of Chinese sensitivity on the subject but of a determination to do something about it is found in two remarkable letters written in January 1860 by the Reverend A. W. Loomis, Speer's successor as head of the San Francisco mission to the Chinese, to the Presbyterian Board of Foreign Missions in Philadelphia. In the first of these letters,[103] Loomis wrote that he had been approached the previous Sunday after services by six Chinese, representing the Chinese district associations, who said that they had some matters that they wished to lay before him. He related that he tried to put them off but that under pressure he agreed to meet with them the next day. At the meeting they told him that his predecessor, Speer, had routinely interested himself in political matters affecting the Chinese and that they now wished Loomis's assistance. They told him specifically, Loomis wrote, that "they would like some laws altered, especially those excluding Chinamen from the privilege of testifying in the courts" and requiring payment of the miners' tax.[104] Loomis related that, while he did not wish to become too involved in politics, he did inform the Chinese leaders that he would try to be of assistance and that in the meantime they should write up petitions expressing their grievances. He told the Board of Foreign Missions that what the Chinese needed was "a good man to lobby for them" in the legislature and that he intended to see if he could locate such a person.[105]

At the end of the month Loomis wrote again to his superiors in Pennsylvania to inform them of the results of his efforts. In this letter,[106] he announced that he had found a lawyer—indeed a former city judge[107]—to attend to the interests of the Chinese in Sacramento, that the heads of the company houses had agreed to his terms,[108] and that the lawyer had already commenced work in the state capital. Loomis's later correspondence with the Board of Foreign Missions makes no further reference to the arrangement,[109] and so one cannot say for how long a period the lawyer-lobbyist remained the Chinese representative in Sacramento. The episode, however, clearly demonstrates the well-developed political consciousness of some Chinese (here the leadership of the most important organizations in the community) at this very early period in the history of the immigration and their willingness to make aggressive use of American institutions to protect Chinese interests. Three cases decided by the California Supreme Court bear witness to the same phenomenon. Two of these arose in the mining districts and involved challenges to the still resented, even if lowered, foreign miners' tax. The third involved a challenge to another discriminatory tax.

Chinese Court Victories in the Mining Districts

Ex parte Ah Pong[110] was a habeas corpus action brought by a Chinese laundryman from El Dorado County. An 1861 revision in the foreign miners' license law had declared that *all* foreigners who were ineligible for citizenship but resided in the mining districts would be considered miners for purposes of the act; they were thus made liable to the tax.[111] The county tax collector had sought to collect the tax from Ah Pong, but he had refused and thereupon been ordered to work on the county roads until the sum was paid off. Upon his refusal to work, he was prosecuted, convicted, and sentenced to twenty days' imprisonment.[112] After his application for a writ of habeas corpus to the county judge of El Dorado County was denied, he applied to the state supreme court, which issued the writ and ordered the case heard on the merits.[113] The petitioner's counsel argued to the court that the statute violated the state constitution on a number of grounds, principally because it was irrational and arbitrary. The court agreed that the petitioner was unjustly imprisoned but chose to sidestep the constitutional question and base its decision on its own somewhat curious construction of the statute. In a terse but unanimous opinion, it ruled that the act could not possibly be held as applying to the petitioner, whatever it seemed by its terms to say. The mere fact that he was Chinese and living in the mining district, it held, could not subject him, a laundryman, to something designated the Foreign Miners' License Tax. "If the act is to be construed as imposing this tax," said the court, "it cannot be supported, any more than could a law . . . which imposed upon every man residing in a given section of the State a license as a merchant, whatever his occupation."[114]

Ah Hee v. Crippen[115] involved a different sort of challenge to the Foreign Miners' License Tax. A Chinese miner brought a replevin action to recover a horse that had been attached by the county tax collector to enforce payment of the tax.[116] The plaintiff first argued that the law conflicted with Article I, Section 17 of the California Constitution, which granted foreigners who were bona fide residents the same rights of possession and enjoyment of property as United States citizens.[117] If native-born citizens had the right to mine lands for gold without paying any license fee or tax, so did foreigners who were bona fide residents. He invoked, in short, a state constitutional right to the equal protection of the laws. Second, he argued that the mining legislation applied only to mining on "public lands," that is, land owned either by the United States or the state of California, and not, as was the case here, to mining on privately owned property.[118]

Interestingly, the District Court of Mariposa County completely accepted the plaintiff's constitutional argument[119] and ordered his property returned because it had been seized illegally.[120] The state supreme court, however, chose, here again, to avoid the constitutional claim and to decide the case on the basis of statutory construction. In an opinion penned by Chief Justice Stephen Field, it affirmed the lower court ruling but on the ground that the legislature must have intended the prohibition against mining without a license to apply only to public lands.[121]

We know nothing about the Supreme Court litigants Ah Pong and Ah Hee other than what is revealed in the opinions themselves and nothing about the origins of their lawsuits. We do not know whether they were aggrieved individuals acting exclusively on their own or at the initiative and with the support of Chinese organizations.[122] We can speak more confidently about the origins of a very important case decided the following year. This too involved a challenge to a discriminatory tax though one with much broader impact than the Foreign Miners' License Tax.

The Chinese Police Tax and the Case of Lin Sing v. Washburn

In early 1862 the legislature empaneled a joint select committee, consisting of three senators and three assemblymen, to confer with the Chinese merchants of California[123] and to report back to the full body on the wisdom of permitting a permanent Chinese presence in the state. The charge was similar to the charge that the legislature had given a decade earlier to the Committee on Mines and Mining Interests, and the 1862 report that the committee issued[124] was, in its uniformly pro-Chinese thrust and tone, quite reminiscent of the earlier 1853 committee report.[125] In view of the quantum growth of Sinophobia in the intervening ten years, the latter is the more striking of the two documents and, in retrospect, seems almost a historical anomaly. Significantly, it was to be the last report sympathetic to Chinese interests to issue from any organ of California state government for the duration of the nineteenth century.

The committee told the legislature that the approximately fifty thousand Chinese then working in California were a distinct economic asset to the state. The Chinese merchants, the report stated, were "men of intelligence, ability, and cultivation, who [had] kindly and promptly [responded to the committee's] many inquiries."[126] They were peaceable, patient, and industrious, and they were helping to build the state "by contributing largely to our taxes, to our shipping, farming, and mechanical interests."[127] Instead of seeking to discourage their presence, the state ought to encourage them to stay and pursue their labors.[128] Nor was there any foundation to the charge that they represented a threat to white interests. No evidence indicated that Chinese were displacing white labor. They did not mingle with whites. Indeed, they did not even have the most basic civil rights, such as the right to testify in court, that were possessed by the lowliest Caucasian. "Certainly we have nothing to fear from a race so contemned and restricted," said the authors.[129]

The committee saw no need for further legislation on the Chinese and took the legislature to task for the hostile laws then on the books, laws which it believed[130] ran counter to the spirit and letter of the treaty with China signed by the United States in 1858.[131] "The present laws in force in regard to this class of our population," the committee declared, "impose upon them quite as heavy burdens as they are able to bear, and, in many instances, far beyond their ability to stand up under."[132] The committee voiced the hope that no more legislation would be enacted "to oppress and degrade this class of persons in our State."[133] Regarding possible legislation, the committee was particularly insistent on one point: the state of California was totally without power to act directly either to exclude the Chinese from its shores or to deny them privileges that it accorded other foreigners. If the legislature was determined to pursue these avenues, it would have to go to the Congress of the United States.[134]

For all of the force of its arguments, the committee's report had practically no impact on the full legislature. Within seven weeks of their receipt of the document, the senate and assembly passed, and Governor Leland Stanford[135] signed, yet another piece of anti-Chinese legislation.[136] Entitled "An Act to protect Free White Labor against competition with Chinese Coolie Labor, and to Discourage the Immigration of the Chinese into the State of California,"[137] the act levied a tax of $2.50 per month, to be called the Chinese Police Tax, on all Chinese residing in the state, except those who were operating businesses, who had licenses to work in the mines, or who were engaged in the production or manufacture of sugar, rice, coffee, or tea. Further, it made employers of the designated Chinese equally liable with them for payment of the tax and provided that the tax collector could demand payment of the tax directly from employers; if refused, the tax collector could auction off their personal property with one hour's notice.[138]

The tax was subjected to legal challenge almost immediately. In June 1862, the San Francisco tax collector sought to collect from Lin Sing, a Chinese merchant resident in the city,[139] the sum of $5, representing apparently the tax due from one of his employees for the months of April and May. Under threat of property seizure, he paid the tax but immediately brought suit before a magistrate for a refund. The magistrate sustained the state's demurrer to the suit, the county court affirmed the magistrate's ruling, and the case of *Lin Sing v. Washburn*[140] went up to the California Supreme Court for review.

In argument before the court, the attorney general of California, Frank M. Pixley, suggested that wealthy Caucasian business interests and the great commercial classes were behind the litigation.[141] To be sure, a segment of the California Caucasian establishment was desperately anxious to promote trade with the Chinese Empire. Moreover, it saw Chinese labor as an industrious and inexpensive tool for the development of the state's resources and viewed anti-Chinese legislation as a threat to the promotion of those goals.[142] There is no credible evidence to support Pixley's claim, however, and there seems every reason to believe that the lawsuit was as the *Daily Alta* put it, a Chinese-sponsored test case.[143] The merchant leaders of the community certainly had every incentive of their own to contest the tax, the onus of complying with which, for all practical purposes, would fall on them. We know through the Reverend Loomis that they had followed the 1862 legislative proceedings very closely and with much dismay. In February he wrote to Philadelphia that the Chinese were in "a great ferment" about the several measures, then pending, to impose new taxes on them.[144] More to the point, the day after Lin Sing filed his complaint, the Sacramento *Record-Union* reported, "The several Chinese organizations in this city and state are making arrangements to test *in the Supreme Court* [emphasis added] the constitutionality of the Police Tax Law." It went on to say that the Sacramento Chinese were negotiating with a local law firm to represent them.[145] The reference must surely have been to the just initiated case.

Lin Sing, like *Downer*, raised important questions concerning the respective power of the state and federal governments in foreign trade and commerce regulation, questions that were still rather unsettled at the time. Arguing the state's case before the court, Attorney General Pixley[146] contended that the California act was a legitimate exercise of the state's police power and constituted no interference with the national power to regulate foreign commerce. He argued that the measure affected the Chinese only after they had landed and taken up residence. Having left their ships, he maintained, the Chinese had left the domain of foreign commerce (and thus the realm of exclusive federal jurisdiction) and had become "part and parcel of the inhabitants of the State."[147] As such, they were subject to state taxation. "The Police of the ocean belongs to Congress. The Police of the land belongs to the States," he declared.[148]

Relying on Chief Justice John Marshall's opinion in the 1827 Supreme Court case, *Brown v. Maryland*,[149] and the opinion of the Court in the 1849 series of cases known as the *Passenger Cases*,[150] the California court concluded that the police tax did in fact interfere with the exclusive federal power over foreign commerce and was for that reason void. In *Brown*, the Supreme Court had struck down a Maryland statute that required all importers of foreign goods by bale or package to take out a license before they could sell the contents.[151] The Court had held that the statute violated the ban on collection of duties by states and interfered with the federal power over foreign commerce. The law purported to operate on goods only after they had come ashore and had thus left the stream of foreign commerce. According to Marshall, however, the right to import included the right to sell, and a tax on the right to sell imported goods was the equivalent of a tax on imports that the states were forbidden to assess.[152] In the *Passenger Cases* the Court had voided New York and Massachusetts statutes taxing alien passengers arriving in the respective states. A state, it said, could not tax a foreigner for the privilege of coming into the state.

The California court read the two cases as standing for the proposition that no state law could interfere in any significant way, directly or indirectly, with the exercise by the national government of its exclusive power over foreign commerce, which to the court included foreign immigration.[153] The law here in question (a "measure of special and extreme hostility to the Chinese," the court called it)[154] had the necessary tendency of diminishing immigration from China and general commercial intercourse with that country. That indeed, its caption made clear, was its purpose. But commerce with China was a subject of interest to the entire nation and for that reason was within the exclusive regulatory authority of Washington. The Chinese could be taxed as other residents, but they could not be set apart as special subjects of taxation.[155] The court saw *Brown* as support for the proposition that the mere arrival on shore of articles of foreign commerce or, in this case, of immigrants, did not suddenly remove them from scrutiny under the foreign commerce clause of the U.S. Constitution.

Chief Justice Field wrote a dissent in which he argued that once the Chinese had landed and taken up residence in the state they had ceased to be part of the stream of foreign commerce and were subject to whatever taxes the state might choose to impose on them.[156] He also wondered how the court could nullify the police tax on the grounds offered without also overruling *People v. Naglee*,[157] which had validated the first law requiring foreigners to pay a license tax for the privilege of working in the mines. It was an interesting question, and indeed another was whether the majority's rationale would not also dictate an overturning of the discriminatory tax imposed on Chinese miners. A possible distinction between the two taxes that the court did not go into was that payment of the miners' tax was made a condition of plying that trade while payment of the police tax was being made a condition of one's very residence in the state.

Lin Sing v. Washburn was the first case in which a Chinese resident of the United States sought to invalidate a state enactment on the grounds that it violated the Constitution or laws of the United States. It would certainly not be the last.

Hints of Hope in the Middle 1860s

The years immediately following the *Lin Sing* decision brought other developments encouraging to the Chinese. In 1865 the California Supreme Court handed down an opinion that narrowed in a small but significant way the scope of the laws prohibiting Chinese testimony. In *People v. Awa*,[158] the court reversed a Chinese appellant's manslaughter conviction on the grounds that a Chinese witness who had wished to testify on his behalf had been unable to do so because of the 1863 statute forbidding Chinese testimony against white persons. Writing for the court, Justice Lorenzo Sawyer ruled that the statute ought to be construed strictly, as he put it, "in favor of life, liberty and public justice."[159] It only prohibited a Chinese person from testifying against a "white person," he noted, and the opposing party in the case, the state, clearly was not a "white person."[160]

In a related development clear signs began to appear around this time that a significant segment of the public was willing to support repeal of the ban on Chinese testimony, at least in criminal cases. Editorials in major newspapers urging repeal began to appear with some frequency,[161] and in 1867, a measure was introduced in the legislature, to a chorus of wide editorial support, to reverse the ban. When in January 1868 the state senate voted overwhelmingly in favor of repeal, the *Daily Alta* expressed the hope that a bill to permit testimony in civil cases would soon follow.[162] Even when the measure failed in the assembly, disappointment with the result was accompanied by confidence that the measure would be reintroduced and passed eventually.[163]

Overshadowing all of these developments was the completion of negotiations in 1868 of a new treaty between the United States and China.

The Burlingame Treaty

In 1867, China asked Anson Burlingame, U.S. minister to the Manchu Court in Peking, to head a goodwill mission to the United States and other western countries.[164] The request was extraordinary, but Burlingame, by his tact and evident sympathy for China, had won the confidence of the Chinese Imperial Court, and so was entrusted with this important assignment. Burlingame and two Chinese envoys arrived in San Francisco in April 1868 and proceeded to make their way across the country to Washington amidst great fanfare.[165] The visit resulted in an agreement between the United States and China to reexamine the 1858 Treaty of Tientsin, which both sides thought was in need of revision.

An amendment to the Treaty of Tientsin was signed in Washington in July 1868. (Official exchange of ratifications would come the following year.) Ever since known as the Burlingame Treaty,[166] it contained two provisions of particular significance to the Chinese in California. An article was added in which both countries recognized "the inherent and inalienable right of man to change his home and allegiance, and also the mutual advantage of the free migration and emigration of their citizens and subjects, respectively for purposes of curiosity, of trade, or as permanent residents."[167] This provision was included at the insistence of the Americans and ran counter to the Chinese Empire's age-old prohibition against the emigration of its subjects. It could only have been interpreted by the Chinese as a ringing endorsement by this country of continued Chinese immigration.[168] Another article provided that "Chinese subjects visiting or residing in the United States, shall enjoy the same privileges, immunities, and exemptions in respect to travel or residence, as may there be enjoyed by the citizens or subjects of the most favored nation."[169]

There is evidence that the Chinese in California followed the treaty negotiations with considerable interest and greeted with enthusiasm the prospect of receiving greater protection from its more liberal terms.[170] Upon learning of the treaty terms the Chinese foreign office itself expressed to Burlingame its hope that after the treaty was put in force "the Chinese in California will cease to be subjected to the ill treatment they have hitherto met with."[171] The treaty, finally, attracted favorable comment in certain sectors of the Caucasian community. The *Daily Alta,* a few days after the signing, expressed the opinion that the "most favored nation" clause might mean the end of the ban on Chinese testimony.[172] The Reverend Speer, living in retirement in New York but still intensely interested in the Chinese in America, predicted that the treaty would "sweep away the legal disabilities to which the Chinese have been subjected on the Pacific Coast" and "permit them to obtain the sheer rights of humanity."[173]

Chinese Testimony and the Fourteenth Amendment

Eventually the "most favored nation" provision of the Burlingame Treaty would prove to be an enormous boon to Chinese litigants, especially in the federal courts, but the full impact of the clause was not to be felt for some time. In the meantime a few California prosecutors were trying to use another provision of federal law to pry open the courtroom door for Chinese witnesses. This was the equal protection clause of the Fourteenth Amendment, an amendment that was added to the Constitution in the same month that the Burlingame Treaty was signed. That clause forbade the states from denying to any persons within their jurisdiction the equal protection of the laws.[174]

San Francisco Assistant District Attorney Davis Louderback had been looking for an opportunity to test the validity of the California statute barring Chinese testimony under the equal protection clause of the Fourteenth Amendment ever since Secretary of State William Seward certified without reservation that the amendment was a part of the Constitution on July 28, 1868. One presented itself in December when a Chinese man was stabbed on a San Francisco street. There were no white witnesses to the incident, and so the prosecution's case rested entirely upon the testimony of the victim. Louderback initiated an action against the assailant in the police court of Judge R. R. Provines and offered the testimony of the Chinese victim in support of the charge. The defense of course objected on the grounds of the California statute. Louderback countered that the statute, which he described incidentally as "a relic of by-gone barbarism" and "a disgrace to our age and times," was void under both the equal protection clause of the Fourteenth Amendment and the Civil Rights Act of 1866, which conferred equal civil rights on all American citizens irrespective of race or color. The newspaper accounts of his argument in court fail to make clear all of its details, but the gist of it appears to have been that the equal protection clause was intended to be construed very broadly, that is to say to cover Chinese, and that a denial to a victim because of race of the right to testify against an assailant was a denial of equal protection. He contended that the Civil Rights Act covered the case as well inasmuch as the second section of the act prohibited "any person" from depriving "any inhabitant" of a state of the substantive rights secured by the act's first section, among which was the right to give evidence on terms of equality with whites.[175]

Judge Provines seemed impressed with Louderback's argument but at the same time indicated a reluctance to accept it and take the bold step of nullifying the state statute. He noted that some of the very issues Louderback was raising were due to be addressed shortly in a case then pending before the California Supreme Court, a case which he thought might very well vindicate the right of all to testify.[176] Opting for the more cautious course, he decided not to admit the testimony.[177]

The following month the California Supreme Court proved wrong Judge Provines's expectations and disappointed as well the hopes of those who thought that the tribunal might continue to be a pathfinder of sorts in the cause of Chinese civil rights. In *People v. Washington*,[178] a curious case, the defendant, a mulatto, had been indicted for the robbery of one Ah Wang, solely on the testimony of Chinese witnesses. Counsel for the defendant moved successfully to set the indictment aside, and the matter went up on appeal. The Supreme Court affirmed on the ground that the Civil Rights Act of 1866 had placed all citizens (and the act had declared all persons born within the United States and not subject to a foreign power to be U.S. citizens) on a level of equality before the law with respect to their personal liberty. The law provided, in pertinent part, that citizens of every race and color, without regard to previous condition of servitude, should have "the same right, in every State and Territory, to make and enforce contracts, to sue, be parties, and give evidence . . . and to the full and equal benefit of all laws and proceedings for the security of person and property, as is enjoyed by white citizens."[179] If white citizens could under California law exclude Chinese testimony, then blacks, like the defendant, born in the United States, could avail themselves of the same privilege.[180]

There was, to be sure, in the language of the opinion something of a nod in the direction of the Chinese. The court raised questions, rhetorical at bottom, about the validity, under Article I, Sections 11[181] and 17 of the California Constitution, of banning Chinese testimony in criminal cases. And it also suggested that the Fourteenth Amendment's equal protection clause might have some bearing on the issue.[182] But the court refused to go any further, and the opinion is devoid of any real reflection of the ironic injustice it was working on one minority group in the effort to vindicate the rights of another. And, on balance, the Chinese could only have perceived the decision as a serious blow to their hopes.

The *Washington* decision did not, however, end legal skirmishing over the admissibility of Chinese testimony in the courts of California. In June 1869 Louderback appeared again in Judge Provines's court, this time assisted by a private attorney, Daniel J. Murphy, to press the case for admissibility. The defendant in this criminal prosecution was charged with assault and battery, and Louderback again offered the testimony of a Chinese witness. This time counsel's argument rested entirely on the Fourteenth Amendment. The amendment, he contended, had extended the protections of the Civil Rights Act of 1866, which he now acknowledged covered only blacks, to all races and placed all races on a level of equality. Judge Provines, however, again refused to receive the witness's testimony, saying that such a decision would cause too much confusion, given the pronouncements of the higher court.[183]

In the fall of the same year significant cracks began to appear in the wall of inadmissibility, first on the civil side of the docket and then on the criminal side. *Welch v. Ah Hund,* was a civil action for damages that had been brought in the Fourth District Court of San Francisco. It grew out of an alleged breach of contract by the defendant, a Chinese resident of the city. Counsel for the defendant sought to tender his client as a witness, arguing (he perhaps took his cue from the *Washington* dicta) that the law preventing Chinese from testifying against whites in civil cases violated both the equal protection clause of the Fourteenth Amendment and Article I, Sections 11 and 17, of the California Constitution. Surprisingly, the court agreed with the Fourteenth Amendment argument and ruled that the testimony should be received.[184] More important, a third effort by Assistant District Attorney Louderback in Judge Provines's police court ended in success.

In November two whites were arrested for robbing a Chinese man on the street. The Chinese victim was the only witness to the attack, and Louderback, conscious no doubt of Judge Provines's sympathies as betrayed by his comments in his court on previous occasions and willing to make one more effort in that forum, filed charges against them. He again brought in private counsel, the firm of Darwin and Murphy, to assist him and left the argument concerning the Fourteenth Amendment to attorney D. J. Murphy.[185]

Murphy's argument was the most elaborate yet made on that head. The language of the equal protection clause was as broad and comprehensive as could be, he declared. Protection was granted to *all,* even to those who did not enjoy the immunity of citizenship, and equal protection included the equal right to testify in court. In support of this view he adduced a passage from a speech made by Senator John Conness of California during the debates on Section 1 of the Fourteenth Amendment. In the context of a debate on the wording of the section, which then already contained the equal protection clause in its present form, Conness had described the abuses the Chinese were subjected to in his state as the necessary consequence of being barred from testifying against whites. He then went on to say, "I am very glad, indeed, that we have determined at length that every human being may relate what he heard and saw in a court of law when it is required of him and that our jurors are regarded as of sufficient intelligence to put the right value and construction on what is stated." The passage, Murphy declared, showed that the specific question of Chinese testimony had been raised and discussed during the debates and supported the broad reading of the amendment's coverage for which he was contending.[186]

Turning to the term "protection," it implied, he said, the security of property and person against violence coming from any source. It also implied that there should be some means of vindicating the right. But the right to this protection would be meaningless if one could not speak against one's attacker in a court of law. Murphy even sought to invoke the authority of *People v. Washington* to support his cause. He argued that the tenor of that decision, although the right of the Chinese to testify was not before the court, suggested that the Fourteenth Amendment had knocked down all barriers to testimony on racial grounds.[187]

A little over a week later Judge Provines yielded to the logic of the prosecution's reasoning and reversed himself on the question of the admissibility of Chinese testimony in criminal cases. He agreed that the phrase "any person" in the Fourteenth Amendment's equal protection clause was broad enough to include Chinese and that the law, in denying Chinese the right to enforce the law's protection by testifying against those who did them harm did not accord them the same quantum of protection that it accorded to whites. "If the one class [whites] has the ability or capacity to have the law enforced and the other has not, certainly *protection* [emphasis in original] is not equal to the two."[188] He allowed as well how in his view even in a civil suit between a white and a Chinese litigant equality of protection was denied if the former could testify while the latter could not.[189] Curiously, Provines sought to limit his holding to the rights of victims of crime or civil litigants to testify themselves against persons of another race. He did not wish to be misunderstood to be saying, he stressed, that Chinese or Indians[190] were generally competent to testify. Equal protection was sufficiently served if "neither the white person, on the one hand, nor the Chinaman or Indian on the other is permitted to call Chinaman or Indian in his behalf as against the other."[191]

Judge Provines's ruling, notwithstanding its curious understanding of equal protection, was the first to say that the Chinese came under that provision of the Fourteenth Amendment. But it had come from the lowest-level court of record in the California system and, unless endorsed by a higher tribunal, could be of only limited utility. For whatever reasons, the ruling was not appealed, and so the occasion did not arise for a higher court to speak. The stage was set, however, for a more authoritative decision on the relevance of the Fourteenth Amendment to the question of Chinese testimony in late March of the following year. On March 24, 1870, the county court of San Francisco, Judge Delos Lake presiding, was presented with the question of the admissibility of Chinese testimony in another criminal case. The court, in order, as it made clear, to get an authoritative decision on the issue from the California Supreme Court, ordered the testimony admitted. The defendant was convicted, and the matter went up on appeal to the high tribunal, with briefs submitted not only by counsel for the appellant and the state attorney general but also by the firm of Darwin and Murphy, of counsel to the state.

The main brunt of the state's case was carried by the private firm, which submitted a closely-argued thirty-eight page brief expanding on the argument made in the November case in Judge Provines's police court. The state attorney general's brief made essentially the same points. The thrust of both briefs was that the criminal law did not offer the same protection to the potential Chinese victim of crime as it did to the potential white victim and that as such it amounted to a denial of the equal protection of the law, guaranteed to all by the Fourteenth Amendment.[192]

The California high court did not rule until January 1871, handing down a decision that can best be described as a hollow exercise in formal logic. The law afforded whites and Chinese exactly the same degree of protection, wrote Justice Jackson Temple for the court. "If a crime be committed against the person or property of a Chinaman," he declared, "that same punishment is meted out to the criminal when convicted, as though the crime had been committed upon a white man."[193] Further, each could take advantage of the same means of proof. Both could use the testimony of whites to convict white defendants. Neither could use the testimony of Chinese witnesses.[194] "The law," he said, "dispenses equal justice to all."[195] Counsel for the state had pressed the point that inequality could surely be found in the fact that when the victim was the only witness, the white man could testify against his assailant whatever his race while the Chinese man could not. But Temple said he found no force in this argument. White victims were permitted to testify against their assailants not because they were victims but because on other grounds they were considered to be competent witnesses. Chinese victims were not permitted to testify because on other grounds their testimony was considered to be unreliable. The fact that both were the victims of criminal conduct was immaterial to the discussion. The Chinese victim's disadvantage was one shared by all who were so circumstanced as to be surrounded at the time of the criminal act by persons incompetent to testify.[196] Judge Temple concluded his opinion with a lengthy discourse on federalism, saying that he could not imagine that the proponents of the Fourteenth Amendment intended it to allow the sort of interference in the internal police affairs of the state, including its discretionary control over trial procedure, as seemed called for by the respondent's argument.[197] One justice dissented, saying that he thought the California act had clearly been abrogated by the passage of the Fourteenth Amendment.

To their credit, several newspapers castigated the high court for its *Brady* decision. "We regret this decision for it opens the door to abuses of the very worst kind," said the San Francisco *Chronicle*. "It places Chinamen outside the protection of the laws of the State, and leaves them to hold their lives at the sufferance of the roughs and rowdies."[198] "It was bad enough . . . that a set of demagogues at Sacramento should enact such a law," the *Daily Alta* declared, "but it is heaping double disgrace on the State to have it upheld on moral grounds by our Supreme Court."[199] And in a later issue it associated itself with a recommendation of the New York *Tribune* that the question of Chinese testimony be brought up to the Supreme Court of the United States for review.[200]

There was no discussion in the *Brady* case of the possible applicability of the recently enacted Civil Rights Act of 1870 to the question before the court. But that act, passed by Congress two months after Judge Lake's trial court ruling and while that ruling was on appeal, had in fact opened up another clear avenue of attack on California's ban on Chinese testimony. The events leading up to the act's passage provide confirmation once again of the political awareness of the Chinese.

The Civil Rights Act of 1870

An opportunity to bring their grievances directly to the attention of representatives of the federal government presented itself to the Chinese leadership in June 1869. In that month the House Ways and Means Committee, accompanied by Senator Roscoe Conkling and ex-Senator Benjamin Wade (Wade was at the time one of the government-designated directors on the board of the Union Pacific Railroad) visited San Francisco as part of a fact-finding tour of the West Coast.[201] On June 25, while in the city, the congressional delegation met with representatives of the Chinese community and with several leading Caucasian merchants and bankers. Journalists were also present.

At the meeting, Fung Tang, a prominent merchant, delivered a prepared address on behalf of the Chinese community. He began by praising the year-old Burlingame Treaty, though he emphasized that the Chinese were still waiting for the just and equal protection it seemed to guarantee. (Fung's complaint was, technically speaking, premature. Though the treaty had been signed by both countries and ratified by the United States, it had not yet been ratified by China and so had not yet entered into force.) He held out the promise of greatly increased commercial intercourse between China and the United States,[202] but made it clear that such a development was contingent on relief from the unjust laws under which the Chinese were suffering. He then stressed three points. First he expressed the opinion that the miners' tax violated the provisions of the Burlingame Treaty. The Chinese were willing to pay taxes cheerfully when taxed equally with others, he declared but disliked being singled out for taxation. Second, he expressed the view that the commutation tax was unfair and inconsistent with America's claim to be a free country. Finally, there was the ban on Chinese testimony. This civil disability was the sorest point of all, for it left the Chinese defenseless with respect to their lives and property and "unable to obtain justice" either for themselves or for others. Fung also entertained questions from the Congressmen, and he concluded with a plea to them to "speak favorably of us to the United States Government."[203]

The congressional delegation appeared moved by Fung's presentation and sympathetic to his complaints; but it promised nothing in the way of concrete action, offering only the hope that the Chinese grievances "like others growing out of the prejudices of men, would be corrected with the advance of public sentiment."[204] But on December 6, 1869, the opening day of the congressional session, Senator William Stewart of Nevada (the same Stewart who as district attorney of Nevada County, California, had prosecuted the case of *People v. Hall*) introduced a resolution:

> That the Committee on the Judiciary be requested to inquire if any States are denying to any class of persons within their jurisdiction the equal protection of the law, *in violation of treaty obligations with foreign nations* [emphasis added] and of section one of

> the fourteenth amendment to the Constitution; and if so, what legislation is necessary to enforce such treaty obligations and such amendment, and to report by bill or otherwise.

Stewart's resolution initially received unanimous approval but upon motion of Senator Sumner was laid on the table pending the constitution of Senate committees.[205] Stewart raised the question of discrimination against the Chinese again on December 22 in connection with discussion of a bill, introduced by Senator Williams of Oregon, to regulate Chinese immigration. Stewart proclaimed his support for any measure aimed at preventing anything other than the free immigration of Chinese, but he suggested that the Committee on Commerce, while it had the Williams bill under consideration, should also "examine the police regulations that California has made." The state imposed a tax of $5 on all immigrants from China, he said, and this was unfair and discriminatory. Congress should legislate to prevent California from imposing "any undue or unreasonable burdens upon these people."[206] And the following month he introduced a bill[207] that addressed most of the concerns that Fung had raised in his meeting with the congressional delegation. It provided in pertinent part:

> That all persons within the jurisdiction of the United States, Indians not taxed or excepted, shall have the same right in every State and Territory in the United States to make and enforce contracts, to sue, be parties, give evidence, and to the full and equal benefit of all laws and proceedings for the security of person and property as is enjoyed by white citizens, and shall be subject to like punishments, pains, penalties, taxes, licenses, and exactions of every kind and none other, any law, statute, ordinance, regulations, or custom to the contrary notwithstanding. No tax or charge shall be imposed or enforced by any State upon any person emigrating thereto from a foreign country which is not equally imposed and enforced upon every person emigrating to such State from any other foreign country, and any law of any State in conflict with this provision is hereby declared null and void.[208]

The opening language, while very similar to Section 1 of the Civil Rights Act of 1866, went further and extended basic civil rights, including the all-important right to give evidence in court, to *all persons*, that is to say not just citizens, within the jurisdiction of the United States. The requirement at the end of the first sentence that all persons be subject to "like . . . taxes, licenses, and exactions of every kind," along with the requirements of the last sentence, assured that the Chinese would be freed of the burden of special fiscal legislation such as the Foreign Miners' License Tax and the police tax.

In his speeches on the floor of Congress, Senator Stewart made it quite clear that his bill was intended for the benefit of the Chinese. Thus on May 20, 1870, he said in explanation of the measure, which in the meantime he had incorporated into a voting rights bill that he was sponsoring:

> We are inviting to our shores, or allowing them to come, Asiatics. . . . For twenty years every obligation of humanity, of justice, and of common decency toward these people has been violated by a certain class of men—bad men. . . . It is as solemn a duty as can be devolved upon the Congress to see that those people are protected, to see that they have the equal protection of the laws, notwithstanding that they are aliens. . . . If the *State courts do not give them the equal protection of the law* [emphasis added], if public sentiment is so inhuman as to rob them of their ordinary civil rights, I say I would be less than a man if I did not insist . . . that this provision shall go on this bill . . . and that we will protect Chinese aliens or any other aliens whom we allow to come here, and *give them a hearing in our courts* [emphasis added]; let them sue and be sued; let them be protected by all the laws and the same laws that other men are.[209]

And a few days later, he declared:

> There are other provisions in it relating to other subjects [besides voting rights]; and for them I congratulate the country, *particularly those provisions which extend the strong arm of the Government to the protection of the Chinese* [emphasis added]; those provisions which protect those industrious, helpless people whom we have invited to our shores; those provisions which go at this late date to wipe out to some extent the infamy that rests upon this nation for having invited the Asiatics to come here, having made treaties for their protection, and then allowed a State in this Union to pass barbarous and cruel laws, to place upon them unjust and cruel burdens, to tax them differently from other people, and collect that tax in a brutal manner.[210]

What precisely motivated Stewart to introduce his measure and work so vigorously for its enactment is difficult to determine. As a man who had lived many years in the California mining districts, Stewart was of course intimately familiar with the discrimination and mistreatment the Chinese were subject to.[211] As attorney in the *Hall* case he had in fact fought to persuade the California Supreme Court to permit the Chinese to testify in the state's courts. But he represented a state whose white population was showing signs of becoming almost as bitterly anti-Chinese as was the white population of California. And in the previous session, he had vehemently opposed a bill introduced by Charles Sumner to naturalize all Chinese residents in the United States. Part of the explanation may be that Stewart had close connections with Collis P. Huntington of the Central Pacific Railroad and had done favors for the railroad during his first term.[212] Even though the transcontinental railroad had been completed by this time, the Central Pacific continued to employ Chinese laborers on other projects and may have wished to promote continued Chinese immigration or encourage Chinese already here to stay. But this is all highly speculative. As his principal biographer makes clear, and as we shall see later on, Stewart was a man who often spoke out of both sides of his mouth on public policy questions, the Chinese question included.[213]

Congress eventually enacted Stewart's measure into law, with minor changes, as Section 16 of the Civil Rights Act of 1870.[214] While the overriding purpose of that act was to protect black voters in the South in the exercise of the franchise and other civil rights, no one in Congress could have had any doubt that Section 16 was aimed at securing the rights of the Chinese. This was equally clear to many outside of Congress, it may be noticed. The San Francisco *Examiner*, for example, a bitterly anti-Chinese paper, delivered itself of a jeremiad against the legislation, describing its sponsor, Senator Stewart, as "a rotten-borough demagogue and panderer to capital" and complaining that Stewart's bill placed the Chinese on precisely the same footing as whites. "Under [Section 16 of the act] no State legislation can apply to a Chinaman which does not apply equally to all people," it declared. "The Radicals have legislated to encourage coolie labor," it went on, "and until the party in power repeal their infamous legislation and treaty and leave the States to discourage Chinese immigration by hostile legislation, it will be in vain for them to say they do not favor it."[215]

Aftermath of the Civil Rights Act

Notwithstanding the to all intents unambiguous language of Section 16 of the Civil Rights Act of 1870, state officials continued to demand the Foreign Miners' License Tax from Chinese miners after the act's passage, and the state's courts continued to be unwilling to admit Chinese testimony against whites. Efforts undertaken by government officials and by private individuals to enforce the act's provisions met with mixed results.

The federal government moved relatively quickly and with effect to put an end to the practice of discriminatory taxation. On December 10, 1870, a federal grand jury in San Francisco returned an indictment against the sheriff of Trinity County for exacting the sum of $4 from Ah Koo, a Chinese miner, in violation of Section 16. The sheriff was eventually convicted of the offense, but no sanction appears to have been imposed, probably because on the day final judgment was entered the sheriff filed an affidavit with the court stating that he had ordered his deputies to cease collecting the tax.[216] When it was discovered that the practice was persisting in another rural county, El Dorado, the U.S. attorney in San Francisco not only secured another indictment but went to the length of having the sheriff arrested and brought to the city for trial.[217] These actions seem to have served as a sufficient deterrent to future attempts to collect the tax.

In May 1871 two prominent members of the Chinese community, involved in civil lawsuits, sought to avail themselves of the privilege that the 1870 federal act had seemingly conferred on them with respect to testimony in court. Li Po Tai, a Chinese herbal doctor with many Caucasian patients, brought a claim for $231 in unpaid bills against a white man in a San Francisco trial court. The first newspaper reports of the launching of the civil action said that the plaintiff was bringing it as a test case. He intended to offer himself as a witness, it was said, and if refused would either seek to have a criminal prosecution brought against the judge under the criminal provisions of the Civil Rights Act of 1870 or would himself bring a civil suit for damages against the same magistrate under the just-enacted Civil Rights Act of 1871.[218] When during the proceedings plaintiff's counsel tendered his client as a witness in his own behalf and was met with the familiar statutory objection, he countered that the California law was in contravention of the Constitution "and the several Acts of Congress to enforce the civil rights of all persons within the jurisdiction for the United States." When argument turned to the *Brady* case, counsel noted that the California Supreme Court ruling pre-dated the Civil Rights Act of 1870 and was therefore not binding on the court. The court took the question under advisement and seemed prepared to rule on it, but before it could, the parties, according to the press, agreed to settle the case thus making the matter moot.[219]

Later in the month another Chinese herbal doctor, involved in a case as a civil defendant, again raised the civil rights issue and this time the court was allowed to render a decision on the claim. *Garrett v. Lou Ci Tat* was a medical malpractice action brought by a Caucasian patient in justice court against the defendant Chinese physician for failure to cure him as promised. At the conclusion of the plaintiff's presentation of his case, counsel for the defendant offered his client's testimony and when the judge initially refused he argued that the magistrate was subjecting himself to liability "under the Ku Klux Act" (the Civil Rights Act of 1871.) This argument was persuasive enough to cause the court to reverse itself and permit the Chinese physician to testify.[220]

A justice court decision in a civil case was of course of little precedential value. That was made manifest a few days later when a police court signaled its unwillingness to follow the decision and refused to admit the testimony of a Chinese who claimed he had been robbed by a white man.[221] And in March 1872, the Twelfth District Court in San Francisco, a higher level trial court, declined, citing the *Brady* case, to hear the testimony of a Chinese woman against a Caucasian murder defendant. The proponent of the testimony, interestingly, was Daniel Murphy, since 1870 the district attorney for San Francisco.[222] Murphy told the local press that he intended to appeal the ruling to the state supreme court and took the first step in that direction by filing a notice of appeal.[223] One suspects that an argument focused narrowly on the applicability of the 1870 Civil Rights Act (as opposed to the Fourteenth Amendment) to the question of Chinese testimony might well have persuaded the California high court to reverse its stance. In the event, the effort was rendered unnecessary by the actions of the California legislature. A revision of the state's penal and civil codes, enacted in 1872, eliminated the ban on Chinese testimony in criminal and civil proceedings.[224] Whether the legislature felt that it was but succumbing to the inevitable is impossible to say.[225]

2 Test Cases in the 1870s

San Francisco's First Anti-Chinese Ordinances

By 1870 roughly a quarter of California's Chinese population lived in San Francisco as opposed to the roughly 8 percent who had lived there in 1860. (The actual numbers had more than quadrupled, going from about 2,700 to about 12,000.)[1] One does not have to hunt very hard for reasons for this large increase in the city's Chinese population. For a variety of reasons San Francisco was becoming a more desirable place to earn a livelihood than the interior of the state, both for new arrivals from China and for the Cantonese immigrants already there. Scratching out a living from the steadily depleting placer deposits of the Sierra foothills was becoming more difficult with each passing year.[2] By the end of the 1860s opportunities for railroad work were dropping off due to the completion of the transcontinental railway. By contrast the city of San Francisco, beginning to emerge as a populous and dynamic commercial and manufacturing center, offered economic opportunities that it had not a decade before.

The Chinese who settled in San Francisco found a variety of employments. Some found jobs in Caucasian-owned manufacturing enterprises. Others started their own businesses or found work with the Cantonese merchants and small business owners who, like their nineteenth-century counterparts in so many other parts of the world, were then beginning to gain a solid foothold for themselves in the local economy. This was particularly so in industries such as clothing and leather goods manufacturing and cigar making, fields then under severe competition from East Coast enterprises and in the process of being abandoned by Caucasian entrepreneurs. Many entered the commercial laundry trade—a trade the

Chinese had introduced—either as employees or as laundry owners. A fair number took positions as cooks or domestic servants in white households. Some operated truck gardens on the city's outskirts while others worked as street vendors, selling fish, vegetables, and other wares on the crowded walkways of Chinatown and elsewhere in the city.[3]

The increase in Chinese residents bred an increase in resentment and hostility in the Caucasian population, especially among the city's workers, who saw the Chinese not only as an alien and distasteful race but as economic competitors. The hostility manifested itself in a number of ways. One was sheer physical violence. It became a common spectacle, for example, to see crowds of young people, often egged on by their elders, pelting new Chinese immigrants with stones as they made their way with their baggage from the docks to the Chinese quarter.[4] Another form of hostility was the development of organized mass opposition to the Chinese and the agitation for anti-Chinese legislation at the local level.

The Lodging House and Basket Carrier Ordinances

At its June 13, 1870 meeting, the San Francisco Board of Supervisors received a petition from Thomas Mooney and Hugh Murray, the president and vice president of the Anti-Coolie Association, demanding that something be done about the Chinese quarter of the city, described as being crowded and contaminated with disease. The petitioners asked the board to appoint its own committee to "ascertain the Chinese mode of living and lodging," to enforce strict sanitary regulations in the district, and most drastically, if somewhat inconsistently, to "provide some means of removing the Chinese beyond the city limits." The board promised to seek information from the health authorities.[5]

The same Thomas Mooney made an appearance the following month at a mass meeting organized by the San Francisco affiliate of the Knights of St. Crispin, a national organization of shoemakers. The stated purpose of the meeting was to organize a "combined movement against the further introduction of Chinese into the labor market of the state."[6] The proceedings were marked by the kind of racial demagoguery that one had by now come to expect at gatherings of this sort. One speaker told his hearers that the choice before the state was between "free and acceptable labor and the vilest system of slavery ever known to enlightened man." The hour had come, he told them, "when you must use those powers bestowed on you by the God of the universe to hurl from your midst this abominable clay-colored race, stained with every crime and abomination known to ancient or modern barbarianism." Calls were heard for legislation at the national and local levels to deter Chinese immigration. Mooney, himself not part of the working class but rather the president of a local bank and a man with pretensions to political office,[7] complained to the group, as he had to the supervisors, about the laxity with which sanitary regulations were being enforced in Chinatown.[8] A week later a much larger group assembled under the auspices of the same organization, constituted itself into a formal organization called the "Anti-Chinese Convention of the State of California," and discussed plans to organize a network throughout the state for the purpose of deterring Chinese immigration. The group also directed its leaders to inform the leadership of the Chinese community that in the group's opinion it was no longer safe for Chinese to come to or reside in San Francisco.[9]

A few days later, on July 18, the board of supervisors convened for its regular weekly meeting. It heard a fairly noncommittal report from the health authorities on living conditions in Chinatown and what might be done to change them. One member, on hearing the report, complained that he had expected a more vigorous and more forthcoming response to "the petition of the Anti-Coolieites" [the Mooney petition] on sanitary conditions in Chinatown. Anti-Chinese feeling was growing, he noted. Bad and unscrupulous persons might be relied on to exploit it if those in authority did nothing to defuse it. It was necessary, he said, "for cool and sensible men to take hold of and manage this question."[10] Perhaps with this kind of consideration in mind the mayor was authorized to appoint a committee of three to confer with the board of health on "the Chinese question."

At the same meeting, the board authorized the printing of an ordinance that made it a misdemeanor for anyone to let rooms or apartments that should contain less than five hundred cubic feet of air for each adult person sleeping or dwelling in them and made it a crime as well for any tenant to dwell or sleep in such a room or apartment.[11] Duly enacted into law at the board's next meeting, it came to be called variously the "lodging house law," the "cubic air law," and "the pure air law." (The *Daily Alta* reported the passage of the ordinance under the headline "More Air to Chinamen.")[12] Many San Francisco Chinese undoubtedly did live in crowded quarters, but the willingness of Chinese laborers to endure discomfort and hardship in order to economize on living expenses was a tendency observable in overseas Chinese communities all over the world. The Chinese had certainly not invited the supervisors to intervene to protect them. Indeed, as later events would show, the Chinese renters this measure was ostensibly designed to protect were thoroughly hostile to it. Like later California laws purporting to be public health and safety measures, this one originated less in the desire to promote the public weal than in the desire to pander to racial resentment and to make life difficult for the Chinese.

The board also considered a second petition it had received from Mooney's Anti-Coolie Association, this one directed at Chinese street vendors. It complained that "hordes of Chinese peddlars," were plying their trade on the city streets without having obtained the proper license. It asked that they be required to wear a badge and also that they be prohibited from exposing their wares on the sidewalk.[13] The board did not act on these requests immediately, but in December it did enact an ordinance making it a misdemeanor for anyone to carry baskets on the city's sidewalks suspended from or attached to poles across the shoulder.[14]

The Chinese fish and vegetable peddlers and the Chinese laundrymen knew perfectly well that they were being singled out for legislative attention by this ordinance, and many, it appears, resented it. One of them determined to have the new measure's validity tested in court. When in January 1871 three Chinese street vendors were brought before the San Francisco police court on complaints that they had violated the law, one of them through counsel demurred to the complaint on the grounds that the ordinance under which he had been arrested was invalid because it had not been properly enacted by the board (they had not declared the carrying of baskets to be a nuisance as they were required to, he argued). The police court agreed with him and ordered him released from custody, but the decision was appealed to the county court, which overruled the lower tribunal.[15] It held that the ordinance was valid since the board of supervisors was empowered generally to provide for the removal of nuisances and obstructions from the city streets and could perfectly well decide that the carrying of poles was an obstruction.[16] The matter did not end there, however. Counsel for the vendor, Ah Wong, shortly thereafter sued out a writ of habeas corpus in the California Supreme Court, and the case was sent to a San Francisco district court for hearing. There the petitioner now alleged not only that the ordinance was beyond the power of the supervisors but also that it was racially discriminatory in intent and effect. Though general in its terms, he argued, it was intended to affect only the Chinese.[17] It was an argument that would be made again and again by Chinese litigants over the course of the next three decades. The district court, after only a day's deliberation, found that the ordinance was constitutional on grounds similar to those that the county court had advanced. It was a proper exercise of the power of the city to promote the public safety, the district court said, citing as authority a California Supreme Court decision granting the city of San Francisco the right to prohibit slaughterhouses.[18]

To the *Daily Alta* the habeas proceeding was an indication of how serious an economic threat the Chinese took the basket ordinance to be and how far they were prepared to go in challenging it. "This ordinance affects the Chinese peddlars considerably and they are using all the means of the law to have the matter fully tested," the paper commented.[19] But it may well have been principle as much as any potential economic impact that drove the Chinese to the courts. The ordinance was in fact not a terribly serious threat to the livelihood of the Chinese street vendors, and those Caucasians who thought that it would drive them out of business were disappointed. They adapted to it without enormous difficulty. Those who wished to retain their poles simply used the city streets, scurrying along them as close to the sidewalk as possible. Or if they used the sidewalks, they carried a single basket slung over their shoulders.[20]

The Anti-Chinese Legislation of 1873

In May of 1873 a San Francisco supervisor laid before his colleagues a set of three proposed ordinances designed to ratchet up significantly the costs of living and working in the city for the Chinese. As the member put it in introducing the battery of laws, "The General Government has so tied our hands by the treaty with China, that we must depend entirely upon local legislation to discourage the immigration of Chinese."[21] One measure was aimed, significantly, at Chinese laundrymen, a logical and likely target for legislation of this sort since Chinese laundries constituted a highly visible symbol—perhaps the most visible symbol—of the Chinese presence in the local economy.

Chinese immigrant entrepreneurs, filling a need that no one else seemed eager to fill, had introduced commercial laundering to California in the early days of the gold rush (as early as 1852 a San Francisco newspaper observed that the washing of clothes in San Francisco was performed largely by Chinese)[22] and quickly achieved a position of dominance in the industry, one that they would maintain for the rest of the nineteenth century.[23] By 1870 there were about 2,600 Chinese laundrymen, comprising proprietors and their laborers, in California, of whom about 1,300 lived in San Francisco, the latter figure representing some 12 percent of the Chinese population of that city.[24] By this time the laundrymen had organized into a powerful guild.

Early in their history the Chinese washhouses in San Francisco, generally joint ventures between several men employing at most a handful of employees (or occasionally none at all), had established a trade association, an association that bore many of the characteristics of the craft guilds that had long been a fixture of commercial life in China. As often tends to be the case with trade associations, the San Francisco guild existed, in part, for the purpose of regulating and limiting competition. Known as the Tung Hing Tong, it developed a strict set of rules on the location of laundries and on the minimum prices laundries could charge. It received and passed on applications for the establishment of new laundries and arbitrated disputes between existing establishments.[25] The organization also came to serve as the defender of Chinese laundrymen against threats from the Caucasian world.[26]

The proposed San Francisco laundry ordinance capitalized on the fact that Chinese laundries were all modest operations that made no use of horse-drawn vehicles. It amended the city's laundry licensing order, which previously had imposed a schedule of fees on laundries ranging from $2 to $15 per quarter depending on how many vehicles they used, to require that laundries employing *no* horse-drawn vehicles in their operation should now pay the highest fees of all.[27]

The other two proposed ordinances breathed a meaner and more vindictive spirit. One, in recognition of the fact that male Chinese wore their hair in a braided queue and that the loss of this queue would entail disgrace and humiliation and of the further fact that Chinese found guilty of violating the lodging house ordinance (which had just begun to be enforced) were choosing to serve jail sentences rather than pay fines, required the county jail to shear the hair of all convicted prisoners to within one inch of the scalp. The final measure compelled all who wished to disinter the remains of deceased persons to obtain the consent of the county coroner. It was well known to the supervisors that the remains of the Chinese who died in this country were often disinterred and their bones returned to their home villages for burial. Such a law offered officials ample opportunity for harassing the Chinese, as its sponsor was well aware. As he put it, if the coroner did not understand how he should discharge his duty, he was sure that someone could be found who would.[28] The possible impact of the two measures on the flow of Chinese immigration was not lost on the general public. The San Francisco *Evening Bulletin* editorialized:

> It is generally known . . . that to deprive a Chinaman of his queue is to humiliate him as deeply as is possible. It is also very generally known, that the bones of no Chinaman are permitted to remain in a foreign land, and that all Chinese, before leaving their country, feel assured that, after death, no matter where they die, their bones will be taken back to mingle with their native sod. So strict are all Chinese on these two points, that it is believed, if they were prevented from wearing their tails here and if after death their

> bones were denied transportation to their native land, the immigration of these superstitious people would be effectually stopped, and a reflux commence from our shores to the Flowery Kingdom.[29]

The Chinese were incensed at the proposed ordinances and a group of them asked the Reverend Otis Gibson, a Methodist minister and head of the church's Chinatown mission, to make their anger known to the board of supervisors. At the June 2 meeting of the board, at which a final vote was to be taken, he appeared and read to the members his translation of a lengthy statement of protest prepared by five named Chinese, as they put it, "on behalf of the Chinese in America." It is a remarkable document, bearing witness once again to the deep sensitivity of many Chinese on the question of racial discrimination. "In California, Oregon and Nevada," the statement read,

> laws designed not to punish guilt and crime, nor yet to protect the lives and property of the innocent, have been enacted and executed discriminating against the Chinese; and the Board of Supervisors of the City of San Francisco . . . has surpassed even these State authorities, in efforts to afflict us, by what seems to us, most unjust, most oppressive, and most barbarous enactments.

The Chinese had throughout their stay in this country been a largely peaceable and industrious people, the statement's authors declared. They had toiled patiently to build railroads, to aid in harvesting California's fruits and grains, to reclaim its swamplands. In the mining regions they had been satisfied with claims deserted by whites. Their presence, the authors noted, had made possible numerous manufacturing industries which could not have otherwise survived on the West Coast. Why, then, they asked, was there such bitter hostility against them? Why were there so many "severe and barbarous enactments" directed against them? "[I]n the name of our country," they went on, "in the name of justice and humanity, in the name of Christianity (as we understand it), we protest against such severe and discriminating enactments while living in this country under existing treaties." Should the discrimination and mistreatment continue, the statement concluded, the Chinese were prepared to recommend that the Burlingame Treaty be abrogated and that all Chinese and Americans be required to leave each other's countries. This, it said on a note of sarcasm,

> will give to the American people an opportunity of preserving for a longer time their civil and religious institutions, which, it is said, the immigration of the Chinese is calculated to destroy! This arrangement will also, to some extent, relieve the Chinese people and

> Government, from the serious embarrassments which now disturb them, and enable them by so much to return to the traditional policy of their sages and statesmen, *i.e.*, "Stay at home and mind their own business, and let all other people do the same."[30]

The statement, however, had no evident effect on the supervisors who went on to enact both the license law and the hair-cutting ordinance.

The Chinese were not alone in reacting negatively to the San Francisco ordinances. A few days after their passage, the *Daily Alta* printed a long excerpt from a sister journal, the *Monitor*, condemning them. It had no sympathy for Chinese immigration, the paper declared, but disliked the means that had been chosen to deter it. These were "partial laws," meant in the main to impose hardship on the Chinese, and as such were "bad in principle and thoroughly un-American." Today it was the Chinese whose ox was being gored, but tomorrow some other group might be the object of partial and discriminatory lawmaking.

> We look with much suspicion upon any legislation, State or municipal, which aims directly or indirectly, at discriminating between the different classes of our population. . . . What we want to see maintained is the grand Republican [the *Monitor* like the *Alta* was a pro-Republican paper] programme of equal rights and equal privileges for all.[31]

The mayor of San Francisco, William Alvord, was also known to be opposed to the ordinances, and on June 9 he returned the license law unsigned and the hair-cutting ordinance with a veto message affixed. He opposed the new schedule of license fees because he felt they were irrational and worked a hardship on the poor. The other measure he thought more reprehensible. Its manifest purpose was to inflict shameful punishment on persons convicted of minor offenses, something that ran counter to a fair criminal jurisprudence. More important, he was convinced that the law violated the Civil Rights Act of 1870 and the treaties between the United States and China. "Though general in its terms [it is] in substance and effect, a special and degrading punishment inflicted upon Chinese residents for slight offences solely by reason of their alienage and race." Finally, he considered the regulation of the affairs of the county jail to be beyond the legislative authority of the supervisors.[32]

The Soon Kung *and* Hung Hai *Cases*

The mayor's veto of the hair-cutting, or as it quickly came to be called, the "queue," ordinance could not be overridden, but the amendment to the laundry license ordinance did eventually become law, though only on a close vote and not without further interesting debate in the legislative chamber. One supervisor moved for the ordinance's indefinite postponement on the ground that "it contemplates an unequal and oppressive tax." Another, having had time for further consideration, expressed his conclusion that the measure was flawed. As framed, its onus would fall on whites as well as Chinese. He suggested that it be redrafted so as to apply to Chinese only.[33]

According to the Reverend Gibson the Chinese laundrymen were deeply upset at the serious economic hardship the new laundry license law threatened and came to him for counsel. His advice to them, so he tells us, was "to go on as before, paying no regard to the law, and see what would be done."[34] It was advice that was easy to heed, at least initially, since in the first months following passage the city authorities made no efforts to enforce the new fee schedule. In early February, however, thirteen Chinese laundrymen, who kept laundries using no horse and wagon, were arrested for failure to pay the $15 quarterly license fee. The arrests caused the *Daily Alta* to comment that their cases would "doubtless give some enthusiastic attorney occasion to air his ideas of equity and practice."[35]

As it would turn out, the *Alta*'s prediction was not far off the mark. The laundrymen hired Henry H. Haight, former Democratic governor of California, to represent them.[36] (Though direct proof cannot be supplied, it seems plausible to assume that they acted through the agency of their guild.) According to Gibson, at his (Gibson's) suggestion, they also caused complaints to be issued against a number of white women who took in laundry in their homes.[37] While the complaints against most of the laundrymen were dropped, one case, against laundryman Soon Kung, was pressed forward to conviction in the police court. From there an appeal was taken to San Francisco county court, where defense counsel again argued that the ordinance was invalid. On July 9 Judge John Stanly handed down a decision completely vindicating this claim.

Stanly rested his decision on the general power of courts to strike down city laws and county ordinances that were obviously unfair or oppressive. Under views widely shared at the time by judges and commentators alike, city and county governments—municipal corporations as they were called—were looked upon as distinctly inferior governmental bodies, possessing limited powers and subject to far-ranging judicial supervision in the interest of protecting individual rights. Thus Thomas Cooley, the author of the leading post-Civil War treatise on constitutional law, *Consti-*

tutional Limitations, advised judges to be extremely cautious and deferential in reviewing acts of the state legislature but to act vigorously to strike down municipal ordinances found to be oppressive, in restraint of trade, or otherwise in contravention of established common-law principles. The leading treatise on the law of municipal corporations gave essentially the same advice. Stanly cited both works in support of his decision as well as a line of pre-Civil War Massachusetts cases.[38]

The San Francisco ordinance was void, in Stanly's view, because it arbitrarily discriminated against the poorer laundry keeper. From its face it appeared that the law's purpose was to make it more difficult for the small laundry operator than for his larger competitor to carry on his business. He thought the injustice of such a purpose was too obvious to require extended analysis. It would be a fine day, he declared, if, "under a form of government which abhors unequal and discriminating laws . . . and which guarantees to all the equal protection of the laws," the courts could not nullify a municipal law, "which discriminates unjustly against the poor, wantonly and unnecessarily adds to their burden, and substantially prohibits them from the pursuit of a useful and worthy calling."[39]

The judge took note of the allegation that, in addition to discriminating against the laundry keeper of lesser means, the ordinance was deliberately designed to fall with special weight upon the Chinese laundry operator, but he did not think he needed to go into the question of legislative motivation in order to reach the conclusion that the law was invalid.

> Suggestion has been made that the order was intended to apply primarily to a race of persons not expressly designated in it. However that may be, this Court has nothing to do with the secret motives or intentions of the body which passed the order.

The fact that the ordinance on its face discriminated against poorer laundry operators was sufficient justification for declaring it null and void.[40]

At the end of 1874 the city of San Francisco revised its general municipal regulations and, to comply with the court's ruling in *Soon Kung* presumably, restored the laundry licensing schedule to the status quo ante.[41] But there matters did not rest. On March 13, 1876, the board of supervisors passed another ordinance requiring all laundries not owning wagons to pay $15 per quarter.[42] It might seem strange at first blush that the San Francisco supervisors would choose to re-enact without material changes an ordinance that the county court had unequivocally struck down two years earlier, but when California lawmakers pondered anti-Chinese legislation, a measure's conformity or lack thereof with prevailing judicial opinion seldom counted for much given sufficient popular pressure. And this was a period of great anti-Chinese agitation.[43]

A few days after final approval of the ordinance a Chinese-language newspaper, the *Oriental* (*T'ang fan kung pao*),[44] reported that Chinese laundrymen had gathered to discuss the newly enacted ordinance and were considering hiring a lawyer to challenge it in court. They were concerned about the ordinance's probable impact on their apparently already narrow profit margins, and, one sees clearly in the article, were very resentful that they were again being racially targeted. One of them is reported saying, "The Americans only know how to deal with the Chinese in hard ways."[45] The leaders of the *hui-kuan* showed the same clear awareness of the ordinance's ultimate purpose in an open letter they sent to their countrymen in Hong Kong in early April. The purpose of the letter was to inform the Chinese of the growing strength of the anti-Chinese movement and of the dangers they would face in this country if they chose to emigrate here. In it they described the various ways in which Caucasian Californians were trying to discourage Chinese immigration. "In the city of San Francisco," they wrote, "the prominent men now want all Chinese laundrymen to pay a heavy tax. They tried to impose the tax once before, but did not succeed. They are now trying it again, and in this and other ways endeavoring to stop all emigration from China to this country."[46]

An opportunity for a court test of the new laundry ordinance soon presented itself as the city's licensing officer moved quickly to enforce it. And when the Chinese laundryman Hung Hai was arrested for engaging in the laundry business without having paid the required license fee, he, acting in all probability with the support of his fellow tradesmen, sued out a writ of habeas corpus in a state trial court.

On May 2, 1876, Judge Samuel B. McKee of the Third District Court struck down the ordinance in an opinion that virtually echoed the earlier views of Judge Stanly and ordered the petitioner released from custody. A city's power to license businesses and professions, said the judge, was one limited by the constitutions of both the United States and of the state and was furthermore limited by the requirement that it be exercised in a reasonable manner. The ordinance's sheer unreasonableness was enough to condemn it in the judge's eyes.

> It exacts from the washerman or washerwoman who have nothing more than a basket in use in the business and cannot afford to employ a horse and wagon, a license fee more than seven times greater than is required from a launderer who employs in the busi-

> ness a horse and wagon . . . and equal to that required from him who may employ in the business ten, twenty or any number of horses and wagons.[47]

This could only be seen as oppressive of the poorer members of the laundering profession, and such unequal treatment by a municipality was forbidden by common principles of jurisprudence.

Like Judge Stanly, Judge McKee had to deal with the allegation that the ordinance had sprung from improper legislative motivation, here made with greater force since counsel for the petitioner had supplied the court with the affidavit of one of the supervisors declaring that the law had been passed with the intention of affecting only the Chinese. McKee, too, did not think that he needed to consider possible bad motivation in order to reach his conclusion. The fact that the measure was "unequal, unreasonable and unjust" in operation and effect sufficed. But he differed with his colleague on the right of courts to inquire into the subject. The motives of municipal legislators could be inquired into, he thought, and if it could be shown that in the exercise of their lawful power to tax or to regulate "a lawful and necessary business" they had passed a statute for ulterior reasons, that would entitle a court to declare the statute void.[48]

The *Hung Hai* and *Soon Kung* cases again reveal the alacrity with which Chinese residents of California resorted to the courts when they felt that their interests were threatened by discriminatory legislation. It may well have been these decisions that prompted this comment from B. E. Lloyd in his 1876 book, *Lights and Shades in San Francisco*. "The Chinese are very punctual in paying taxes, licenses, and all just public demands," he wrote, "but when the municipal authorities . . . indulge in a little legislation specially aimed at the pocket of the heathen, they generally avail themselves of the yankees' argument, 'Why?', have the matter tested in the courts, and if victorious, as they commonly are, hide their faces in their broad sleeves and laugh over their success."[49] The cases ended the efforts of San Francisco to use differential business taxation as a means of discouraging a Chinese presence.[50] But differential taxation was but one weapon in what proved to be a rather sizable armory, and the *Soon Kung* and *Hung Hai* decisions did not in the least deter San Francisco, other cities in the state, or the state legislature from reaching for other weapons before the decade was over.

The Case of the Twenty-two Chinese Women

On August 24, 1874, a little over a month after the county court rendered its decision in *Soon Kung*, the steamer *Japan* arrived in the port of San

Francisco from Hong Kong with a full load of passengers, almost all of them Chinese. When the vessel arrived, the commissioner of immigration, a state official, and his agents boarded it in order to inspect the passengers. They examined the eighty-nine Chinese females on board and determined that some twenty-two were prostitutes. Pursuant to California law, he ordered the ship's captain to detain them on board pending receipt of a $500 bond for each of them from the ship's owner, the Pacific Mail Steamship Company, or, failing that, to return them to China at the next sailing. This order set in motion a chain of events that would soon bring another, very different, set of Chinese complainants into court.

Unlike the basket carriers or laundrymen or indeed any of the other Chinese litigants discussed in this work, these litigants probably did not reflect any broad community sentiment, nor is it likely that many Chinese saw their legal action as advancing any broad community interest. (It is probable in fact that quite the contrary held true.) But the "Case of the Twenty-two Chinese Women," as the case that grew out of these events came to be called, a case pursued probably for narrow if not unsavory reasons, was destined to produce legal principles of considerable importance to the community as a whole. It eliminated once and for all any hope that those opposed to the Chinese might have harbored that the states could use any supposed reserved rights over foreign immigration to halt Chinese immigration at the gates. It also provided the occasion for a federal court to suggest for the first time that the Chinese might derive very broad protections indeed from the Fourteenth Amendment to the United States Constitution. And it would be under the banner of these principles that virtually all later Chinese civil rights litigation would proceed.[51]

It seems appropriate here to say a word about Chinese prostitution, the background against which the "Case of the Twenty-two Chinese Women" unfolded. Chinese immigration had its unsavory side. For a variety of reasons, including no doubt the inhospitality of the surroundings, most Chinese men, if married, did not choose to bring their wives to California. If unmarried they elected not to marry or build families in the state. The large bachelor society, predictably, created a large demand for prostitution, and, just as predictably, an industry grew up to satisfy the demand. Large numbers of young women were recruited by Chinese procurers from rural districts of China, often under false pretenses, and were transported across the sea to work as prostitutes in San Francisco, the mining districts, or other regions where Chinese congregated.[52] Like prostitutes in other parts of the world, once in California these women faced a generally unhappy existence, exploited, abused, and some kept in a state of virtual enslavement by their masters. Prostitution flourished on a grand scale in all sectors of California society in the nineteenth century, especially in the city of San Francisco. Prostitutes came from all racial and ethnic backgrounds and plied their trade in all ethnic enclaves. But Chinese prostitution was always a topic of special concern to Caucasian California. Caucasians often acted and spoke in fact as if the problem were peculiar to the Chinese.[53] It was the subject of repeated, horrified comment in the press and of endless declamation in various legislative corridors. On more than a few occasions it was the object of special legislative attention. In 1866 for example the California legislature enacted a statute declaring Chinese houses of prostitution (but only these) to be public nuisances and providing a variety of remedies for their abatement.[54]

Chinese prostitution was of course a problem and was perceived as such by many Chinese. Apart from humanitarian considerations, responsible leaders of the community could not help but see that the presence of so many prostitutes in their midst furnished grist to the mills of their enemies, who were fond of pointing to it as but further evidence of Chinese moral degeneracy. These leaders cooperated with the authorities in prostitution abatement campaigns. Occasionally, they mounted campaigns of their own.[55] In 1868, for example, the leaders of the district associations proposed a solution to the problem. They addressed a memorial to the governor, deploring the traffic and exhorting him to use his influence with the steamship companies to see to it that no Chinese woman be allowed to book passage in Hong Kong unless she could present a certificate of good character signed and sealed by an agent they should designate in that port.[56] There is no evidence that the governor seriously considered this suggestion, but in 1870 the legislature passed a statute making it unlawful to bring into the state any "Mongolian, Chinese, or Japanese female" without first presenting to the commissioner of immigration evidence that she was a voluntary immigrant and was a person of correct character.[57] And in 1874 it amended its immigration law, which required a $500 bond for certain kinds of immigrants—paupers, convicted criminals, the handicapped, others thought likely to become public charges—to add to the list anyone found by the commissioner of immigration to be a "lewd or debauched woman."[58] (That the two statutes were in conflict—the one barring absolutely the admission of immoral women, the other conditioning their admission on the giving of bond—does not seem to have occasioned comment.) It was, it appears, under the authority of the latter statute that the commissioner ordered the twenty-two women detained on board the steamship *Japan* on August 24, 1874.

The day after the commissioner of immigration issued his detention order, someone—accounts differ as to who he was—retained a former judge, Leander Quint, as attorney and made application for a writ of habeas corpus in the California Supreme Court. It issued the writ and transferred the matter to the Fourth District Court in San Francisco for hearing.[59] At the hearing, which went on for several days, the commissioner of immigration testified that the women were prostitutes and were being detained pursuant to state law. (It was clear that it was the bonding statute that he had chiefly in mind, but at times he seemed to suggest that he was relying on the other statute as well.) When pressed by counsel for the women to supply the grounds on which he based this conclusion, he responded that it was based on his observations of the women's demeanor and manner of dress and on the evasive and unsatisfactory responses they had given to questions put to them about their marital status. The Reverend Otis Gibson, who had lived in China for many years before coming to San Francisco, lent support to the commissioner's views. Gibson testified that the style of dress worn by several of the women detainees—handkerchiefs around the head and gaudy-colored garments embroidered with silk—corresponded with the type of dress worn by courtesans in China. He opined that at least half of those who had been detained were prostitutes.[60]

The captain of the *Japan* was called by counsel for the petitioners and stated that he had had occasion to observe the women during the voyage over and that they had deported themselves in exemplary fashion. He also produced certificates signed by the U.S. consul in Hong Kong and the emigration officer in that port certifying that all of his passengers were voluntary emigrants and that they had not been induced to leave by fraud.[61] He claimed that the women had been interviewed by these officials before departure and would not have received these documents had the issuers not been satisfied as to their respectability.[62] A number of the women themselves took the stand. All testified that they were married and had come to California either to meet or to rejoin their husbands. The testimony, it must be said, was less than convincing and was substantially undermined by the fact that none of the alleged husbands came forward to claim his bride.

The Pacific Mail Steamship Company was separately represented at the hearing by Thomas Bergin of the well-established San Francisco law firm of McAllister and Bergin. The company was reaping large financial rewards from the passenger trade with China and, whatever its belief about the morality of the women, doubtless had little sympathy for an attempt by any state to assert such expansive controls over foreign immigration.[63] Bergin sought to focus the court's attention on the legal as opposed to the factual issues, namely that the California statute gave enormous discretion to a state official to determine who should and who should not enter California. He suggested as well that local law ran counter to the Burlingame Treaty and, interestingly, Section 16 of the Civil Rights Act, which protected persons against special enactments. These issues, he argued, transcended the mere individuals who were involved in the case.[64] But the court found that the statutes were constitutional and, satisfied that the evidence showed that the women were prostitutes, remanded them back to the custody of the master of the steamship.

On that same day, August 29, counsel for the women made application for another habeas writ in the California Supreme Court, alleging that they were about to be deported to China and asking the high court itself to rule on the important legal questions the case raised. The chief justice granted the writ returnable before the Supreme Court and ordered the women into the custody of the city coroner. A little more than a week later, after hearing oral argument, the appellate tribunal handed down its decision. Addressing the only points that had apparently been raised, it held that the California bonding statute offended neither the due process clause of the Fourteenth Amendment, nor Article VI of the Burlingame Treaty, which provided that Chinese subjects visiting or residing in the United States should have the same privileges and immunities with respect to travel and residence as the citizens of the most favored nation. The California law was general in application and did not discriminate against the Chinese, the court declared, and it found no violation of due process in the summary adjudicative powers vested by the statute in the commissioner of immigration. It analogized them to the summary powers of inquiry and decision often vested by statutes in quarantine or health officials. It was aware of no decision holding such laws unconstitutional under the concept of "due process."[65] The matter was far from concluded, however. One of the women sued out yet another writ of habeas corpus, this time in the federal Circuit Court for the District of California.[66] The hearing on the petition took place September 16 and 17 before a federal panel consisting of Circuit Court Judge Lorenzo Sawyer, District Court Judge Ogden Hoffman, and Supreme Court Justice Stephen Field, in San Francisco to sit as a circuit judge. (At the time Supreme Court justices were obliged to periodically hear cases in the circuits for which they were responsible.)

Justice Field did most of the questioning during oral argument and dominated the proceedings.[67] A colloquy with counsel for the state made clear that he thought the case raised major issues of constitutional law and gave an unmistakable clue as to the direction of his thinking on them.

Field seemed most upset by the law's latent particularism, a topic on which, as he had shown a year earlier in the *Slaughter-House Cases*,[68] he harbored very strong views. These cases had been brought by a group of New Orleans butchers displeased by a state law requiring that all butchering work be done on the grounds of a single corporation. They alleged that it violated the privileges and immunities clause of the Fourteenth Amendment ("No State shall make or enforce any law which shall abridge the privileges or immunities of citizens of the United States") and the amendment's due process and equal protection clauses. By a five to four vote the Court held that it didn't. Field, along with Justices Joseph Bradley and Noah Swayne, wrote vigorous dissents. Field contended that the measure, by granting special privileges to one group of businessmen, violated the privileges and immunities clause. The other dissenters agreed with Field but maintained that it violated the due process and equal protection clauses as well.

That the statute in question in this case was aimed specifically at the Chinese had been acknowledged by government counsel. But, according to Justice Field (if the newspaper accounts of his remarks are reliable), since the incorporation of the Fourteenth Amendment into the Constitution, states were prohibited from singling out foreigners for special treatment of this sort.[69] In the *Slaughter-House Cases* Field had argued that the privileges and immunities clause of the Fourteenth Amendment protected citizens against unequal and partial legislation in the lawful pursuits of life.[70] He spoke now of other provisions of that Amendment. He noted that the Fourteenth Amendment's due process and equal protection clauses used the word "person" as opposed to "citizen." This, he said, proved an intention to place foreigners on a level of equality with citizens in certain respects at least. "I have no doubt," he declared, "that the State can exclude all dangerous persons; but the idea is that whatever protection the law gives shall be uniform and shall extend to all classes."[71] American prostitutes, he noted, were able to come and go as they pleased. The statute in question clearly raised the question whether the state of California was not here trenching on the exclusive control over foreign commerce vested in the Congress by Article I, Section 8 of the Constitution. And there was nothing terribly controversial about Field's contention that the Fourteenth Amendment's due process and equal protection clauses applied to noncitizens as well as citizens. What was surprising was Field's suggestion that these clauses had application to the California statute.

Justice Field announced the court's ruling on September 21. The tribunal had decided that the petitioner was unlawfully detained and must be discharged. The opinion was bottomed principally on federal commerce clause considerations. Field acknowledged that under the Constitution, the states retained, as a matter of self-defense, the power to exclude from their territory certain classes of immigrants entirely, criminals, for example (and by that he meant convicted felons) or those afflicted with incurable disease. They could furthermore condition the entry of those who were likely to become a public charge—for example, the insane—upon the payment of security. But the right of the states to exclude foreigners was narrowly limited to these few instances. Beyond that, control over immigration was exclusively the preserve of the federal government.[72] And Field thought that the California statute clearly encroached on that preserve. A state could not exclude foreigners merely because of the supposed immorality of their past lives or professions unless that immorality had resulted in conviction for a felony. Where a state thought that certain kinds of foreigners would disregard its laws and be injurious to its peace, declared Field, "the remedy lies in the more vigorous enforcement of the laws, not in the exclusion of the parties."[73]

Field recognized that the law at issue was a manifestation not only of a desire to exclude Chinese prostitutes but of a dislike for Chinese immigration in general. For his part, he felt that there was ground for the feeling, consisting in the probable unassimilability of the Chinese, but he admonished the state that if their immigration was to be stopped it must be stopped by the federal government, where the whole power over the subject lay. The state could not "exclude them arbitrarily, nor accomplish the same end by attributing to them a possible violation of its municipal laws,"[74] especially not in the case of the Chinese since their right to immigrate to the United States was grounded firmly in international treaty. As for California's desire to rid itself of lewdness, he confessed that he had little respect "for that discriminating virtue which is shocked when a frail child of China is landed on our shores, and yet allows the bedizened and painted harlot of other countries to parade our streets."[75]

Field thought that there was another view of the case, one, as he put it, "founded upon the legislation of Congress since the adoption of the Fourteenth Amendment," that entitled the petitioner to be discharged from custody.[76] The first section of the amendment, said Field, in addition to designating who were citizens of the United States and forbidding legislation abridging their privileges and immunities, had also enacted that no state should deprive *any person* (the distinctive term "citizen" having been dropped, he noted) of life, liberty, or property without due process or deny to *any person* the equal protection of the laws. The effect of this provision was to place all persons whether high or low, native or foreign, on a plane of civil equality. "Discriminating and partial legislation, favoring particular persons, or against particular persons of the same class, is now prohibited," he declared.[77] And, he went on, equality of protection not only implied equal access to the courts, but also equal exemption "with others of the same class from all charges and burdens of every kind."[78] It was the first time that any judge had made so explicit what was implicit in the wording of the Fourteenth Amendment's due process and equal protection clauses, namely that they embraced within their coverage aliens as well as citizens.[79]

It was in conformity with these principles, Field explained, that Congress had enacted the Civil Rights Act of 1870, which, among other things, declared that the states should not impose taxes or charges on any class of immigrants that it did not equally impose on other classes of immigrants. From Field's comments during oral argument, it was clear that he thought the problem with the statute was that it was only designed to affect lewd and debauched women who were Chinese. But by its terms it was not aimed at any particular racial group. How then could it be found to be in conflict with the federal law? Only by a somewhat tortuous reasoning process, it must be said. Making the right of an immigrant to land contingent on the giving of a bond by a third party was the imposition of a charge, Field reasoned. But it was only imposed upon certain classes of foreigners coming to California *by ship*, leaving foreigners of the same class who arrived in the state by land exempt from similar charges. Therein, according to Field, lay the inequality of charge made illegal by the act of Congress.[80]

Field's colleagues did not share his view of the case. They thought of it strictly as a commerce clause case and considered that it had nothing to do with the Fourteenth Amendment. Furthermore it appears that Judge Sawyer at least did not even share his view of what the commerce clause mandated, considering that states still had wide berth to regulate foreign immigration,[81] but under the law the opinion of a single Supreme Court justice, sitting on circuit, became the opinion of the court, no matter what the views of his colleagues on the panel.

Field, anxious to have a United States Supreme Court ruling on the questions raised by the *Ah Fong* case, suggested, at the conclusion of his reading of his opinion, that counsel make arrangements to have the matter sent up to the high court on a writ of error for a quick decision.[82] Since a writ of error could only be used to review a final adjudication by a state supreme court, one of the petitioners was not released but was allowed to sue out a writ of error in the U.S. Supreme Court, contesting the judgment of the California Supreme Court. Matters did not move quickly, however. It was not until January of 1875 that the record in the case, now called *Chy Lung v. Freeman,* was received in the U.S. Supreme Court and still another year before the case was argued. In the meantime Congress, acting in response to pressure from western representatives, had passed a statute forbidding the importation of women for purposes of prostitution. In furtherance of this objective it imposed new inspection duties on consular officials in Hong Kong, and, on this side of the ocean, vested in federal port officers the right to inspect incoming vessels in order to keep out prostitutes and felons convicted of nonpolitical offenses.[83]

On March 20, 1876, practically two years after the circuit court ruling in *Ah Fong,* the Supreme Court handed down its decision. On the same day it decided two cases from other states raising practically identical issues of state versus federal power over immigration. In *Henderson et al. v. Mayor of New York et al.* and *Commissioners of Immigration v. North German Lloyd*[84] it nullified laws from, respectively, New York and Louisiana that required the owners of vessels landing foreign passengers to give bonds for every such passenger in the sum of $300, conditioned to indemnify the states against their becoming public charges. These were attempts by the states to regulate foreign commerce, it held, and as such were incursions on an exclusive federal legislative domain. The California statute under review in *Chy Lung* was different in that it did not apply to all foreign immigrants but only to those determined by a state official to fit a certain description. This did not make it any less intrusive on federal prerogatives or any less constitutionally infirm in the Court's view. The California law, in vesting so much uncontrolled discretion in a state official, gave the official, by the wrongful exercise of that discretion, the power to complicate the foreign relations of the United States. The California law gave carte blanche to a silly or a wicked state official, it said, to keep out of the state individual foreigners no matter how distinguished or to subject them to extortion thereby bringing disgrace upon the United States and perhaps even involving it in a serious international dispute.[85]

Chy Lung and its companion cases represented the most extensive and definitive Supreme Court opinions yet on the subject of the right of the states to regulate foreign immigration, and decisions since then have added little to the principles the high court set forth in that case. These cases represented a sharp departure from previous precedent, which was equivocal on the subject and open to the interpretation that states still possessed considerable authority in this public policy area. The three Supreme Court decisions made it abundantly clear that the states had virtually no power to affect it directly. (Field had spoken in *Ah Fong* of the reserved power of the states to exclude foreigners as a precautionary measure against the increase in crime or pauperism. The high court implied it was skeptical that any such power existed.)[86] As the Court put it in *Chy Lung:* "The passage of laws which concern the admission of citizens and subjects of foreign nations to our shores belongs to Congress, and not to the States. It has the power to regulate commerce with foreign nations: the responsibility for the character of those regulations, and for the manner of their execution, belongs solely to the national government."[87] As noted above, the decisions effectively ended any hope the state of California might have had of itself controlling the flow of Chinese immigration. The Court had nothing to say in *Chy Lung* about Field's views on the relevance of the Fourteenth Amendment or the Civil Rights Act of 1870 to the issue before it. Nor did Field himself seize the occasion to restate his views. Perhaps on reflection he realized that the facts of this case did not present him with the best platform from which to press his beliefs concerning the relation between those provisions and "partial and discriminatory legislation."

The State and Federal Legislative Hearings of 1876

The year 1876 was marked by other events of major significance to the Chinese, most notably the launching of two inquiries on the subject of Chinese immigration by the state and national governments. The month following the *Chy Lung* decision, a special committee of the California Senate held, amid great fanfare, two weeks of public hearings on the subject. It concluded—not surprisingly given the composition of the legislature and the temper of the times—that the immigration was an unmitigated evil and sent a memorial to the U.S. Congress asking that body to act forthwith to suppress it.[88] Six months later a committee of the United States Congress (formally designated "the Joint Special Committee to Investigate Chinese Immigration"), empaneled in response to pressure from western legislators, traveled to San Francisco to conduct an even more comprehensive and important investigation of its own.[89]

The congressional committee opened its hearings in San Francisco on October 18 and adjourned a month later. During that time it heard from 130 witnesses, some reasonably informed, others merely engaging in racial stereotyping. The record of the proceedings takes up almost thirteen hundred printed pages. Though the bulk of the testimony that was heard inclined against the Chinese, a fair number of witnesses, principally businessmen employing Chinese laborers and the two Protestant missionaries most active in the community, the Reverend Gibson and the Reverend Loomis, stepped forward to speak in their favor.[90] In its final report, however, the federal panel echoed the recommendations of the state body.

Holding up the specter of imminent inundation by hordes of low-wage workers uninterested in if not incapable of assimilation (it concluded on the basis of the ethnological testimony that it had received that "there is not sufficient brain capacity in the Chinese race to furnish motive power for self-government"),[91] the committee urged that steps be taken by the executive and legislative branches of the national government to "restrain the great influx of Asiatics to this country."[92]

The congressional investigation did produce one useful benefit for the Chinese. It brought the leadership of the community into contact with two Caucasians who would prove to be valuable allies in the future. When word reached leaders of the Chinese district associations that a congressional committee was preparing to visit the West Coast, they sought to secure an attorney to be their representative before the body. Because of intense hostility existing in the state at the time, they could initially find no one. When they reported this fact to the committee chairman, Senator Oliver P. Morton of Indiana, he asked a California businessman with legal training with whom he was acquainted, Frederick A. Bee, to take on the task.[93] Bee agreed, and a prominent local attorney, Benjamin Brooks, without having been solicited, volunteered to assist him.[94]

Benjamin Brooks had come to California with the gold rush but immediately entered into law practice. He soon established a reputation as a leading land-title lawyer, specializing in the litigation of Spanish land-grant claims. By 1876 Brooks was one of the leading members of the San Francisco bar.[95] Frederick Bee was born and raised in New York State. He studied law but does not ever seem to have practiced there. He too came to California at the time of the gold discovery. He spent his first years in California in the mining districts, first as a miner, then as a merchant. He later became involved in a range of large business ventures, including the construction of the first transcontinental telegraph line and the establishment of the Pony Express. Bee's name first became linked with the Chinese in 1855. During that year, according to his obituary, while he was residing in the mining county of El Dorado, he came to the defense of some Chinese gold miners who were being "roughly treated" by whites and "assisted them in maintaining their rights." The obituary gives no further particulars on the incident. What added things Bee might have done for the Chinese in the years immediately following or what in particular caused Senator Morton to think of him as a possible representative before the Joint Congressional Committee cannot be documented.[96]

The motivation that led the two to offer to take on the thoroughly unpopular task of representing the Chinese seems to have been complex. Brooks told the committee that he had had no previous connection with the Chinese.[97] Bee apparently had employed Chinese workers before in his business enterprises. To judge from their comments before the committee, both men thought that Chinese workers, particularly agricultural workers, had been and would continue to be crucial to the economic development of the state. Both also were aware of the fact that the anti-Chinese movement was spearheaded by members of the white working class and saw it, especially in its more violent manifestations, as a symptom of a broader movement that threatened property and the established civil order. Both too, however, appear to have been genuinely moved by admiration for the Chinese, and to have been genuinely repelled by the unequal treatment to which the state of California and its municipalities were subjecting them.[98]

A Challenge to the Lodging House Law in Federal Court

The year 1876 witnessed the passage of significant new state and local legislation aimed at the Chinese. It will be remembered that in 1870 the San Francisco Board of Supervisors, largely in response to pressure from the extreme anti-Chinese faction in the city, had passed an ordinance (the so-called "lodging house" or "cubic air" ordinance) regulating the amount of space to be allocated to the tenants of lodging houses and imposing the alternative penalties of fine or imprisonment on violators. It had also passed an ordinance, calling for the shearing of the hair of male prisoners committed to the county jail to within one inch of the scalp in order to encourage Chinese violators to pay fines rather than choose the alternative of confinement in jail. The latter measure, as noted however, had been vetoed by the mayor.

In April of 1876 the California state legislature passed its own cubic air law.[99] Within days the San Francisco Board of Supervisors passed again the previously rejected "queue" ordinance.[100] As the Sacramento *Record-Union* commented when the ordinance was first being considered, "The resolution was intended as a blow at Chinese pig-tails."[101] It along with other provisions for the governance of the county jail received the board's final approval on June 12 and was signed by the mayor two days later.[102]

Since its original enactment in 1870 the city had enforced its own cubic air ordinance only in sporadic fashion. The first arrests under the ordinance had not been made until May of 1873.[103] No arrests were made in either 1874 or 1875 or in the first months of 1876. But in April of that year, whether or not in response to passage of the state lodging house law is not clear, enforcement began again in earnest.[104] Since an 1873 San Francisco court decision had made clear that it would be exceedingly difficult to convict the proprietors of lodging houses of violating the law, the effort was directed at the lodgers themselves.[105] As in 1873, Chinese lodging houses were the only targets.[106] The police invariably made their forays into the Chinese quarter in the dead of night, with officers occasionally using ladders to gain access to the premises. Once inside a building they took precise measurements of the premises and arrested any tenants found to be sleeping in rooms with less than the required space. We may take as fairly typical one raid conducted on the night of June 21. As the San Francisco *Evening Bulletin* described it the next day:

> A posse of officers made a descent last night on a Chinese lodging house on Clay street between Dupont and Stockton. Fifty six lodgers were captured in rooms as follows: six men were captured in a room containing but 1584 cubic feet of air; seven in a room of 2160; 8 in a room of 2310; 6 in a room of 1800; 9 in a room of [2374 or 2574-print illegible]; 6 in a room of 2359 1/2; 9 in a room of 2574; 1 in a room of 95; and seven in a room containing 2184 feet.[107]

The paper went on to report that of the fifty-six men arrested thirty-three had paid over $10 as bail, which they had forfeited, the others were taken to the police court, where they were promptly tried, convicted, and sentenced either to pay a $10 fine or to serve five days in the county jail.[108]

As the city's enforcement efforts mounted, so too did anxiety and consternation among the ostensible beneficiaries of the city's police measures, the ordinary Chinese lodgers. They soon brought their concern to the attention of the district associations. This was a logical development. The *hui-kuan* presidents had several times during the past year given clear evidence of their willingness to act forcefully to protect Chinese interests. They had, for example, on two occasions called upon the city authorities in the strongest terms to protect the Chinese against Caucasian violence, noting on one of these occasions that the Chinese were prepared to defend themselves if that protection was not forthcoming.[109] They had also during the first week of April 1876 addressed an open letter to the American public, defending the Chinese presence in the United States but offering to assist in the effort to restrict immigration if that would prevent the Chinese from suffering the abuses and indignities daily heaped upon them, as the Chinese Six Companies presidents put it, "in this so-called Christian land."[110]

On April 29, 1876, the *Oriental* reported that some Chinese who had been arrested under the lodging house law had been passing out fliers in Chinatown urging the community to hire a lawyer to represent them. In response, representatives of the Chinese Six Companies had invited these men to discuss the matter with them. The representatives, according to the journal, evidenced a great deal of timidity about acceding to these requests. They pleaded that their funds were limited and the number of Chinese likely to be arrested under the ordinance vast. They did not think they would be able to defeat the unlimited power of the government. They recommended that the Chinese population ignore the law, counting on the inability of the city's prisons to deal on a continuing basis with the large volume of persons likely to be found in violation of the ordinance.[111] Given this rather footless stance, it is surprising that two weeks later the same newspaper reported that the Chinese Six Companies had hired "a prestigious lawyer" to challenge the lodging house law.[112] There is no way to determine who this prestigious lawyer was or exactly what instructions the Six Companies gave; in any case, the lawyer took no immediate action. Raids and arrests under the lodging house law continued apace during the summer months and into the fall, and there is no record of the initiation of any legal action aimed at stopping them.[113]

Interestingly, the summer did see a court challenge to the queue ordinance though only the sketchiest of accounts can be provided concerning its origins and course. The *Bee,* a Sacramento paper, reported on June 22 that the Chinese were quite displeased with the San Francisco queue ordinance and were preparing to test its constitutionality in court. They were acting, according to the paper, with the support and assistance of Caucasians. ("Some tawney-haired humanitarian sentimentalists have come to the rescue of the Mongol in this matter," was the way the *Bee* put it.)[114] There is no record of when suit was filed, but the San Francisco *Chronicle* of August 25, 1876, noted that the Judiciary Committee of the board of supervisors had met the previous day to consider a request from the sheriff of San Francisco that he be defended in a suit filed against him designed to test the validity of the queue ordinance. The sheriff claimed that two Chinese arrested for violating the cubic air law had secured from a local court an injunction forbidding him from cutting their hair and that they had succeeded in raising the general question of the measure's validity before that tribunal. He further stated that he had been refused help by the district and county attorneys' offices. The committee, according to this report, ordered the county attorney's office to assist him.[115] The same newspaper reported several weeks later, on September 16 (under the headline "The Sheriff vs. John's Queue") that the court had sustained a demurrer to the complaint of the two Chinese. According to this account, the court rejected allegations that the ordinance in question was directed solely at the Chinese, that it was cruel and unusual punishment, and that it was beyond the legislative power of the board of supervisors. The court found the measure, rather, to be a legitimate prison sanitary regulation and one that was being applied equally to all prisoners.[116] The newspaper accounts make no mention of the involvement of Six Companies or any other Chinese organization in the initiation or maintenance of this lawsuit.

Frederick Bee and Benjamin Brooks had made a point of criticizing the cubic air and the queue ordinances in remarks they made before the Joint Special Committee in October.[117] And Brooks, in a post-hearing brief that he submitted to the committee in January 1877, directed harsh comments at both measures. He claimed that the cubic air law was not called for by any public necessity, and, although it was habitually violated by the majority of the white population, was never enforced against anyone but the Chinese. It had no assignable motive, he said, other than "malice, hatred and ill will. . . . Supplemented as it is by the Cue Cutting [*sic*] Ordinance, it is a palpable violation of the treaty, the constitution, and the inalienable rights of man," he declared.[118] But by the time Brooks filed his brief the city had again ceased enforcing the ordinance.

No arrests at all were made during 1877[119] or in the first month of the succeeding year, but in February 1878, for reasons that are not entirely clear, the city authorities decided to resume enforcement of the law. And the arrest on February 26 of some twenty-nine Chinese lodgers was the catalyst that sent the Chinese into court. The next day Bee and Brooks, along with another local attorney, D. W. Douthitt, filed a petition for a writ of habeas corpus in the United States Circuit Court in San Francisco on behalf of one Ah Wing (or Chin Ah Win), one of those arrested in the February 26 raid.[120] The habeas application attacked the state lodging house law, which since its enactment had superseded the city's own ordinance as the basis for all enforcement efforts. It alleged that the measure, the basis for the petitioner's incarceration, was enacted solely for the purpose of being enforced against the Chinese and that it in fact was enforced only against them and, as such, was in violation of the Constitution of the United States, of treaties existing between the United States and China, and of federal law. Statutory provisions specifically mentioned were Section 16 of the Civil Rights Act of 1870 and Section 1 of the Civil Rights Act of 1871, both included in the most recent codification of the federal statutes, the Revised Statutes of 1875, as Sections 1977 and 1979, respectively.[121] Section 1977 of the Revised Statutes conferred on all persons within the jurisdiction of the United States the same right to the "full and equal benefit of all laws and proceedings for the security of persons and property as is enjoyed by white citizens." Section 1979 made persons acting under color of law who subjected others within the jurisdiction of the United States to the deprivation of rights secured by the Constitution or laws of the United States liable to those injured in an action at law, suit in equity, or other proper proceeding for redress.[122]

The matter did not come up for oral argument until April 15, the petitioner having meanwhile been admitted to bail.[123] To judge from the (admittedly quite fragmentary) accounts in the city's newspapers, Brooks and Douthitt do not seem to have presented as forceful a case as they might have against the law. Instead of offering evidence that would have tended to prove the allegations of discriminatory motivation and enforcement contained in their habeas complaint, they did nothing more than expand on those allegations, asking the court to take judicial notice of the discriminatory enforcement pattern which they claimed existed. The tribunal was not impressed. Speaking in open court both for himself and for his colleague Circuit Judge Sawyer, District Judge Hoffman declared that the court had no right to inquire into the motives of the legislature and disclaimed any knowledge that the law in question was being enforced only against the Chinese. The measure, so far as the court could see, was only a public health and safety regulation well within the realm of legislative competence.[124]

The case was far from a total loss for the Six Companies. The court did admonish counsel for the city and state that the city must enforce the law fairly and impartially and could not restrict its enforcement activities to the Chinese. The city was further advised that the police could only act on probable cause and had no right to break in at random to see if people were violating the law. If the law were abused in the administration, there were available remedies, it suggested.[125] And, in a rather unusual move, the court as much as invited counsel for the Chinese to return to the federal bench to challenge the San Francisco queue ordinance. "I cannot deny that there has been oppressive legislation against the Chinese," Judge Hoffman declared. "The law requiring jailors to cut off queues, which is equivalent to a mutilation of Chinamen is undoubtedly discriminatory in its action," he went on, "and if it should come up for consideration I should say that it is unconstitutional."[126] The Chinese would act quickly enough to take Judge Hoffman up on his implied invitation. Meanwhile a group of Chinese litigants were calling upon the circuit court to decide another important question but one still not definitively settled, namely whether Chinese residents in the United States had the right to become U.S. citizens.

A Test Case on Naturalization: In re Ah Yup

The *Ah Wing* decision was handed down on a Monday. By the end of the week the press was reporting that a group of Chinese merchants had retained Frederick Bee and Benjamin Brooks to aid them in obtaining certificates of naturalization in the United States Circuit Court in San Francisco and that applications could be expected shortly.[127] Although direct proof is lacking, the involvement of Bee and Brooks in the case, both now universally recognized as chief Caucasian counselors to the Six Companies, makes it difficult to resist the conclusion that this case too, like *Ah Wing,* was undertaken with the encouragement and support of the Six Companies' leadership. It was not the first time that a California federal court had been asked to address the question of Chinese naturalization, but it was clear that something of a different order of magnitude was in the works here, something looking toward an authoritative opinion of record. The *Chronicle* noted that in anticipation of the applications the court had invited members of the local bar to offer their views on the issue that these applications raised.[128] The applicants doubtless knew that they faced an uphill struggle.

As was noted in the previous chapter, since the beginnings of the immigration a widely shared assumption had existed in the white community that Chinese could not become naturalized U.S. citizens. The assumption was not without foundation during most of the period we have been discussing. The first federal naturalization statute, enacted in 1790, restricted the right of naturalization to "any alien, being a free white person,"[129] and that language remained in the statute (which underwent several other modifications) up to the Civil War. These words had led the great antebellum jurist and legal commentator, Chancellor James Kent, to express doubt as early as 1826 as to whether "any of the tawny races of Asia" could be admitted to citizenship under the statute.[130] The situation became somewhat more complex after the Civil War. In 1870, driven no doubt by the logic of the great post-Civil War amendments and of the war itself, Congress amended the law to extend the naturalization privilege to "aliens of African nativity, and to persons of African descent."[131] But the amendment still left the naturalization rights of other nonwhites, at best, under a cloud. In 1875 things took an odd, though probably unintended, turn for the better so far as the Chinese were concerned, when the federal statutes were codified for the first time. The codifiers left out of the basic naturalization provision the phrase "being a free white person" so that it now simply read: "An alien may be admitted to become a citizen of the United States in the following manner."[132] A separate section of the Revised Statutes affirmed that the naturalization provisions should apply to "aliens of African nativity and persons of African descent."[133] But the following year, in a bill designed to correct errors and omissions that had occurred during codification, Congress, while leaving the wording of the basic naturalization provision unchanged, added the words "being a free white person" to this other section so that it now read "The provisions of this title shall apply to aliens [being free white persons, and to aliens] of African nativity and to persons of African descent."[134]

In December of 1875, with the law in this somewhat confused posture, a number of Chinese had sought to file declarations of intention to become citizens, the first step in the naturalization procedure, in the federal courts in San Francisco.[135] It is unclear whether these Chinese applicants or, for that matter, the courts were aware of the amendment to the law enacted in February. In any event some of those who applied were turned down while others were allowed to file their declaration of intention, albeit with a warning from the court clerks that their applications might be denied when they sought their final papers later on.[136] The filing of the applications, it should be noted, sent a shudder down the collective spine of the Caucasian community, and resulted, among other things, in the introduction in Congress the following month of a bill by Congressman John Luttrell of California, declaring in no uncertain terms that nothing in the naturalization laws should be construed so as to permit the naturalization of Chinese or Mongolians.[137] The bill, however, was never enacted into law.

It so happens that we know the identities of three of the December 1875 applicants and perhaps something of their motivation in seeking naturalization. One, Hong Chung, was an officer of one of the *hui-kuan*, the Sam Yup company. Another, Chock Wong, was the publisher of the Chinese-language newspaper, the *Oriental*. A third was a young man of no particular renown by the name of Chin Tin.[138] Testifying four months later before the California State Senate Committee, Hong Chung, offered some revealing comments on his (and perhaps others') reasons for taking out his first papers and on the attitude of his compatriots toward the question of U.S. citizenship. He told the legislators that a great many Chinese desired to become citizens and remain in the United States, and in response to the query whether, once naturalized, they would become candidates for public office, he responded: "May be; I don't know. They are going to become citizens. I like to be citizen. American man make no good laws for Chinaman. We make good laws for Chinaman citizens."[139] Neither Hong Chung nor Chock Wong took any further action on their applications, but on March 26, 1878, Chin Tin, more than two years now having elapsed since the filing of his declaration of intention, appeared in the United States District Court to apply for admission to citizenship. But District Judge Hoffmann denied the application, basing his decision on the amendment of February 18, 1875 to Section 2169 of the Revised Statutes. Chin's attorney took exception to the ruling, thereby laying the groundwork for an appeal to the circuit court.[140]

On the morning of April 22, 1878, three young Chinese—Ah Yup, Li Huang, and Leong Lan—arrived in the circuit court, accompanied by Frederick Bee, seeking to be naturalized. Circuit Judge Sawyer said that he would like to hear argument on the matter and set a hearing for that afternoon, with argument on the appeal of Chin Tin subsumed therein. In oral argument Brooks, who took the role of spokesman for the Chinese, contended that the term "white persons" was vague and indeterminate and could not be taken in a literal sense since in the class of persons called "white" could be found individuals of every hue from the lightest blonde to the most swarthy brunette, some in fact demonstrably darker than the Chinese.[141] Several members of the bar, including a former justice of the Supreme Court, were present, on the other hand to argue that the naturalization law used plain language which should be understood in its ordinary sense.[142] Another attorney called Sawyer's attention to the amendment of February 1875 to the naturalization law and to Judge Hoffman's denial of Chin Tin's application.[143]

Sawyer rendered his decision a week later. Referring, curiously, to the petition before him as "the first application made by a native Chinaman for naturalization," he ruled that Chinese were excluded from the privilege under federal law. The words "white person" had a well-settled meaning in common popular speech and in scientific literature, Sawyer observed, and were seldom if ever used in a sense so comprehensive as to include individuals of the Mongolian race.[144] More to the point, Sawyer was able to adduce considerable evidence that Congress had used the words "white person" in the naturalization laws with the specific intent in mind of excluding Chinese.[145] He noted, for example, that at the time of the 1870 amendment to the law an effort undertaken by Senator Charles Sumner of Massachusetts to strike the words "white person" from the naturalization statute had been successfully opposed on the very ground that this would admit Chinese to citizenship.[146] Furthermore, he was able to show that this consideration had been adverted to when Congress in 1875 voted to restore the words "white person" to Revised Statutes, Section 2169 after they had been omitted in the original codification (although Sawyer observed, correctly, that it would have made more sense to have inserted these words in another section of the law.)[147] During the litigation Bee had told the San Francisco *Chronicle* that the Chinese were prepared to take their case all the way to the Supreme Court of the United States,[148] but the thoroughness and cogency of Sawyer's opinion apparently convinced them that an appeal would have been an exercise in futility.[149] Another more promising litigation avenue beckoned in the meantime.

An Important Victory in the Federal Courts: Ho Ah Kow v. Nunan

The Chinese returned to Judge Sawyer's court four days later with a civil suit for damages against the sheriff of San Francisco, Matthew Nunan, on behalf of a man named Ho Ah Kow, a cubic air ordinance violator who had recently had his queue cut off in the county jail. Five days later identical complaints were filed on behalf of three other former Chinese prisoners.[150] One San Francisco paper was convinced that all three cases—*Ah Wing, Ah Yup,* and now the attack on the queue-cutting ordinance—were part of a general legal offensive, devised by the Six Companies and their attorneys, a belief that is not implausible.[151]

The *Ho Ah Kow* complaint, somewhat curiously given the fact that the case followed logically and upon the heels of *Ah Wing,* sounded only in tort, alleging simply that the sheriff had mutilated the plaintiff's person without any authority and had caused him intense humiliation and suffering.[152] It made neither a constitutional nor a statutory civil rights claim. Only in later pleadings did counsel for the plaintiff, J. E. McElrath as attorney of record and Benjamin Brooks as of counsel, raise the constitutional claim, though even then they did not develop it very fully.[153] The plaintiff's case, according to the pleadings, rested on two foundations: first, that the board of supervisors had acted in excess of the powers it had been delegated by the state legislature in enacting the hair-cutting ordinance; second, that the ordinance denied to the Chinese the equal protection of the laws. The powers of the supervisors, it was alleged, did not include the right to regulate the duties of the sheriff, a state officer, or the affairs of the county jail. The board's right to prescribe punishments was also limited (the cutting of prisoners' hair should be seen as a punishment, counsel argued). The board could prescribe no punishments other than fines and imprisonment and had no powers to prescribe punishments for violations of state law. (Ho Ah Kow had been convicted under the *state* cubic air law.) The lawyers also claimed that the San Francisco ordinance under which the plaintiff's hair had been cut was passed out of hostility to the Chinese and out of a desire to penalize them in particular.[154] The case was not submitted for decision until October and was referred then, upon written briefs, to Supreme Court Justice Field in his capacity as circuit justice.[155] The matter would stay under submission for almost nine months. In the meantime a number of other Chinese who had had their queues cut off in the county jail filed similar suits in circuit court against the sheriff.[156] And in September, counsel for the Chinese was able to procure an injunction from a state court, ordering the sheriff to desist from cutting the hair of Chinese prisoners, pending the outcome of the federal lawsuit.[157]

The wait proved worthwhile for the Chinese. The opinion that Justice Field read in open court on July 7, 1879, was a complete vindication of their cause. Field accepted the plaintiff's argument that the queue ordinance was beyond the board of supervisors' power. In response to the city's contention that this was a mere sanitary measure he noted that, under state law, the power to prescribe sanitary regulations for the county jail inhered in the board of health. But in Field's mind the claim that this was a sanitary measure was mere pretense. He had no doubt that the mandatory cutting of prisoners' hair should be seen as a punishment, a measure, as he put it, designed to add to the severity of the prisoner's confinement. But the board of supervisors had no authority to add to the punishments which the legislature had prescribed for violations of state law.[158]

Field found the plaintiff's other objection to the ordinance equally valid. He was as expansive on the point as the plaintiff's attorneys had been terse. The ordinance was, he declared, "special legislation on the part of the supervisors against a class of persons who, under the constitution and laws of the United States, are entitled to the equal protection of the laws."[159] The class character of the legislation was no less manifest because of the law's general terms. That the ordinance was intended to operate with special severity upon the Chinese was acknowledged by the supervisors on passage and was so understood by all. The reason that had been urged for its adoption, after all, he noted, was that only fear of losing his queue would induce the Chinese convicted under the lodging house law to pay his fine. Field did not think there was any need for judicial reticence given this state of affairs.

> [W]e cannot shut our eyes to matters of public notoriety and general cognizance. When we take our seats on the bench we are not struck with blindness, and forbidden to now as judges what we see as men; and where an ordinance, though general in its terms, only operates upon a special race, sect or class, it being universally un-

> derstood that it is to be enforced only against that race, sect or class, we may justly conclude that it was the intention of the body adopting it that it should only have such operation, and treat it accordingly.[160]

Once a measure was so characterized, Field had no doubt as to where judicial duty lay. Restating the principles he had first announced in *In re Ah Fong,* he affirmed that the equal protection clause of the Fourteenth Amendment applied to all persons and not just to citizens. That provision, he declared, forbade "hostile and discriminating legislation by a state against persons of any class, sect, creed, or nation, in whatever form it may be expressed."[161] The clause ensured, among other things, that no one while within the United States, regardless of country of origin, race, or color, should be subject to charges or burdens not equally borne by others or suffer greater or different punishments for criminal offenses. It ensured also that the courts should be open to all on the same basis for the security of person or property, the enforcement of contracts, and the redress of wrongs. And that prohibition on differential treatment applied to all instrumentalities of state government, including the subordinate legislative bodies of counties and cities.[162]

Section 16 of the Civil Rights Act of 1870 (Section 1977 of the Revised Statutes of 1875) was equally dispositive of the issues before the court. That law—which had been passed, Field noted again, in implementation of Fourteenth Amendment principles—gave all persons within the jurisdiction of the United States the right to the same benefit of laws and proceedings for the protection of person and property as was enjoyed by white citizens and banned differential punishments, pains, penalties, and exactions.[163]

As he had before in *Ah Fong* Field acknowledged the widespread community sentiment against the Chinese and again admitted a certain sympathy for that viewpoint and a certain hope that some way could be devised to prevent further immigration. But, the "remedy for the apprehended evil," he made clear, lay only with the national government. The state and its municipalities, he cautioned Californians, were without power to address the issue either directly or indirectly, by, for example, passing "hostile and spiteful" legislation of the kind before the court.[164]

Reaction to the decision in the California press was generally furious. "Every thinking person on the coast is perfectly satisfied that, at the present rate, American institutions in California will be displaced eventually by Asiatic barbarism. . . . There is no measure that legislative ingenuity could devise . . . that would not be pronounced unconstitutional by Judges Field and Sawyer or by any other judges that could be named," the *Chronicle* thundered.[165] Justice Field was such a zealous advocate of the Chinese, the *Examiner* said, that there was no need for a Chinese litigant to employ counsel in any case where he sat as a judge.[166] And the *Morning Call* asked sarcastically, if the Chinese queue was protected by the Fourteenth Amendment, why then Hindu immigrants shouldn't be protected in the custom of *suttee*.[167] But the Sacramento *Record-Union* struck a more moderate tone. Noting that it was notorious that the ordinance in question had been passed for the express purpose of inflicting a cruel and unusual punishment upon the Chinese, it congratulated the court for striking the measure down. The paper proclaimed its support for stopping Chinese immigration but said it would never sanction any treatment of the Chinese that was not "manly and just and honorable."[168]

Ho Ah Kow's significance for the future struggles of the Chinese can hardly be exaggerated. In the first place it said clearly that certain important provisions of the Fourteenth Amendment to the Constitution—the equal protection clause and, by necessary implication, the due process clause as well—applied to noncitizens as well as citizens and that the Chinese could make claims under it. This holding took on particular importance for the Chinese in light of the ruling in *Ah Yup*. It is true that Justice Field had expressed virtually identical views in the *Ah Fong* case. But that was a commerce clause case, and his attempt to use it as a forum to express his opinions concerning the reach of the Fourteenth Amendment had a strained quality that weakened the case's potential for influencing subsequent decision making. As noted above, the Supreme Court completely disregarded Field's Fourteenth Amendment views when it reviewed the case on appeal. With *Ho Ah Kow*, the court clearly had before it a Fourteenth Amendment claim, and that lent much greater force to Field's declarations.[169]

Ho Ah Kow was important, obviously, too, for its clear pronouncement that race or ethnic identity could not be the basis for the differential allocation of governmental burdens and, less obviously, for its suggestion that a law's surface neutrality did not immunize it from Fourteenth Amendment scrutiny. Even a superficially neutral measure could offend against the concept of noninvidious treatment embodied in the equal protection clause and the federal civil rights laws. The Chinese would oblige the federal courts to develop this notion further in a series of cases they would bring a few years later. Before that, however, they would be forced to deal with a series of state laws, about which there could be no pretense of governmental neutrality.

II

THE DECADE OF THE 1880s

Seeking the Equal Protection of the Laws

3 The California Constitutional Convention and Its Aftermath

The California Constitution of 1879

The original California constitution had been adopted in 1849 when the population of the state was approximately fifty thousand and the only industry of any consequence was mining. As the state's population began to grow and its economy and social structure became more complex, voices could be increasingly heard urging the summoning of a new constitutional convention to revise the fundamental law. As early as 1857 a popular vote had been taken on the question but had failed to garner the requisite number of votes. Efforts undertaken in succeeding years also failed to generate sufficient support, but the matter was never allowed to die. And in September 1877, supporters of constitutional revision were able at length to win a majority in a statewide plebiscite on the issue.[1] The state legislature responded in March of the next year by passing a resolution calling for a convention to frame a new constitution and setting June 19 as the date for the election of delegates.

It was the misfortune of the Chinese that the successful movement for constitutional revision should coincide almost exactly with the rise to prominence of the California Workingmen's party, the largest, most vociferous, and most influential anti-Chinese movement in California's history. And it cannot be doubted that the efflorescence of this movement had a greater impact than anything else upon the course that the former movement took. The party was first and foremost the creation of one man, Dennis Kearney, a demagogue of extraordinary power. Kearney had arrived in San Francisco from Ireland in 1868 as a merchant seaman and in 1872 had become proprietor of a draying business. In this early phase of his life he manifested no particular solicitude for the working population but by the fall of 1877 he had thrust himself into the leadership of the city's anti-Chinese forces. In a series of fiery speeches delivered in vacant sandlots to large assemblies of workers, Kearney denounced the Chinese presence in California in the most intemperate of terms. He urged his audiences to organize to "vote the moon-eyed nuisance out of this country" and suggested that the use of force would be warranted if peaceful means did not succeed in accomplishing that objective. (Kearney advised all of his followers to carry muskets and ammunition.) The Chinese laborer he described as a curse to the country and a menace to American liberties. Each harangue ended with the cry, "The Chinese must go!"[2] In October the loosely knit movement crystallized into an organization calling itself the Workingmen's party. The party drew up a platform calling for the expropriation of large landholdings, the permanent wresting of the reins of government from the hands of the rich, where it allegedly lay, the confiscatory taxation of wealth, and most important, the ridding of the country once and for all of Chinese laborers.[3]

The Kearney agitation caused great alarm in the Chinese community. On November 3, 1877, the presidents of the *hui-kuan* sent a strongly worded letter to Mayor A. J. Bryant. "Large gatherings of the idle and irresponsible element of the population," they noted, "are nightly addressed in the open streets by speakers who use the most violent, inflammatory and incendiary language, threatening in plainest terms to burn and pillage the Chinese quarter and kill our people." They demanded from the mayor protection to the full extent of his power in "all our peaceful, Constitutional and treaty rights against all unlawful violence." As they had done in 1876, they informed him that they would not intervene to prevent their countrymen from defending themselves if attacked.[4] They were not alone in their apprehension. Many in the upper and middle classes, including those on record as opposed to the Chinese presence in California, were alarmed by the violent tenor of Kearney's remarks and by what they saw as his party's thinly veiled threats against the institution of private property. The city authorities made several efforts to silence Kearney and his co-leaders in the fall of 1877 and early winter of 1878, arresting them twice for incitement to riot and bringing one (unsuccessful) criminal prosecution against them. In the meantime Kearney's party was growing daily in numbers and in political influence. And it was beginning to spread to other California municipalities. In March 1878, for example, Workingmen's party tickets were successful in winning all the municipal offices they contested in Oakland and Sacramento.[5]

As noted earlier, the election of delegates to the state constitutional convention had been set for June 19. Kearney and his followers viewed with relish the prospect of participating in the drafting of a new state constitution, and the Workingmen's party fielded candidates for convention seats in constituencies across the state. For a time the party held out the hope that it would win a clear majority of the delegates and work its political will without opposition in the convention proceedings. As it happened, the Workingmen candidates won only the San Francisco seats and lost rather decisively elsewhere in the state. Nonetheless the party's delegates constituted a third of those who convened in Sacramento in late September to begin the convention's work and were by far the largest partisan voting bloc present.[6]

Given this array of forces and the temper of the times, it took no exceptional political perspicacity to see that the subject of the Chinese would be made a large item on the convention's agenda. (One Workingmen's delegate told the assembly that he considered the Chinese the main reason the convention had been called into existence.)[7] Early in the proceedings a Committee on the Chinese was empaneled and charged with the task of drafting provisions for inclusion in the new constitution. John F. Miller, a San Francisco businessman, was appointed to the chair.[8] Miller was known to be quite hostile to the Chinese, but he was not allied with the Workingmen's faction, and some of the convention's less radical elements harbored the hope that he would serve as a moderating force in the committee's deliberations. The report which his committee presented to the full convention on December 9 was, however, anything but moderate. It recommended the incorporation in the new constitution of an article that would have prohibited all further Chinese immigration into California and placed the Chinese population remaining in the state, in effect, beyond the pale of the law. It was as extraordinary a measure as had ever before or has ever since been introduced for consideration before an American deliberative body, and there is no better way to gauge the depth, the intensity, and the sheer ferocity of Caucasian animus against the Chinese than by examining its nine separate provisions.

Section 1 gave the legislature power to impose conditions upon the residence in the state of aliens thought to be detrimental to its well-being and to remove them from the state if necessary. Section 2 forfeited the charter of any corporation that should employ in any capacity foreigners ineligible for citizenship. The third section made such foreigners ineligible for all public employment. Sections 4 and 5 forbade all further Chinese immigration into California. Section 6 deprived the Chinese of the right to sue or be sued in the state's courts and disbarred any lawyer who sought to appear for or against them in any civil proceeding. It also, for good measure, denied them the right to be granted licenses to carry on any trade or business, the right to fish in the state's waters, and the right to purchase or lease real property anywhere in the state. Section 7 permitted the legislature to exclude the Chinese from any portion of the state it saw fit to. Section 8 forbade the state's public officers from employing Chinese in any capacity whatsoever and made anyone who had ever done so ineligible to stand for election. Section 9 denied anyone employing Chinese the right to vote.[9]

Although the vast bulk of the delegates to the constitutional convention were anxious to appeal to the overwhelmingly anti-Chinese sentiments of their constituents and were sympathetic to the effort to incorporate anti-Chinese language in the new constitution, many were clearly put off by the immoderate, if not outlandish, character of the proposed provisions. During debate on the article, some pointed out that certain sections—those purporting to stop Chinese immigration into the state—were in clear conflict with the settled federal constitutional principles while noting that others were at the least constitutionally suspect.[10] The immoderate character of the proposed legislation, one delegate argued, was enough to tarnish severely California's image and thereby undermine its efforts to win support from its sister states for federal exclusion legislation. Another was courageous enough to speak to the injustice and plain inhumanity of many of the article's provisions, those especially that forbade the employment of Chinese by corporations and that made it impossible for the Chinese to carry on a business or to fish in the state's waters. These, he argued, would have the effect of condemning to starvation "one hundred and twenty-five thousand aliens who have been brought to our shores under treaty rights."[11]

Eventually some of the most radical provisions of the article were excised, but even in its toned-down form the measure that was approved as Article XIX, captioned "Chinese," of the proposed new constitution was severe enough. It declared the presence of the Chinese to be dangerous to the well-being of the state and bade the legislature to do all in its power to discourage their immigration into California. It prohibited corporations from employing Chinese and forbade their employment on any public work—state, county, or municipal—except as a punishment for crime. Section 4 of the article mandated the delegation to the state's cities and towns of the power "for the removal of Chinese without the limits of such cities and towns, or for their location within prescribed portions of those limits."[12] The convention added anti-Chinese language to other parts of the constitution as well. Article I, Section 17, part of the so-called California Bill of Rights, provided that foreigners of the white race or of

African descent who were eligible to become citizens should have the same rights with respect to property as native-born citizens, by implication denying the same equality of protection to those thought not to be eligible for citizenship, that is, the Chinese.[13] Article II, Section 1, for example, confirmed the franchise to all male citizens of the United States, native-born or naturalized, but went on to declare that "no native of China, no idiot, insane person, or person convicted of any infamous crime . . . shall ever exercise the privileges of an elector in this State."

The convention concluded its work on March 3, 1879, and submitted the proposed new constitution to the electorate for approval. The document contained of course many other provisions besides those affecting the Chinese, and some of these, especially those concerning banks, railroads, and taxation, proved quite controversial. Many of the state's newspapers, fearful that the new provisions would drive capital away from the state, campaigned zealously against adoption of the new constitution.[14] Few had much to say about the Chinese article although the Sacramento *Record-Union* observed that the drafters appeared not to have heard of the equal protection clause of the Fourteenth Amendment. "This [clause] covers the case of the Chinese completely," the paper wrote, "and prevents the adoption of any discriminating and hostile legislation in their regard."[15] The election on the new constitution, held on May 7, turned out to be close: 77,959 voted in favor of adoption, 67,134 against.

In the wake of the approval of the new constitution the San Francisco *Morning Call* noted that it would now become the duty of the next legislative session to devise appropriate legislation to implement that document's anti-Chinese provisions.[16] The California legislators who convened in Sacramento on January 5, 1880, needed no prompting in this regard and stirred to the task with enthusiasm. The session would in fact prove to be the most Sinophobic in the state's history.

The Corporations Bill and the Tiburcio Parrott *Case*

The second section of Article XIX, which prohibited corporations from employing Chinese, was generally considered to be the most important anti-Chinese provision in the new constitution. In February the legislature added two new sections to the Penal Code in implementation of Section 2 of the article, the constitutional provision that forbade the employment of Chinese by the state's corporations. The first made it a misdemeanor punishable by fine or imprisonment in the county jail, for any officer, director, or agent of a corporation to employ "any Chinese or

Mongolian" in any capacity for any work whatever. The second imposed criminal liability on the offending corporation itself and prescribed that the corporation should forfeit its charter, its franchise, and all its corporate rights upon a second conviction.[17] During debate a number of legislators had objected to the measure on the grounds that it conflicted with the Burlingame Treaty and the U.S. Constitution, but the majority's rejoinder was that the legislature should not concern itself with the constitutionality or unconstitutionality of measures before it, that matter being the proper province of the courts. The opinion ventured by a few that state legislators too had an obligation to uphold the Constitution seems to have been almost casually brushed aside.[18]

In the wake of the bill's passage Dennis Kearney, then out of the city, telegraphed his followers in San Francisco to see to it that the directors of corporations continuing to employ Chinese workers be hunted up forthwith and arrested.[19] Shortly, delegations of workers were confronting various San Francisco employers demanding that they discharge their Chinese employees.[20] The agitation had its effects. The *Alta* reported a few days later that several San Francisco woolen mills and an Oakland jute mill had discharged all of their Chinese employees. One of the woolen mill owners insisted, however, that he was acting only out of respect for law, and as an interim measure—until the law's constitutionality could be tested—and not because of pressure from the sandlot. He expressed the view that the measure would "fall to pieces" once subjected to a court test.[21] The potentially enormous impact of the corporation law (hundreds of California corporations employed thousands of Chinese) and the fact that the measure took effect immediately upon passage virtually assured that a test would be soon in coming. It would arise in the quicksilver mining industry.

Quicksilver or mercury is an element that amalgamates readily with gold and is therefore very useful in placer mining. Even before the discovery of gold at Sutter's Mill in 1849, California had found that it was blessed with substantial deposits of the metal. The gold rush rapidly accelerated the industry's development, and the state rose quickly to become a leading producer of mercury both for domestic consumption and for export. The price that the metal commanded on the world market, however, was subject to large fluctuations, and the business was attended with a great deal of risk.[22] Mercury producers came to rely heavily on Chinese laborers first because many of them, former gold miners, were skilled in the hydraulic mining techniques that were used in mercury production but also because they could be employed at wages that the producers felt would allow them to remain profitable.

One area with substantial mercury deposits was Lake County, not far north of San Francisco. Almost immediately upon passage of the corporations bill, one mercury producer in the county shut down operations completely, claiming that it could not remain solvent if it were forced to pay the wages that appeared necessary to attract white workers.[23] Another, the Sulphur Bank Quicksilver Mining Company, just as quickly became the object of a criminal proceeding. On February 20, a week after enactment of the bill, a former member of the California legislature swore out a complaint against the president of the company, one Tiburcio Parrott, in the police court of San Francisco, alleging that his firm had willfully employed a Chinese worker (named in the complaint) in violation of the law.[24] Pursuant to the complaint a warrant was issued and the president duly arrested. The next day he filed a petition for a writ of habeas corpus in the United States Circuit Court for the District of California claiming that the law under which he had been arrested was in violation of the U.S. Constitution and the Burlingame Treaty.[25] Given the rapidity with which this prosecution was mounted and the fact that the company in question seems to have been disposed to comply with the law, it appears probable that this was a collusive legal action, aimed at forcing a quick determination of the corporation law's constitutionality.[26]

Oral argument on the Parrott petition commenced on March 6 before a panel consisting of District Judge Ogden Hoffman and Circuit Justice Lorenzo Sawyer.[27] The state, testimony no doubt to its view of the importance of the case, was represented by a team of lawyers, including the attorney general, the district attorney for San Francisco and three other private attorneys specially retained for the occasion. Appearing for Parrott was the McAllister and Bergin law firm. Also present in the court was Delos Lake, a former state court judge. Lake informed the court that he had been retained by the Chinese consulate in San Francisco for the purpose of representing the Chinese and asked its permission to intervene on their behalf. It was well known, he said, that the law in question was aimed at the Chinese and that the Chinese were therefore an interested party, entitled to separate representation. The court agreed.[28] A word concerning the San Francisco Chinese Consulate, then a still quite new diplomatic outpost of the Ch'ing Empire, seems appropriate at this point.

The Chinese government, motivated in large part by concern for the tenuous positions of Chinese nationals living in the United States, had determined in 1875 to establish a regular and permanent diplomatic presence in this country, but it did not act on that decision until 1878. In the early part of that year the government dispatched a diplomatic mission to the United States, a mission that arrived in San Francisco in July. In September the head of the mission, Ch'en Lan-pin, officially presented his credentials as minister to the United States to President Rutherford B. Hayes, and in November Ch'en informed the Department of State that he was establishing a consulate in San Francisco and appointing as consuls a relative, Ch'en Shu-t'ang, and the man who, since the congressional hearings of 1876 had become the Six Companies' official spokesman to the Caucasian world, Frederick Bee.[29] It was clear from the outset that one of the consulate's principal tasks would be protection of the local Chinese community against the excesses of Sinophobia, though exactly how its role should relate to that of the Six Companies remained rather unclear.[30] It was apparent too from the consulate's intervention in the Parrott case that it was prepared to move vigorously to discharge that task.[31] Indeed, it had given token of its willingness to act aggressively on behalf of the local Chinese community even before that.

As it happens, the corporations bill was not the only item on the consulate's agenda in the early months of 1880. It was at the time more concerned about fending off an effort then underway by city authorities to remove the Chinese population from its customary place of abode in San Francisco. On February 21, the day on which Parrott filed his habeas petition, the San Francisco Board of Health passed a resolution officially declaring Chinatown to be a nuisance, and on February 24 the city's health officer had posted a notice in Chinatown informing the population that they would in thirty days be removed en masse from the area.[32] "All the power of the law," it read, "will be invoked . . . to empty this great reservoir of moral, social and physical pollution, which . . . threatens to engulf with its filthiness and immorality the fairest portion of our city."[33] The San Francisco *Examiner* commented that with the Chinese gone the central portion of the city would be opened up for major commercial and residential development. Indeed, the paper said it had been informed by the city's health officer that capitalists stood ready to purchase and develop the whole area once the Chinese had been evacuated.[34] Thanks to actions undertaken by the consulate, the health authorities' pronouncements proved more bluster than serious threat. Immediately upon learning of the board's proposed action, Ch'en Shu-t'ang had written to Delos Lake, asking for an opinion on its legality. Lake had replied that the authorities would be acting totally beyond their powers if they proceeded with their plans and that individual property owners in Chinatown would be privileged to resist them with force if necessary.[35] The consulate made the correspondence available to the local newspapers, which printed it, and the health authorities announced soon thereafter that they would not press ahead with their plans. But to return to the federal circuit court and *Tiburcio Parrott.*

California's case for the corporations law's validity hinged entirely on the concept of a state's reserved power over corporate affairs. The *Dartmouth College* case,[36] notwithstanding its acknowledgment of the fact that corporations were the mere creations of the law, had suggested that corporate charters were contracts and, all other things being equal, unalterable once issued. In the wake of that decision most states had taken care to make clear, either through general legislation or through the wording of individual corporate charters, that they reserved to themselves the right to alter, amend, or repeal corporate charters. If the state of California had the right completely to revoke a corporate charter, counsel argued, it a fortiori had the right to impose any conditions that it wished on a corporation's operations. Those could include limitations as to the kinds of workers the corporation could employ. The law should not be seen as operating against the Chinese but only against the law's creature, the corporation.[37]

Hall McAllister, though counsel for the mining corporation, put his stress on the law's impact upon the Chinese. It was this he claimed that made it infirm. He had several strings to his bow. He argued first that the California statute was an encroachment upon the general rights that resident aliens possessed under general rules of international law. Under these rules, he said, aliens had the right to labor in the foreign states where they resided. The statute was furthermore in conflict with the Fourteenth Amendment equal protection clause. The amendment by its terms applied to "persons" and not just citizens, and the concept of equal protection of the laws excluded partial and discriminating legislation against a particular class, exactly the sort of legislation that the court had before it. McAllister drew the court's attention to the Civil Rights Act of 1870. That law gave to all "persons" within the jurisdiction of the United States the same right to make contracts and the right to the same benefit of legal proceedings as was possessed by white citizens. It also mandated that they should be subject to like penalties, taxes, licenses, and exactions and no other. The cutting off of employment rights to the Chinese, he argued, was an exaction or penalty put specially upon them and as such forbidden by the law. He also mentioned a complementary piece of legislation, the Civil Rights Act of 1871, which gave persons a civil remedy for violations of their federal constitutional or legal rights committed under color of law. McAllister finally argued that the act was in conflict with the Burlingame Treaty, which guaranteed to the Chinese the same rights with respect to residence as were enjoyed by citizens of the most favored nation.[38]

Delos Lake, counsel for the Chinese, pursued some of the same themes and added some new ones. The enactment in question clearly violated the Fourteenth Amendment equal protection rights of the Chinese. It denied to them the right that others had to enter into employment contracts with corporations. He adduced in support of his cause the just decided Supreme Court case of *Strauder v. West Virginia*.[39] In that case the high court had invalidated on Fourteenth Amendment equal protection grounds a West Virginia statute barring blacks from sitting on juries. The decision, said Lake, made clear that blacks stood on the same footing as whites with respect to their civil rights and that no discrimination could be made against them by law because of their color. Like McAllister, he contended that it was clear from the use of the term "persons" in the Fourteenth Amendment that Chinese were entitled to invoke that constitutional provision as well as blacks. It was also clear that the California statute before the court discriminated against them because of their color in the exercise of their civil rights. It came therefore under the principle enunciated in *Strauder*. The notion that the state was merely using its reserved police power to regulate corporations Lake dismissed as mere pretense. It was well known, said Lake, that the purpose of the enactment in question was to "enforce the departure of the Chinese by starvation." There had never been, he declared, such a bold, bald attempt to legislate a people out of the state. Lake also contended that the law trenched on Chinese Fourteenth Amendment due process rights, since to deprive a person of the right to labor was to deprive him of his property.[40]

Lake argued that the law infringed as well on the Fourteenth Amendment equal protection and due process rights of corporations. (Corporations were persons, he maintained, and as such were entitled to invoke that provision's protections.) The law allowed individuals to enter into contracts with Chinese but forbade that same right to corporations. It also, by forbidding corporations from employing Chinese, prevented them from putting their property to its best and most advantageous use, thereby depriving them of that property without due process of law.[41]

Judges Hoffman and Sawyer handed down their decision on March 22. The petitioner, they ruled, was entitled to be discharged from custody. Though neither judge thought there could be the slightest doubt about the unconstitutionality of the California statute before them, each wrote a lengthy opinion explaining in detail the basis for the result the court had reached. The two opinions differed somewhat in emphasis. Hoffman thought the California statute unconstitutional on two separate grounds:

first, that it violated the rights of corporations (though not in the way argued for by Lake); second, that it violated the rights of the Chinese. Sawyer was less sure on the first point.

Hoffman described the state's assertion that it was completely unrestrained in its power to deal with corporations as a claim "well fitted to startle and alarm."[42] He was prepared to admit that states had considerable right to regulate corporate affairs for the benefit of corporate shareholders, their creditors, or the general public, but this right was limited by constitutional principle. It must be reasonable, and sheer oppression or wrong could not be inflicted under the guise of regulation. A state could not, for example, deprive a corporation of property or contract rights that had already vested in it. The statute in question was not reasonable in Hoffman's view. It denied to corporations the right to contract with employees of their choosing on terms mutually agreeable to both. If this kind of interference were accepted, he asked, what would prevent the state from prescribing a rate of wages, of hours of work, "or other conditions destructive of the profitable use of corporate property."[43] The right of corporations to be free of arbitrary and oppressive state interference was analytically separate from any rights that the Chinese might possess under treaty or the Constitution, he emphasized. The California statute would be equally offensive if it forbade the employment of Irish or Germans instead of Chinese. Corporations, he declared, "may stand firmly on their own right to employ laborers of their choosing, and on such terms as may be agreed upon, subject only to such police laws as the state may enact with respect to them, in common with private individuals."[44]

But the treaty rights of the Chinese were quite clearly involved in the case at bar, Hoffman pointed out, and even if one were prepared to accept the state's argument concerning its reserved power over corporations, the legislation before the court must fall on that account. The statute was, according to Hoffman, clearly designed to force the Chinese out of the state of California and was thus in open and contemptuous violation of the right that Chinese possessed under the Burlingame Treaty to reside in the United States with all of the privileges, immunities, and exemptions possessed by other foreign nationals.[45] The end purpose of the statute was made totally transparent, in Hoffman's view, when one looked at the article of the state constitution under which it had been enacted. That article's title boldly proclaimed that it was directed at the Chinese. Its second section forbade corporations from employing Chinese, thereby imposing corresponding restrictions on the right of the Chinese to labor for their own subsistence and increasing the likelihood that they would become paupers, criminals, or mendicants, while its first section directed the legislature to pass laws for the removal of persons liable to become paupers or mendicants.[46]

Sawyer thought there was considerable plausibility to Hoffman's view that the California law trenched impermissibly on corporate rights, but he preferred to bottom the court's decision on the law's impermissible interference with the individual rights of the Chinese. He agreed with the point made explicitly by Lake and implicitly by McAllister that the law did not really have as its object the regulation of the affairs of corporations. It was in truth aimed at the Chinese, its ultimate purpose being to exclude them from a wide range of employment, thereby driving those in the state away and deterring others from coming.[47] That, he said, was "the object, and the only object, to be accomplished by the state constitutional and statutory provisions in question."[48]

Like Hoffman he saw the law as being squarely in conflict with the Burlingame Treaty. Article VI of that treaty stipulated that the Chinese while in the United States should enjoy the same "privileges, immunities and exemptions" in respect to residence as were enjoyed by the citizens and subjects of the most favored nation. The words "privileges and immunities" were used in the U.S. Constitution, Sawyer noted, and had acquired a clear and generally agreed upon meaning in constitutional discourse. Article IV, Section 2 specified, "The citizens of each State shall be entitled to all Privileges and Immunities of Citizens in the several States." As used in this provision of the Constitution, the weight of judicial authority made clear, the term referred to those privileges that free persons living in a free society would deem to be fundamental. Any list of such fundamentals would have to include, among others, the right to acquire property, to engage in a trade or business, and to labor for subsistence. Both the majority and the dissenting justices in *The Slaughter-House Cases* had agreed on this point, Sawyer noted. (They had, however, disagreed on the meaning of the privileges or immunities clause of the Fourteenth Amendment, a point Sawyer did not stress.)[49] He had no doubt that the same meaning was equally applicable to the words as used in the treaty with China. The right to labor ("this absolute, fundamental and natural right," Sawyer called it) was guaranteed Chinese immigrants by the treaty to the same extent that it was granted by the state to other foreign nationals. A state constitutional provision or statute that purported to restrict that right for the Chinese and not for other classes of aliens was in clear violation of the treaty.[50]

The law in question, Sawyer noted, was also in conflict with the equal protection clause of the Fourteenth Amendment and the federal law, Section 16 of the Civil Rights Act of 1870, enacted to give effect to that constitutional provision. (He agreed with Field's view, expressed in *Ho Ah Kow,* that the Fourteenth Amendment, because of the use of the term "person," applied to the Chinese.) He thought it required little in the way of argument to show that the Chinese did not enjoy the equal protection of the laws or, to use the statute's words, "the full and equal benefit of all laws and proceedings for the security of persons and property" as was enjoyed by white citizens where, as he put it, "the laws forbid their laboring, or making and enforcing contracts to labor, in a very large field of labor which is open, without limit, let or hindrance, to all citizens and all other foreigners, without regard to nation, race, or color."[51] *Strauder* he considered to be especially on point, for the Supreme Court had been dealing with a law that discriminated *on the basis of color* and had made clear that the amendment and the act conferred on people of color the right to be free of "unfriendly legislation against them distinctively, as colored."[52] This right, Sawyer stressed, was wholly independent of treaty stipulations "and would exist without any treaty whatever, so long as Chinese are permitted to come into and reside within the jurisdiction of the United States."[53]

Sawyer concluded by calling attention to the fact that there were in the statutes of the United States civil and criminal provisions designed to give effect to the equal protection clause of the Fourteenth Amendment. Section 1979 of the Revised Statutes (the codification of Section 1 of the Civil Rights Act of 1871) provided a civil remedy either at law or in equity for infractions of the amendment. The petitioner, he remarked, might have incurred liability under this statute had he discharged the Chinese worker for whose employment he was now under arrest.[54] Section 5519 made it a crime for two or more persons to conspire to deprive any class of persons of the equal protection of the laws. This he commended to the consideration of those who were disposed to go from place to place "to compel employers to discharge peaceable and industrious Chinamen engaged in their service."[55]

Since at the time federal circuit court judgments in habeas cases could not be appealed to the Supreme Court, the opinion of Judges Sawyer and Hoffman in effect ended the debate about California's power to limit Chinese employment rights—a point the governor was compelled to make in response to an inquiry from leaders of the San Francisco Workingmen's party, in the wake of the federal court decision, concerning what steps the state had taken to appeal it to the Supreme Court.[56] Most organs of public opinion seemed to be of the view that an appeal would have been an exercise in futility in any case, considering the inherent weakness of the state's position. The staunchly Republican Sacramento newspaper, the

Record-Union, commented that the result in the case was exactly as was to be expected and that the same fate awaited every other anti-Chinese measure under legislative consideration. The state had no power to discriminate against the Chinese and the sooner this was realized the sooner the public fisc would cease to be wasted on fruitless legislation and litigation. Help on the issue of Chinese immigration, if that was what was wished, could only be found at the federal level.[57] The *Examiner,* a Democratic and bitterly Sinophobic paper, echoed these views exactly. "There ought to be a cessation," it commented, "of the vain, ill-advised, mischievous and actually obstructive legislation and action which, while aimed at the Chinese, harms only the cause that is at the bottom of the agitation." Only by electing the right legislators to Congress would California solve the Chinese question.[58]

Other Anti-Chinese Measures

The opinion of the federal circuit court did nothing at all to dampen the legislature's enthusiasm for anti-Chinese lawmaking. As the reporter for the *Daily Alta* had noted perceptively at the outset of the twenty-third session, "The Senate and the Assembly apparently intend to sacrifice themselves to almost every measure which has for its object anti-Chinese legislation whether constitutional or unconstitutional, and in defiance of the Federal Constitution and national treaties."[59] On April 3, a little over a week after the court handed down its decision in *Tiburcio Parrott,* the governor signed a bill, passed in implementation of the first section of Article XIX of the state constitution, making it the duty of local governments to pass laws providing for the removal of Chinese residents beyond town or city limits or in the alternative to set aside discrete portions of the city for Chinese residence.[60] Later in the month the legislature passed laws declaring that no license to transact any business or pursue any occupation should ever be granted to any alien not eligible to become a state elector[61] and forbidding the same class of aliens from taking fish from the state's waters for purposes of sale.[62]

Among the measures, ranging from the vicious to the merely spiteful considered but not passed during the session were: a bill, in effect seeking to override the Civil Rights Act of 1870, which would have prohibited the conviction of criminal defendants on uncorroborated Chinese testimony,[63] a bill, introduced by the author of the corporation measure, making it a felony for the Chinese to follow any occupation at all,[64] a bill imposing a tax on all Chinese residents and authorizing the governor to use the state militia to collect it,[65] a bill forbidding the keeping of account books in any language other than English,[66] and a bill to impose a tax on a product used by Chinese laundries to make starch (the sponsor alleged that cheap starch gave Chinese laundries an unfair advantage over white-owned establishments).[67]

In re Ah Chong

The law regarding fishing in the state's waters, not surprisingly, came up soon enough for a court test. Chinese had been involved in the salt and freshwater fishing business in California almost from the beginning of the immigration, selling part of their catch domestically and exporting the rest to China. Recent archaeological findings, in fact, suggest that it may have been the Chinese, and not as previously thought, the Italians, who pioneered the commercial fishing industry in the state.[68] In the year 1880 there were over one thousand Chinese involved in the trade in the greater San Francisco Bay Area.[69] On May 22 six Chinese fishermen were arrested in the town of Vallejo, at the north end of San Francisco Bay, for taking fish from the bay waters and offering them for sale.[70] In short order the Chinese consulate, acting through Delos Lake and Thomas Riordan, an associate of Benjamin Brooks and a man who would eventually come to assume the status of principal attorney representing the Chinese, sued out writs of habeas corpus on behalf of the six in the federal circuit court.[71] The petition contained the by now usual averments that their incarceration was illegal since the law under which they were being held was in contravention of the Fourteenth Amendment, Section 1977 of the Revised Statutes, and the Burlingame Treaty.[72] Oral argument was had before Sawyer on May 31 and the court delivered its opinion on June 9. The outcome was not surprising.

The state adduced the so-called "common property" doctrine, sanctioned by the United States Supreme Court in the 1876 case of *McCready v. Virginia*,[73] in defense of the fishing law. That case raised the question of whether the state of Virginia could make it a crime for residents of other states to farm oysters in Virginia waters. The petitioner, who had been convicted under that statute, claimed that the act was void under the interstate comity clause of the Constitution. The court, however, sustained the measure, declaring that Virginia owned, on behalf of its citizens, the marine resources in its territorial waters and that the right that Virginia citizens possessed to farm oysters came not from their citizenship alone but from *their citizenship and property combined.* Since the right to harvest marine resources was ultimately a property right and not a mere privilege and immunity of citizenship, the state could exclude all others except citizens, the ultimate owners of the resource, from enjoying the right. California now argued that its own law was analogous to the Virginia measure. Since, under the authority of *McCready*, it could forbid citizens of other states from fishing in its waters, a fortiori it could forbid aliens from doing the same thing.[74]

Sawyer, however, was not moved by this argument. Taking a somewhat broader view of the term "privileges and immunities" than the one he had advanced in *Parrott*, he now interpreted it to mean any favor granted by the government.[75] And that decided the issue. He conceded that the state could exclude all aliens from fishing in its waters, but if it permitted one class of aliens to enjoy that privilege it must grant the same right to others whose governments had negotiated treaties containing a most favored nation provision.

> To exclude the Chinaman from fishing in the waters of the state, therefore, while the Germans, Italians, Englishmen, and Irishmen, who otherwise stand upon the same footing, are permitted to fish *ad libitum*, without price, charge, let or hinderance, is to prevent him from enjoying the same privileges as are "enjoyed by the citizens or subjects of the most favored nation."[76]

He also thought that the law's differentiation between Chinese and non-Chinese aliens violated the Fourteenth Amendment equal protection clause. To subject the Chinese to imprisonment for fishing in the state's waters while exempting non-Chinese aliens from any punishment for doing the same thing was, he said, to subject them to "different punishments, pains, and penalties" and thereby to deny them the equal protection of the laws.[77] The thrust of previous equal protection analysis (including Sawyer's own) had been to establish an equality of legal-rights privileges between aliens and citizens. Sawyer now extended the concept to bar discrimination between different classes of aliens.[78]

Sawyer made clear in his opinion that he did not think the measure in question had anything to do with fisheries policy or the conservation of natural resources. He saw it, he said, as an anti-Chinese measure, on the same footing with the measure that had been voided in *Parrott* and with other similar measures enacted by the 1880 session of the California legislature, and he took a certain delight in pointing out how the Sinophobic passions of that body had led it into some very sloppy draftsmanship in the case of the measure then before him. As he noted, women were ineligible to become electors under the California Constitution. And so by the literal terms of the act French, English, and Irish women resident in the state could not take fish (for sale) from the state's waters. Such infelicities in expression, he declared, were "illustrative of the crudities, not to say absurdities, into which constitutional conventions and legislative bodies are liable to be betrayed by their anxiety and efforts to accomplish, by indirection and circumlocution, an unconstitutional purpose which they cannot effect by direct means."[79]

Although neither *Ah Chong* nor *Parrott* had specifically addressed the constitutionality of other provisions of the state constitution or of the other anti-Chinese measures the legislature had enacted, the decisions had, in the opinion of many, at the very least, left those measures under a cloud. In May of 1880, for example, when the San Francisco Board of Supervisors sought advice on a petition it had received from a state assemblyman urging it to enforce the act providing for the removal of the Chinese outside the city, its judiciary committee reported to the full board, and citing *Parrott*, that it did not think such action was within the power of local government.[80] (This law remained on the books, however, and, as we shall see, an attempt was later made to implement it.)

In re Wong Yung Quy

Though not an outgrowth of measures passed in the constitutional convention or in the subsequent legislative session, one final Chinese-sponsored civil action decided by Judge Sawyer's court in 1880 deserves to be mentioned. It may be seen as additional evidence of the Chinese willingness to use the courts to challenge treatment felt in any way to be unfair or invidious. The case holds a certain amount of significance as well for the important jurisdictional issue it settled—at least in the California federal circuit.

It will be recalled from chapter 2 that as early as 1873 the city of San Francisco had come close to enacting a law touching on the Chinese custom of exhuming the remains of their countrymen, after the lapse of several years, for reburial in China. That measure would have required that anyone seeking to exhume remains obtain a permit from the county coroner. The ordinance, however, failed to pass the board of supervisors. In 1878 the state legislature, under the spur of pressure from the San Francisco Anti-Monopoly Association, a well-known anti-Chinese organization, took up a similar measure. Its sponsors frankly avowed that they saw it as a powerful potential tool for deterring Chinese immigration. Noting how deeply rooted was the Chinese desire to see their remains buried in their native soil, one of the bill's chief supporters commented that "to throw obstacles in the way of perpetuating [this custom] was to effectively exclude them from the country."[81] Another declared his belief that the Chinese had inured themselves to threats of violence and were "only vulnerable through their superstitions."[82] The measure as ultimately enacted was captioned, "An Act to protect public health from infection caused by exhumation and removal of the remains of deceased persons."[83] It made it unlawful to disinter remains anywhere in the state without first obtaining a permit from local authorities and conditioned the granting of that permit on enclosing the remains in a metallic casket (an expensive proposition) and the payment of a $10 fee. Significantly, it exempted from the requirements of the act the removal of remains for the purpose of reinterments within the same county.[84]

The act went into effect on May 1, 1878, and during the first year of its operation the Chinese apparently complied with its provisions. In the fall of 1879, however, a Chinese by the name of Wong Yung Quy, acting without the support of any Chinese organization but perhaps with the collusion of state officials, initiated a test of the measure.[85] Claiming that he wished to exhume the remains of his cousin who had been buried two years earlier, he presented the local health authorities with the requisite death certificate and with a wooden, rather than a metallic, burial case, which apparently was acceptable. He refused, however, to pay the $10 fee, and was therefore denied a permit. He proceeded, nonetheless to disinter the remains of his cousin, whereupon he was promptly arrested, judged guilty of having violated the act and sentenced to a term in the county jail. From there he sued out a writ of habeas corpus and brought the matter before Judge Sawyer's court. In his petition he contended that the act in its practical effects applied to Chinese only and had been passed for that purpose (an affidavit from the superintendent of disinterments disclosed that some 97 percent of those receiving permits under the act were Chinese). The law, he argued, unlawfully discriminated against the Chinese in violation of the Fourteenth Amendment, impermissibly burdened foreign commerce between the United States and China, and, finally, conflicted with Article IV of the Burlingame Treaty, which declared that Chinese residents in the United States should be free of all disabilities on account of their religious faith (the claim was that the exhumation custom was religious in origin).[86]

As a preliminary matter Sawyer had first to dispose of an important challenge to the jurisdiction of his court. The federal Habeas Corpus Act of 1867, as noted above, had for the first time extended federal habeas corpus protection to persons in *state* custody, but it did not settle the question of when the remedy could be invoked. Traditionally at common law the writ of habeas corpus was available only to test the legitimacy of pre-trial incarceration and could not be used as a substitute for appeal once a person had been convicted of an offense. The California attorney general now insisted that under that principle Sawyer's court was without jurisdiction to hear the Wong Yung Quy complaint. The court, however, echoing a view just then beginning to crystallize in the Supreme Court, distinguished between cases in which the allegation was that an error in the proceedings had led to a flawed judgment and cases in which it was alleged that the state court judgment had been entered without any authority at all. The former class of cases, it agreed, were not susceptible to habeas corpus review in federal court but the latter were. A habeas petition which claimed that the law under which the petitioner was incarcerated was unconstitutional and therefore void deserved to be classed under the latter head, Sawyer said.[87] Inasmuch as a fair number of future Chinese civil rights actions would be brought as habeas corpus attacks on state court judgments this was a not insignificant ruling by the federal circuit court.

Judge Sawyer rendered his decision on the merits on May 24, 1880. Generally so sensitive to Chinese allegations of discriminatory treatment, this time he found the Chinese claims to be completely without merit. The remains of deceased persons could not be considered exports, he explained, and the law could not be considered a regulation of foreign commerce. Conceding that Chinese religious precepts mandated that the remains of the deceased be reburied in China and that the Burlingame Treaty protected them in their religious observances, nothing in the law unduly restricted the performance of that religious rite.[88] The Fourteenth Amendment equal protection claim he considered to be equally without foundation. There were no restrictions in the act which did not apply to all alike, whether foreigners or citizens. If it disproportionately affected the Chinese, it was not because that was its intent but rather because the Chinese, due to their national or religious customs, were more involved than other nationalities in the exhumation of their dead. The crucial fact was that there was nothing in the law to set it apart from the canon of traditional police power measures. Indeed it seemed to him a well nigh classic instance of police power regulation. The exhumation of the dead had always been considered a proper subject of municipal regulation, he commented, in all times and among all civilized nations. The measure was in the final analysis much more like the law he had sustained in the cubic air case than the ordinance his court had struck down in *Ho Ah Kow*. "The exhumation and removal of the dead is not a matter of public indifference, harmless in itself, like the wearing of the hair, as in the *Queue* case," he noted.[89]

4 The Laundry Litigation of the 1880s

Both *Tiburcio Parrott* and *Ah Chong* had laid emphasis on the Burlingame Treaty as a very large bulwark protecting the Chinese against hostile state and local laws. While the treaty existed, said Judge Ogden Hoffman in *Parrott*, the Chinese had the unfettered right to immigrate to this country and while here to labor and pursue trades on the same basis as other foreigners. At the same time, he noted that modifications in the treaty could be negotiated by the federal government at any time. Even as he spoke, the national administration was in the process of such negotiations, and later in the year the United States and China reached agreement on a modification under which the United States became entitled, unilaterally, to suspend the coming of Chinese laborers into the country for a period of ten years. Soon after Congress passed a statute in implementation of the treaty. This and successive laws enacted later in the 1880s would bring the Chinese into repeated legal conflict with the federal government. We shall defer our consideration of these extraordinarily interesting cases until Part 3, however, and continue here our discussion of the Chinese confrontation with state and local authorities over their right to the equal protection of the law, a struggle that continued into the 1880s. The first and main area of conflict would be the commercial laundry trade, a line of business that, as noted, the Chinese had pioneered and one in which a large number of them worked.[1]

The San Francisco Laundry Legislation of 1880

We discussed earlier the license fee legislation aimed at Chinese laundries enacted by the San Francisco Board of Supervisors in the years 1873 and 1876 and the cases that arose out of those measures.[2] The subject of Chinese laundries would continue to agitate Caucasians in later years. The opponents of the Chinese raised the issue before the joint congressional committee in the fall of 1876, pointing to the Chinese washhouses as yet another evidence of the baleful effects of Chinese immigration. They produced as a witness the fire marshal of San Francisco, who testified that the Chinese were as a race careless in the use of fire, that fires were more frequent in Chinatown than anywhere else, and that Chinese washhouses, scattered as they were throughout the city, were a general menace to the community's fire safety.[3] And an insurance man was produced who testified that the Chinese caused insurance rates to go up dramatically wherever they went in the city and that his insurance company had ceased writing policies in Chinatown because of the fire hazard.[4] The testimony was, it may be noted, far from convincing. The marshal could offer no hard evidence to back up his assertions,[5] and the insurance man, on close questioning, admitted that the reason his company had ceased insuring Chinese property was the fear of incendiary fires started by white arsonists.[6] He also stated that in his opinion the Chinese were more careful with fire than any other people he knew.[7] In addition, counsel for the Chinese were able to produce another insurance man of long experience in San Francisco who testified that the Chinese were no more prone to start fires than anyone else and that insurance rates in Chinatown were no higher than in any other part of the city. "I am certain that for fifteen years there has not been a single building entirely destroyed in the Chinese quarter," he declared. He also stated that Chinese laundries paid no higher rates than non-Chinese washhouses and that there was no lack of insurers anxious to write policies on Chinese property.[8]

Chinese laundries were thrust into the public consciousness the summer following the congressional investigation, when a considerable number of them became the chief target of rioters in one of the largest anti-Chinese civil disturbances in the city's history.[9] Then, two months later, whether stimulated by these events it is impossible to say, the San Francisco *Post*, a leading organ of Sinophobic opinion, published a series of lengthy articles on the subject of Chinese laundries.[10] The paper could muster no sympathy for the laundrymen whose stores had been burned or damaged by the rioters. Rather, the gist of the series was that Chinese laundries in the aggregate constituted a nuisance desperately in need of abatement. It contrasted the Chinese washhouses unfavorably with the hundred or so "French laundries" that still existed in and around the city. The Chinese establishments, it claimed, echoing themes sounded by the city and state in their argument before the congressional committee, were fire hazards and invariably raised insurance rates on and depreciated the value of property in their vicinity. "In this matter of Chinese laundries," the journal declared, "the concurrent testimony of city officials and those interested in real estate and insurance matters proves that the business as now conducted is dangerous to the health and security of the city, costly to its treasury and detrimental to large private interests."[11] And it cited approvingly the views of one observer who recommended that a law be passed requiring that laundries be constructed of brick[12] and of another that laundries be compelled to locate in the suburbs, where, as he put it, "other laundries than Chinese generally are."[13] The recommendations would prove prophetic although it would take three years for the prophecy to come to fruition.

Early in the morning of February 5, 1880, a devastating fire, the first of such magnitude in such an establishment, broke out in a Chinese laundry in San Francisco. A worker just arising from sleep had apparently been careless with a candle and had ignited clothes hanging in one of the laundry's drying rooms. Before the fire could be put out it had taken the lives of ten laundry workers.[14] A fire that takes ten lives is of course a most serious matter and serious accidents are often a stimulus for public health and safety measures. Predictably, however, what might have served as the occasion for a general consideration of ways and means to improve the fire safety of public laundries came to be seen first and foremost as another opportunity to strike at the Chinese. At the first meeting of the board of supervisors following the fire Charles Taylor introduced a measure requiring that all buildings—the phrasing is significant—"erected and used by Chinese as laundries" should be constructed of brick or stone with walls not less than 8 1/2 inches thick. At the same meeting another resolution was introduced calling upon the city attorney to furnish his opinion "as to whether or not [the board] has the legal right to restrict and confine the keeping and carrying on of laundries by the Chinese to a certain designated portion of this city and county" and, if he determined it did, to prepare an appropriate ordinance, leaving the boundaries blank, to be filled in by the board.[15]

Within a few days the city attorney reported back to the board of supervisors that it could under its police power, order Chinese laundries to a certain restricted district of the city if it determined, after investigation, that that was necessary to protect the population against fire or against the spread of contagious diseases.[16] The supervisors chose not to act on the city attorney's opinion, but at their February 17 meeting they did pass the Taylor resolution, amended however at the sponsor's insistence to apply to all laundries since as he put it the limitation of the measure's application to the Chinese might render it constitutionally vulnerable. In its final form the measure provided that "all buildings erected and used as laundries, within the corporate limits of this city and county, on and after March 1, 1880, shall be constructed but one story in height, with brick or stone walls, not less than twelve inches in thickness." It also stipulated that all doors and windows should be metal or metal-covered, something of a bizarre provision, it may be said, in an ordinance designed to promote fire safety.[17]

The ordinance in this phrasing seemed aimed only at laundries yet to be built. But three months later, on May 24, the board passed another ordinance that applied to existing laundries as well. This measure made it unlawful for anyone "to establish, maintain or carry on a laundry" within the corporate limits of the city and county without having first obtained the consent of the board of supervisors, "except the same be located in a building constructed either of brick or stone." Violators of the order were made subject to fines up to $1,000 and imprisonment up to six months in the county jail.[18] It also forbade the raising of scaffolding on any rooftop without supervisorial consent. (Rooftop scaffolds for the drying of clothes were a conspicuous feature of many Chinese laundries. In no surviving report concerning laundry fires in San Francisco, however, are rooftop scaffolds listed as a contributing cause.)[19]

In spite of their eventual neutral formulation, it seems fairly clear that the February and May laundry ordinances were motivated more by racial antipathy than by any simple concern for promoting the public safety.[20] The initial discussions in the board make it clear that had it not been for qualms about the constitutionality of such wording, the measures would have applied only to Chinese laundries.[21] The supervisors must have clearly understood how the laws, even when neutrally formulated, could be used to oppress the Chinese. The Chinese washhouses were small, low-cost operations and were virtually all conducted in wood frame buildings. Brick structures were few and far between in the neighborhoods outside the central business district where many of the Chinese laundries were located. Removing to premises with brick structures, assuming they could have been obtained, would probably have raised the cost of operations to a prohibitive point for most. Constructing new brick buildings to comply with the ordinance would have been out of the question for any but the wealthiest laundries. Virtually all Chinese laundries, then, wishing to stay in business would be relegated to the discretion of the board.

The Ah Din *and* Ah Ling *Cases*

The supervisors, in passing their ordinances, did not reckon on the extent of the opposition they would provoke among the Chinese laundrymen or on the determination of their guild, the Tung Hing Tong, to put up resistance.[22] The initial response of the laundrymen was to continue in operation in disregard of the laws and force the city to bring criminal prosecutions against them. Such enforcement was not long in coming.

Toward the end of the month of June the assistant engineer of the city's fire department filed a criminal complaint in the police judges court of San Francisco against a Chinese laundryman by the name of Ah Din, charging him with maintaining a wooden laundry without having obtained the consent of the board of supervisors. At the hearing on the complaint the laundryman was represented by Thomas Riordan, the man who had represented the Chinese fishermen in *Ah Chong*. Riordan demurred to the complaint on the grounds that the ordinance was unconstitutional. The court overruled the demurrer but agreed to receive written arguments on the issue, and the case was submitted on that basis.[23]

Riordan made numerous claims in his brief: that the ordinance was beyond the powers vested in the board under the state Consolidation Act, which set forth the powers of municipal bodies; that it was unreasonable, unjust, and oppressive; that it deprived the defendant of vested rights; that it deprived him of his property without due process of law; that it was "class legislation" aimed only at the Chinese. The court was not prepared to rule on most of these claims, but the vested rights argument did strike a responsive chord, and on August 24 it ruled the ordinance invalid on that basis. The court seemed bothered by the fact that someone who had invested a great deal of funds in the fitting out of a wood frame laundry might now find that investment rendered worthless by a negative supervisorial vote. This, said the court, would be a deprivation of property without due process of law.[24]

The decision of a police judges court, a tribunal at the bottom rung of the judicial ladder, was of limited precedential value and certainly did not settle the question of the laundry ordinance's validity. The city continued to view the law as valid and to enforce it. A new opportunity to test the ordinance presented itself the following year when another Chinese laundryman, Ah Ling, was convicted of violating the ordinance in the police court. This time the defendant appealed the judgment to the superior court of the city and county. Counsel for the defense was again Thomas Riordan. Riordan was at the time under retainer to the Chinese consulate but appears here to have been acting at the behest of the Tung Hing Tong.[25]

On May 7, 1881, the superior court ruled flatly that the San Francisco ordinance was unconstitutional and reversed the conviction.[26] The decision, while endorsing the view that the measure interfered with vested rights, was much more broadly based than the lower court judgment of the year before. The newspaper account of it is worth quoting in full. The ordinance, Judge T. W. Freelon said,

> is oppressive, discriminating, unreasonable and arbitrary, and gives special privileges to such and only such as the Board of Supervisors may desire capriciously or in its unrestrained discretion to favor. It is in restraint of trade and it tends directly and necessarily to the creation of monopolies. It is unconstitutional because it does not operate equally and uniformly on all those who are within the same category. It confers special privileges on those who have the capital to build or have brick or stone buildings. It is an unwarranted and unauthorized interference with vested rights. It deprives a class—that is the poor—from following a useful and necessary sanitary pursuit and gives it exclusively to individual or corporate capital.[27]

The reasoning and the language here, it will be noticed, resonate with that of Judges Stanly and McKee in the mid-1870s laundry license cases discussed in chapter 2, *Hung Hai* and *Soon Kung*.[28] As in those cases, the court did not think it necessary to reach the claim of racial discrimination. Had there been no Chinese presence in the United States and had the ordinance been directed purely at smaller Caucasian-owned laundries, it presumably would have met the same fate. As we shall see, however, the last word had yet to be heard on the validity of the May 1880 supervisorial laundry order.

The First Federal Laundry Case: In re Quong Woo

The following year the city put yet another potential obstacle in the way of Chinese laundries wishing to carry on business. On May 8, 1882 (two days, as it happened, after Congress passed the first Chinese Exclusion Act), Supervisor John McKew introduced a new and supplementary laundry ordinance. It required all laundries seeking to operate within a designated district of the city to obtain the consent of the board of supervisors and conditioned that consent on the recommendation of twelve residents of the block where the laundry was located. The boundaries of the proposed zone encompassed all of Chinatown and the central business district and fully one half of the residential districts of the city. Some two hundred Chinese laundries, the bulk of those then operating in San Francisco, were within the zone.[29] Before the measure became law the term "residents" was changed to "citizens and taxpayers."[30] (Not wishing to let the obvious escape its readers' notice, the *Evening Post* commented, "This will prevent Chinese from recommending their fellow countrymen for a license.")[31] The board of supervisors had been receiving complaints from time to time from some Caucasian property owners that Chinese laundries were depreciating the value of their real estate,[32] and the law may simply have been intended to address the concerns, real or imagined, of these property owners. But the measure clearly harbored the potential of having much more far-reaching consequences. Opponents of the Chinese viewed it as tantamount to a sentence of death on a large part of the Chinese laundry industry. If the ordinance withstood the test of a judicial investigation, the *Post* predicted, there would soon not be "any Chinese laundry between Larkin and Ninth streets and the waterfront [the stated boundaries of the laundry district]."[33]

In the weeks following passage of the law a number of laundry operators, all bearing European names (mainly French, it seems), succeeded in obtaining the requisite number of signatures and secured permits from the board of supervisors. The only Chinese who appears to have applied saw his petition denied when several subscribing citizens withdrew their signatures after being subjected to pressure from an anti-Chinese organization.[34] Having the continued pursuit of their livelihoods depend on the goodwill of white San Franciscans was of course an intolerable situation from the Chinese perspective, and on July 18 the *Post* reported to its readers that it had learned that the laundrymen were determined to fight the laundry law in court. "While the Chinese despise our laws and violate them . . . with impunity, they are not slow to invoke them in their own behalf, and in the case of every law which may work to their prejudice they call to their aid all the resorts which our legal system provides," the paper commented with mixed admiration and annoyance.[35]

To bring this legal challenge the laundrymen retained in addition to Thomas Riordan, the McAllister and Bergin firm as well. The means settled on was a habeas corpus action in federal court. On July 25 one Quong Woo, a laundryman who had operated a business in the affected area for eight years and who had been arrested for violating the ordinance, petitioned for a writ of habeas corpus in the Circuit Court for the District of California. The petition alleged that the supervisors knew and expected that no Chinese subject could obtain twelve signatures and that the true purpose behind the laundry ordinance was, by imposing impossible conditions, to make it impossible for Chinese laundrymen to carry on their trade. The ordinance was but another manifestation of the long-standing Caucasian antipathy toward the Chinese race and was in clear contravention of the Burlingame Treaty, Section 1977 of the Revised Statutes of the United States, and of the equal protection clause of the federal Constitution.[36] The habeas writ was granted, argument was heard a week later, and two weeks later the circuit court rendered its decision.

Supreme Court Justice Field, sitting then in San Francisco in his capacity as a circuit magistrate, delivered the opinion of the court. Although in the one previous case in which he had had occasion to consider a Chinese challenge to a local ordinance, *Ho Ah Kow v. Nunan,* he had laid great stress on the racial hostility that lay behind the measure, here he did not deem it necessary to go into the claims of racial discrimination. The ordinance was null and void on quite other grounds. It threw obstacles that a municipal body was simply not empowered to throw in the way of the pursuit of an ordinary and inherently harmless trade.

Field's opinion was premised mainly on the common law of municipal legislatures. He agreed that municipal governments had large powers to regulate the conduct of businesses. It was perfectly within their power, for example, to ensure that businesses were conducted in such a way so as not to endanger the public health and safety or to be offensive to the senses or to disturb the neighborhood in which they were conducted. ("All business must be so conducted as not to endanger the public safety and health.")[37] They could also license trades either where the nature of the business demanded special training or in order to raise revenue. But what they could not do was to use the licensing power as a means of prohibiting the exercise of any ordinary or inoffensive trade or business. Nor could conditions be annexed to the issuance of licenses which would tend toward such a prohibition.[38] (Field characterized the conceptualization of laundries implicit in the ordinance as businesses threatening good morals or dangerous to the public safety as "miserable pretense.")[39] To do so would be an abuse of authority that flew in the face of well-established doctrine with respect to the powers of municipal bodies.[40] A fortiori was it an abuse of authority to make the exercise of the ordinary trades or avocations of life depend upon the favor or caprice of other private individuals whose actions, as he put it, could not be controlled by any legal proceeding.[41] And, Field pointed out, the Chinese, by virtue of the treaty between China and the United States, stood in exactly the same status with respect to these principles as did native citizens. Those rightfully in the country[42] had the right to "follow any of the lawful ordinary trades and pursuits of life, without let or hindrance from the state, or any of its subordinate municipal bodies, except such as may arise from the enforcement of equal and impartial laws."[43] Field made no reference to the petitioner's constitutional claims in his opinion.

In the United States Supreme Court: Ex parte Tom Tong

Field had stressed in his decision that it was within the legitimate power of municipal bodies to seek to ensure that businesses were conducted in such a way as not to endanger the public health, safety, or peace. "If [a laundry] be conducted in a manner that is offensive or dangerous, the supervisors may direct the manner to be changed, and prescribe regulations for its prosecution," he had said.[44] In the immediate aftermath of the *Quong Woo* decision the San Francisco supervisors adopted a detailed and comprehensive laundry ordinance, Order No. 1691, the first of several that it would adopt over the course of the next three years. The rationale for the measure as stated in its preamble was that the "indiscriminate establishment" of laundries posed a threat to the public health and safety and depreciated the value of surrounding property.

The ordinance first set forth the boundaries of a new laundry district, larger than the one described in the *Quong Woo* ordinance. It required that anyone seeking to operate a laundry within the district receive certification from the health officer of the city that his premises were properly drained and from the board of fire wardens that all heating apparatuses were in good condition and did not pose a threat to surrounding property. In addition, it required that laundry operators receive the written consent of the board of supervisors. Other provisions forbade the employment of persons with contagious diseases and the washing and ironing of clothes between the hours of 10 P.M. and 6 A.M. and on Sunday.[45] Passed in October 1882 the measure went into effect in January 1883,[46] and the city moved quickly to implement it, arresting one hundred Chinese laundrymen for violations within a few weeks of passage.[47]

Frustrated perhaps by an inability to obtain the requisite permissions (see below), suspicious in any case of any regulation that vested in Caucasian officials such unfettered discretion to determine whether they should be allowed to pursue their trade, and emboldened, no doubt, by the string of successes they had had to date in challenging the city's laundry laws, the Chinese laundrymen set about to test this measure too. In short order the McAllister and Bergin firm had sued out a writ of habeas corpus and brought the matter before the federal circuit court. The petitioner, Tom Tong, a laundryman who had been in business for twelve years, alleged that neither the board of supervisors nor any of the public officials would grant him the authorizations specified in the ordinance.[48] He argued that the ordinance was merely a device to avoid the *Quong Woo* decision and that its real purpose was to drive the Chinese out of the laundry business.

The measure left too much discretion in officials and in the board of supervisors, prescribing no standards that the Chinese laundrymen could conform to and represented an attempt by a municipal legislature to turn an essentially harmless business into a public nuisance. The city for its part claimed that the ordinance was nothing more than a normal police power measure, designed to promote the public health and safety.[49]

A circuit court panel consisting of Circuit Judge Lorenzo Sawyer and District Judge Hoffman heard the case, but the judges were unable to agree on an outcome. Sawyer thought the laundryman's point well taken. The new ordinance had to his mind not obviated the objections made to the ordinance invalidated in *Quong Woo.* Instead of being made subject to the pleasure of twelve citizens, the right to pursue the laundry trade was now being made to depend upon the unconstrained and unguided discretion of the board of supervisors. Hoffman disagreed.[50] The judges then sought to send the case to the United States Supreme Court for resolution under provisions of the Revised Statutes of 1875 that permitted lower court panels to send cases to the high court when the judges could not agree on a decision. The case was taken under submission by the high tribunal, but it decided on May 7 that it lacked jurisdiction to address the questions on the merits. As it interpreted the relevant code provisions,[51] only in criminal, as opposed to civil, proceedings could it review divisions of opinion that arose before the entry of final judgment. A habeas corpus action, it determined, was in its essence a *civil* proceeding.[52]

In June the city, for reasons having exclusively to do with the public fisc, repealed Order 1691 and enacted a new laundry ordinance. Under Order 1691 the city license collector was forbidden to issue laundry licenses to applicants unless they could show a copy of a resolution from the board of supervisors authorizing them to operate. The Chinese laundrymen had been either unwilling or unable to procure supervisorial authorizations and the license office had ceased to collect fees from them. Unwilling to suffer the indefinite loss of the some $1,650 in license fees per quarter that the Chinese laundrymen paid, the supervisors decided to unhinge the issuance of laundry licenses from the laundry order's substantive health and safety provisions.[53] Under the new order the issuance of a license was made dependent only upon the payment of the prescribed fee. In all other respects the new laundry ordinance, designated Order No. 1719, was identical to the old.[54]

An opportunity to test this measure—or at least one part of it—soon arose when a laundryman, Woo Yeck, was arrested for violating that provision of the ordinance that forbade the washing of clothes at night and on Sunday. Through counsel for the laundrymen's guild, Thomas Riordan, he brought a habeas challenge to the ordinance in San Francisco Superior Court. This court, after hearing argument, found the ordinance to be valid.[55] Riordan then obtained a new habeas writ from the state supreme court, made returnable, for reasons that are not entirely clear, in the Superior Court of Alameda County, a county that lay across the bay from San Francisco. This court, by contrast, found the provision of the ordinance under which the petitioner had been arrested to be void. It represented, said the court, an unwarrantable interference, as the court put it, "with the natural and inalienable right of every individual . . . to life, liberty and the pursuit of happiness, and to acquire, hold and enjoy property." Comprehended within these general rights was the specific right of the individual to labor during any hours of the day or night. The state could legislate to protect the community against fire and to protect the public health but it could not prescribe the hours during which businesses could be held open nor the number of hours that laborers could work.[56] The opinion is of course a well-nigh classic statement of the ideology of economic substantive due process, a doctrine then beginning to crystallize in state courts across the country.

There was no provision at the time for the appeal to the state supreme court of habeas corpus rulings by lower courts, and so the net result of all of the legal maneuvering that had taken place was two conflicting decisions by courts of equal authority on the extent of the city's ability to regulate laundry hours. It was a situation that could have been satisfactory to neither side. The city sought an opportunity to raise the question directly with the high court, and one was quickly found. Apparently certain white laundry proprietors also objected to the limitation on the hours of their operation, and one Emil Moynier agreed to become the subject of a test case. Arrangements were made with the chief of police for him to be arrested, whereupon he immediately filed a petition for habeas corpus in the California Supreme Court itself and was released on bond. The city submitted the same brief that it had in the *Woo Yeck* case, and counsel for the laundrymen's guild was permitted to enter the case as amicus curiae, submitting the same brief that he had used in the lower court case.[57] A three-judge panel of the California Supreme Court handed down its decision February 8, 1884.

The judges saw no merits whatever to the petitioner's claims. Individuals might have a constitutional right to acquire property and pursue and obtain happiness in whatever way they chose, but this right was neatly counterbalanced by the right of municipalities, guaranteed in the state constitution, to make such regulations as they deemed necessary to protect the public health and safety. The ordinance, with its provisions relating to drainage and fire safety, were a classic exercise of this municipal right. As to the claim that the limitations placed on hours of operation exceeded the bounds of the police power, the judges simply said that they were in no position to declare that these limitations were not a legitimate part of a rational health and safety scheme.[58]

Now having the sanction of the state supreme court, the city authorities moved quickly to enforce the night and Sunday hours provisions of Order 1719. The laundrymen were not resigned, however, to let matters rest there and quickly embarked on several new legal tacks. Their attorney, Thomas Riordan, first sought to raise the issue of the order's validity before the full California Supreme Court, filing a petition for a writ of habeas corpus on behalf of an arrested Chinese laundry worker by the name of Soon Hing, but the court adhered to the rule declared by the three-judge panel and refused to grant the writ. He then sought relief in the federal courts. On March 3, 1884, Riordan filed a habeas application on Soon Hing's behalf with the federal circuit court, raising now for the first time the claim of racial discrimination. The supervisors, he claimed, had passed Order 1719 "for the purpose and with the intent to oppress the Chinese engaged in the laundry business, and not from any sanitary, police or other legitimate purpose." The two-judge circuit court panel was divided on whether a writ should issue and on April 7 filed a certificate of opposition of opinion.[59]

Shortly afterward Riordan filed the record of the proceedings in the Supreme Court of the United States, preliminary to asking that tribunal to review the lower court ruling. Alfred Clarke, who had represented the city in the lower court, was now appointed special counsel by the board of supervisors, with authority to do whatever was necessary to demonstrate the validity of the laundry order. He would remain chief lawyer for the city and county of San Francisco in all future litigation involving Chinese laundries. Clarke was convinced that the Supreme Court lacked jurisdiction to review the lower court ruling, but being anxious to obtain a definitive judgment as quickly as possible from the high tribunal on the validity of the order, he arranged for the bringing of a parallel test case, again as in *Moynier*, involving a French laundry owner, Francis Barbier, convicted of operating his business during the night hours. (Since Soon Hing's conviction for violating Order 1719 the board of supervisors had enacted, in October 1883 and then in March and April 1884, a series of new laundry orders, Nos. 1746, 1762, and 1767, each identical to its predecessor in its substantive provisions but each defining new laundry district boundaries. It was under the last of these, Order 1767, that Barbier was convicted.) Barbier challenged the constitutionality of the ordinance in a habeas action in San Francisco Superior Court, but the court rejected his petition. His attorneys thereupon sought review via writ of error in the U.S. Supreme Court, and counsel for the city and for Barbier submitted the case to that tribunal for decision on written briefs in October 1884. After some complex maneuvering by counsel for the Chinese laundrymen, the Court, reversing an earlier decision, agreed to decide the Soon Hing case as well.[60]

In January 1885 the Supreme Court handed down its decision in *Barbier v. Connolly*.[61] Two months later it decided *Soon Hing v. Crowley*.[62] The two decisions, both authored by Justice Stephen Field on behalf of a unanimous court, were a complete vindication of the city's position. Field gave short shrift to Barbier's claims that the limitation on working hours unconstitutionally deprived him of the right to labor and acquire property and impermissibly discriminated between those engaged in the laundry business and those engaged in other kinds of work. He found the contested section of the ordinance to be purely a police regulation reasonably calculated to reduce the risk of fires at night. As such it was a matter completely outside the ken of the federal courts. He rejected out of hand the Fourteenth Amendment claim of partial legislation. The ordinance contained no invidious discrimination against anyone similarly situated. All persons engaged in the laundry business within the affected district were subjected to the same burdens and requirements.[63] Although he rejected the constitutional attack on the San Francisco law, Field did seize the occasion to set forth in the fullest fashion yet, although in *dictum* to be sure, the Fourteenth Amendment jurisprudence that he had begun to develop as early as *Ah Fong*.

> The Fourteenth Amendment, in declaring that no State "shall deprive any person of life, liberty, or property without due process of law, nor deny to any person within its jurisdiction the equal protection of the laws," undoubtedly intended not only that there should be no arbitrary deprivation of life or liberty, or arbitrary spoliation of property, but that equal protection and security should be given to all under like circumstances in the enjoyment of their personal and civil rights; that all persons should be equally entitled to pursue their happiness, and acquire and enjoy property; that they should have like access to the courts of the country for the protection of their persons and property, the prevention and redress of wrongs, and the enforcement of contracts; that no impediment should be interposed to the pursuits of any one, except as applied to the same pursuits by others under like circumstances; that no greater burdens should be laid upon one than are laid upon others in the same calling and condition. . . . Class legislation, discriminating against some and favoring others, is prohibited.[64]

Since no one on the Court wrote any separate opinion distancing himself from these views, the justices were in effect giving their approbation to the view first broached by Justices Field, Bradley, and Swayne in the *Slaughter-House Cases*, namely that the Fourteenth Amendment was designed, among other things, to guarantee equality of right in the lawful pursuits of life.[65] Now, however, the class of beneficiaries of the amendment's terms had been expanded to include aliens as well as citizens, an expansion made possible doctrinally by the shift in focus from the privileges and immunities clause of the amendment to its due process and equal protection clauses.[66]

Soon Hing had made much the same sorts of objections to the ordinance under which he had been convicted, and in *Soon Hing v. Crowley* Field dealt with them in much the same way. The personal liberty guaranteed by the Constitution was not absolute, he pointed out, but rather was subject to all sorts of restrictions in the interests of promoting the public weal. "However broad the right of every one to follow such calling and employ his time as he may judge most conducive to his interests, it must be exercised subject to such general rules as are adopted by society for the common welfare," he declared. The liberty guaranteed by the constitution was "liberty regulated by just and impartial laws."[67] This brought him to the additional claim, indeed the principal claim made by Soon Hing, that the ordinance in question had sprung from hostility against the Chinese and not from a concern for the public safety. There was nothing either in the language of the ordinance or in the record of its enactment that tended to sustain these allegations, Field declared. "The rule is general with reference to the enactments of all legislative bodies that the courts cannot inquire into the motives of the legislators in passing them except as they may be disclosed on the face of the acts, or inferrible from their operation, considered with reference to the condition of the country and existing legislation."[68] Indeed, he noted, even if the legislative motives were as alleged, the ordinance would not be infirm "unless in its enforcement it is made to operate only against the class mentioned."[69]

The White *Habeas Corpus Cases*

The city's power to broadly regulate the laundry business had now been confirmed by the highest court in the land. But the full extent of this power had still not yet been settled. A question remained, for example, concerning the validity of the original laundry ordinances passed by the board of supervisors in the winter and spring of 1880—Order No. 1559, providing that new laundries be constructed of brick or stone and No. 1569, providing that existing wooden laundries obtain supervisorial permits in order to continue operation. A superior court, it will be remembered, had voided Order 1569 in a decision handed down in May 1881[70] and, by implication, had left Order 1559 under a cloud. Counselor Clarke, heartened no doubt by the trend of court decisions, now determined to have these remaining questions brought to a quick and favorable resolution. The vehicle he chose for doing this was again the prosecution of a Caucasian laundry owner. As will appear later, the subject may not have been an altogether unwilling defendant.

On January 1, 1885, E. White, the proprietor of two very large laundry establishments in San Francisco, was arrested for violating Order 1559 and Section 67 of Order 1587, identical in language. For reasons that are not entirely clear, the matter did not come up for a hearing in the police court, however, until March 9, at which time the defendant was duly convicted and sentenced to a fine of $5 or five days in jail. Immediately his attorney A. C. Searle sued out a writ of habeas corpus in the California Supreme Court. The cause was submitted on written briefs, the petitioner's alleging that the orders were unreasonable, that they unjustly discriminated between persons engaged in the laundry business and those engaged in the bakery business and likewise between the wealthy and the poor. (The *Ah Ling* case was offered as authority in support of these views.) It also argued that the orders had been repealed by implication by subsequent supervisorial legislation, in particular Orders 1719 and 1767, which it was alleged were designed to cover the whole subject of laundry legislation.[71]

On June 2 a three-judge supreme court panel handed down a terse opinion dismissing the writ, saying only that in light of the *Barbier* and *Soon Hing* cases it had no doubt of the city's power to pass such ordinances and that nothing in Orders 1719 and 1767 suggested that they were meant to repeal the earlier laundry legislation. Nothing in these later ordinances, the court said, dealt with the materials out of which laundry buildings were to be constructed.[72]

The California Supreme Court having given its sanction to Order 1559, Counselor Clarke now pressed forward with the prosecution of a number of Chinese laundrymen under the related Order 1569, among them one Chin Yen. The *Chin Yen* case was argued in police court on June 18, L. H. Van Schaick, a former judge under retainer to the Tung Hing Tong, appearing on behalf of the Chinese laundryman, and arguing against the constitutionality of the ordinance. As events were taking shape, it appeared as if this case would be the vehicle for testing the validity of Order 1569, but the city, revealing its now well-established preference for seeing these issues raised in the context of cases involving Caucasians, moved to short-circuit the process. On June 23, while *Chin Yen* was still under submission, the redoubtable E. White was again brought into justice court, this time on the charge of "maintaining" (as opposed to "constructing") a wooden laundry without supervisorial permission, in violation of Order 1569. He was convicted the next day, and, in what was now taking on the aspect of familiar ritual, sued out a habeas writ in the superior court of Judge T. K. Wilson, the magistrate who in November 1883, had confirmed the validity of supervisorial Order 1719.[73] This time White appeared *in propria persona.*

Judge Wilson handed down his decision a week later. He was unable to agree with the decision of his colleague Judge Freelon in the *Ah Ling* case, he said. The ordinance was good and valid and well within the power of the municipality to enact. He found full authority for it in those provisions of state law that conferred on municipalities the power to pass regulations designed to promote public sanitation and fire safety. The law in question was purely a fire safety measure, in his view. Nor was it special legislation and for that reason constitutionally infirm. All engaged in the same business were subjected by it to the same restrictions. He did not think there was any force to the argument that the law discriminated improperly in favor of entrepreneurs wealthy enough to build brick buildings and against smaller businesses. The same reasoning might be applied, he said, to any other measure limiting the right to erect wooden buildings within certain sections of the city, and yet no one could seriously contest the supervisors' power to pass such an ordinance.[74]

Counselor Clarke chose this juncture to render a report to the board of supervisors on his tenure as special counsel in the laundry litigation. It was an impressive record of success he could point to. He had prevailed in the end in every contested case and had secured judicial sanction, in most instances from the court of last resort, for practically the full range of the city's laundry legislation. "The result of [the recently completed] litigation," he told the board on July 8, "has been the complete vindication and demonstration of the municipal police legislative power."[75] There was still one outstanding unresolved matter, namely the validity of Order 1569. On this question there was still a conflict of authority. But, though he did not mention this in the report, plans were already in the works to remedy that situation.

On July 13 E. White, now represented by counsel, filed a petition for a writ of habeas corpus in the California Supreme Court, challenging anew his conviction under Order 1569. The petition made exactly the same arguments that White had made in the superior court proceeding. But two days later his attorney, R. M. Swain introduced a significant new argument in the conclusion of the printed brief he filed with the court. It is worth quoting at some length:

> There is no doubt but the law in question was aimed at the Chinese laundries. . . . If this law is sustained, it places all of this industry in jeopardy. A Chinaman has no vote, so, perhaps, while a Chinaman would be refused permission to keep a laundry, a white man would experience no difficulty in obtaining such permission. If Chinese laundries are to be closed, of course monopolies will flourish, and the laundry business will be carried on by such monopolies, founded upon the ruins of the present laundry system. The certificate of the Health Officer, obtained for each laundry, shows the sanitary condition perfect. That of the Fire Wardens shows there is no danger to be apprehended from fire; but here comes in an oppressive law and places this legitimate, licensed business at the mercy of men elected to a political office by a political party, at a time when to be opposed to the Chinese is considered popular and a test of party loyalty.[76]

It at first glance seems an exceedingly strange argument for the Caucasian laundryman to make, but it becomes less curious if a document filed in the court a few days later is to be believed. This document sought to put the whole of the White litigation in a new light.

On July 20 L. H. Van Schaick, who had received leave of court to enter the new White habeas corpus case as amicus curiae on behalf of the Tung Hing Tong, filed an affidavit, charging that the several White cases were in effect collusive actions, orchestrated on both sides from beginning to end by Clarke. He alleged that in the first White action—that which had resulted in the Supreme Court decision sustaining the validity of Order 1559—Clarke had "made and prepared the briefs used by both the petitioner and [the] respondent" (he claimed to have received this information from White's attorney in the action, A. C. Searle).[77] He alleged further that in the June 1885 proceeding—that which had resulted in the superior court decision affirming Order 1569's constitutionality—Clarke had again acted as sole attorney for both sides, preparing all relevant papers. (It will be remembered that White appeared in this proceeding *in propria persona.*)[78] Finally he charged that R. M. Swain was appearing in the pending White proceeding at the request of Clarke (he had been so informed by Swain, he claimed) and further that the brief Swain had filed five days earlier was a copy of the brief which he (Van Schaick) had filed in the *Chin Yen* proceeding in the San Francisco police court. The brief was being used, he stressed, without his knowledge or consent.[79]

In response to the filing of this affidavit the court issued an Order to Show Cause requiring White to come forward with reasons why, in light of the allegations made in the affidavit, his habeas petition should not be dismissed. But there is no record of any hearing ever being held on the matter. The last-dated item to be found in the supreme court case file is a stipulation dated August 14, 1885, and signed by Van Schaick, the San Francisco district attorney and the city and county attorney, indefinitely postponing the hearing both on the Order to Show Cause and on the underlying habeas petition.[80] It seems safe to say in light of what happened later that by this point all parties had agreed that the better course would be to let the *White* case die and to have the issue of Order 1569's validity adjudicated in the context of a different proceeding. A Chinese laundryman would shortly initiate just such a proceeding, and in this case there would be no doubt in any quarter about the true adversariness of the parties.[81]

Yick Wo v. Hopkins

Prompted no doubt by the California Supreme Court decision of June 2, 1885,[82] sustaining the validity of Order 1559 and Judge Wilson's superior court decision upholding Order 1569, large numbers of Chinese laundrymen had during the summer petitioned the board of supervisors for permission to operate in wooden buildings.[83] Among these was a laundryman by the name of Yick Wo (or Yick Wo Chang according to some court documents), who had been continuously operating his laundry at the same location in San Francisco for twenty-two years.[84] He had previously received from the health officer and the Board of Fire Wardens the requisite certificates concerning proper drainage and fire safety called for under local law.[85] Like all other Chinese who applied for permits during this period, he had been denied permission to operate by the board of supervisors.[86] On August 22, 1885, Yick Wo was arrested for continuing to operate his laundry without supervisorial permission in violation of Section 1 of Order 1569. (It was one among numerous arrests of Chinese laundrymen that took place during this period.)[87] He was convicted of the offense the same day in San Francisco police court, and on August 24 his attorneys filed a petition for a writ of habeas corpus in the California Supreme Court.[88]

Yick Wo's habeas corpus petition, drafted by the Tung Hing Tong attorneys Van Schaick and Smoot, attacked the ordinances under which the petitioner had been imprisoned on several grounds.[89] They were, they said, no longer in force, having been repealed by subsequent laundry laws or, in the alternative, had lapsed by virtue of nonenforcement. They were unreasonable and thus never valid. They represented an improper attempt by a municipal body to declare something a nuisance.[90]

These claims were urged with some force, but, the petitioner's attorneys laid equal, if not greater, emphasis on the potential for racial discrimination that the ordinances harbored. The very vagueness of the order (it seems sensible to speak in the singular since in terms of content only one law was before the court) opened the way to such discrimination, it was alleged. The order, the attorneys noted, in no way informed the applicant what he needed to do in order to secure supervisorial consent. It permitted "discrimination by indirection."[91] Or, as they put it somewhat more colorfully elsewhere in the petition, the Chinese laundrymen were compelled by the order "to seek the haven of supervisorial consent without chart or compass to protect [them] against the sunken rocks of discrimination."[92] Moreover, it was alleged, none of this had happened by accident. The orders providing for special permission of the board in order to operate a laundry, Yick Wo's lawyers argued, had been adopted "for the purpose of discriminating against him and his countrymen, and . . . [was] enforced so as to accomplish that result."[93]

To add force to the argument Van Schaick and Smoot brought certain statistical claims to the court's attention. Since enforcement of the ordinance had begun in earnest, they alleged, some 150 Chinese had been arrested for violating the ordinance while 80 similarly situated Caucasian laundry proprietors had been left unmolested. Moreover, some 200 Chinese laundrymen had petitioned the board of supervisors for permission to continue in business without success while not a single petition presented by a non-Chinese was denied.[94] As constituted and enforced, the ordinance deprived the petitioners of their federal constitutional rights under the Fourteenth Amendment and discriminated against them in violation both of Section 1977 of the Revised Statutes of 1875 and of the treaty between the United States and China.[95]

In a Memorandum of Points and Authorities that he submitted to the court, special counselor Clarke denied that there was any substance to the petitioner's state law claims. Nothing in the long and complex history of the city's successive laundry legislation, he contended, would entitle anyone to conclude that the 1880 prohibition against operating in wooden buildings without supervisorial approval had been repealed by subsequent legislation. He dismissed as well the petitioner's claim that the denial of Yick Wo's application amounted to a legislative declaration of nuisance, contending that rather what was involved was the exercise of that discretion that municipal bodies possessed to regulate the conduct of business in promotion of the public health and safety.[96]

In a separate brief[97] Clarke dealt with the petitioner's allegations of racial discrimination. The city, in its response to Yick Wo's habeas petition had admitted the substantial accuracy of Yick Wo's statistical allegations although it claimed that one white laundry owner had been denied a permit and it implied the reason the eighty-odd Caucasian laundries had been left unmolested while the Chinese were being prosecuted was that they (the white laundries) did not have scaffolds on the roof.[98] Clarke now sought to qualify and to explain the city's admissions.

Clarke argued in the first instance that they were immaterial and ought to be disregarded.[99] If they were not, he contended that they were capable of entirely beneficent explanation. If Chinese laundries were being treated differently by the city authorities it was because they were different. The key was the presence or absence of scaffolding. (Clarke submitted for the court's consideration photographs of some seven Chinese laundries, Yick Wo's included, all showing buildings with scaffolds on the roof.)[100] This explained both the different pattern of granting permits and the differential pattern of arrests under the ordinance. He had been given to understand that two Caucasian laundry owners had received permits from the board, he said. He could not say how many other might have as well, but he could say for certain that none of the wooden laundries owned by Caucasians had scaffolding on the roof whereas this was "one of the objectionable features of the Chinese laundries championed by the Tung Hing Tong."[101]

Scaffolding was also, according to Clarke, the key to explaining the differential pattern of arrests. The Chinese laundry owners who had been arrested had scaffolding on their roofs while the Caucasian laundry owners did not.[102] "The police department, in attempting to enforce the laundry order," said Clarke, "have not perpetrated the absurdity of arresting some harmless widow who had no scaffold on her roof, but finding scaffolds on the roof of Yick Wo and 200 of his countrymen, they arrested them."[103]

But the scaffolds were certainly not the only reason for denying the Chinese laundrymen permission to operate. Clarke portrayed Chinese laundries, without exception, as a menace to the well-being of the city of San Francisco. "The capital of $200,000 invested by the Chinese consists of a few bars of soap and a few gallons of water in each of their three hundred wash houses, a lease or tenancy of a rookery which would not bring a ground rent from a white tenant but for which they pay a very high rent."[104] Elsewhere he sought to depict all Chinese laundries as so many tinderboxes waiting to burst into flame. Some wooden laundries were well ventilated and well drained and had taken every precaution against fire, Clarke contended, while those owned by the Chinese were "constructed in the cheapest manner, of rough redwood boards, not even painted on the outside, not even bearing on the inside the momentary protection against fire which a coat of plaster would give."[105]

Clarke spent considerable time maligning the Chinese laundrymen's association, seeming to imply that the association bore responsibility for all the ills the laundries were causing. He depicted it as a kind of "state within a state," exercising strict control over its constituents and determined at all costs to block every attempt of the municipality of San Francisco to interpose regulations of its own. "Would any city in China," he asked rhetorically, "tolerate an invasion of Americans setting up a *Tung Hing Tong* in opposition to the local government, and the location of 300 firetraps all over the city, thereby jeopardizing the safety of life and reducing the value of property."[106] Indeed he declared, if Yick Wo would disaffiliate from the organization and remove the scaffolding from his roof, he would stand in better posture before the courts of justice.[107]

There was no substance whatsoever, Clarke declared, to the charge that the San Francisco Board of Supervisors had any wish to persecute the Chinese. He pointed out that that same board had granted permits to operate to a number of Chinese employment agencies.[108]

Despite the elaborate briefing by both sides of the federal issues raised by Yick Wo's complaint, it was the state law issues almost exclusively that the California Supreme Court addressed in the decision that it handed down on December 29.[109] The court held that the municipal legislation in question was a classic exercise of the police power, well within the authority conferred on the board of supervisors by the state constitution and state law. The business of conducting a laundry, it said, involved the constant use of fires "under circumstances, and perhaps by persons, liable to result in conflagrations." On the other hand there would be instances in which it would be clear that the laundry could be conducted without presenting any danger to surrounding property.[110] It saw nothing wrong in letting the supervisors be the final judges of these facts. The court also rejected the claim—a rather weak one without doubt—that Order 1569 (and Section 58 of Order 1587) had been repealed by implication by the enactment of subsequent laundry legislation, noting that there was no express repeal of the 1880 legislation in any later laundry law and that the law did not favor the repeal of statutes by implication. The various laundry laws could be reconciled in their provisions, it held.[111]

The court dealt with the petitioner's federal claims in the tersest fashion. With regard to his contention that his Fourteenth Amendment rights had been violated, it said simply "we think the principles upon which contention on that head can be based have in effect been set at rest by the cases of *Barbier v. Connolly* . . . and *Soon Hing v. Crowley*."[112] The claim of infringement of treaty rights fared no better. "A regulation which applies alike to all persons engaged in a given pursuit, without distinction as to nationality, residence, age, sex, or condition, is not, when otherwise regular and valid, subject to the criticism of being in violation of treaty obligations," it declared.[113] The California judges had nothing to say specifically concerning the federal statutory claim.

The matter was far from over, however. Yick Wo's attorneys,[114] believing no doubt that they were more likely to be addressed in that forum, sought now to raise the Chinese laundrymen's federal claims in the United States Circuit Court in San Francisco. In early January they brought an action in that tribunal, asking it to enjoin the chief of police of the city and county from arresting Yick Wo and other similarly situated Chinese laundrymen. The court heard vigorous oral argument on the substantive issues raised, but Judge Sawyer decided the case on a procedural point, holding that the weight of authority was that a federal court had no jurisdiction to enjoin proceedings first commenced in a state court.[115] The decision closed off one potential avenue of review. But another means of bringing the claims of the Chinese laundrymen to the federal court's attention, the writ of habeas corpus, had yet to be explored. And, from the perspective of the attorneys for the Chinese, an eminently suitable *habeas* petitioner was ready at hand.

On the same day that the circuit court declined to exercise jurisdiction in Yick Wo's injunction action, another Chinese laundryman of long experience, Wo Lee, was convicted in police court of operating a laundry in a wooden building without supervisorial permission, and upon failure to pay the requisite fine was committed to the custody of the San Francisco sheriff. Like Yick Wo he had been in business continuously in the same location for over twenty years (twenty-five years to be exact). His premises had likewise passed inspection by the Board of Fire Wardens and by the health officer. He filed immediately in the circuit court a petition for a writ of habeas corpus, a petition that, save for its allegations of fact concerning the petitioner, was identical in content and form to Yick Wo's California Supreme Court petition. In response, the city offered copies of the relevant San Francisco ordinances and the record of the petitioner's conviction in the police court. It also included the set of admissions it had presented the California Supreme Court.[116]

The case was submitted without oral argument, and a decision issued quickly from the circuit court. Sawyer minced no words in expressing his strong dislike for the city ordinance in question. It was to his mind but a variant of the law he had wanted to, but had been unable to, nullify in *Tom Tong*. The right to carry on a "harmless and necessary occupation," he observed, was here being made to depend not upon any prescribed conditions but "upon the consent or arbitrary will of the board of supervisors."[117] Laws of this sort tended to frustrate the exercise of this fundamental right and were inherently suspect from a constitutional standpoint, he declared, citing as authority his own and Field's opinion in the *Quong Woo* case and a recent decision of the Maryland supreme court. In the case of *City of Baltimore v. Radecke*,[118] that court had voided a Baltimore ordinance giving the mayor complete discretion to determine who should be able to use a steam engine in the operation of a business.[119] All the more infirm was the ordinance, from Sawyer's perspective, if from the generality of its terms and the arbitrary discretion it vested in elected officials, it permitted the supervisors to engage in racial discrimination. And Sawyer was clearly convinced that that was its necessary tendency, if not its specific purpose. He took notice of the petitioner's uncontradicted claim that all Chinese applicants had been denied permission to operate while all Caucasian applications had been granted and as well of "the notorious public and municipal history of the times."[120] That the law in its execution as so far revealed meant prohibition of the laundry trade to the Chinese, he said, "must be apparent to every citizen of San Francisco who has been here long enough to be familiar with the course of an active and aggressive branch of public opinion and of public notorious events." And if, he asked rhetorically, it was clear that the purpose of the ordinance was to drive out the Chinese laundrymen, *and not merely to regulate the business for public safety*, did this not disclose a case of violation of the provisions of the Fourteenth Amendment and of the treaty between the United States and China?[121]

Notwithstanding this apparent uncompromising condemnation of the ordinance, Sawyer here, as in the *Yick Wo* case, declined to take any steps to undo what the California Supreme Court had done. In the first place, Sawyer noted, his court did not have such power. The federal circuit court, though it had concurrent jurisdiction with state courts to review the questions being raised by the Chinese laundrymen, had no appellate power over the state supreme court and could not make its decision binding on that court. Nor did Sawyer think it would be appropriate for him to hold officially that the state court had erred on, as he put it somewhat incongruously, a matter open to reasonable doubt,[122] especially when the avenue to an authoritative review of the state supreme court decision lay fully open. It was, Sawyer said, a case that seemed peculiarly proper to be left to the final decision of the United States Supreme Court, and he expressed the hope that both parties would cooperate to procure a speedy decision from that tribunal.[123] Steps in the direction of obtaining such a result were immediately forthcoming. On January 29, Yick Wo filed a writ of error in the California Supreme Court seeking from the United States Supreme Court the review of the decision in his case. On the same day the federal circuit court entered an order allowing an appeal of its decision in *Wo Lee.*

There would be no oral argument in the cases before the U.S. Supreme Court. Rather, both were submitted to the Court for decision entirely on the basis of the written record that had been accumulated in the lower courts and the written arguments of the parties. The brief filed by the attorneys representing the Tung Hing Tong (Hall McAllister was now listed as the lead counsel of record), harped again on the chief points made by counsel in the California Supreme Court in the *Yick Wo* habeas corpus case although in a somewhat more focused and pointed fashion (whether this betrayed the presence of McAllister's hand in the drafting it is impossible to say). Counsel again argued that under the ordinance the exercise of what they dubbed a "harmless and necessary occupation" (a phrase that had been used by Sawyer in his opinion on circuit and that certainly would have resonated positively with Supreme Court Justice Stephen Field who had used essentially the same phrase to describe the laundrymen's trade in his *Quong Woo* opinion)[124] had been made dependent upon the "arbitrary will" of a legislative body, this, it was alleged in violation of natural right.[125] But the attorneys laid heavy emphasis on the allegation of discriminatory enforcement, an issue, they reminded the Court, that the state court had sidestepped.[126] The admissions as to the number of laundry petitions granted and denied and the number of arrests under the ordinance, made by the city in the state supreme court and the federal circuit court and now part of the record, were again brought forcefully to the court's attention.[127] The two allegations—of a bad law and of discriminatory enforcement—of course went hand in hand, as counsel for the petitioner and appellant sought to suggest in this passage:

> This is not the case of a valid or constitutional law enforced or administered in an unconstitutional manner. It is a law of unfinished growth and stands as if it read: "Clothes washing for hire, in buildings not made of brick or stone, is prohibited; but this law is not to be enforced against those who, from time to time, we the lawmakers shall except from its operation." With such a measure, providing in terms for the insertion of illimitable provisos and exceptions, it is not only the privilege, but it would seem to be the duty, of the courts to scrutinize its operations closely, and declare the Act itself a nullity, because it establishes a system by which forbidden results can be and are accomplished without any possible redress to the persons aggrieved.[128]

But the lawyers did take pains to argue that even a valid or neutral law, if enforced in a discriminatory fashion, ran afoul of the Fourteenth Amendment, citing as authority two recently decided civil rights cases, *Ex parte Virginia* and *Neal v. Delaware*, and Field's dictum in *Soon Hing v. Crowley* on the discriminatory enforcement of neutral laws.[129] They asked the court that "the ingenuity of human hostility . . . not be allowed to triumph over and destroy the natural and conventional rights entrusted to and sacredly sheltered by the sword of justice."[130]

The city (Clarke and an attorney by the name of H. G. Sieberst were on the brief) relied heavily on the brief it had submitted to the California Supreme Court, including large excerpts from it in its U.S. Supreme Court argument. The federal court was thus bade to consider the scaffolding on the Chinese laundries and their allegedly more dilapidated condition and greater tendency to fire, as reasons for the differential treatment of white and Chinese laundrymen. (The photographs that had been submitted to the California court in *Yick Wo* were included with the brief. There was no photograph of Wo Lee's laundry in the batch.) The same allegations were made concerning the pernicious influences of the Tung Hing Tong. The city did seek to bolster its case with some new assertions. It now insisted that two and only two permits had been granted to Caucasian laundrymen, but an excerpt from the California Supreme Court brief that it chose to include contained the statement made in that court that it didn't know for certain how many Caucasians had received permits.[131] It also now claimed that all white laundrymen who were operating without permits were under arrest and awaiting trial.[132] Finally, it sought to link Chinese laundries with the spread of opium and with the corruption of children and servants through the traffic in lottery tickets—yet another reason demonstrating the expediency of regulating *these* laundries, as the lawyers put it.[133]

The city again forcefully and indignantly rejected the accusations of discrimination leveled against it by the Chinese laundrymen. Indeed, according to Clarke and Sieberst, San Francisco was a veritable haven for the Chinese. "The city of San Francisco has not oppressed the Chinese. On the contrary, she has taken them under her wing and protected them when they were abused and driven out of other places."[134]

The decision of the Court, handed down May 10, 1886, and authored by Justice Stanley Matthews, mentioned scaffolding not at all. It was, in fact, in substance and in tone (if not in result) remarkably similar to Sawyer's opinion on circuit in *Wo Lee*. Justice Matthews, like his circuit bench colleague, considered the San Francisco laundry ordinances to be very bad law indeed, and for much the same reasons. In essence it was bad because it offended the constitutional principle that the exercise of fundamental rights, including the right to pursue a profession or trade not be made subject to the exercise of arbitrary governmental power. The Fourteenth Amendment, Matthews declared, citing Field's opinion in *Barbier v. Connolly* (a case Matthews said the California Supreme Court had misread) required that all persons should be equally entitled to pursue their happiness and acquire and enjoy property and that the law should lay no greater burdens upon one set of persons in the same calling and condition than it did on others. Conversely, it forbade "class legislation," that is to say, laws that favored some and discriminated against others with respect to the exercise of these rights.[135] And, Matthews stressed, these constitutional rights were as applicable to Chinese aliens as they were to U.S. citizens. The Fourteenth Amendment to the Constitution, he declared, was not confined to the protection of citizens but rather applied to all *persons* within the territorial jurisdiction of the United States.[136]

The San Francisco ordinances clearly offended these principles in Matthews's view. He differed entirely with the opinion of the California Supreme Court that they vested a not unusual discretion in the board of supervisors. In his view they seemed rather to confer upon the city legislators "naked and arbitrary power" to give or withhold consent, with no guidance whatsoever as to how that power should be exercised.[137] They prescribed no rule for the operation of laundries to which all interested in pursuing that profession could conform. Rather they made all such persons, in Matthews's choice phrase, "tenants at will under the supervisors of their means of living."[138] And the idea that one might be compelled to hold one's means of living at the mere will of another was from a constitutional standpoint, Matthews said, intolerable.[139] Like Sawyer, he thought the San Francisco laws not dissimilar to the ordinance that the Maryland Supreme Court had voided in *Radecke*, and he quoted at length from that decision.[140]

But, having all but declared the San Francisco ordinance void on its face for all of the above-cited reasons, Matthews, as he came to the end of his opinion, edged away from that conclusion and embarked on a different line of constitutional analysis that focused on the application rather than on the content of the law. The Court was not obliged in the cases before it, said Matthews, to hypothesize about the abuses to which ordinances of this sort might lead. It had here a real live instance of such abuse in the administration of the San Francisco laws. For the evidence of the ordinance in operation disclosed an unequal and oppressive administration of the law. The record showed, the Court pointed out, that while all Chinese subjects had been denied supervisorial consent to pursue "their harmless and useful occupation," eighty others not Chinese had been permitted to carry on the same business under similar conditions.[141] The conclusion could not be resisted, said Matthews, that no explanation for this differential treatment existed "except hostility to the race and nationality to which the petitioners belong."[142] But such discrimination constituted a denial of the equal protection of the laws in violation of the Fourteenth Amendment. As Matthews put it in words that have since been repeated numerous times in American constitutional discourse: "Though the law itself be fair on its face and impartial in appearance yet, if it is applied and administered by public authority with an evil eye and an unequal hand, so as practically to make unjust and illegal discriminations between persons in similar circumstances, material to their rights, the denial of equal justice is still within the prohibition of the Constitution."[143] The lower court decisions in *Yick Wo* and *Wo Lee* were accordingly reversed and the petitioners ordered discharged.

Yick Wo has acquired its place in constitutional history for its early endorsement of the principle that racially discriminatory enforcement of the law offended the constitutional mandate of equal protection just as much as did a law that discriminated in its terms. But, as should be clear from the account above, the decision is more than simply an indictment of a neutral law unfairly applied. Notwithstanding the references to laws "fair on their face and impartial in appearance," the Court clearly thought it had before it a very flawed piece of legislation. Indeed a good two-thirds of Justice Matthews's opinion is given over to an analysis of just how bad a law the San Francisco ordinance was. A law that vests total and seemingly unconstrained discretion over access to the laundering trade in a municipal legislative body is, he makes abundantly clear, inherently suspect. But it would be wrong to stint the decision's race relations jurisprudence.

In the end the basis of the Court's holding was not the facial invalidity of the law but rather its conviction that there had been racial discrimination in the law's administration. In reaching this conclusion the court relied mainly, it is clear, on the admissions made by the city's attorneys separately in both the *Yick Wo* and *Wo Lee* cases concerning the numbers and racial identities of those who had received laundry permits and those arrested for operating wooden laundries without permits.[144] It was, after all, on its face a rather startling fact that not a single one of some two hundred Chinese laundries, some having been in business for many years, a good many of them having already received fire and sanitation clearances, would have been deemed suitable to continue in operation. These numbers, the Court concluded, at least raised the presumption of a pattern of hostility toward the Chinese, and threw on the city the burden of rebutting that presumption by some convincing show of evidence. One may speculate as to why the city's attempt to do this was unpersuasive to the justices.

San Francisco's principal explanation for the disparity in the treatment of white and Chinese laundries was that the Chinese laundries had scaffolding on the roof while the Caucasian laundries did not, but a number of factors must have worked to make the Court suspicious of this claim. There was no documentation tending to show that rooftop scaffolding was the reason the supervisors had denied laundry permits to the Chinese applicants, only the bare assertion by the city's lawyers. The assertion was itself undermined by references elsewhere to other factors—the general condition of Chinese laundries or their membership in the laundry guild—as explanations for the city's negative attitude toward Chinese laundries. Scaffolding, moreover, was not an absolute bar to obtaining a laundry permit. It could be waived by the supervisors presumably if they found a scaffolded building to be nonetheless safe and sound.[145] There was too the city's failure to offer any convincing proof that the law was being enforced against white-owned laundries. Under the ordinance's terms *all* wooden laundries, even those without scaffolding, needed to obtain supervisorial permission, and yet, according to counsels' admissions, some definite number of Caucasian operators of wooden laundries who did not have permits had been left unmolested.[146] The contradictory assertion made in counsels' brief that all white laundrymen who were not in compliance with the law were under arrest was made without any accompanying supporting documentation and must have seemed suspicious in light of the numerous other passages in the brief purporting to show why there were many good reasons for treating white and Chinese laundrymen differently. Finally, one cannot neglect the broad and hostile generalizations about Chinese laundries, sprinkled so liberally throughout the Clarke and Sieberst brief. These must surely have undermined the city's argument that it was administering the law with a fair and even hand and that it was only the obstinate refusal of the Chinese to remove their scaffolding that prevented them from getting permits from the supervisors.[147]

Reaction to the Decision

Reaction in the Caucasian press to the Supreme Court ruling was, not surprisingly, thoroughly hostile. It was the San Francisco *Evening Bulletin* that ran the longest and most vitriolic editorial. The concept of equal protection of the laws was fine in theory, it said, but it could only be based on an equality of habits, acquirements, and tendencies. The problem with the Chinese was that they had habits and tendencies that made their laundries dangerous. It was susceptible of proof, the paper declared, that similarly situated Chinese and white laundries presented different risks. Thus the need had arisen for "different rules for the conduct of washing" when entrusted to the different races. But, according to the *Bulletin*, these were facts to which "judicial Bourbonism" was determined to turn a blind eye. Or, as it put it seizing on another historical allusion, "The Delphic oracle at Washington intimates that we can do nothing to bridge the chasm which separates [the Chinese] from the modern races of men. We can do nothing to elevate or reform them, for that would be discrimination, contrary to the Fourteenth Amendment." All that was left to the beleaguered Caucasian majority in the paper's opinion was the total exclusion of the inferior race.[148] The Chinese, of course, took a very different view of the decision. There was a great fusillade of fireworks in Chinatown to greet the decision, and, according to one newspaper, the residents of the quarter seemed wild with delight.[149]

Although the Court had not in so many words declared the San Francisco laundry ordinances unconstitutional, the local newspapers, reflecting no doubt a widely shared view, were convinced it had.[150] And in October 1887 the city enacted a new, comprehensive laundry law, one, to judge from its terms, meant to supersede all previous legislation on the subject. It retained many of the provisions of earlier legislation, including the ban on night and Sunday work, but it made the operation of laundries conditional solely on the passing of inspections by the city's health officer and Board of Fire Wardens, eliminating the requirement of supervisorial approval.[151]

The Case of Tie Loy v. Stockton

During the fall of 1885 and early winter of 1885–86, as the *Yick Wo* and *Wo Lee* cases were making their way through the courts, several other California cities passed laundry laws of their own. The catalyst for the passage of many if not all of them seems to have been the unprecedentedly fierce anti-Chinese agitation then convulsing the state. (During this period many towns forcibly drove out their Chinese inhabitants. Several Chinatowns were burned. Town after town passed resolutions demanding that the Chinese leave.)[152] Municipal politicians were under considerable pressure to demonstrate their sympathies with the statewide movement, and this was one way of showing it. The sponsors of these laundry laws made little effort to conceal the fact that they were being enacted primarily in order to vex the Chinese. The experience of Stockton, a city about fifty miles from San Francisco, is illustrative.

Early in 1885 the *Evening Mail*, Stockton's main newspaper, had run a series of editorials complaining that the city's Chinese laundries, all located in the town's center, were letting their dirty water drain onto their premises and demanding that the city take forceful action against them. It found itself unmoved by the local health officer's explanation that the Chinese laundries had no alternative since the city had not yet provided a sewerage system for that part of the city.[153] It also did not think that enforcement need be made to weigh very heavily on white establishments:

> In the case of industries and enterprises conducted by white persons, and which for obvious reasons it would be desirable to encourage, by general consent spontaneously given, a point would be strained in favor of the offending parties. But, in the name of Heaven, does anybody suppose that the interests of the city require that Chinese wash-houses should be fostered and encouraged? . . . If we really hate the Chinese as we profess, and desire as earnestly to rid ourselves of their presence as we pretend, why not strain the point the other way in their case? A Chinese nuisance of equal intrinsic rankness with one of Caucasian origin is infinitely more offensive because of the repulsiveness of the association.

The paper also suggested that the city look into the possibility of forcing all Chinese washhouses to move out of the city to Stockton's original Chinese quarter, by then an uninhabited area of marshes and sloughs to the city's southwest.[154]

Stockton did pass an ordinance in late February requiring all washhouses to run their waste water through underground sewers into large receiving sewers or a slough of running water or tidewater. (The city presumably had agreed to build such facilities.)[155] But that was not enough for the *Evening Mail*, and when in September the city of Watsonville passed an ordinance making it illegal to carry on a laundry anywhere within the city limits, the *Mail* thought that Stockton could learn a lesson from the experience of that municipality. It noticed that as a consequence of the passage of the law Watsonville's Chinese were desperately looking around for a place to locate and might have to leave the area entirely. Stockton should follow suit. The key point was to see to the enactment of laws that the Chinese could not live under and then strictly to enforce those laws. "This is the best way of all of settling the Chinese question," said the journal.[156] The paper expanded more on this strategy a few weeks later:

> How can the Chinese be got out, it is asked. Easily enough. Pass an ordinance declaring that no house having the general reputation of

> a house of ill-fame shall be permitted within specified limits, embracing the Chinese quarter. This would dispose of prostitutes. Then enforce the state law against gambling. . . . Next declare that no wash-house shall exist within limits prescribed so as to except the laundry on American street . . . and in general make it so interesting for John that he would gladly prefer residence in the old Chinatown on the south side of Mormon slough.[157]

As if acting on cue, a city councilman in short order persuaded his colleagues to order an ordinance drafted "for the purpose of making circumstances so disagreeable to the Chinese that they would abandon their places in [the new] Chinatown." Since class or partial legislation was forbidden and therefore no law could be aimed overtly at the Chinese, the councilman suggested that the city attorney proceed by making a thorough tour of Chinatown in order to inventory, so to speak, potentially objectionable Chinese customs and then draft legislation, general in its terms, to "prohibit them if possible and thus disgust the Mongolians."[158] The upshot of all of this was the introduction in the city council of a legislative package on October 26 consisting of an anti-gambling measure, a law prohibiting the smoking of opium, one forbidding open fires in houses, and a law banning laundries from most of the city. "Four ordinances, whose object is to drive the Chinese from the city" was the *Evening Mail*'s unartful summary of the package. Three of the measures were passed immediately and sent on to the mayor for signature. The proposed laundry ordinance, however, was referred to committee for a redrawing of boundaries when it was discovered that a white-owned-and-operated laundry had inadvertently been included in the district from which laundries were to be banned. (It was located right next door to a Chinese washhouse.)[159]

It is interesting, given the temper of the times, that the Chinese laundry ordinance occasioned something of a sharp division in the city government. One member objected that the measure would work an unjustified hardship on the Chinese and pointed out that Chinese laundry owners or those from whom they rented their property had spent a great deal of money to comply with the city's recently enacted sewer law. A supporter of the law retorted that the whole purpose of the law was to work hardship on the Chinese and thereby to get rid of them. The San Francisco laundry ordinance which had just been declared constitutional pointed the way to a viable legal strategy for accomplishing that end, he declared.[160] In the end, on December 14, 1885, the measure passed over the veto of the mayor. It forbade the operation of any public laundry within any part of Stockton except the original Chinese quarter. In the debate that preceded the vote to override the veto a member attributed the measure to the popular hysteria of the moment. "It is an idea of the American people to go crazy once a year on skating rinks, roller coasters and so forth, and this time they have gone crazy on the anti-Chinese sentiment." He predicted flatly that it would not stand up if challenged.[161]

The prediction proved accurate. Even as he prepared to arrest all of the city's Chinese laundrymen, Stockton's city attorney told the press that the laundrymen had retained counsel and that he expected two habeas corpus actions to be filed, one in state and one in federal court, for the purpose of testing the law.[162] Within days this happened. A Caucasian proprietor, though one who employed mainly Chinese, sued out a writ in state court on January 26, 1886. On the same day, a Chinese washhouse owner, Tie Loy, did the same thing in the federal circuit court in San Francisco. Some interesting testimony was heard in the state court action. The former health officer of Stockton testified, for example, that he had examined the laundry in question and other laundries in the vicinity and had found them to be in good sanitary condition, all having installed drainage systems in conformity with the recently enacted law. From a public health standpoint he said he preferred public laundries inasmuch as they were more likely than private homes to use disinfectants in their wash water and to have better drainage.[163] Further proceedings were stayed, however, pending the outcome of the federal case.

Tie Loy made no specific claim of racial discrimination in his petition. He argued simply that the ordinance, if enforced, would make it impossible for him to carry on a perfectly legitimate business. The area set aside for laundries, he claimed, was "uninhabited and uninhabitable," consisting, he said, "of large fields of low swampy lands subject to overflow," used in the main for cultivation and pasturage. There were no buildings to be found in it suitable for use as laundries. The ordinance was, he said, beyond the power of the council to enact and contravened the U.S. Constitution and the treaty between the United States and China.[164]

Judge Sawyer, who heard the case, handed down his opinion on February 16.[165] If he had felt constrained some weeks earlier in the case of Wo Lee to defer to the opinion of the California Supreme Court concerning the legitimacy of the San Francisco laundry law, he felt no such reticence with regard to the Stockton ordinance. This ordinance, in his view, could make no pretense to be an effort to regulate the laundry business. Its purpose rather seemed to be to extinguish it. "It absolutely destroys, at its chosen location, an established ordinary business, harmless in itself, and indispensable to the comfort of civilized communities."[166] It was an attempt to treat the occupation of laundering as if it were a nuisance, like a slaughterhouse or a place for the storage of gunpowder. But that would not stand up to analysis. A washhouse was clearly not a nuisance either per se or prima facie. It could only become one through gross negligence in its operation.[167]

The right to labor in the laundering trade, as in any other essentially harmless trade, Sawyer declared, was "one of the highest privileges and immunities secured by the constitution to every American citizen, and to every person residing within its protection," and the Stockton law clearly interfered with this right.[168] (Sawyer treated this proposition as if it were settled constitutional law. The chief authority he cited for it, however, was the dissenting opinions of Field, Swayne, and Bradley in the *Slaughter-House Cases.*) The ordinance also violated the due process clause of the Fourteenth Amendment, he said, inasmuch as it arbitrarily deprived the laundrymen of their property, and the equal protection clause since it discriminated against one group of tradesmen while leaving others unhindered in their pursuits.[169]

Sawyer condemned the Stockton ordinance because in his view it violated the rights of all, non-Chinese and Chinese alike, but the judge made quite clear that he fully understood its particular purposes. "No one can in fact doubt the purpose of this ordinance," he declared. "It means, 'The Chinese must go;' and, in order that they shall go, it is made to encroach upon one of the most sacred rights of citizens of the state of California,—of the Caucasian race as well as . . . of the Mongolian."[170]

The Equal Protection of the Laws: A Note on Doctrine

The Chinese laundry decisions rest ultimately of course on a general concept of equal protection and unquestionably stand for the proposition, now a bedrock principle of constitutional jurisprudence, that race is presumptively an unlawful basis for the distribution of governmental burdens or benefits. They are also a tribute to judicial willingness to defend the rights of unpopular minorities in the face of popular pressure. But they are too, in an important sense, an enduring tribute to what we may call the judicial Jacksonianism of the post-Civil War period. As the historian Carl Degler points out, the cardinal principle of Jacksonianism, a dominant strain in American political thought throughout the nineteenth century, was economic freedom or, more precisely, freedom from economic discrimination by government. Boiled down to its essence the Jacksonian credo said "that no one should obtain rights or privileges from government which no one else enjoyed. In practice this meant that the state should not favor one class or individual over any other in economic endeavors."[171] A major corollary of this principle was that individuals should be free from the effects of legislative favoritism as they sought to advance themselves economically through the pursuit of one of the so-called ordinary trades or avocations of life. According to this view, as Eric Foner notes, all Americans could obtain social advancement and mobility if they were frugal, worked hard, and were unhampered by unequal laws.[172] Andrew Jackson himself put it this way: "[If government] would confine itself to equal protection, and as heaven does its rains, shower its favors alike on the high and the low, the rich and the poor, it would be an unqualified economic blessing."[173]

Jacksonian ideology continued to loom large in the post-Civil War period, perhaps nowhere more than among American judges, and one can see Jacksonian attitudes reflected in the Chinese laundry decisions, both those discussed here and in chapter 2 (as indeed one can see these attitudes reflected in the *Ah Chong* and *Parrott* cases discussed in chapter 3) at every level of the American judiciary.[174] And for good reason. The laws the Chinese were contesting in these cases, quite apart from their racial motivation, were easily assimilated by the men of the bench to classical models of economic favoritism. It would be a fine day, said Judge Stanly of the San Francisco Police Court in the very first Chinese laundry case, the 1874 case of *People v. Soon Kung* discussed in chapter 2, if, "under a form of government which abhors unequal and discriminating laws . . . and which guarantees to all the equal protection of the laws", the courts could not nullify a municipal law, "which discriminates unjustly against the poor, wantonly and unnecessarily adds to their burden, and substantially prohibits them from the pursuit of a useful and worthy calling." In the 1881 *Ah Ling* case the San Francisco superior court spoke derisively of a law that gave special privileges to such and only such as the board of supervisors might desire capriciously or in its unrestrained discretion to favor. The ordinance in question, said Justice Field in *Quong Woo*, was null and void because it threw obstacles that a municipal body was simply not empowered to throw in the way of the pursuit of an ordinary and inherently harmless trade, making it depend, as it were, upon the favor or caprice of other private individuals, individuals whose actions, as he put it, were beyond control by any legal proceeding.[175]

The principal legal basis for these decisions was the supervisory power which judges thought they were entitled to exercise over the actions of municipal corporations under traditional common law principles. Under those principles they thought it their right to strike down municipal laws found to be arbitrary or oppressive. In later laundry cases another basis for decision was increasingly cited—the Fourteenth Amendment—which many believed had constitutionalized the right to be free of arbitrary interference with the pursuit of a trade or occupation.[176]

Justices Field, Bradley, and Swayne had pressed this point of view vigorously in the *Slaughter-House Cases* but had been unable to win over their brethren, who had opted instead for a narrow reading of the amendment. Within a relatively short period of time, however, the Court reversed itself on the question of the amendment's scope. In *Barbier*, decided a dozen years later, it said that the Fourteenth Amendment's due process and equal protection clauses were intended to protect all against invidious and unequal treatment in the ordinary pursuits of life, among which were clearly included their economic pursuits.[177] This was technically dictum, but by the time the important Chinese laundry cases came up in the federal courts, the judges were treating it as if it were the settled holding of the court. Such convictions pepper Lorenzo Sawyer's opinions in *Wo Lee* and *Tie Loy*. That Sawyer was not overreaching or misreading the high court was made clear shortly, in *Yick Wo*. The Fourteenth Amendment, Justice Matthews declared in that case, required that all persons should be equally entitled to pursue their happiness and acquire and enjoy property and that the law should lay no greater burdens upon one set of persons in the same calling and condition than it did on others. Conversely, it forbade legislation that, for no good reason, favored some and discriminated against others with respect to the exercise of these rights.[178] Discrimination on the basis of race was one type of discrimination "for no good reason." In sum, then, when the Chinese laundrymen argued in court that California municipalities were interfering with their right to pursue a livelihood or to advance themselves economically, they could count on a sympathetic hearing from the judges.

5 The Struggle for Access to the Schools

It was a different right that Joseph Tape, the Chinese father of Mamie Tape, sought to vindicate when he appeared with his daughter at San Francisco's Spring Valley Primary School in the mid-1880s. If the Chinese laundrymen of California were attacking laws that they saw as aimed at putting them out of business, Tape was seeking to secure for his daughter and for all other Chinese children the right of access to the state's public schools. His efforts, which would eventually take him to the state's highest court, would reveal that the men responsible for educating the state's young were as bigoted and narrow-minded as any other public officials. To understand the California Supreme Court case of *Tape v. Hurley*, it is first necessary to know something about the prior history of California's treatment of its nonwhite school children and about earlier efforts of the Chinese to gain access to public education.

The Early History of Racial Segregation in the Schools

California began to make specific provision for the education of its nonwhite children in 1860. In that year the legislature amended the existing school law to provide for the strict segregation of "Negroes, Mongolians, and [American] Indians." Children belonging to these ethnic groups were not to be admitted to the public schools under any circumstances. Indeed, the superintendent of public instruction was empowered to withhold funds from school districts that violated this prohibition. At the same time school district trustees were given the discretion to establish separate schools for minority children.[1] Six years later an act passed requiring the trustees to establish separate schools if the parents or guardians of ten such children should apply for them. The act also permitted districts to admit nonwhite children to white schools when it was impracticable for them to establish separate schools, provided, it stressed, that a majority of the white parents made no objection.[2] In 1870 the state of California enacted a new comprehensive school law. This measure, like its predecessors, provided for the education of children of African and American Indian descent in separate schools, but, whether by intention or by accident, it failed to make any explicit provision for the education of Chinese children.[3]

In an extremely interesting case brought in 1873, *Ward v. Flood,* the parents of a black child living in the city of San Francisco challenged the 1870 law on grounds that it violated the newly enacted Thirteenth and Fourteenth Amendments to the U.S. Constitution, in particular the equal protection clause of the latter amendment. They argued, as had the black parents in the memorable pre-Civil War case of *Roberts v. City of Boston,*[4] a case brought under the Massachusetts Constitution, that forcible separation stamped blacks with the "odious distinction of caste" and reinforced deep-seated public prejudices. But the California Supreme Court, quoting liberally from the decision of the Massachusetts court in that case, held that the separation of the races for educational purposes was a reasonable exercise of the police power.[5] The California court did, however, go out of its way to affirm that all children in the state were entitled to receive instruction at the public schools as a matter of state constitutional right and that the state's "colored children" could only be excluded from white schools when separate schools were in fact available for them to attend.[6] The following year the state amended its school law to provide that Indian children and children of African descent should be admitted to white schools if separate schools were not available for them. It made no mention at all of the children of the Chinese.[7]

Early Chinese Attempts to Gain School Access

Nineteenth-century Chinese California was overwhelmingly a bachelor society, and children never made up more than a very small percentage of the total population. But from the beginning some members of the community had demonstrated an interest in having their children educated. In August of 1859, for example, thirty Chinese parents living in San Francisco had petitioned the city's board of education to create an elementary school for their children. In response the board agreed to hire a teacher to teach Chinese students in a room rented from the Presbyterian Chinese mission.[8] This arrangement lasted with some interruptions for about a decade, but it was terminated in 1871, the school board claiming there was not sufficient interest on the part of Chinese parents to continue it. After the closing of this school some Chinese children continued to be educated in private schools, chiefly ones operated by Protestant missionaries.[9]

The next systematic efforts of the Chinese to gain access to the schools that can be documented occurred in the mid- and late 1870s, by which time there were over two thousand Chinese children of school age living in the state.[10] The *Ward* case, with its broad assertion of a right to an education irrespective of color—that and the sheer growth in the population—may have served as the catalyst for these efforts.[11] In early 1875, about a year after the *Ward* decision was handed down, an eight-year-old Chinese girl applied for and was admitted to a public elementary school in Sacramento by vote of the city board of education.[12] The event was deemed worthy of comment by the *New York Times*. The San Francisco *Examiner* predicted that more applications could be expected. "John Chinaman," it said, "is not slow in taking advantage of American institutions where they can be made of service to him."[13] Whether this in fact happened cannot be ascertained.

On February 12, 1877, an article appeared in the bilingual San Francisco newspaper, the *Chinese Record*, pointing to the fact that Chinese taxpayers were contributing several thousand dollars annually to the support of public education but because of race prejudice were not being allowed to send their children to the public schools. Like the Chinese, the Chinese-language version of the article noted, blacks had originally been prevented from attending public schools, but they had challenged the discriminatory rule and had won. (This was of course a slight misrendering of the *Ward* case. The black parents in that case had not been seeking access to the schools but access to nonsegregated schooling.) The Chinese, said the paper, should follow the example of the blacks.[14] Six months later thirty San Francisco Chinese merchants followed up on this suggestion. They submitted a petition to the board of education requesting it to open a school for Chinese children. "Your Honorable State," it read, "levies poll and other taxes for the support of education, and makes no difference between natives and foreigners. If from the first, Chinese and Americans had been placed on the same footing in the schools, it would have been in accordance with right and justice, and there would have been subsequently no distinction; but your Honorable State has established schools of all grades, and has not admitted Chinese, which is contrary to the original intention (that they should be open to all)."[15] The petition was denied.

Having been rebuffed by the board of education, the Chinese decided to take their case to the state legislature. The following March a petition bearing some 1,300 signatures, including those of the principal Chinese merchants of Sacramento and other cities as well as San Francisco, was submitted to the state assembly demanding that Chinese children be allowed to attend public schools on the same basis as the children of other foreigners. It noted that the Chinese paid poll taxes in excess of $42,000 per year in San Francisco.[16] The petition was ignored by the assembly, and when later in the session several Caucasians submitted another petition complaining about the treatment the Chinese had received and asking the body to consider their appeal, it too was given similar treatment.[17] Two years later the legislature opened up a new opportunity for the Chinese by again amending the California school law.

The 1880 Revision in the School Law

In its 1880 session the legislature undertook a major revision of the education sections of California's Political Code. Among other things it struck the word "white" out of the general admissions provision of the law so that the new law, codified as Section 1662 of the Political Code, read simply: "Every school, unless otherwise provided by law, must be open for the admission of all children between six and twenty-one years of age, residing in the district." It also repealed that section of the code which called for the education of black and Indian children in separate schools.[18] Since these measures were passed during the most Sinophobic session in the history of the California legislature, it seems safe to assume that they were probably not intended in any sense to benefit the Chinese. (Their purpose seems rather to have been to abolish separate schools for Negroes and Indians.) Nevertheless, the change in language was of potentially great significance for the Chinese. For the first time in over a decade Chinese children had, by arguable implication at any rate, been brought within the coverage of the state's school law and been placed on the same footing with all other racial groups when it came to school access. It is not clear why the Chinese did not use this revision in the law as basis for a new appeal to the school authorities or, perhaps more pertinently for an appeal to the courts. They had by this time given the clearest evidence of their willingness to go to law to advance their rights and had seen some of their efforts crowned with success. The explanation may simply be that they were preoccupied with litigation on too many other fronts at the time. The first efforts to exploit the new law would in fact not come until some three years after its enactment.

Initiation of the Tape Litigation

On September 16, 1884, shortly after the commencement of the new school year, the San Francisco *Evening Bulletin* reported that a Chinese by the name of Joseph Tape had sought to enroll his eight-year-old daughter, Mamie, in San Francisco's Spring Valley Primary School but that the school had refused to admit the child. As one might gather from the name, Joseph Tape was not a typical Chinese immigrant. Tape, according to a court affidavit that he later filed, had arrived in California in 1869 and sometime shortly thereafter had decided to discard his queue and adopt the American style of dress. He eventually met and in 1875 married a Caucasian woman, Mary M. Tape (he apparently also took her name), the marriage being solemnized in the Reverend A. W. Loomis's First Presbyterian Church. The child in question was born the following year. Joseph Tape spoke fluent English, was a Christian, and for the previous seven years had been engaged in the draying and expressing business in the city.[19]

Upon being rebuffed by the Spring Valley School officials, Tape complained to San Francisco School Superintendent Andrew J. Moulder, who in turn sought advice on the matter from State Superintendent of Public Instruction William Welcker. Welcker replied that in his view "Mongolian children" could not become public school pupils under any circumstances. Under the state constitution, he said, public education was reserved for those who could become U.S. citizens and the law was clear that the Chinese could not. The laws were against the Chinese in this and in other respects, he said, and were intended to discourage and not encourage Chinese immigration. He noted that a similar question had been put to him the previous year from a county in the interior of the state and that he had reached the same conclusion. This was far from the end of the matter.[20]

Within the next two weeks two events occurred which prompted Superintendent Moulder to again solicit advice from the state schools chief on the Tape application. The first was a ruling by the federal circuit court that Chinese born in the United States were U.S. citizens. (The case is discussed in the next chapter.) The second, linked to the first, was a strongly worded letter from the Chinese consul, Frederick Bee, which Moulder received on October 4. The consulate, said Bee, had learned of Joseph Tape's attempt to enroll his child in the public schools and of the denial of his application. The reasons that the school authorities had given for the refusal, said Bee, were inconsistent with the treaties, Constitution, and laws of the United States. This was especially so in the present case, said Bee, making oblique but obvious reference to the Tape application, in view of the fact that the child in question was native-born. He felt it his duty, he said, to "renew the request to admit the child, and all other Chinese children resident here who desire to enter the public schools under your charge."[21] Two days later Moulder contacted State Superintendent Welcker to ask whether, in light of the recent federal court decision on citizenship, he wished to modify his ruling on the admissibility of Chinese children. (Welcker's original decision, it will be remembered, was that only those eligible for citizenship could be admitted to the schools.) Welcker immediately wrote back that he saw no need at all to modify his ruling. Since when, he asked, did state officials have to take notice of a newspaper report of a federal court decision, especially when the decision had nothing to do with Chinese school attendance? Besides, Welcker said, it was a question in his mind whether a federal court "has the power to condemn the state of California to undergo the expense of educating the children of Chinese when the presence of such foreigners is declared by the Constitution to be dangerous to the well-being of the State."

Superintendent Moulder disclosed the Welcker letter's contents to the local press and made clear that he was completely in sympathy with the state superintendent's decision. He observed to a reporter for the San Francisco *Chronicle* that the Chinese were perjurers all and that "if admitted [to the schools] would doubtless soon overrun our schools, to the exclusion and detriment of the white children." He declared publicly that he would continue to deny the sons and daughters of Chinese admission to the public schools and so informed Consul Bee on October 11.[22] Circuit Judge Lorenzo Sawyer, it should be noted, was not particularly amused by Welcker's animadversion on the authority of the federal courts. "How will that do as a specimen brick from the wisdom of the School Master General of the Great State of California?" he asked his friend Judge Matthew Deady of Oregon. "Have you any such learned pundits in the State of Oregon? If not please import Welcker." The state, he noted, did not scruple to get all the taxes it could out of the Chinese for the purpose of educating American and white foreign children. He wondered what Welcker might have to say on that score.[23]

The San Francisco Board of Education, which under the law had ultimate authority in these matters, did not itself officially confront the question of the admission of Mamie Tape to the public schools until its meeting of October 21, 1884. At that meeting Moulder read to the members his correspondence with Bee and Welcker and asked for the board's endorsement of his actions. A lively debate ensued, fueled in part, possibly, by the revelation made by one member that he had been called upon by an attorney for the Chinese, William F. Gibson, the son of the Methodist missionary to the Chinese the Reverend Otis Gibson, who said that the Chinese intended to go to court if the consulate's petition was turned down. The board eventually passed a resolution, prohibiting all school principals, under pain of immediate dismissal, from admitting any "Mongolian child," either male or female, to any public school in the city. The vote was not unanimous. At least one of the eleven school board members voted against the resolution, explaining that since the Chinese might now be allowed to vote (referring, one presumes, to the citizenship decision) they certainly ought to be educated.[24]

The next morning members of the Tape family began to lay the groundwork for the test case Attorney Gibson had promised. Mamie Tape, accompanied this time by her mother, again presented herself for enrollment in the Spring Valley school. She was met by the school principal, Jennie M. Hurley, who refused to entertain her application, citing as grounds the fact of her Chinese descent and the just enacted board of education resolution.[25] On October 28 Gibson filed in the Superior Court of the City and County of San Francisco an application for a writ of mandate, to be directed to Principal Hurley, Superintendent Moulder, and the members of the school board, ordering them to have Mamie Tape examined for purposes of determining her qualifications for admission to the elementary school. The application simply alleged, without elaborating on the points, that by law and custom children had the right to be accepted into the public schools nearest their residences. The court issued an alternative writ requiring the defendants to either admit the child or show cause why a peremptory writ should not issue requiring them to do so. The defendants moved to quash the writ on November 21, alleging that the board could not admit Mamie Tape "or any other Mongolian or Chinese child" because no provision had been made in the law for the education of such children. They alleged also that the Chinese as a race had filthy living habits and were prone to fatal and contagious diseases, implying that Chinese children shared these traits and thus might present a danger to other children if admitted to the public schools.[26] The case was submitted on these pleadings.

The Superior Court Decision

Judge James Maguire of the superior court delivered his decision in the case in open court on January 9. The several newspaper accounts of what the judge said differ somewhat, but all agree on the main points he made. The only reason the school authorities urged against the admission of Mamie Tape to the public schools was that she was Chinese and as such was excluded from the benefits of free public education even though all other races were entitled to these benefits. But, said the judge, he knew of no California law susceptible to this construction. Furthermore, if there were such a law it would violate the equal protection clause of the Fourteenth Amendment. That clause according to the decision in *Ward v.*

Flood meant that the measure of rights within the state should be equal and uniform for all persons according to their respective conditions. If the state declared, as California did, that all children had a right to an education, it could not exclude one group of children without violating the clause. But the state by positive enactment had declared that all children were entitled to receive instruction at the public schools, and the court would not read that to mean all white children. Maguire granted that there was force in the objection that the mixing of the Caucasian and Chinese races in the schools was fraught with danger, but that argument, he said was one better addressed to the legislature. The courts could only enforce the law as it existed. The court, said Maguire, was prepared to issue a peremptory writ of mandate, ordering Mamie Tape's admission to the Spring Valley school. A former member of the school board was present to hear Judge Maguire and rose to remind the court of the board's policy to dismiss summarily any school principal who admitted Chinese pupils to her or his school. Maguire responded that if that happened the members of the board voting for the dismissal would be summarily held in contempt.[27]

The day after Maguire spoke a newly formed unofficial body calling itself the Legislative Committee and consisting of some of the most important education officials in the state, including the president and several members of the San Francisco school board, the superintendent of the city's schools, and several principals, held its first meeting. (The group grew out of a meeting of the State Teachers Association. Its purpose seems to have been to make recommendations to the state legislature on changes in school law.) Judge Maguire's decision was high on its agenda. One member of the group said he didn't see what harm there could be in admitting Chinese to the public schools, but the consensus seems to have been that the proper course of procedure was to induce the legislature to create separate schools for Chinese pupils. A member of the San Francisco Board of Education, who had attended the meeting, told an *Alta* reporter afterward that it would be wiser for the San Francisco school board to use its limited funds for this purpose than to spend them pursuing an appeal of the decision.[28] Superintendent Moulder and his supervisor, State Superintendent Welcker, it soon turned out, did not share this view on the wisdom or feasibility of an appeal.

The San Francisco Board of Education took up the Tape case again at its January 14 meeting. In the wake of Judge Maguire's ruling, Attorney Gibson had again submitted a petition asking that his client be admitted to school, but Superintendent Moulder insisted that the board continue the fight against the admission of Chinese children. If the superior court decision were allowed to stand, he said, dire consequences would follow. The Chinese were a nation of liars and would perjure themselves en masse, claiming they were born in this country, and would overrun the schools. (Moulder treated the decision as if it only applied to Chinese born in this country.) Chinese girls were all prostitutes, he added, and only wished to attend school so that they could learn English and thereby increase their market value. He predicted massive white flight from the public schools should the Chinese be allowed to commingle with white pupils. Moulder read a letter from State Superintendent Welcker, who likewise strongly recommended an appeal. He expressed full confidence that the lower court decision would be overturned. After some discussion the board voted to carry the matter to the state supreme court.[29]

In the California Supreme Court

As had happened in the lower court, there was no oral argument before the California Supreme Court in the case of *Tape v. Hurley*. The parties submitted the case on written briefs, which set forth in greater detail than they had in the trial court pleadings their legal and constitutional arguments. William Gibson deployed several powerful arguments in support of the Tape child's claim. There was the plain language of Section 1662 of the Political Code, with its requirement that the schools be open to "all children." And he was able to cite cases from other jurisdictions to the effect that laws of this sort were to be construed broadly to embrace children of color even when not specifically mentioned. These cases, he argued, were evidence of "the tendency of the present age," which he said was not to make any distinction between school children except according to their level of study.[30] He cited also the "most favored nation" provision of the Burlingame Treaty, maintaining that so long as the children of other aliens were permitted to attend the state's public school, the children of the Chinese had to be extended the same privilege.[31] Finally he raised what he may have considered his most important point, namely Mamie Tape's claim under the equal protection clause of the Fourteenth Amendment. Drawing heavily on the reasoning and language of the California court in *Ward v. Flood*, he argued that for purposes of the case at bar, the clause meant that once a state established schools, the right to attend them could not be denied to persons within its jurisdiction on account of race or color.[32] Gibson ended his brief with an appeal to the justices' native pride. The Civil War Amendments had been adopted, he said, to promote equality before the law for all Americans and to end discrimination once and for all on account of race. "By their adoption our country placed herself in full harmony with the spirit of the age," he declared. "Shall California, the freest, the most liberal, and in many respects the most enlightened of American commonwealths, now give the signal for retreat?"[33]

Gibson's was the very model of a persuasive appellate brief on a major public policy issue. The state's by contrast was rather lackluster. It did make one plausible point—that it was unrealistic to suppose that the 1880 session of the California legislature could in any way have wanted to have benefited the Chinese—but did not really develop it. It failed utterly to come to grips with any of the major legal or constitutional issues raised by the case and dealt with in such detail by Gibson. Altogether it had the look of something that had been hastily slapped together by lawyers who were not really convinced that they had much of a case.

The California Supreme Court had little difficulty in deciding the case in favor of Gibson's client. It chose to disregard all arguments concerning the Fourteenth Amendment and the treaty with China and to base its decision upon the Political Code alone. It viewed the matter as one of the straightforward application of a statute whose terms were transparent. The legislature had spoken clearly and unambiguously on the question of the admission of children to the state's schools, said the court, and effect had to be given to its intent. The Political Code said that the schools were to be open to all children between the ages of six and twenty-one, only allowing the trustees discretion to exclude children of vicious habits or suffering from contagious disease. There was no allegation that Mamie Tape fit either of these descriptions, and there was no reason why she should not be admitted to the schools. It therefore unanimously affirmed the lower court's writ of mandate that she be admitted to the school, modifying it only so as to make it run against Principal Hurley alone.[34]

The Aftermath of Tape

In anticipation no doubt of an adverse ruling from the high court, state school officials, it emerged, had been lobbying the legislature since early in the 1885 session for a law establishing separate schools for Chinese children.[35] These efforts yielded results. A few days after the *Tape* decision the state education law was amended to read:

> Trustees shall have the power to exclude children of filthy or vicious habits, or children suffering from contagious or infectious diseases, and also to establish separate schools for children of Mongolian or Chinese descent. When such separate schools are established Chinese or Mongolian children must not be admitted into any other schools.[36]

Acting on this authority, the San Francisco Board of Education established a separate primary school for Chinese children in Chinatown. Fifty-four pupils were enrolled in the school by the end of its first full year of operation. The number rose to ninety-two the following year.[37] Some seventeen years later, in 1902, the Chinese brought a challenge in federal court to the law permitting the segregation of Chinese pupils, alleging that it was arbitrary and motivated by racial hostility and as such conflicted with the equal protection clause of the Fourteenth Amendment. The court, however, relying on the growing body of authority that had by that time accumulated upholding the doctrine of "separate but equal" in the sphere of education, rejected it without much discussion.[38] The practice of segregating the Chinese school children of San Francisco continued until well into the twentieth century.[39]

In April of 1885, shortly after the board of education gave notice of its intent to open a separate Chinese school, the mother of Mamie Tape, a woman of obviously little formal education, wrote a long letter to Superintendent Moulder, upbraiding him and his confreres for their handling of the case. "You have," she wrote, "expended a lot of the Public moeny foolishly, all because of a one poor little Child." It complained bitterly, as well, of the suffering the board's actions had caused her and her child. The letter's pained and eloquent close summed up well not only her own deep hurt but also, in a sense, the real significance of the whole affair.

> May you Mr. Moulder, never be persecuted like the way you have persecuted little Mamie Tape. Mamie Tape will never attend any of the Chinese schools of your making! Never!!! I will let the world see sir What justice there is When it is govern by the Race prejudice men! Just because she is of the Chinese descend, not because she don't dress like you because she does. Just because she is descended of Chinese parents I guess she is more of a American then a good many of you that is going to prewent her being Educated.[40]

It is unclear whether Mamie Tape ever attended the primary school, the creation of which had been the direct result of her lawsuit.

During the same period that Chinese litigants were waging the courtroom battles described in this and the preceding chapters, battles aimed in the main at vindicating federal rights against hostile local action, others were simultaneously engaged in litigation of a very different character—often before the very same tribunals. Here their foe was the federal government itself and their object to test the limits of that government's racially discriminatory immigration policies or, in one case, to force that government to live up to its commitment to protect Chinese residents against mob violence. Those cases that arose out of the federal anti-Chinese immigration legislation of the 1880s and 1890s raised novel and extraordinarily interesting questions of constitutional law and stretched into the first years of the twentieth century. As more than one commentator has noted, they went a long way toward establishing the foundations of modern U.S. immigration law. We return now to the beginning of the 1880s and to the treaty revision that set all of these events in motion.

III

THE DECADE OF THE 1880S

Court Contests with the Federal Government

6 Federal Exclusion Act Litigation

The First Phase

The Fifteen Passenger Bill and the Revision of the Burlingame Treaty

Calls for federal action to end Chinese immigration began to be heard from western representatives in Congress as early as 1867. In that year Congressman Johnson of California introduced a resolution in the House of Representatives, directing the Judiciary Committee to inquire whether Congress could by legislation prevent the immigration of "Chinese and other inferior races" into the country.[1] Several measures to limit or halt the Chinese influx were introduced in the House or Senate during the 1870s but none could muster enough votes to pass either body. Pressure from the western states was inexorable, however, and, since there was in effect no countervailing pressure, it became clear by the end of the decade that Congress would respond in some fashion to it. The California senate, in a memorial on the evils of Chinese immigration that it had sent to Congress in 1877, had suggested that one way to curb Chinese immigration, pending negotiation of the abrogation of the Burlingame Treaty, would be to pass legislation limiting to ten the number of Chinese passengers who could be landed by vessel at any U.S. port.[2] A measure along exactly these lines was passed by both houses of Congress in 1879. Dubbed the "Fifteen Passenger Bill," it limited the number of Chinese passengers who might be brought to the United States in any one vessel to fifteen.[3] The bill was greeted with wild enthusiasm by many Caucasians on the West Coast but drew an agitated remonstrance from the Chinese minister to Washington. The minister, in a conversation with Secretary of State Evarts, called it offensive and insulting and protested that it in effect abrogated the Burlingame Treaty. The minister said that he was particularly offended by the derogatory remarks concerning the Chinese made by members in the course of the congressional debates.[4]

President Hayes, on grounds that it amounted to a virtually complete ban on Chinese immigration and therefore to an unprecedented attempt by the legislative branch to nullify a treaty with a friendly foreign power, vetoed the Fifteen Passenger Bill. In his veto message he made clear, however, that he did not object to the principle that something might need to be done to limit Chinese immigration, only to the manner in which the congressional bill sought to accomplish that end. He raised the possibility of making a modification of the Burlingame Treaty as a preliminary to dealing with the Chinese immigration question.[5]

At the opening of the second session of the 46th Congress, which convened December 1, 1879, Hayes reported that the government of China had indicated its willingness to consider revising the Burlingame Treaty's free emigration provisions as a way of easing tensions with the United States,[6] and in early 1880 the administration dispatched the former president of the University of Michigan, James Angell, to Peking for the purpose of negotiating just such a modification. After prolonged negotiations Angell succeeded in accomplishing what the administration wanted. The new treaty, signed at Peking on November 17, 1880,[7] permitted the U.S. government, whenever it determined that it should be in its interest to do so, to *suspend* for a reasonable period of time, but not absolutely to prohibit, the coming of Chinese laborers into the United States. At the same time it reaffirmed the right of Chinese laborers already in the United States to "go and come of their own free will" and again guaranteed them all the "rights, privileges, immunities, and exemptions" accorded to the citizens or subjects of the most favored nation. Indeed new language was added pledging the United States to devise measures to protect those rights and privileges should they be threatened by the actions of others.[8]

The new treaty entered into force on July 19, 1881, and the United States Congress wasted little time in acting on its provisions. In March 1882 it presented to President Arthur a Chinese immigration bill which, among other things, called for the suspension of the immigration of Chinese laborers for twenty years and called for the establishment of an internal passport system as a means of identifying those Chinese laborers who were entitled to reside in the United States. Arthur found both of these provisions objectionable and vetoed the measure.[9] Enough votes could not be mustered to override the presidential veto, but by changing the period of suspension to ten years and eliminating the passport provision Congress was able to obviate the administration's objections, and on May 6, 1882, the president signed a revised bill into law.

The innocuously titled "Act to Execute Certain Treaty Stipulations Relating to Chinese" was the first federal immigration statute to single out an ethnic group by name for invidious treatment. It represented, to say the least, a dramatic reversal in the historic American policy of open immigration.[10] Premised on the view, as stated in its preamble, that the coming of Chinese laborers into the United States endangered "the good order of certain localities," the act suspended the immigration of Chinese laborers, skilled and unskilled both, for a period of ten years and imposed severe criminal and civil penalties on any who should abet a violation of this ban.[11] At the same time, in accordance with the 1880 treaty provisions, it guaranteed to Chinese laborers who were in the United States on November 17, 1880, the date of the treaty's signing, or who should have come into the country by August 4, 1882, ninety days after the act went into effect, the right to stay in the country and to travel from and to it at will. For the purpose of affording these laborers evidence of their right to leave the United States and return, it provided that the collectors of customs at U.S. ports should make lists of Chinese laborers sailing for foreign destinations and furnish them with certificates of identification.[12] Under the act Chinese not of the laboring classes, merchants for example or students, who wished to immigrate to the United States had to obtain a certificate from the Chinese government identifying them as such.[13] Finally, taking the occasion to eliminate once and for all any doubt there might still have been on congressional intent concerning Chinese naturalization, the act included a provision forbidding any state or federal court from admitting any Chinese to citizenship.[14] Such in broad outline was the act that initially was called the Chinese Restriction Act and that eventually would be known as the first Chinese Exclusion Act. The law was quite detailed. It ran to some two and a half folio pages of closely printed text in the U.S. Statutes at Large and purported to establish a complete and clear set of guidelines for the regulation of Chinese immigration. As events would soon show, however, it failed to address many important points. These would have to be settled by the courts.

The major California newspapers greeted the passage of the 1882 act with great enthusiasm, declaring that it heralded the beginning of the end of Chinese immigration and all the controversy that had engendered. "We can look on this rush of servile immigration with a good deal of equanimity," trumpeted the *Daily Alta California*, "because knowing it is the last."[15] "The Chinese question is not settled," said the *Morning Call*, "but it is fairly on the way to settlement."[16] According to the *Chronicle*, the act was not perfect but it was the best that could be gotten and if it proved to be flawed in any particular it could easily be amended.

"As it stands," that paper said, "it leaves no further excuse for injecting the Chinese question into either State or national politics."[17] (How laughably premature this prophecy was would be revealed in very short order.) The *Post,* on the other hand, an extremely Sinophobic paper, as noted above, had expressed great skepticism as the act was nearing passage that it would go far toward solving the state's "Chinese question." It would not remove the Chinese then in California, the paper pointed out. They fully intended to stay. And in a remarkably illuminating passage it went on: "It will not prevent the Chinese from washing our soiled linen, manipulating our cigars, manufacturing our shoes, making our clothes, baking our bread, cultivating our fields and gardens, [or] grading our railways." It would not cause housekeepers to dismiss their Chinese servants. What was needed, the paper said, was good white workers to replace the Chinese, but they were hard to find.[18]

Enforcement of the Exclusion Act: The First Phase

At the outset it looked as if the implementation of the Chinese Exclusion Act might proceed with a minimum of difficulty. On May 19, 1882, the secretary of the treasury issued a circular officially informing the various collectors of customs at ports throughout the United States of the terms of the Exclusion Act and indicating in a general way what form the certificates should take that were to be issued under Section 4 of the act to Chinese laborers departing the country. As the date approached at which the free immigration of Chinese laborers would end and when no further guidance on the question of laborers' certificates seemed forthcoming from the Treasury Department, the Chinese consulate in San Francisco decided itself to seize the initiative. Sometime in early June the consul general arranged a meeting with the collector of customs and proposed to him that the consulate issue to those Chinese laborers who wished to return to China certificates of identification and that on the basis of these the collector then issue his own certificates to the returnees. The collector agreed with the proposal, whereupon the Chinese consulate, at its own expense, printed blank forms, containing on the same sheet both a consular certificate of identification (styled a "Chinese Consular Passport") and a collector's certificate. These went into use for outgoing Chinese on June 6 and appear to have been liberally issued by the collector's office. On August 8 the treasury's own laborers' certificate forms reached the collector's office in San Francisco with the directive that they replace the forms devised by the consulate.[19] On that same day the American steamship *City of Sydney* arrived in San Francisco from Australia, carrying a largely Chinese crew, the first Chinese laborers, as it happened, to seek to enter the United States after August 4, 1882, the day the window on free immigration officially closed. The vessel's arrival would provide the occasion for the first litigation under the Exclusion Act.

First Cases under the 1882 Exclusion Act

Upon arrival in San Francisco harbor the master of the *City of Sydney* sought to land his Chinese crewmen but was refused permission to do so by the collector of customs on the grounds that the crewmen were laborers and were required by the 1882 act to possess certificates of identification. The vessel proceeded to dock, but the Chinese crewmen were forced to remain on board (some appear to have been removed to another vessel in the harbor). Ten days later a petition for a writ of habeas corpus was filed on behalf of the detained crewmen in United States circuit court by the law firm of McAllister and Bergin, the same firm that had just finished representing the Chinese laundrymen in their successful challenge to the McKew laundry ordinance (*In re Quong Woo*). The action was being brought, reported the San Francisco *Morning Call,* at the behest of the Chinese consulate, which, the paper said, viewed the matter as an important test case under the new federal law.[20]

The habeas petition, filed in the name of one Ah Sing, a cabin waiter, alleged that the petitioner was a seaman by occupation, that he had come to California six years earlier, and that he had left the state aboard the *City of Sydney* on May 8 on a voyage from San Francisco to Australia and back. He alleged that he was being restrained of his liberty in violation of the Constitution of the United States and the Burlingame Treaty.[21] The master of the *City of Sydney,* in his return to the writ, admitted the facts stated in the petition and the detention of the petitioner as alleged. In his defense he pleaded both the Exclusion Act, which by its express terms forbade masters of vessels from bringing Chinese laborers ashore from any foreign port or place and, more pertinently, the refusal of the collector of the port to permit him to land the crew.[22] The matter came on for hearing August 21 before a panel consisting of Supreme Court Justice Stephen Field, then sitting, as noted in chapter 4, as a circuit justice in San Francisco and Circuit Judge Lorenzo Sawyer.[23]

Though the dispute was nominally between the Chinese crewmen and the master of the *City of Sydney* or rather between the crewmen and the owners of the vessel, the Pacific Mail Steamship Company, the company made clear at the hearing that it bore no animus toward the petitioner or his countrymen (the captain would have landed the petitioner had the collector not prevented him from doing so). It was only anxious to know its duties under the new law. It did not seek to argue that the petitioner *should* not be landed. That role was left to the United States district attorney, who was permitted to intervene in the matter. He argued vigorously that the Chinese seamen should not be permitted to land without the descriptive certificates mentioned in Section 4 of the act. If they were, he contended, nothing would prevent masters of vessels from leaving their crews in Hong Kong and taking on a crew of prohibited laborers, thus subverting the purposes of the act. McAllister, for his part, argued that the law had not been officially promulgated so far as the petitioner was concerned. The collector of the port, he noted, had not been officially informed of the act's passage until May 19, eight days after the *City of Sydney* left San Francisco. He also argued that inasmuch as the petitioner had never left the *City of Sydney*, a ship flying the American flag, during the whole of its voyage, he had in fact never left American territory.[24]

Field handed down his decision on August 27. The question presented, he declared, was whether the 1882 act applied to the petitioner. To his mind the answer to the question was fairly simple. It did not. That followed straightforwardly from the wording of the legislation. It prohibited masters of vessels from landing Chinese laborers "from any foreign port or place." To Field that plainly referred to Chinese laborers embarking at foreign ports, not to Chinese who might be aboard a vessel when it touched at a foreign port. To conclude otherwise, he stated, would in effect force masters of vessels carrying Chinese seamen to put them ashore at any foreign port they touched and refuse to return them to their ports of embarkation, an act that would violate the law governing the obligations of masters to merchant seamen.[25]

Field agreed with McAllister's argument that in contemplation of law an American vessel was deemed to be part of the territory of the United States. It was agreed that the petitioner had never left the ship and had legally therefore never ceased to reside on American territory. It would be exceedingly odd, he declared, if an act of Congress would be seen as depriving someone of a right he had acquired under a treaty the United States had solemnly entered into. "The object of the act of Congress," said Field, "was to prevent the further immigration of Chinese laborers to the United States, not to expel those already here."[26]

It turned out that Ah Sing was the only Chinese sailor who had remained aboard the *City of Sydney* during its entire voyage. All of the others had gone ashore in Sydney for several hours while the ship was in that port. Their status was addressed in a separate opinion handed down two days later. Field thought it no different from that of the Chinese cabin waiter. The crewmen, Field noted, had left the ship with the captain's permission. They were still bound by their contracts to return to the ship.

They had given no indication to do otherwise. A Chinese laborer working on an American merchant ship, said Field, could not be held to lose his residence in the United States by virtue of a few hours' stay in a foreign country.[27] Such a result would be both unjust and absurd and it was a general principle of jurisprudence that laws should be construed so as to avoid leading to unjust or absurd results. There was, moreover, he stated, a practical reason for avoiding giving the Exclusion Act a narrow or hard construction. Such a construction, he opined, could not help but bring the act into disrepute and invite efforts for its repeal. "The wisdom of its enactment," he said, "will be better vindicated by a construction less repellent to our sense of justice and right."[28] It was an extraordinary misreading of the climate of public opinion on Field's part, as events would shortly show.

The Case of Low Yam Chow, *the Chinese Merchant*

The arrival in San Francisco two weeks after the *City of Sydney* of another vessel raised a new issue for the court. The *City of Rio de Janeiro* was completing a voyage from Panama, and among its passengers was a Chinese merchant by the name of Low Yam Chow who had resided in that country for some years and who was also associated with a Chinese business enterprise in San Francisco. When he sought to land he was refused permission on the grounds that he did not have the Chinese governmental certificate required of Chinese other than laborers under Section 6 of the 1882 act. The same firm that had represented the Chinese laborers in the previous litigation, McAllister and Bergin, now sued out a writ of habeas corpus on his behalf, and this matter, like the previous one, was brought before the federal circuit court for review. At the hearing on the writ the government argued strenuously that the only evidence that was admissible to prove the petitioner's merchant status was the certificate of identification called for under Section 6 of the act, but this objection was overruled and the petitioner was permitted to present other proof that he was a merchant.[29] On September 5, Justice Field handed down the court's decision.

In Field's view the Exclusion Act could not be viewed in isolation but, rather, had to be seen in the context of the several treaties the United States had entered into with the Chinese Empire. The Burlingame Treaty had proclaimed the principle of free immigration for all classes of Chinese. The 1880 revision of that treaty had modified that commitment so far as laborers were concerned, but *only* with regard to laborers. By its express terms it excluded other classes of Chinese from the modification and reaffirmed the continued right of free immigration for these other classes. The 1882 act was framed in conformity with the 1880 treaty and was aimed only at modifying the immigration rights of Chinese laborers. Section 6 of that act was to be seen against this background. That section, it was true, did say that Chinese other than laborers should obtain certificates of identification from the Chinese government but, according to Field, the certificates were to be seen as means for these classes of Chinese to prove their status and not as a means of restricting their entry. To hold otherwise would, he said, be to impute to Congress an intent to overthrow clearly established treaty rights.[30] (Field's reliance on the treaties as an independent source of rights is quite striking in light of the position he was to take later.)

Having come this far Field might, it seems, have gone on to affirm the general principle that Chinese seeking to enter the country as merchants could establish their status by any ordinarily admissible evidence, but he seemed instead to wish to place his decision on another, less broad footing. Section 6 of the 1882 act called upon the Chinese government to state all manner of particulars about the holders of certificates, but the petitioner did not reside in China and therefore in cases such as the one before the court it would be unreasonable to call upon the Chinese government to make such affirmations. He repeated what he had said in the earlier cases, that all laws were to be construed so as to avoid unjust or absurd conclusions.[31] The act would be construed in light of its overriding purpose, which was to eliminate competition with the Chinese laboring classes and not so as to put any unnecessary or embarrassing strain upon commercial relations with China, which, he noted, was large and on the increase. (The Chinese consulate had amply documented this in a statement it had furnished the court.) Federal officers, "possessed of more zeal than knowledge," he remarked with obvious irritation, seemed to be determined to bring about exactly the latter result. Chinese merchants who resided outside of China at the passage of the Exclusion Act would not be required to produce certificates from the Chinese government establishing their status. They could prove that by any legitimate means.[32] On this basis the petitioner was ordered discharged from custody.

District Judge Ogden Hoffman, who sat on the case with Field, associated himself with Field's practical jurisprudence. "[T]he friends of the law do it the best service," he wrote, "by giving to it a reasonable and just construction, conformable to its spirit and intent and the solemn pledges of the treaty, and not one calculated to bring it into odium and disrepute."[33] Some weeks after the decision, the *Morning Call* commented that the Treasury Department intended to act in accordance with the court's ruling and permit Chinese merchants who did not come directly from China to enter the United States without the certificate normally required. This opened the prospect of great abuse, the paper opined, adding that perhaps thought should be given to excluding all Chinese and not just laborers.[34]

Who Is Chinese?

In August 1883 the federal Circuit Court in Massachusetts handed down a decision on another novel question under the Exclusion Act. The United States attorney in Boston brought an information against the master of a British vessel for landing a Chinese laborer in that port. The man was a carpenter who had shipped aboard in Manila under articles that required him to stay with the vessel until it should return to Britain but who had left it in Boston without the master's knowledge or permission. The master pleaded guilty to the information subject to the opinion of the court on whether an offense had been committed under the facts as stated. The court might very well have determined that the master had not, under these facts, either landed the man or permitted him to land, but it chose to dismiss the charges on another ground. The man, it turned out, had been born in the British territory of Hong Kong, and the court held that he was not a *Chinese* laborer within the meaning of the Exclusion Act. The act, it reasoned, was inextricably bound up with the 1880 treaty between the United States and China and had been passed to carry into effect rights the United States had acquired under that treaty. Seen in that light it could only apply to Chinese laborers who were the subjects of the Chinese government. But the laborer in question in this case was a subject of the British monarch.[35]

The Massachusetts court's decision soon became known in California,[36] and it was inevitable that the same question should soon be brought up for decision there. A few weeks later it was although under circumstances that can best be described as puzzling. When the steamship *Arabic* arrived in San Francisco at the beginning of September from Hong Kong, applications for writs of habeas corpus were filed in the circuit court on behalf of two laborers detained on board. The petitions alleged that the laborers had been born in Hong Kong and were therefore British subjects. At the hearing on the writs it emerged that one of the men had already been permitted to land while it could not be clearly established from the other whether he in fact wished to press his claim.[37] These cases were therefore dismissed before any arguments on the merits could be heard, but later in the month a laborer was found who was willing to press the claim of British nationality. On September 20 an application for a writ was filed for Pong Ah Lung, a laborer born in Hong Kong and detained aboard the SS *Oceanic*. Argument was had on the merits of the claim, and on September 24 Justice Field and Judge Sawyer rendered their decision, Field writing for the court.

The Massachusetts court had erred, Field declared, in finding that the only purpose of the Exclusion Act had been to carry treaty stipulations into effect. The act's purpose was to exclude laborers of the Chinese race regardless of the country to which they might owe allegiance.[38] The treaty of 1880 had been negotiated so as to enable the United States to legislate with respect to laborers who were subjects of the Chinese emperor. Otherwise the Chinese government would have had just cause for complaint. It was not supposed, said Field, that any European government, having Chinese laborers as subjects, would complain about their exclusion from the United States, and so it was not deemed necessary to negotiate any treaty modifications with them. This held particularly true for Great Britain since the British colony of Australia itself excluded Chinese laborers.[39] The framers of the law, declared Field, knew perfectly well that the colony of Hong Kong was capable of pouring thousands of Chinese laborers into the United States and thereby defeating the act's purposes.[40]

The available evidence would seem to indicate that the Chinese consulate, which had lent its support to, if it had not in fact actually sponsored, the first cases brought under the 1882 Exclusion Act was opposed to the bringing of these. During the pendency of the proceedings several local papers reported that the consulate was hostile to the cases. They speculated that the consulate did not desire a decision from the California Circuit Court on the question, preferring to rest content with the Massachusetts decision.[41] The Chinese consul, Frederick Bee, was present at the hearings on the first habeas petitions and according to press reports manifested a decided coolness toward the petitioners' claims.[42] The consulate, on the other hand, was quite supportive of the litigants in the several habeas corpus cases that were brought in the district court the following month when the steamship *Rio de Janeiro* made port.

The Son of the Chinese Merchant

One of the Chinese passengers who was detained aboard ship was a minor who had arrived in San Francisco armed with both a certificate issued by the Chinese government describing him as a "trader" and with a letter from his father, directed to the father's business partners in San Francisco, asking them to initiate his son into the business they jointly owned. The youth was represented in the proceeding by Thomas Riordan, the laundrymen's attorney and the man who had represented the Chinese fishermen at the consulate's behest in 1880. The San Francisco *Chronicle* noted that Consul Bee was also present to assist the petitioner.[43] District Judge Hoffman ordered the youth discharged from custody on the same day his petition was filed on the grounds that the Exclusion Act was not intended to apply to the children of Chinese merchants.[44]

The Case of Chin Ah On *and Others*

The petitions of the other litigants—some five in number—were not quite so quickly disposed of. They were heard together, on October 29. The *Evening Bulletin* noted that a large crowd of Chinese spectators was present in Judge Hoffman's courtroom for the hearing and that the attorneys for the petitioners, among them Thomas Riordan, were seated at the side of Bee and Tsing Hoy, the vice-consul and interpreter of the consulate.[45] The petitioners made a variety of different claims. Two petitioners claimed to have come in order to take positions in the mercantile establishments of relatives. Three produced merchants' certificates issued by an official in Canton but based their claims for permission to land as well on the ground that they had resided in the United States on November 17, 1880, the date of the signing of the treaty (the argument being presumably that residence at that date was enough to confer a right to land irrespective of one's status as merchant or laborer). Evidence was heard on all of these points, the petitioners seeking to prove the validity of their certificates (the vice-consul testified to their authenticity) or the fact of their residence in the United States on the date in question, the government contending in the alternative that the certificates were not in the proper form or that the petitioners were in fact laborers and not merchants at all. Because of the variety of claims before the court and the haphazard order in which they were argued the hearing became something of a jumble. Hoffman decided on the basis of what he had heard in court that one of the petitioners was an ordinary laborer and ordered him remanded to custody for return to China. He took the other cases under submission. A week later he rendered his decision.[46]

Notwithstanding the evidence that had been presented on the petitioners' merchant status, Hoffman chose to treat all the petitioners as laborers who were resident in the United States on the date of the conclusion of the 1880 treaty but who had gone to China before the 1882 act was passed. The question, he said, was whether on these facts they could land without presenting the laborers'certificates required under the 1882 act.[47] He felt compelled to say that they could. The treaty of 1880, he noted, secured to Chinese then resident in the United States the right to go and come of their own free will. The law of 1882 confirmed such laborers in their treaty rights but in addition imposed the requirement that they present laborers' certificates upon their return. But, said the judge, that would be a reasonable requirement only if limited to Chinese laborers with a right to reside who left the United States after the 1882 act was passed, when certificates were available for the taking. To apply it to Chinese who had left the United States before the law went into effect would be to practically deny them the rights secured them by the treaty. Before the court would impute to the Congress an intent to violate a treaty with a foreign power, said Hoffman, it would require clear and unequivocal evidence of that intent. Hoffman thought that the Congress had probably failed to provide for laborers in such status as the petitioner's.[48] This was the first pronouncement of a court of record on what came to be known as the issue of "former residence." It would by no means be the last. The matter would be a vexatious one and would continue to consume the time of the courts for the next several years.[49]

In the months immediately following the *Chin Ah On* decision the pace of habeas corpus activity increased markedly in the federal courts of California, prompting both the district and circuit courts to complain that these Chinese cases were making it impossible for them to handle other judicial business.[50] The cases fell for the most part into three classes: pleas of "former residence," (many petitioners were able to prove their claims by bringing into court the books of the *hui-kuan* showing the payment of the departure tax assessed by the companies), applications based on documents furnished by the Chinese government certifying to the petitioner's merchant status ("Canton certificates" was the term used for them), and applications by the children of Chinese merchants.[51] Some of these cases appear to have been actively supported, if not actually sponsored by the Chinese consulate; others seem to have been brought by the litigants themselves, or, in the case of workers, possibly by their employers, independent of any consular involvement.[52] Most were decided without a written opinion. A few, however, gave the courts the chance to say more about the doctrines laid down in the *Chin Ah On* case.

A week after that decision, for example, the district court decided that a Chinese laborer who left the United States after the 1882 act went into effect and who knowingly failed to apply for the certificates provided for under Section 3 of the act could not enter the United States on a claim of former residence.[53] In the very important case of *In re Leong Yick Dew*,[54] decided in February 1884, the circuit court clarified a point that the earlier opinions had left rather murky, to wit at what precise point in time the certificate requirement should become operative. The court now said that

that point should be the time when it first became physically possible to obtain certificates. Although the Treasury Department certificates did not arrive in San Francisco until August 8, 1882, the court noted that the Chinese consul began issuing temporary certificates on June 6, 1882. It decided that this date should be the cutoff date. Chinese laborers who left the United States after it without obtaining laborers' certificates would not be permitted to return. At the same time the circuit court, for the first time officially, endorsed the district court principle of former residence. Chinese who left before June 6 could still seek to land on that ground alone.[55]

The 1884 Amendment to the First Exclusion Act

Disturbed by what they perceived to be the too liberal interpretation the lower federal courts were giving the 1882 Exclusion Act, Pacific Coast representatives in Congress soon began to lay plans for its revision. The *Daily Alta* reported as early as December 1883 that a group of Pacific Coast Senators and Representatives had recently convened for the purpose of devising ways to curb "loopholes" in the 1882 law, a law which the paper commented had given way at virtually every point where its strength had been tested.[56] These efforts soon bore fruit. In July of 1884 Congress passed and the president signed into law a series of amendments to the 1882 legislation.

The most significant changes in the law wrought by the 1884 amendments had to do with the act's certification procedures, those applying to laborers and to non-laborers alike. Section 4 of the 1882 act was changed so as to provide that the laborer's certificate should show, in addition to the information called for under the 1882 act, the individual, family, and tribal name of the laborer and when and where he had pursued his occupation. Moreover, it was provided that the certificate should be "the only evidence permissible" to establish the laborer's right of re-entry.[57] Section 6 of the original act, the section that dealt with the entry rights of Chinese other than laborers, was thoroughly revamped. The certificates called for by this section were, it was now said, to be issued by the government of the place from which the non-laborer came rather than, as before, "under the authority of [such] government." In the case of merchants (the term "merchant," it was now made clear, did not include "hucksters," "peddlers," and fishermen), it was specified that their certificates should include, in addition to the data already called for, information on the nature and value of the business they carried on. Merchants' certificates were now to be visaed by U.S. diplomatic representatives in the country from which the merchant came, and it was made the duty of these representatives to look into the truth of the statements set forth in the certificates. As with the laborers' certificates the merchants' certificates were to be the sole evidence permissible to establish a right of entry into the United States, but the U.S. government was to be free to controvert them.[58] Finally, to eliminate any doubt about the applicability of the exclusion legislation to the whole of the Chinese race, to codify, as it were, the decision of Justice Field in the circuit court case of *In re Ah Lung*, the 1884 act confirmed that its provisions should apply to "all subjects of China and Chinese, whether subjects of China or any other foreign power."[59] The Chinese legation to the United States protested vehemently against the changes wrought by the 1884 law, alleging that it seemed to be aimed at depriving the Chinese government of its right to issue passports to its own people, putting all real authority into the hands of U.S. officials in China, and that by redefining "merchants" to exclude peddlers and dealers in fish it went well beyond the terms of the treaty of 1880, which had only distinguished between merchants and laborers.[60]

In re Ah Quan

On July 27, 1884, the *Oceanic* docked in San Francisco, the first ship carrying Chinese to arrive since the enactment of the 1884 amendments. Laborers possessing return certificates were allowed to land, but a good number of the Chinese passengers were detained on board. In short order some thirty habeas writs, raising a variety of legal claims, had been sued out on their behalf in the U.S. Circuit Court, and it was clear immediately that the federal bench in San Francisco would soon have to say authoritatively what the 1884 act meant. During the course of the hearing on the writs it was agreed by all concerned that the court should proceed with one of the cases and leave the others in abeyance pending a decision.[61] According to the local Caucasian press, the case was the one which the Chinese consulate thought "as likely, in its presentation . . . to raise nearly all the questions liable to be raised . . . under the amended Restriction Act."[62] Lyman Mowry, an attorney for the consulate (three attorneys were present for the consulate at the hearing), said the case had been brought to get an interpretation of Sections 3, 4, and 6 of the new act.[63] The selected petitioner, Ah Quan, argued that he had a right to land on two separate grounds, because of former residence and because he was a merchant. He had neither a Section 4 (laborer's) nor a Section 6 (merchant's) certificate and sought to prove both statuses by other means (through "parol evidence" in the language of the law) something which he was entitled to do under the existing interpretation of the 1882 act. The U.S. attorney argued strenuously that the purpose of the 1884 amendments was to compel all Chinese henceforth to present certificates evidencing their status. Parol evidence, he said, was now no longer admissible. The question then was to what extent the 1884 act had altered the petitioner's rights.[64]

A circuit court panel consisting of Circuit Judge Sawyer and District Judge Hoffman handed down its decision on August 7. The court, said Sawyer, had decided to stand by its previous decisions on the rights of both laborers and merchants. It would continue to interpret the certificate requirement of Section 4 as applicable only to those laborers who departed the country on or after the date when it became possible to obtain one, June 6, 1882. The plea of former residence was still acceptable and still provable by any relevant evidence by those who left before that date. There was nothing in the amendatory act, said Sawyer, that required a construction more unfavorable to Chinese laborers than the one it had given the 1882 act in *Leong Yick Dew*.[65] The court's construction of the original act in that case was before the congress when it passed the 1884 amendments, Sawyer noted, and if that body had intended to overrule the circuit court's interpretation, it would have done so by clear and convincing evidence. The court found no such evidence in the new act. Similarly, Chinese other than laborers who left China or any other foreign country before July 5, 1884, would still be permitted to prove their right to enter the United States upon such evidence as the court had previously allowed.[66] The holding of Judges Sawyer and Hoffman, as it would turn out, would remain the law of the circuit for a little less than two months. What changed everything was the arrival of Justice Field in San Francisco in late September for one of his regular stints as a circuit judge.

In re Chew Heong

The local press had anticipated Field's arrival with great interest. The *Evening Bulletin* noted that a number of cases raising important questions under the amended Exclusion Act were on the circuit court's docket, and it anticipated that Field's presence would permit the tribunal to address them in more authoritative fashion than had theretofore been possible.[67] One was the habeas corpus case *In re Chew Heong*. It raised anew the question of the impact of the new law on the right to use parol evidence to prove former residence.

The Chinese laborer Chew Heong, who had left the United States before the passage of the first Exclusion Act and perforce, therefore, before any certificate was required, was seeking to land on this ground, offering to prove his former residence through the testimony of others. He was of course entitled to do this under the authority of the recently issued opinion in *Ah Quan*. Field's presence permitted the authorities to bring the issue of previous residence up again for reconsideration, however, and this they proceeded to do. The Chinese consulate, recognizing the importance of the question (there were apparently some twelve thousand Chinese laborers similarly situated) again, as in the earlier *Ah Quan* case, retained a bevy of powerful counsel to press the laborer's claim.[68] The United States was itself also well represented. A reporter for the *Morning Call*, present at the hearing on Chew Heong's habeas petition, observed, "There were present in court all the forensic force that the Government employs to defeat the machinations of the cunning Celestials who wish to gain a foothold in this country, as well as all the legal artillery employed by the latter to storm the Government defenses."[69]

The hearing on Chew Heong's habeas petition took place before the full circuit panel (Field, the circuit judge, and the two district judges) and stretched over two days. Argument revolved entirely around the question of Congress's intentions in enacting the 1884 amendments to the Exclusion Act. At the close of the proceeding Field announced that he intended to rule for the government although he indicated that all of his colleagues on the panel disagreed with him. He suggested that the decision when handed down would therefore be ripe for appeal to the U.S. Supreme Court (at this time habeas decisions of the lower courts could only be appealed to the U.S. Supreme Court if heard by a multimember panel and if there was disagreement among the panel judges).[70]

Field read his relatively short opinion from the bench on September 29. He thought Congress's purpose in enacting the 1884 law was quite clear. It was to eliminate the practice followed by some of the lower courts of receiving parol evidence of previous residence, a practice that had led to the overcrowding of court dockets, and to affirm that henceforth the certificate should be the only means of proof for *any* Chinese laborer seeking to re-enter the United States, including those who left the country before the original law took effect.[71] If this interpretation caused any hardship, that was for Congress to correct, not the judiciary, Field declared.[72]

Circuit Judge Sawyer dissented and was joined in the dissent by District Judges Hoffman and George M. Sabin. (The fact that there were three votes against Field's one meant nothing. In cases of a divergence of view the law provided that the opinion of the presiding judge should be deemed the opinion of the court.)[73] He insisted, as he and Judge Hoffman had in *Ah Quan*, that the congressional legislation ought, if possible, to be construed in such a fashion as not to destroy treaty rights and that such a construction was possible if the certificate requirement were held to apply only to such laborers who left the United States when it was possible to obtain certificates.[74] There was no divergence of viewpoint in the other important opinion concerning Chinese rights handed down by the court that day.

Citizenship by Birth: The Case of Look Tin Sing

The habeas corpus case of *Look Tin Sing* raised the novel and interesting question of whether a Chinese person born in the United States was, by virtue of that fact alone, a citizen of this country. The first Exclusion Act had made it clear that Chinese could not become naturalized citizens, but the question of citizenship by birth remained unsettled. The petitioner in this case was a lad of fourteen who had been born in Mendocino, California. His parents lived in the northern California coastal town of Mendocino where his father had been a merchant for some twenty years. The father had sent his son to China for an education when he was nine, but when he returned from that country and sought to enter the United States, he was prevented from doing so by the immigration authorities, who claimed he was an alien barred from entering the country by the terms of the exclusion legislation. They ordered him detained aboard ship pending deportation to China, whereupon his parents, very probably with the financial support of the consulate or some domestic Chinese organization, retained counsel who sued out a writ of habeas corpus on the boy's behalf. In their petition, counsel, relying on Section 1 of the Fourteenth Amendment, argued that Look Tin Sing was a U.S. citizen by virtue of birth on American soil and as such was entitled to enter the country. The section provided, in pertinent part, that "all persons born or naturalized in the United States, and subject to the jurisdiction thereof, are citizens of the United States and of the State wherein they reside."

The case attracted a great deal of attention in the San Francisco legal community, and, before the hearing on the petition, Justice Field invited all interested members of the bar to submit their views on the constitutional questions the case raised. Whether in response to this call or at the behest of the parties, an impressive array of legal talent did in fact appear in Field's courtroom to argue the case for and against the petitioner.[75] John Norton Pomeroy, a jurist of some note, then on the law faculty of the Hastings Law College, was the primary spokesman for those opposed to the petitioner's claim. He argued at the hearing that the key term was "subject to the jurisdiction thereof." The boy, said Pomeroy, was only partially subject to the jurisdiction of the United States when he was born in this country. He owed his primary allegiance to the Emperor of China. What he acquired at most by birth in this country was the right to renounce his allegiance to China and declare his allegiance to the United States once he attained the age of majority. As authority for the view that the children born to foreign nationals in the United States were not U.S. citizens he cited a dictum to that effect by Justice Samuel Miller in the *Slaughter-House Cases.* Miller, speaking of the citizenship clause of Section 1, had said, "The phrase, 'subject to its jurisdiction' was intended to exclude from its operation children of ministers, consuls and citizens or subjects of foreign states born within the United States."[76] The United States district attorney, for his part, advanced the rather extraordinary view that even if the petitioner were a citizen by birth he was still excluded from landing in the United States by the Exclusion Act.[77]

Several attorneys argued the case for the petitioner, including William M. Stewart, the former Senator from Nevada, now a private citizen with a law practice and residence in San Francisco. Counsel for the petitioner contended that the plain language of the Fourteenth Amendment settled the matter. Stewart contended that a ruling adverse to the petitioner would cast doubt upon the citizenship of many persons of European ancestry born in the United States of parents who were not naturalized. The question before the court was completely different from the question of Chinese restriction.[78]

Field rejected the Pomeroy view and ruled on September 29 that Look Tin Sing should be allowed to land. The language of the Fourteenth Amendment was sufficiently broad to cover the petitioner, he said. The words "subject to the jurisdiction thereof," said Field, not citing much in the way of authority, were meant to except from citizenship the children of the diplomatic representatives of foreign countries and those who were born here but who later renounced their allegiance to the U.S. government.[79] For reasons unknown he chose not to speak to Justice Miller's dictum in *Slaughter-House* concerning the meaning of the term, itself uttered without citation to authority. As to the district attorney's claim that the petitioner could be excluded even if he was a citizen, Field seemed nothing short of incredulous. It was beyond the power of Congress to exclude a citizen of the United States from this country for any cause other than crime, he declared in no uncertain terms.[80]

Several newspaper accounts of the *Look Tin Sing* hearing reported Field as announcing at its close that he intended to rule for the petitioner on the understanding that his colleague Sawyer would rule against him, thereby making it possible to appeal the case to the U.S. Supreme Court for a final and authoritative opinion. (As noted above at the time a division of opinion in the circuit tribunal was the only basis for appeal to the high court in habeas cases.) But Sawyer elsewhere denied that there was any such understanding, and in fact the circuit court opinion was unanimous.[81] The important constitutional question raised by the case would not be addressed by the Supreme Court until almost the end of the century. The Chinese in the meantime were laying plans for an appeal to the tribunal of the adverse decision in *In re Chew Heong*.

Chew Heong Appeals to the Supreme Court

A Notice of Appeal to the Supreme Court was filed in the *Chew Heong* case on October 1, and the matter was quickly briefed and submitted by counsel for the two sides.[82] The Supreme Court handed down its opinion a scant two months later.[83] The treaty of 1880 between the United States and China, wrote Justice John Marshall Harlan for the majority, was a part of the nation's domestic law. It conferred upon Chinese laborers like the petitioner, those that is to say who were in the country on November 17, 1880, the right to go from and come into the United States at their pleasure.[84] Congress could of course disregard the treaty and withdraw that privilege, but the Court would require the clearest evidence that Congress wished to do this before reaching that conclusion. Harlan did not find such evidence in his review of the 1882 and 1884 immigration legislation. To be sure the third section of both the original and the amended version of the law made the right of Chinese laborers to re-enter the United States contingent on the production of the certificate provided for under the section, but, said Harlan, it would be both unreasonable and unjust to conclude that Congress meant that requirement to apply to laborers who were absent from the country when it enacted these laws and who were therefore physically incapable of procuring such certificates. "What injustice could be more marked," Harlan wrote, "than by legislative enactment, to recognize the existence of a right, by treaty, to come within the limits of the United States and, at the same time, to prescribe, as the only evidence permissible to establish it, the possession of a collector's certificate, that could not possibly have been obtained by the person to whom the right belongs."[85] "*Lex non intendit aliquid impossibile* [the law does not intend anything that is impossible to do] is a familiar maxim of the law," Harlan noted.[86]

The 1880 treaty, the 1882 act, and the 1884 amending act should and could be construed so as to harmonize with one another, said Harlan. Taken together they meant that a Chinese laborer to whom a certificate had been issued under the 1882 act could re-enter the United States only upon producing that certificate. Similarly, a laborer who had been issued a certificate under the 1884 act had to produce the certificate called for under that act in order to re-enter. Chinese laborers like the petitioner, however, who resided in the United States at the time of the treaty but who left the United States before the 1882 legislation was passed could re-enter the United States upon a proof of prior residence alone. Such a construction, he said, preserved treaty rights and at the same time gave full effect to the congressional legislation.[87]

As important as the Court's decision was for its holding on the specific issue before it, the decision was equally important for its endorsement of the more general principles, first articulated by the California Circuit Court in the early Exclusion Act cases, that the treaty of 1880 was to be taken seriously as an independent source of rights and that congressional exclusion legislation was to be construed, if at all possible, in such a fashion as not to violate those rights.

Justice Field, who had had a large hand in fashioning the circuit court law just adverted to, wrote a lengthy dissent, strikingly harsh both in tone and in substance. His colleagues were distorting the plain intent of Congress in their reading of both the 1882 and the 1884 acts, he insisted. The manifest purpose of both acts (the second act eliminated all doubt on this point, he stressed), was to require certificates of identification from all Chinese laborers who had a right to re-enter the United States. And such a construction of the laws was possible, he opined, without doing any violence to the treaty of 1880. The right of re-entry guaranteed by that treaty, he maintained, was meant to apply only to those Chinese laborers who were in the United States on the date the treaty was signed *and* who continued their residence in the country afterwards. It did not apply to Chinese like the petitioner who left the country in 1881 to take up residence elsewhere and who now sought to return. Such a construction eliminated all conflict between the treaty and the congressional legislation in his view.[88] But even if the congressional acts did conflict with the treaty, then they were to prevail as the last expression of the sovereign will.[89]

This seemed a rather different judge from the one who had addressed the subject of Chinese exclusion in the circuit court cases decided a year earlier. In those cases, it will be remembered, Field had spoken of the necessity of construing the exclusion law so as to avoid producing unjust, oppressive, or absurd results. He had laid great stress on the United States-China treaties and on the need to reconcile the treaties and the law. Indeed his Supreme Court dissent was much harsher than the opinion he had rendered on circuit in the same case. He offered in the opinion something of an explanation for his new point of view. It had resulted, he said, from subsequent reflection on relations between the United States and the Chinese Empire.[90] The treaty between the United States and China had proven to be entirely one-sided, he said. China had not lived up to her side of the bargain. In the first place she had done nothing to ensure that the emigration of her subjects was truly voluntary. The majority of Chinese who immigrated to the United States, said Field, adopting the rhetoric of the extreme Sinophobic party, came in effect as coolie slaves.[91] Secondly, the freedom of trade and residence in China that the treaty promised U.S. citizens had proven illusory. The consideration for emigration from China had failed, and the United States, Field seemed almost ready to say, would be justified now in disregarding the treaty.[92]

The Status of Chinese Merchants under the 1884 Act

One question that *Chew Heong* did not address was the effect of the amended Exclusion Act on the travel rights of resident Chinese merchants. That question had been simmering between the Chinese legation in Washington, the State Department, and the collector of customs in San Francisco for some time and remained still unsettled as of the date of that decision. A word by way of background on this dispute.

It will be remembered that in the 1882 circuit court case of *Low Yam Chow* Justice Field had ruled that Chinese merchants returning to the United States, as opposed to those seeking to enter for the first time, did not need to produce the certificates called for under Section 6 of the original Exclusion Act but could prove their merchant status by any legitimate means. Acting on this decision the Chinese consulate in San Francisco began to issue identification certificates to departing merchants (Chinese consular certificates or consular passports they came to be called), and for a time the customs officials in San Francisco accepted them as sufficient to allow re-entry into the country. Then in early 1884 the collector of customs in San Francisco informed the Chinese consul general that he intended to issue certificates of his own to departing merchants and would no longer accept the consular certificates, but after a protest from the Chinese legation in Washington he was overruled by the secretary of the treasury.[93] The matter did not end there, however. When the 1884 act went into effect, the collector, without waiting for any directions from Washington, announced that in view of the changes in the law nonlaborer Chinese returning to the United States, including merchants, would henceforth need to furnish him with certificates issued in China by the Chinese government. Another protest from the Chinese legation caused the secretary of the treasury again to overrule the collector, this time in the form of an official circular addressed to all customs officers directing them to accept certificates issued by Chinese consulates in the

United States.[94] Another circular, issued on January 14, 1885, approximately a month after the Supreme Court decision in *Chew Heong,* said simply that Section 6 of the 1884 act was not to be seen as applying to Chinese merchants who were lawfully in the United States at the date of the 1880 treaty. They would continue to be able to re-enter the country on any evidence satisfactory to the collector that they were not Chinese laborers.[95] The two circulars by themselves, however, were not enough to resolve the problem on the ground in San Francisco. The *Evening Bulletin* of January 22 reported the collector as being unwilling to say whether he would follow the secretary's instructions.[96] It seemed clear that a court test would sooner or later be necessary to clear the air.

A number of habeas corpus cases involving persons claiming to be Chinese merchants were at the time making their way through the federal courts in San Francisco. One involved a man who had arrived in San Francisco in July 1884 but who had been refused permission to land on the ground that he did not possess a Section 6 certificate. His contention was that he was a partner in a well-known Chinatown firm and was returning to the city after a sojourn of several years in British Columbia, where his firm had a branch. Judge Hoffman of the district court heard the case on January 14, 1885, and, confessing his uncertainty on the questions raised, ordered the petitioner remanded to custody with the understanding that the case would be appealed to the circuit court.[97] In March 1885 the case came on for a hearing before that tribunal. According to one organ of local opinion the attorneys representing the man were in the employ of the Chinese consulate and were seeking through the vehicle of this case to obtain an authoritative ruling on the status of all Chinese similarly situated.[98] Just such a ruling came down from Judge Sawyer at the end of the month.

Section 6 of the amended Exclusion Act required Chinese of the exempt classes who were "about to come to the United States" to procure a certificate of identification containing certain specified information from the Chinese government. The question before the court, said Sawyer, was whether that clause was meant to apply to Chinese merchants domiciled in the United States.[99] The question was to be decided, he continued, in light of the principles affirmed by the court in *Chew Heong,* and bearing in mind those principles the answer had to be no. The Supreme Court had said emphatically in that case that acts of Congress were to be construed so as not to bring them into conflict with treaty stipulations. Under the Treaty of 1880 merchants continued to have the right to go from and come into the United States at will. To require merchants who, like the petitioner, had their residences and businesses in the United States to obtain certification of their status from representatives of the Chinese government in China (it must be borne in mind that that was the construction put upon the statutory language by the collector) was to ask them to do what was at best impracticable, at worst impossible. Persons in the United States were in the best position to ascertain the merchant status of Chinese merchants there resident. Such means of identification would often not be available in China. To adopt the construction of the statute urged by the U.S. attorney, said Sawyer, would render legal and treaty rights nugatory. Section 6 of the amended Exclusion Act, the court held, was not applicable to resident Chinese merchants who left the United States for temporary purposes, intending to return, either before or after the Exclusion Act was passed. This was the construction, the court noted, that had been adopted by the executive department.[100]

Other Judicial Developments in 1885

The San Francisco federal courts handed down only one other significant opinion on Chinese restriction during the remainder of 1885. *In re Jung Ah Lung*,[101] brought in Judge Hoffman's district court in April, raised new, complex, and interesting questions. The petitioner, another Chinese laborer denied permission to land, had first come to California in 1876. Shortly after his arrival he had converted to Christianity and had begun to attend the Chinatown Methodist mission of the Reverend Otis Gibson. He had left San Francisco after two years and had moved to New York City, where he became proprietor of a laundry. He had returned to China in October 1883, in possession of the laborer's certificate provided for under the first Chinese Exclusion Act. He alleged that his certificate had been stolen from him by river pirates in China, and he sought to re-enter the United States on the strength of an entry in the customs house register, which showed that a certificate had in fact been issued to a man bearing his name and of his physical description, and on the testimony of witnesses who knew him. He was represented in the litigation by the Reverend Gibson's son, William F. Gibson, the same attorney who had represented the Chinese child Mamie Tape in her successful effort to be admitted to the San Francisco public schools.

S. G. Hilborn, the U.S. attorney, intervened first with an attack on the very right of the district court to hear the petitioner's case. Hilborn alleged that Jung Ah Lung was not being restrained of his liberty within the meaning of the habeas corpus act and more important that the decision made by customs officials that he did not have a right to land concluded the matter and precluded further inquiry into it by the court. (The moving force behind this legal stratagem seems to have been the new collector of customs, who was determined to have this latter point pressed.)[102] In a published opinion issued October 13 Hoffman rejected both contentions. He thought it obvious that the detention of the petitioner aboard ship at the instance of the authorities of the port was a restraint of his personal liberty within the act's intention. As to the U.S. attorney's second claim, Hoffman thought it extraordinary that anyone should be trying to oust the federal courts of their ancient right to inquire through the writ of habeas corpus into the lawfulness of such restraints and vest it in a "purely executive officer," who, he noted, was not authorized to administer oaths or subpoena witnesses. Until he received the clearest directive to the contrary from Congress, he would assume that Chinese persons, like all others in the country irrespective of color, were entitled to avail themselves of the benefit of the great writ.[103]

Having rejected the challenge to its jurisdiction the court then went on to address the merits of the petitioner's claim. Gibson was able to present an impressive case. He introduced into evidence the entry in the customs register containing Jung Ah Lung's physical description and showing that a certificate had been issued to him. He produced two witnesses who said they could identify the petitioner as a man who had attended the San Francisco Methodist Church in 1876. Another witness, who had served as a missionary in China, identified him as a churchgoer in that country as well and testified that his story about river pirates was credible.[104] For his part the U.S. attorney chose simply to stand on the position that under the law a laborer's certificate was the only evidence admissible to show a right to re-enter the United States.[105] Hoffman found the petitioner's evidence both admissible and persuasive and ordered him discharged the same day.[106]

The district court findings were affirmed by the circuit court, and the U.S. attorney soon filed an application for the allowance of an appeal to the Supreme Court, an application that was duly granted. The lower court transcript was filed in the Supreme Court, and the matter was set for hearing on January 25, 1886.[107] But for reasons that are not clear the cause lay in limbo for two years and briefs were not actually submitted until well into the high court's October 1887 term; and the Supreme Court did not hand down its decision until February 1888. Though the decision, chronologically speaking, belongs to a later phase in the legal history of Chinese exclusion, a phase we address in a later chapter, topically it is related to this phase, and we discuss it here.

Justice Blatchford, writing for the majority, affirmed the conclusions and the reasoning of Judge Hoffman. He saw nothing in the language of either the 1882 or 1884 acts to support the argument advanced by government counsel that Congress wished by those measures to divest the federal courts of jurisdiction to issue habeas writs in Chinese immigration cases or to vest final reviewing authority in customs officials.[108] On the merits, Blatchford fell back on the principle announced by the court in *Chew Heong* that the certificate provisions of the 1884 act were not retrospective. The rights and duties of Jung Ah Lung, who had departed the United States in October 1883, were to be adjudged under the 1882 and not the 1884 act. The relevant section of that act, he observed, did not specify that the certificate was to be the only evidence acceptable to establish the right of re-entry. The district court, therefore, had been correct to receive the secondary evidence that it did.[109] Justices Harlan, Field, and Lamar dissented on the effects of the nonproduction of the certificate (in their view the 1882 act made the certificate the only evidence acceptable) though not on the jurisdictional questions.[110]

A Summary of Developments through 1885

The district and circuit court decisions in *Jung Ah Lung,* handed down, respectively, in November and December of 1885, mark something of a watershed in the history of litigation under the first Chinese Exclusion Acts. With this case the first phase of Chinese exclusion litigation may be said to have come to a close. No decision of any consequence having to do with these laws would be rendered by the San Francisco courts or any other federal court for the next several years. If one were to draw up a balance sheet of the litigation brought by the Chinese in the period, one would have to say that the gains exceeded the losses by some modest but important measure. The decisions suggested that the courts were on the whole prepared to give the exclusion legislation a reasonable, even liberal interpretation, one that would not impose unnecessary hardship on the Chinese. They had ruled that Chinese merchants domiciled in the United States did not have to procure certificates in China before returning to the United States. Both the San Francisco courts and the U.S. Supreme Court had ruled that neither the 1882 nor the 1884 law was to be given retroactive application. And so Chinese laborers who left the United States before either law went into effect were to be permitted to prove their previous residence by secondary evidence and were not to be bound by the certificate provisions of the 1882 or 1884 acts. In *Jung Ah Lung* the courts had decisively rebuffed the attempt by U.S. immigration officials to oust them of jurisdiction over Chinese immigration claims. Particularly striking in these early decisions was the judges' insistence that the treaty of 1880 be taken seriously as a source of individual Chinese rights and that acts of Congress be construed in such a fashion so as not to vitiate those rights. At the same time, it must be pointed out, the courts from the very beginning had made it clear that Congress, if it was so minded, was perfectly free unilaterally to override treaty provisions.[111]

The Chinese consulate, which had supported many of the cases discussed in this chapter, must have derived some modicum of satisfaction at the results this litigation had achieved. The federal court decisions had taken some of the edge off the exclusion laws.[112] This satisfaction, however, could only have been tempered by alarm at a problem of another sort that was at this time increasingly occupying the consulate's attention: raw violence directed against Chinese residents in the western states. The problem had first erupted in a dramatic way in the fall of 1885, and the winter of 1885–86 would see the breaking on the West Coast of a wave of anti-Chinese violence unparalleled in American history. The next phase of Chinese exclusion grew directly out of that episode, and we turn our attention now to it and to the major Supreme Court case it engendered.

7 Seeking Federal Protection against Mob Violence

The Unusual Case of Baldwin v. Franks

The Anti-Chinese Hysteria of 1885–1886

There was of course nothing new about anti-Chinese violence. Outbursts of violence, individual and collective, directed at the Chinese had punctuated California history from the beginnings of the immigration. Occasionally these had taken on the dimensions of full-scale riots. To give but a few examples, in 1871 a major disturbance in Los Angeles had taken nineteen Chinese lives.[1] A mob drove the Chinese out of Watsonville, California, a town near Monterey, in 1875.[2] And, as noted in chapter 4, there was large-scale rioting directed at Chinese laundries in San Francisco in the summer of 1877.[3] (In each of these incidents, it is worthy of note, the Chinese either sued or threatened to sue the perpetrators or the municipalities for compensation for their losses.)[4] The fall and winter of 1885–86, however, would prove to be a season of special ferocity. In September 1885, one of the worst race riots in nineteenth-century American history took the lives of twenty-eight Chinese laborers in the frontier town of Rock Springs, Wyoming, and left the Chinese section of town destroyed.[5] (An extremely detailed and angry account of the Rock Springs incident appeared several months after the event in the San Francisco Chinese newspaper, the *Oriental.*)[6] In the same month three Chinese residents of Squak Valley in Washington Territory were killed in a large vigilante attack on their rural campsite. In early October a hostile crowd invaded the Chinese section of Seattle and threatened the inhabitants. In November mob action forced all Chinese out of the neighboring city of Tacoma.[7] These were the most serious incidents, but there were lesser, alarming occurrences of anti-Chinese violence elsewhere in the West throughout the fall of 1885 and into the winter of 1886.[8] Even when there was no outright violence, there were threats and intimidation. The main newspapers of Washington, Oregon, and California of the day are in fact filled with reports of mass meetings in towns and cities of every size, demanding the expulsion of the Chinese.[9]

Representatives of the Chinese community had reacted quickly and forcefully to these events. The incident in Rock Springs provoked a major diplomatic confrontation between the Department of State and the Chinese legation in Washington, D.C.[10] Protests and pleas for help followed quickly on the heels of the other major incidents as well. In the wake of the first Washington disturbances Consul Bee telegraphed the governor of Washington Territory, expressing fear that another Rock Springs might break out in his jurisdiction and demanding greater protection for the Chinese.[11] Similarly, after the Tacoma riot, the Chinese minister to Washington contacted Secretary of State Thomas F. Bayard asking that immediate countermeasures be taken including the initiation of legal action against wrongdoers.[12]

As the disorders spread in the late fall and early winter, Chinese pleas became more urgent. (On February 7, 1886 a Seattle mob again invaded the Chinese quarter and routed the Chinese out of their homes.) On February 13, 1886, Lee Kim-wah, president of the Chinese Six Companies telegraphed the Chinese legation in Washington: "[T]he condition of our countrymen on this coast is deplorable in the extreme. The Chinese have been driven out of many towns, the people burning our dwellings, robbing our property and murdering our people [with impunity]."[13] He asked the minister to contact the president to demand that federal troops be sent to protect the Chinese. Several days later the Chinese minister called on Secretary Bayard and laid before him a batch of telegrams and newspaper clippings from California which lent credence to the Six Companies' view that a concerted effort seemed to be afoot in the state to drive the Chinese out of all of its towns and cities.[14]

Federal authorities came part of the way toward meeting Chinese demands. Grover Cleveland's administration dispatched an army escort to Rock Springs in the wake of the riot to protect Chinese representatives who were conducting an investigation. In the midst of the Washington disturbances President Cleveland issued an ultimatum to the territory's white inhabitants threatening to send troops if the disorders did not cease.[15] In his first annual message to Congress, Cleveland adverted to Rock Springs and other anti-Chinese riots in the West and declared that "all the power of [the federal government] should be exerted to maintain the amplest good faith toward China . . . , and inflexible sternness of law in bringing the wrongdoers to justice should be insisted upon."[16]

What the national government would not do, however, was to admit that it had any responsibility, or, for that matter, any right, to go any further. Representatives of the Chinese legation had from the very outset of the anti-Chinese violence of the 1880s insisted that the national government, as opposed to the states, had ultimate responsibility for the safety of Chinese residents in the United States and was bound to take positive steps—including the initiation of legal action against wrongdoers—to assure the protection of Chinese lives and property. The legation also claimed that the national government was under a duty to provide monetary compensation to the anti-Chinese riot victims. These claims were invariably rebuffed by the U.S. government. It denied any liability to compensate riot victims, insisting that the prosecution of criminal misdeeds of the sort complained of was, because of the American federal system of government, a matter exclusively within the jurisdiction of state authorities.[17] When Cleveland spoke of bringing wrongdoers to justice, he had in mind the actions of local, rather than federal, officials.

From the Chinese perspective this was an entirely unsatisfactory state of affairs. Local authorities might prosecute ordinary criminal acts directed at individual Chinese from time to time. But given the temper of the times in the West, it seemed to the Chinese entirely unrealistic to expect local authorities to use municipal law to blunt what were in effect the manifestations of a quasi-political movement enjoying wide societal support—especially when these local authorities were themselves more often than not in the movement's vanguard.[18] The Chinese felt that the national government was both empowered and bound to do more than it was doing. The United States had after all pledged in Article III of the Treaty of 1880 to devise measures to protect Chinese residents should they be threatened by ill treatment at the hands of others. Their frustration at the inaction of the national authorities grew as anti-Chinese incidents multiplied.

Incidents in Nicolaus and Oregon City

The small town of Nicolaus lies about twenty-five miles northeast of the state capital, Sacramento. In the late nineteenth century much of Nicolaus's agricultural land was given over to the growing of hops, and a fair number of Chinese workers were employed in the industry. Like practically every town in California it had its anti-Chinese club. On the 6th of February, 1886, the club notified the Chinese workers on five hop farms just outside of town that they had ten days to leave the vicinity or suffer serious consequences. When the Chinese refused to comply with the ultimatum, a group of local vigilantes decided to make good on the threat. At three in the morning on February 18, a band of men wearing masks visited the hop ranches in question, broke into the residences of some forty-six Chinese hop-workers, forced them out of their beds, and drove them to a wharf on the Feather River, where the steamer *Knight* was lying at anchor loading wheat. At this point accounts of the incident become fragmentary and confused, but it appears that the white citizens of Nicolaus had raised a sum of money to pay fares on the steamer and sought to negotiate passage with the vessel's captain. The captain refused to accept money for his unwilling passengers but at length agreed to take them on board and ferry them out of the area. They were put on a barge that the steamer was towing, to the great amusement and applause of a crowd of onlookers, and at midafternoon were disembarked downriver to the state capital.[19] Another incident, remarkably similar in character, occurred four days later in Oregon City, Oregon, a town on the outskirts of Portland. There a band of masked men raided the Chinese quarter in the middle of the night, rousted the Chinese from their homes and forced them aboard a riverboat, this one bound for Portland.[20] These acts rivaled in contempt for law some of the outrages then being perpetrated in the southern states by the Ku Klux Klan and its allies and were to the Chinese yet another reminder of the seeming hollowness of the federal pledge to protect the Chinese against mob violence.

Chinese Diplomats Visit Nicolaus

On February 21, Ching-Ping, Chinese vice-consul at San Francisco, and his secretary, in the company of a deputy U.S. marshal, visited Nicolaus and conducted interviews. The next day the two Chinese arrived in Sacramento. The vice-consul reported that he had been in the course of a visit to Red Bluff and other towns to inquire into anti-Chinese disturbances in those locales when the events at Nicolaus had occurred. While in the state capital he sought to make arrangements for the Nicolaus refugees. One gathers from the newspaper reports of his stay in Sacramento that he was quite upset about what had happened in Nicolaus and elsewhere and that he was frustrated that the law was not more quickly coming to his aid.[21] His frustration must have intensified when news of the February 22 outbreak in Oregon City reached him. And it was perhaps at this point that the decision was made, probably by Chinese diplomatic representatives in conjunction with local Chinese leaders to seize the initiative. In short order two legal actions were undertaken which, in effect, were designed to force the federal hand.[22]

Initiation of Criminal Proceedings

The Chinese of the Portland area retained a Portland law firm, one of whose members was the former U.S. district attorney for the state, to assist them in the initiation of criminal proceedings against the perpetrators of the Oregon City outrage.[23] A complaint was filed, arrests were made, and on March 2, Judge Matthew Deady, Federal District Judge for Oregon, summoned a grand jury. The Portland action was soon upstaged, however, by a parallel criminal proceeding beginning to unfold in California.

On March 8, 1886, there appeared in the Sacramento courtroom of B. N. Bugby, a commissioner of the Circuit Court of the United States for the District of California, a Chinese resident of Nicolaus going by the name of John Sing. He swore out a complaint charging Thomas Baldwin, a native of Nicolaus, and some fifteen other white men of conspiring to expel him and a number of fellow Chinese from the town and thereby to deprive them, as the complaint put it, of their right to the equal protection of the law.[24] On the basis of this complaint Bugby issued a warrant charging Baldwin and his companions with the unspecified crime of conspiracy and directing the U.S. marshal to take them into custody. On March 12, Deputy U.S. Marshal J. C. Franks arrived in Nicolaus, arrested the accused and took them immediately back to Sacramento.[25] They were brought before Commissioner Bugby the next day for an initial appearance, and March 16 was set as the date for preliminary examination.

News about the arrests spread quickly, and on March 16 a large crowd gathered in Commissioner Bugby's office for the hearing. The accused retained former Attorney General A. L. Hart and Grover Johnson, a leader of the California anti-Chinese movement, to represent them. (Coincidentally, two mammoth state anti-Chinese conventions, in one of which Johnson was playing a significant part, were underway in the state capital at this time.) There was no official U.S. government representative present, but a private attorney, A. C. Hinkson, of the Sacramento firm of Armstrong and Hinkson, a firm clearly under retainer to the Chinese, appeared to state the case against the accused. The official warrant for the arrest of the accused had spoken only of the general crime of conspiracy. It now emerged for the first time that the specific federal statute they were accused of violating was Section 5519 of the Revised Statutes of 1875. This seemed an odd choice. The statute, part of the Civil Rights Act of 1871,[26] made it a crime for individuals to conspire to deprive others of their right to the equal protection of the law. But the statute had been declared unconstitutional by the U.S. Supreme Court in the case of *United States v. Harris* decided three years earlier.[27] In *Harris* the Court had overturned the conviction of a group of white Tennesseans, convicted of violating the law for beating several blacks in criminal custody and killing one of them. The statute, said the Court, was aimed at purely private conduct and as such was not within Congress's power to enact under the Constitution. It was the same line of reasoning that would lead the court in its following term, in the *Civil Rights Cases*,[28] to declare unconstitutional Section 1 of the Civil Rights Act of 1875,[29] which established civil and criminal penalties for racially motivated interference with anyone's full and equal enjoyment of public accommodations and conveyances.

Needless to say, Attorneys Johnson and Hart demanded their clients' immediate release. To buttress their demand they produced a telegram from S. G. Hilborn, the U.S. attorney in San Francisco, under the same day's date, informing them that Judge Lorenzo Sawyer intended to telegraph Commissioner Bugby that Section 5519 was unconstitutional. The strong implication was that he would also shortly direct the commissioner to drop the case. "If case not promptly dismissed," Hilborn wired, "get continuance and I will attend to it."[30] The argument on the other side was rather weak. Hinkson made reference to Article VI of the Burlingame Treaty, which assured to Chinese living in the United States the same privileges and immunities with respect to residence and travel as those enjoyed by citizens of the most favored nation, but he did not elaborate very compellingly on how this provision worked to salvage an unconstitutional statute.[31]

Commissioner Bugby could not have helped but be impressed with the strength of the defendants' argument but indicated he was not disposed to dismiss the case without specific instructions from Judge Sawyer. They were not to come. Later in the hearing another telegram to Hart and Johnson from U.S. Attorney Hilborn disclosed that Judge Sawyer had elected simply to call Bugby's attention to the section's unconstitutionality, without mandating any particular outcome to the proceeding. Bugby determined that he would not dismiss the charges and remanded the defendants to the custody of the U.S. marshal.[32]

Habeas Corpus Hearings

Events now began to move quickly. The lawyers for the accused, no doubt as a precaution, had filed a petition for a writ of habeas corpus in

Sawyer's court the previous day and on March 16 a writ issued, returnable March 18. Not content with this avenue of relief, however, they decided to pursue a parallel course in the state courts. On the next day, March 17, they filed an application for a habeas writ in Sacramento Superior Court. Judge Van Fleet issued the writ, returnable the same day, but on hearing oral argument, decided that the case came within the rule of the pre-Civil War case of *Ableman v. Booth*[33] which had held that no state court could issue a writ of habeas corpus to release prisoners held in federal custody, and that he was without authority to consider the matter further.[34] The stage was now set for the hearing of the federal petition.

On the afternoon of March 18, Deputy Marshal Franks brought Thomas Baldwin before Judge Sawyer for the hearing on his habeas petition. (Attorneys for all sides had previously agreed that all of the Nicolaus defendants save one should be released and that one should be allowed to represent the class.) Hilborn was present as the nominal representative of the U.S. government, but it quickly emerged that the real responsibility for the conduct of this litigation on the government side now rested with private attorneys in the employ of the Chinese.[35] Hilborn engaged in some preliminary sparring with counsel for the petitioners on the form of the habeas petition but had nothing to say on the merits. Vice-Consul Bee, on the other hand, was present in court and informed the court that he had retained Hall McAllister to represent the Chinese interest in the case but that business engagements prevented him from being present. He asked that the hearing on the merits of the petition be postponed until the following week when McAllister could appear. The request was granted, but due to other continuances, the hearing did not take place until March 30.[36]

At the habeas hearing that took place on March 30 before Circuit Judge Sawyer and District Judge George Sabin, McAllister set forth for the first time in full the theory of the case against the Nicolaus conspirators. To be sure, McAllister conceded, the United States Supreme Court in *Harris* had nullified Section 5519 insofar as it applied to the conviction of the white Tennesseans. But, McAllister contended, the Court had voided the statute only insofar as it purported to apply to actions of citizens of the United States against other U.S. citizens. In *Harris* the Court had simply said that the ordinary criminal acts of one citizen against another were, under prevailing notions of federalism, the peculiar province of the states and could not be brought under the jurisdiction of the national government either on Thirteenth, Fourteenth, or Fifteenth Amendment grounds. (These were the supposed constitutional bases of the statute according to the attorneys for the government in *Harris*.) But, said McAllister, in the instant case, the prosecution rested on a wholly different set of constitutional premises. It was firmly established, he noted, that the national government had plenary powers to enter into treaties with foreign governments and that these treaties once concluded were the supreme law of the land. It was equally clear that under the "necessary and proper" clause of the Constitution (Art. I, Sec. 8) Congress had full power to pass legislation in implementation of agreements concluded by the national government. The United States had concluded treaties with the Chinese Empire in 1868 and again in 1880. Both treaties guaranteed subjects of China the right to reside and carry on trade in the United States and secured to them "all rights, privileges, immunities, and exemptions" enjoyed by the citizens of the most favored nation. The 1880 treaty had further pledged that the United States, should Chinese residents meet with ill treatment at the hands of other persons, would "devise measures" to protect them and to secure the aforesaid rights. Here, declared McAllister, was ample constitutional basis for the application of Section 5519 to the conspiracy in question in the case before the court. The statute could be viewed, post hoc as it were, as a measure taken in discharge of U.S. treaty obligations. McAllister did not contend that Congress had the Chinese in mind in enacting Section 2 of the Civil Rights Act of 1871, the source from which Section 5519 derived—such a claim would have found no support in the statute's legislative history—but that was not crucial to the argument. He seemed rather to be operating on the well-accepted principle that a law general enough in its terms could have unforeseen beneficiaries.[37]

For good measure, although he did not press the matter, McAllister threw in two other provisions of the Revised Statutes of 1875 which he claimed sanctioned a conspiracy prosecution against the Nicolaus group: Sections 5508 and 5336.[38] Section 5508 made it a federal crime for two or more persons to conspire to injure or oppress any citizen in the exercise of any right secured by the U.S. Constitution or for two or more persons to go in disguise on the highway or in the premises of another for the purpose of hindering that person in the free exercise of rights so secured. Section 5336 punished, among other things, conspiracies to hinder the federal government in the execution of its laws. (Both of these issues were to be forcefully argued on appeal. At this stage of the proceeding, however, they were distinctly in the background.)

Former Attorney General Hart, for the petitioners, vigorously contested these claims. Congress could not limit the powers of a state over ordinary criminal offenses, he declared, by the adoption of a treaty. If the McAllister argument were accepted, then in his view, it must follow that every crime or offense committed against a Chinese person in any state would have to be tried in a federal court. According to Hart, tortured and specious logic was being offered to try to salvage an obviously void and unconstitutional law. There appears to have been little questioning from the bench during oral argument and thus little indication from the judges as to the direction in which they might be leaning. But at the conclusion Circuit Judge Sawyer promised that the court would render its decision the next day.[39]

A large crowd assembled in Judge Sawyer's courtroom on March 31. Conspicuous in it were a number of leaders of the Chinese community. A reporter had commented in the previous day's San Francisco *Evening Post*: "The Chinese are basing high hopes on the result. . . . If the prayer for the writ is denied and the petitioner remanded, it will open the way to retaliatory arrests in every town in the state from which the Chinese have been evicted."[40] Sawyer sounded a similar note in the half-hour opinion which he read in open court.[41] The issue before the court, he declared, was "one of vast consequence to the entire Chinese population of the United States, and of the utmost importance to the peace and good order of society throughout the entire Pacific Coast."[42] Paying scant heed to the other sections of the Revised Statutes being offered as basis for the prosecution, he went straight to Section 5519 which he correctly recognized as the heart of the Chinese case.

> If this section . . . is valid as to Chinese subjects residing in the United States, and embraces the acts set out in the petition and return, then the acts of all public meetings throughout the land looking to, and providing for, depriving Chinese subjects of the rights, privileges, immunities, and exemptions secured to them . . . by means popularly known as "boycotting," or any other coercive means, no matter in what form, or through what channels applied, are criminal, and all those participating in them must be subject to the very severe penalties denounced by the statute.[43]

Sawyer found that the section did in fact apply to the Chinese and that as so applied it was saved from constitutional infirmity. Sawyer was persuaded by McAllister's argument concerning the availability of the treaty-making power as constitutional basis for the application of the enactment to the Chinese. The national government's treaty-making power was broad indeed, Sawyer affirmed, and easily comprehended the subject matter of the several treaties the United States had entered into with the Chinese Empire. These agreements secured to the Chinese a large array of rights, privileges, and immunities. That among these were the rights to select a place of residence and to pursue a lawful vocation at the place so selected seemed unarguable to him. (Sawyer relied heavily on his own opinion in the *Parrott* case[44] for the proposition that the right to pursue a lawful vocation was among the privileges secured to the Chinese by treaty.) He attached special importance to Article III of the Treaty of 1880 which read in full:

> If Chinese laborers, or Chinese of any other class, now either permanently or temporarily residing in the territory of the United States, meet with ill treatment at the hands of any other persons, the government of the United States will exert all its power to devise measures for their protection, and to secure to them the same rights, privileges, immunities, and exemptions as may be enjoyed by the citizens of subjects of the most favored nation, and to which they are entitled by treaty.[45]

Here two points stood out. First, the national government had voluntarily assumed the obligation to take affirmative steps to secure Chinese rights, privileges, and immunities. And secondly, it had undertaken to secure these rights against invasion not only by unfriendly state legislation but as well by *individual persons.* Section 5519 and the prosecution in the Nicolaus case could be seen as the government's discharge of the obligation it had undertaken by solemn international compact. Thus, Sawyer concluded, "[t]he case of the Chinese residents of Nicolaus is clearly distinguishable from that of United States citizens arising under the Fourteenth Amendment, considered in the case of *U.S. v. Harris* and rests upon other and further provisions of the national constitution."[46]

As to the argument advanced by counsel for the petitioner that if the Chinese view were accepted—namely, that they were protected by federal law against ordinary criminal acts—then this represented a severe undermining of the presumed state authority over its own citizens, Sawyer countered that the state had not in this instance surrendered power over its own citizens in their dealings with each other but only in their dealings with foreigners, a *legitimate* subject of national concern. And, Sawyer emphasized, this was a perfectly rational policy. "It is presumed that the state will protect its own citizens," he observed, "while long experience shows that it will not always protect foreigners against the prejudices and hatred of citizens."[47]

Sawyer recognized, however, that he now confronted an additional problem. It could be argued with great plausibility that Congress had the power under the Constitution to pass a law limited in its terms to protecting Chinese aliens resident in the United States in their treaty rights.

It might also plausibly be argued that the protection of the Chinese could be seen as coming under the general language of Section 5519 of the Revised Statutes. What clearly could not be maintained, however, was that Section 5519 was limited to the protection of Chinese rights and privileges. The statute clearly embraced other things as well, and it was precisely these other things that had caused the statute to fail constitutional muster in *Harris*. The question therefore now arose whether the inclusion of improper subject matter in the statute had vitiated the statute for *all* purposes. Or could the constitutional be separated from any unconstitutional parts of the law?

The U.S. Supreme Court had scarcely dealt with the issue of statutory separability or severability before the Civil War but had handed down a number of important opinions on the question in the immediately preceding decade. Sawyer touched on most of these—lightly, it must fairly be said—in his analysis. The case on which he most heavily relied was *Packet Co. v. City of Keokuk*.[48] In this 1877 opinion the high tribunal had sustained against challenge on commerce clause grounds a city ordinance of Keokuk, Iowa, which provided for the charging of fees to vessels moored on the city's wharves on the Mississippi River. Conceding that the ordinance as drafted was subject to a broad interpretation, which would make it constitutionally infirm (it charged fees for docking on the unimproved river bank as well as at the city's wharves), the court chose to give it a narrow interpretation, which brought it well within the bounds of constitutionality. The Court had said in *Keokuk*: "Statutes that are constitutional in part only, will be upheld so far as they are not in conflict with the constitution, provided the allowed and prohibited parts are severable."[49] Sawyer read the case as standing for the proposition that courts ought to go out of their way to find such severability of parts, and he did not experience too much difficulty in finding it in Section 5519 so far as it applied to the case at bar. The key was the ethnic distinctness of the Chinese.

> Chinese subjects residing in the United States constitute a separate, distinct independent class, with distinctly defined and easily recognized limits; and it is not readily perceived why the *class* may not be easily segregated, and the provisions of the statute held constitutional and valid and be fully enforced as to that class, even though void as to other persons and classes, relying on other provisions of the constitution, easily recognized, and without difficulty segregated.[50]

Sawyer recognized, however, that he was not on the firmest of grounds in reaching this determination. There was authority supportive of the view that courts ought not to go out of the way to carve constitutional enclaves out of statutes that were in the aggregate unconstitutional and that the principle of severability ought to be sparingly applied. He was frank in acknowledging this. But he felt constrained, he said, to resolve doubts in favor of the validity of the statutes as it was sought to be applied in the instant case.[51] Sawyer noted that his associate, Judge Sabin, "though with doubt and hesitation," dissented from his ruling, and he assured counsel that a certificate of division of opinion would be made and a writ of error allowed to the U.S. Supreme Court if either party desired it.[52] Indeed he practically invited such a motion. This was a matter which ought quickly, authoritatively and finally to be determined by the Supreme Court. "The specific questions now presented are questions of too vast consequence to be finally determined by a subordinate court," he declared. If a writ of error was taken, he added, the prisoner would be allowed to go at large on his own recognizance. In the meantime he suggested that the government not prosecute "other similar cases" until an authoritative decision could be had.[53] Following upon Sawyer's suggestion, a joint request for a certificate or division of opinion was made by both sides. The request was granted, and the prisoner Baldwin was freed on his own recognizance.

Sawyer sent the case record and opinion on to the Department of Justice with a plea that it be docketed and submitted at the Supreme Court's present term. "I can imagine no case that so urgently requires prompt action," he wrote. "This whole coast is inflamed by active men who are organizing to perpetrate similar outrages. If there is any law making such action criminal, it ought to be authoritatively declared."[54] Stipulation was obtained from counsel to place the case immediately on the Court's calendar and to submit it for decision on the basis of written briefs.[55] Within a month the matter was briefed and under submission.

The Argument on Appeal

Former Attorney General A. L. Hart did not deal with the severability question at all in his argument to the high court. His brief on appeal simply restated the position which counsel for the Nicolaus detainees had repeatedly made in the proceedings below. Section 5519 of the Revised Statutes, under which the plaintiff-in-error was being prosecuted, Hart argued, was unconstitutional and void for all purposes. The subjects upon which Congress could legislate were clearly specified in the Constitution. Upon these it could legislate generally without reference to the persons whose rights it sought to protect. Upon other subjects, however, it could not legislate at all. Conspiracies by private persons against other private persons lay beyond the reach of congressional power. Such conspiracies as well as the underlying offenses were the exclusive preserve of the states. Nor had the conclusion of treaties with China changed the picture. "It was not intended [by the Burlingame Treaty]," Hart declared, "to create the possibility of two systems of municipal law, the one passed by Congress and enforced in the Federal Courts and applicable to Chinese alone; the other passed by the Legislatures of the States, enforceable in the State courts and applicable to citizens as well as aliens."[56] Acceptance of the opposite view by the court would amount to an endorsement of the position that it was possible, by entering into a treaty, to change the nature and form of the U.S. government, a manifest absurdity.

McAllister took an interesting tack in his argument. As noted earlier, in the proceedings below, he had raised the question of the applicability of two other federal laws, Sections 5508 and 5336 of the Revised Statutes, to the Nicolaus incident. But the argument had not been pushed very far and discussion of the provisions had been completely overshadowed by the debate on Section 5519. (In his opinion Sawyer had devoted a scant few lines to them without reaching any firm conclusions.) McAllister now chose to highlight these statutes and to press vigorously for their applicability. His analysis of them consumed the first two-thirds of this brief.

Section 5508, which derived from the Civil Rights Act of 1870,[57] provided for the punishment of those who conspired "to injure, oppress, threaten, or intimidate any citizen in the free exercise or enjoyment of any right or privilege secured to him by the Constitution or laws of the United States" and of those who went in disguise on the highway, or on the premises of another with intent to hinder the exercise of such rights. There was no question about the statute's constitutionality, and, relying on the premise that the right to reside on American soil and to pursue a peaceful avocation were federal rights secured to the Chinese by the several treaties with China (by the laws of the United States, in other words), McAllister submitted that the actions of the Nicolaus mob were on their face a violation of the statute's terms.[58] Section 5336 derived ultimately from the Act of July 31, 1861, a measure passed in the wake of the Southern Secession.[59] It provided for the punishment of those who conspired to overthrow the government of the United States or "to oppose by force the authority thereof" or "by force to prevent, hinder, or delay the execution of any law of the United States." Conspiracies to deprive the Chinese of their treaty rights were in effect conspiracies to prevent, hinder, or delay the execution of federal laws, in this case treaties, he contended. And here he was able to call to his aid the authority of a well known and highly respected member of the federal bench. As noted above, on

March 2 U.S. District Judge Matthew Deady had empaneled a federal grand jury for the purpose of hearing cases against the Oregon City anti-Chinese rioters. In instructing the grand jury members later in the month he had told them that if they found that any of the parties brought before them had maltreated or intimidated the Chinese for the purpose of compelling them to leave their rightful places of residence that would amount to an attempt to prevent the execution of federal laws and would come within the terms of Section 5336.[60]

On the question of Section 5519's constitutionality, McAllister did little more than embellish on the argument which he had made to Judge Sawyer, founding authorization for the statute on the treaty-making provisions of the original Constitution. The *Harris* case, he argued, had addressed a completely separate issue and ought to be limited as authority to the single point it decided. And he cited the authority of the great constitutional commentator Thomas Cooley for the proposition that a legislative act might be clearly void as to some categories of cases and clearly valid as to others.[61]

The Supreme Court Decision

Despite the pleas for urgent action, it was almost a year before the Supreme Court rendered its decision. Chief Justice Morrison R. Waite delivered the opinion of the Court on March 7, 1887.[62] At the outset he conceded the validity of a major point advanced by counsel for the Chinese. He was fully convinced of Congress's plenary power to legislate to protect Chinese interests in this country. "That the United States have power under the Constitution to provide for the punishment of those who are guilty of depriving Chinese subjects of any of the rights, privileges, immunities or exemptions guaranteed to them by . . . treaty, we do not doubt," he wrote.[63] What the Court had to decide, however, according to Waite, was not whether Congress could legislate to protect the Chinese but whether it had in fact done so in the sections of the Revised Statutes under consideration.[64] He addressed each section in turn, giving most attention to Section 5519, which, as he noted, was clearly the main basis for the prosecution.[65]

The Court was not persuaded by McAllister's attempt to salvage the section for the purpose of protecting the Chinese. To be sure, the Court accepted the principle that a statute could be in part constitutional and in part unconstitutional and that the constitutional part might be capable of enforcement. But such would be the case, in the Court's view, only where the parts were so distinctly separable that each could stand alone and where the Court could find that the intention of the legislature was that "the part pronounced valid should be enforceable, even though the other part should fail."[66] The problem with Section 5519 was that it had no parts. "A single provision, which makes up the whole section," Waite wrote, "embraces those who conspire against citizens as well as those who conspire against aliens."[67] The case of *United States v. Reese*[68] offered guidance on the question. There two Kentucky election inspectors had been indicted under Sections 3 and 4 of the Civil Rights Act of 1870, which punished voting inspectors for any wrongful refusal to receive the votes of citizens. There was nothing in either section to limit its operation to wrongful refusals to accept votes on the basis of race or color, something that Congress would have been constitutionally empowered to do, and for this reason they were held to be void. They were too broad in their coverage, comprehending subject matter that was both within and without the jurisdiction of the Congress. The Court there had refused to limit the statute by construction so as to make it operate only on that which Congress might rightfully prohibit, holding that to do so would be "to make a new law, not to enforce an old one."[69]

Packet Co. v. Keokuk, the case on which Sawyer had relied to find severability,[70] presented a problem for this line of reasoning. There, as in *Reese,* one had a single statutory provision, broad enough to be applied in constitutional and unconstitutional fashion, but the Court had allowed the ordinance to stand. But for Waite the crucial distinction was that *Keokuk* involved the contestation of a civil ordinance regulating wharfage fees and not a penal statute.[71] Apparently stricter application of the severability test was appropriate when penal laws were in question.

With respect to Section 5519, one final point needs noticing. The Court commented that it had not been called upon to decide, and was not deciding, whether Section 5519 was separable to the extent that it could be enforced in a territory even though it could not be enforced in a state.[72]

The Court found that Sections 5508 and 5336 were simply not applicable. By its language Section 5508 punished those who conspired to injure or intimidate "citizens" in the exercise of their rights, but in its second part it used ostensibly more general language, making it a crime to go on the premises "of another" with intent to hinder that person's free exercise of federally protected rights. According to Waite the second part was of a piece with the first and was limited in its application to wrongs committed against "citizens," which the Chinese clearly were not.[73] As to Section 5536, which made it a crime to interfere by force with the execution of any law of the United States, the Court held that to come under the section, force must be brought to bear directly against the government, the application of force against private individuals in frustration of federal governmental purposes being insufficient.[74]

Justices Harlan and Field dissented from the majority opinion. Harlan was convinced of Section 5508's applicability. The use of the term "another" instead of "citizen" in the latter clause of the section, he wrote, showed that in respect of the rights and privileges secured by the section, Congress had in mind the protection of persons whether citizens or not. (In this sense the section's language was a little like that of the Fourteenth Amendment.) Baldwin and his confederates had certainly gone "on the premises of another" with the intent to interfere with rights secured by the law of the land.[75]

Field, albeit somewhat tentatively, associated himself with Harlan's interpretation, but he preferred to found his dissent, a powerful and plausible one, on Section 5336. The third clause of that section, which punished conspiracies to prevent by force the execution of any law of the United States was clearly applicable in his view. The stipulations of the various treaties with China, guaranteeing to Chinese aliens in this country the rights of residence and labor, were in his view the law of the land, operating by their own force and requiring no further legislative action for their enforcement. "The right or privilege being conferred by the treaty," he went on, "parties seeking to enjoy it take whatever steps are necessary to carry the provisions into effect. . . . Those who wish to reside here select their places of residence, no congressional legislation being required to provide that they shall enjoy the rights and privileges stipulated. . . . All that is needed, is such legislation as may be necessary to protect them in such enjoyment."[76] And that, according to Field, they had in Section 5336's provision punishing conspiracies to hinder by force the execution of federal laws. The Nicolaus conspirators well knew, as everyone did, that Chinese aliens were guaranteed the rights of residence by solemnly executed national compact. Their actions, Field argued, were aimed not just at their particular victims but at Chinese *as a class*. Their purpose was to nullify the rights conferred on this class of persons by a treaty executed by the national government. What could be a clearer case of a conspiracy against the supremacy and authority of the United States.[77] Field sounded an alarming note at the end of his opinion.

> The result of the decision is that there is no national law which can be invoked for the protection of the subjects of China in their right to reside and do business in this country, notwithstanding the language of the treaty with that empire. . . . Their only protection against any forcible resistance to the execution of these stipulations in their favor is to be found in the laws of the different states. Such a result is one to be deplored.[78]

Press reaction to the *Baldwin* decision was varied. Several eastern newspapers, while not objecting to the decision, took Congress severely to task for not passing laws to protect the Chinese, commenting that it was vain to expect that they could secure protection from the western states.[79] Needless to say, the opinion stirred lively comment on the Pacific Coast, some of it, surprisingly, sympathetic to the Chinese cause. The Sacramento *Record-Union*, for example, a Republican paper which like all organs of opinion on the coast was urging severe restrictions on Chinese immigration but which was terrified of vigilantism and mob violence, deplored the decision, commenting that Justice Field had stated the correct view of things.[80] The *Daily Alta California*, a like-minded journal, also supported Field's dissent but added that Congress should pass laws to make good on its treaty obligations to the Chinese.[81] Perhaps more consonant with general public opinion was the editorial which appeared the day after the decision in the San Francisco *Evening Post*. "This decision is a subject for congratulation, without regard to the merits of the particular case involved," wrote the *Post*, heaving a giant sigh of relief as it were that the judicial branch was at last beginning to turn a deaf ear to Chinese complaints. "It is desirable, of course, that affairs like that at Nicolaus should be prevented," the paper continued, "but it is not desirable that United States courts should have a *confirmed* habit of interfering with the legal machinery of California whenever the interests of a Chinaman are involved. We can take care of ourselves and our Chinamen, too."[82]

Baldwin was, jurisprudentially speaking, a very long shot indeed. The Chinese were calling on the Court to resurrect a statute three years dead and buried, something rarely attempted in constitutional litigation. When the Chinese entered the legal lists, it was normally with firmer hopes of success. But the times were extremely dangerous, and, with no other avenues of recourse seemingly available, it was urgent that some action be taken.[83] Initiating litigation, even on frail grounds, if it did nothing else, may at least have seemed to them to serve as a signal to white society that they did not intend to remain supine in the face of the ominous forces that threatened them. (It is worth noting that at the same time the *Baldwin* case was progressing through the courts, a group of Chinese merchants were pressing an action for damages for negligence in the circuit court against the city government of Eureka, California, for failing to protect them and their property against a mob.)[84] And of course it must be remembered that, despite the odds, the Chinese prevailed in the first phase of the litigation, and that though they lost on appeal, they did not come away completely empty-handed. For the Court had made clear that it was reserving judgment on whether Section 5519 could be enforced in the territories. This was significant as some of the greatest outrages perpetrated against the Chinese, the Rock Springs massacre for example, had occurred in federal territories. Much more important, the Court had declared unequivocally that it was entirely within the constitutional authority of the Congress to enact legislation providing for the punishment of those who were guilty of depriving Chinese subjects of any of the rights of privileges that had been guaranteed them by treaty. With this dictum in mind, perhaps, the Chinese minister left a memorandum at the State Department on March 18, 1887, containing the draft of some provisions of a proposed new treaty between China and the United States. The draft envisioned a much more active role for the federal government in the protection of Chinese residents in the United States. In his gloss on its provisions, the minister suggested that Congress enact a law imposing the death penalty on anti-Chinese conspirators. The Supreme Court in its *Baldwin* opinion, the minister remarked, had sanctioned the spirit of his suggestions.[85]

The Supreme Court may have removed all constitutional obstacles in the way of federal legislation to protect the Chinese, but it could do nothing to remove the political obstacles standing in the way of such laws. Congress was in no mood to consider any such measures. Fortunately, rioting and violence against the Chinese did subside somewhat toward the end of the year, and Congress, grudgingly and without admitting any liability, did eventually appropriate a total of some $425,000 for the compensation of the survivors of the Rock Springs, Wyoming riot and of other anti-Chinese disturbances. The money was distributed to victims and survivors under the supervision of the San Francisco consulate.

8 Federal Exclusion Act Litigation

The Second Phase

The Scott Act and the Chinese Exclusion Cases

THE EXCLUSION TREATY OF 1888

Events like the massacre in Rock Springs and the expulsion of the Chinese from Nicolaus and other western towns during the winter of 1885–86 convinced the Chinese government that there was no hope of achieving security for Chinese laborers in the United States and that it would have to take steps of its own to limit emigration. As the Chinese foreign office put it in a note to the British minister at Peking, "[The] prejudice of the people of the United States against the Chinese laborers is so intense that it is next to impossible to remove it."[1] Accordingly, on August 3, 1886, the foreign office presented the U.S. State Department with a proposal for a new treaty under which the imperial government would prohibit its subjects from emigrating to the United States and deny Chinese laborers who had returned to China the right to go back to that country unless they had family, property, or monetary claims outstanding there. In exchange it proposed that the U.S. government promise to take new steps to assure the safety of Chinese still resident in the United States.[2]

The negotiation of a new accord proved difficult and took many months. The main sticking point was the right of return of Chinese laborers who had once been in the United States. Under the old treaty, of course, this right had been guaranteed. The United States initially insisted on an absolute prohibition on the return of all laborers, while the Chinese wished to make an exception for those who had property or relations in the United States. There was also considerable discussion of what steps the U.S. government should take to protect its resident Chinese. At length, in March 1888, the two sides reached agreement. The new treaty provided that for a period of twenty years the immigration or return of Chinese laborers was to be prohibited. An exception was made for Chinese laborers who had wives, children, or parents in the United States or property or debts of at least $1,000. The United States, for its part, reaffirmed its obligation to secure protection for the persons and property of Chinese resident in the United States. The Senate amended the agreement to make explicit what was already implicit in it, namely that the treaty's prohibition applied even to Chinese who possessed return certificates, but made no significant substantive changes. On May 12, 1888, China's minister to the United States, Chang Yin-huan, informed Secretary of State Thomas Bayard that the amended agreement met with his approval and that he was forwarding it to his government for ratification.[3] Then matters began to unravel. When news of the new accord reached China in the summer of 1888 it met with a storm of opposition, especially in Kwangtung province. It was attacked in newspaper editorials and there were mass demonstrations against it. The agreement was also denounced by Chinese in the United States.[4] Shaken by all of this the Chinese foreign office informed the U.S. minister to Peking in September that it would refuse to ratify the agreement unless the immigration limitation period was shortened and more liberal provisions were made for the return of Chinese laborers with property in the United States.[5]

THE PASSAGE OF THE SCOTT ACT

In the meantime, before affairs reached this juncture, the U.S. Congress, in a move probably designed to put pressure on the Chinese government to end its delays, had already enacted legislation to implement the treaty's terms. The measure was approved by the two houses on September 11 and signed by the president on September 13. By its terms it was to go into effect upon the exchange of ratifications between the two countries.[6] When shortly afterward it became clear that the Chinese government was not going to ratify the treaty, the Congress took matters into its own hands. Congressman William Scott of Pennsylvania, chairman of the Democratic National Campaign Committee (it was a presidential election year and the electoral votes of the western states were expected to be crucial) quickly introduced a bill to accomplish unilaterally through legislation the results the United States was seeking to accomplish through diplomatic negotiation. A short measure, it provided that no Chinese laborer, irrespective of former residence in the United States, should ever enter the country. It forbade the issuance of any new return certificates and voided all then in existence. The bill, it will be noted, was harsher than the new treaty in two respects. It permanently forbade the immigration of laborers instead of suspending it for twenty years, and it made no allowance for the return of laborers with property holdings or family. The bill passed the House without debate and without a single dissenting vote.

The Scott bill did provoke some debate in the Senate. A few senators complained that this was the first time in American diplomatic history that legislative action was being used to scuttle a treaty with a friendly power. Secretary of State Bayard was greatly distressed with the congressional action and sought to persuade President Cleveland to veto the measure. ("The treatment of the Chinese question by Congress is most discreditable and mortifying," he wrote to a friend. "It has depressed and disgusted me greatly.")[7] Cleveland, however, bowing to what he perceived to be irresistible forces, decided to sign the measure, and the Scott bill became the Scott Act on October 1.[8]

There were mass demonstrations up and down the state of California to celebrate the passage of the Scott bill. The Democratic State Central Committee ordered a one-hundred gun salute. The chairman of the Republican State Committee, not to be outdone, urged Congress to pass a yet harsher law, under which all Chinese residents would be required to register and carry on their persons certificates of identification. If found without one they would be subject to immediate deportation.[9] As had happened with each preceding restriction measure important Caucasian voices were again heard saying that now, at long last, the Chinese question was settled. "Every bill that has thus far been framed succumbed to the artifices of the slave-dealers and their lawyers. In the Scott bill we have a law that is invulnerable," the assistant United States attorney responsible for Chinese immigration cases was quoted by a reporter for the *Morning Call* as saying.[10]

Consul Bee expressed outrage at the enactment, which he termed an insult to China and to the Chinese in the United States. "The law is a discrimination against a class, and as such reflects no credit on the boasted American freedom." As to what was to be done about it, he would wait, he said, for instructions from his government.[11] Judge Hoffman, the senior federal magistrate then in town, predicted that the Chinese would soon seek to test the measure in court.[12]

CHAE CHAN PING V. UNITED STATES

News of the Scott Act's passage was quickly disseminated in the Chinese community and occasioned much commotion in the population, as well it might have. The effect of the act was of course to make it impossible for any Chinese laborer then in the United States to ever visit China and return to this country.[13] (Given the manner in which immigration officials were interpreting the law, it must have planted doubts in the minds of merchants about their own return prospects as well.) The great mass of the Chinese community resident in the United States was thus now to be faced with the unpleasant choice of permanent separation from family and friends or a permanent return to the mean existence of their native land. The only question was how and when the challenge would be brought.

One contemporary estimate put the number of Chinese holding return certificates at the time of the Scott Act's passage at thirty thousand.[14] Among these were several hundreds actually en route at the time to the United States. In his message to Congress approving the act, President Cleveland had suggested that in the interest of justice and fairness some allowance ought to be made for them. He was vague, however, as to what he had in mind.[15] The collector of customs for the port of San Francisco did not seem disposed to be flexible. He did allow some hundred Chinese who arrived in the port on September 30, the day before the act went into effect, to land, but on October 4 he had posted on the doors of the Customs House a notice stating that "the Chinese Exclusion Act is in full force and operation . . . and it applies to Chinese laborers who have arrived in the United States since its passage."[16]

The first ship carrying Chinese with return certificates to arrive in San Francisco after the passage of the act was the steamship *Belgic,* which made port on October 7. The collector informed the Chinese passengers on board that their certificates were null and void and that they would not be allowed to land. The Chinese consul general, who had met the ship, registered his strong protest and telegraphed the news of what had happened to the legation in Washington.[17] Attorneys for the Chinese now had the makings of a test case but, it appears, did not wish to begin proceedings until Circuit Judge Lorenzo Sawyer then away in Oregon returned to San Francisco. (Beginning proceedings in the circuit court instead of the district court would eliminate one level of judicial review and shorten the time it would take the case to get to the Supreme Court.) District Judge Hoffman, however, seems to have been anxious to start events in motion and on October 11 summoned Thomas Riordan (described in the paper that reported the story as "the attorney for the Six Companies") and suggested that he make application in the district court immediately for two habeas writs, one for a prior resident aboard the vessel, the other for a "certificated Chinese," thereby bringing both issues up for decision. Before Riordan could act on this suggestion Judge Sawyer returned so the habeas proceeding was begun in his court.[18]

The man chosen by the Chinese to test the new federal law was as well suited as any to do so. Chae Chan Ping had first arrived in California in 1875 and lived there continuously until June 1887 when he had sailed for China, in possession of a laborer's return certificate, duly issued by the collector of the port of San Francisco. He left China for San Francisco on September 7, 1888, aboard the *Belgic* and arrived in that city a month later. He had thus been at sea when the Scott Act went into effect and had had no notice of its passage. Recognizing that the decision would inevitably be appealed to the U.S. Supreme Court and anxious to get an authoritative ruling from that tribunal as soon as possible, Judge Sawyer moved immediately to hear the case. On October 12 and 13, in a courtroom jammed with both Caucasian and Chinese spectators, Sawyer and District Judge Hoffman heard a battery of attorneys for the Chinese attack the Scott Act as, variously, a deprivation of rights indefeasibly vested in the petitioner under the treaty (the certificate, it was urged, was a contract between the petitioner and the United States government) and an ex post facto law. The U.S. attorney argued vigorously against all of these contentions.[19] Two days after the close of argument Sawyer handed down the court's decision.

To call the petitioner's certificate a contract, said Sawyer, would be an abuse of language. It was only evidence of his identity. If there was any contract in this whole affair it ran only between the government of the United States and that of China, and any rights that the petitioner had were derivative of the treaty those two countries had entered into and congressional laws passed in pursuance thereof. But, he went on, it was a well-recognized principle of American constitutional jurisprudence that acts of Congress were on the same plane and entitled to the same judicial respect as treaties and if a treaty and law conflicted the latter of the two prevailed.[20] Sawyer gave equally short shrift to the contention that the act was an ex post facto law. Ex post facto laws were those that made criminal acts that had been legal when performed. But the exclusion act could not be construed as criminal legislation. It simply represented a change in public policy by the Congress of the United States.[21] In a couple of places in the opinion Sawyer noted that he had reservations about the wisdom and justice of the legislation before him, but he made clear he had no doubt as to its constitutionality.[22]

The Chinese who heard Sawyer read his decision greeted it with "weeping and wailing," commented the reporter for the *Evening Bulletin*. "Their great hope that the new exclusion law would be killed [has] received its death blow." he said. Conversely, there was great enthusiasm among the Caucasians present. None reacted more enthusiastically than C. C. O'Donnell, a notorious anti-Chinese agitator. "I have been preaching the anti-Chinese gospel for a great many years, and I tell you it's quite pleasant now to know that the battle is about over." He suggested that the next item on the agenda ought to be the removal of the Chinese in San Francisco outside the city limits.[23]

The same day the court handed down its decision Riordan filed a notice of appeal to the U.S. Supreme Court. To pursue the appeal the Chinese retained two lawyers of national renown, George Hoadley, the former Democratic governor of Ohio and a seasoned Supreme Court advocate, and James Carter of New York, one of the giants of the late nineteenth-century American bar. Hoadley and Carter argued the case orally for the appellant and filed a very lengthy brief on his behalf. Carter filed a separate, shorter brief, summarizing its main points. Harvey Brown and Thomas Riordan weighed in with a short brief of their own.

Although the question of Congress's right to override treaties had never been presented to the Court in quite so precise a form as it was in this case, the tribunal had spoken to the matter generally on several previous occasions and had left little doubt as to what its answer was.[24] Indeed, in the same term in which it decided *Chew Heong*[25] it had held unequivocally that treaties were on no higher a plane than federal laws and could be modified or repealed by Congress at will.[26] What was still quite unclear, however, was what effect the abrogation of a treaty might have on rights or privileges obtained under it. Counsel for the Chinese concentrated on this question in their arguments. They contended that the appellant had a vested right to return to the United States and that he could not be divested of this right by mere legislation. They cited, among other authorities, the old case of *Society for the Propagation of the Gospel v. New Haven*[27] which had said that the termination of a treaty does not divest property rights already vested under it. "Is the liberty of those who enjoy or have been promised our hospitality less sacred, less entitled to legal protection than their property?" asked counsel.[28] In the alternative they argued that the appellant had a contract with the U.S. government under which it had covenanted with certain Chinese laborers that they should be able to return to this country if they left and that the government could not now go back on this promise. As authority for this position they relied heavily on *The Sinking Fund Cases*, decided in 1878, where the Court had affirmed that the United States was as a matter of "due process" constitutionally bound to honor its own contracts, notwithstanding the fact that the "impairment of contracts" clause of the Constitution applied by its terms only to the states.[29]

The basic argument of all three briefs filed by the United States was the same: the appellant's residence in the United States was a matter of permission or indulgence and not a matter of right and this permission was revocable at any time at the will of the Congress. As the solicitor general put it in his brief, "The law gave him the privilege, and the repeal of the law has taken it away."[30]

Justice Stephen Field, appropriately enough, delivered the opinion for a unanimous Court on May 13, 1889. It was quite plain, Field conceded at the outset, that the 1888 act was in clear contravention of the 1868 and 1880 treaties with China, but, he went on, that fact in and of itself was of no consequence since the Court had already said that treaties could be contravened by congressional acts. A certain moral obloquy might attach to one nation's disregarding its solemnly undertaken obligations to another, but, Field noted, "[t]his court is not a censor of the morals of other departments of the government."[31] But was there anything in the Constitution that would prevent the Congress from divesting the appellant and others similarly situated of the right he had been granted to leave the United States and return? Not at all, Field declared. The appellant was an alien and it was unthinkable that the United States did not have the plenary power to exclude aliens from its territory. To say otherwise would be to say that it was not invested with the full attributes of national sovereignty. If the United States could exclude paupers and criminals from its shores, there was nothing that would prevent it from excluding foreigners of a different race, unwilling to assimilate with the Caucasian population and perceived to be a danger to its peace and security.[32] The power of exclusion being an incident of sovereignty, it could not be limited by treaty on behalf of anyone. What Chinese laborers with return certificates had obtained prior to the act of October 1888 was a license, "held at the will of the government, revocable at any time, at its pleasure."[33] The only rights created by treaty that might survive the passage of abrogating legislation, declared Field, were such as were connected with property. And, he went on, "Between property rights not affected by the termination or abrogation of a treaty, and expectations of benefits from the continuance of existing legislation, there is as wide a difference as between realization and hopes."[34]

Two months after the decision the Chinese minister wrote to Secretary of State James G. Blaine, expressing his complete surprise at the conclusion the Supreme Court had come to in the case. "You will pardon me Mr. Secretary," he declared, "if I express my amazement that such a doctrine should be published to the world by the august tribunal for whose members by personal acquaintance I entertain such profound respect. It forces upon me the conviction that in the three years I have resided in this country, I have not been able fully and correctly to comprehend the principles and systems of your great government." He expressed the hope that some way could be found to compensate any Chinese who would suffer losses as a result of the treaty's breach.[35]

WAN SHING V. UNITED STATES AND *LAU OW BEW V. UNITED STATES*

Chae Chan Ping had established beyond doubt that no Chinese of the laboring classes should ever be allowed to enter or return to the United States once departed. What had not been dealt with in the decision was what effect if any the 1888 act had had on the return rights of merchants. Two cases decided by the Supreme Court in 1891 addressed that question. One, a case whose origins and procedural history are somewhat murky, involved a Chinese youth who had arrived in San Francisco on August 7, 1889, seeking to land on the grounds that he was a returning merchant. He was refused permission and through a friend petitioned for a writ of habeas corpus. At a hearing conducted by a court commissioner the petitioner introduced testimony tending to show that he was the son of a San Francisco merchant who had assisted the bookkeeper in his father's business before returning to China, but the commissioner was not convinced and recommended that he be remanded to custody pending return to China. This recommendation was confirmed by the circuit court, and the decision went up to the Supreme Court on appeal. On May 11, 1891, Justice Field handed down the Court's decision. (What the petitioner was doing in the almost two years that elapsed between the application for the habeas writ and the Supreme Court decision is quite unclear from the record.)[36]

The appellant's case, Field declared, rested entirely upon his ability to show that he was not a laborer. By the act of July 5, 1884, he went on, it was provided that a Chinese not of the laboring classes seeking to enter the United States should obtain the permission of the Chinese government or of the government of the foreign country of which he might at the time be a subject. Indeed that was made the sole evidence permissible to establish a right of entry. This clause, said Field, disposed of the question before the Court. The petitioner had presented no such governmental certificate.[37] The total effect of the anti-Chinese legislation enacted by the Congress during the previous decade, said Field, was that no Chinese laborer should henceforth ever enter the country and that all other Chinese, except diplomats, would have to produce a Chinese governmental certificate or a certificate from the foreign country of which they happened to be subjects, properly visaed by a U.S. representative, in order to enter.[38] Field here seemed to be rejecting the gloss put on the Chinese Exclusion

Acts by Judge Sawyer in the circuit court case of *Ah Ping* and indeed the one he himself had expressed in the 1882 circuit court case of *Low Yam Chow,* two cases discussed in chapter 6. Under the interpretation of the exclusion legislation adopted in those cases Chinese merchants having their commercial domicile in the United States or in countries other than China were not to be required to procure certificates from the Chinese government establishing their character as merchants but were to be free to prove their merchant status by any legitimate means.

Several months after the *Wan Shing* decision came down, another occasion arose to obtain clarification on the question of the return rights of domiciled Chinese merchants. In this instance the facts were not in dispute. Lau Ow Bew, a Portland, Oregon merchant of some seventeen years standing, had arrived in San Francisco on August 11, 1891, after a temporary visit to relatives in China. He had in his possession proof of his merchant status issued to him on his departure by the collector of the port. He was nonetheless refused permission to land on the grounds that he did not possess the certificate specified in the 1884 act. He promptly applied for a habeas writ in the district court, and the U.S. attorney sought and was granted leave to intervene. The case, said the San Francisco *Chronicle,* was being brought by the Chinese Consulate "to secure an interpretation of the decision rendered by Justice Field."[39]

The United States Circuit Court for the Northern District ordered the petitioner remanded to custody, citing the authority of *Wan Shing.*[40] An appeal to the Ninth Circuit Court of Appeals followed shortly thereafter, but that court affirmed the decision of the district court, holding likewise that *Wan Shing* had already settled the question of merchants' return rights.[41] Counsel for the Chinese thereupon made application for a writ of certiorari to the Supreme Court of the United States, asking that court to review the lower court decision under the new discretionary jurisdiction conferred on it by the recently enacted Evarts Act.[42] (Prior to that legislation all cases were appealable to the Supreme Court as a matter of right.) In an opinion handed down November 16, 1891, the Court ordered the writ to be issued, citing the gravity and importance of the question raised by the case. Commenting on *Wan Shing,* the Court declared that in that case the appellant appeared not to have obtained commercial domicile in the United States in the first place or, if he had, to have forfeited it by his absence from the country for so long a period of time. Upon that state of facts, said the Court, the precise question of the return rights of domiciled Chinese merchants had not presented itself for definitive disposition.[43] The attorneys for the Chinese had managed to overcome a rather large procedural obstacle and the status of Chinese merchants under the

1888 act was now in a posture to be argued anew (or perhaps, better said, argued fully for the first time) on the merits.

In their brief, counsel for the Chinese argued that Section 6 of the 1884 act was not intended to apply to Chinese merchants domiciled in this country who went to China on brief visits. They laid great stress on the words appearing in the section, "and who shall be about to come to the United States," contending that they seemed clearly aimed at Chinese merchants domiciled in China who were seeking to come to this country for the first time. To suppose otherwise, they declared, would be to ascribe a certain lack of logic to Congress. How, they asked, could a government official in China be expected to certify that Lau Ow Bew was a merchant in Portland?[44] In support of their interpretation they were able to introduce no less an ally than the U.S. Treasury Department, which, it turned out, had adopted exactly this view of things in the regulations it had issued on July 3, 1890. Treasury had there suggested that Chinese merchants about to leave the United States on temporary business should, before leaving, supply themselves here with papers showing their merchant status.[45] It was a deftly constructed legal argument, and it struck a responsive chord in the high court. On March 14, 1892, Chief Justice Fuller, speaking for a unanimous bench, ordered the petitioner, Lau Ow Bew, discharged from custody.

Beginning with the proposition that statutes should be interpreted in such a fashion as not to lead to unjust or absurd conclusions—a proposition which the chief justice noted Justice Field had himself cited in the circuit court case of *Low Yam Chow*—Fuller went on to analyze the relevant statutory provision.[46] Section 6 of the amendatory act of 1884 declared that "every Chinese person, other than a laborer, who may be entitled to come to the United States, and who shall be about to come, should be so identified by the Chinese government." But, accepting the argument of counsel for Lau Ow Bew, the Court held that Chinese merchants going to China for temporary purposes, and with the intention of returning, could not be fit into this category without running afoul of the above-stated principle of construction. Congress could not have intended, the Court declared, that resident Chinese merchants should lose rights guaranteed by treaty if they failed to produce evidence which circumstances would have made it difficult if not impossible to obtain.[47] The Court cited Sawyer's *Ah Ping* decision with approval and again sought to distinguish *Wan Shing*, holding that the Chinese subject in that case was either a laborer or by virtue of prolonged absence had forfeited his merchant domicile in the United States. Unlike Lau Ow Bew, he was not in the position of a merchant returning to a commercial home he had temporarily left.[48] It was a significant victory for the Chinese, but, as events would have it, it would be far overshadowed by another opinion handed down the following year by the high tribunal. It is to this decision, probably the most important Exclusion Act decision ever handed down by the Court, that we now turn our attention.

The Geary Act and Its Aftermath

THE ORIGINS OF THE GEARY ACT

In the late fall of 1890 a congressional delegation consisting of members of the Senate Committee on Immigration and the House Select Committee on Immigration and Naturalization traveled to the West Coast to gather information on the administration of the Chinese Exclusion Act and to inquire whether further legislation on the subject was necessary. Its efforts were part of a more general investigation of federal immigration law and policy that the Congress had commissioned in March of that year.[49] The subcommittee visited Seattle, Portland, other cities in Washington and Oregon, and San Francisco and heard extensive testimony from a large number of witnesses, private citizens, local government officials and federal officers involved in the enforcement of the exclusion laws. In contrast to the 1876 congressional hearings, when no Chinese witness appeared, in these hearings a number of West Coast Chinese testified. As a result the hearings provided a window not only on the functioning of the restriction legislation but also on the Chinese communities on the Pacific Coast. The general impression given by the federal officers who testified was that the exclusion laws were functioning reasonably well and that no major legislative changes were necessary. Many did, however, complain about inadequate funding and asked for additional manpower to implement the laws.[50]

The subcommittee never reported to the full Congress, but in March 1891, Congressman Herman Lehlbach, the sole House member on the panel, summarized its findings and recommendations for his chamber. Noting that the original Chinese Exclusion Act, which had suspended the immigration of laborers for ten years, was not due to expire until May of 1892 (or, in the opinion of some, not until July 1894), Lehlbach said the subcommittee did not feel any need to recommend any specific legislation at that time. The drafting of a bill to replace the original act, he said, could be safely left to the next session of Congress. As to what ought to be incorporated in such legislation, the subcommittee, he said, saw no need to recommend any radical revision in the existing law. It would be sufficient, it thought, to re-enact the 1882 act and to provide greater resources for its implementation. It did recommend that the act be amended to make permanent, rather than temporary, the exclusion of Chinese laborers.[51]

Notwithstanding the generally moderate tone of the subcommittee report, Pacific state representatives in the first session of the Fifty-second Congress seized the occasion of the impending expiration of the 1882 act to paint a picture of an immigration system on the verge of collapse and to demand a further tightening of the screws. Again, as in the past, members of the body were regaled with tales of Asian hordes waiting to inundate the country and of prophecies of the imminent collapse of Western civilization if new and more radical measures were not adopted.[52] Representative Charles Felton, a Californian, said the Congress was presented with a straightforward question of whether the Eastern or the Western type of civilization would survive on the Pacific Coast. The Chinese, he declared, were a race both cunning and intelligent, persistent and patient, industrious and frugal. In addition they were without fear of God, without conscience, and devoid of sympathy. As such there was no competing with them, "however low the type," as he put it, by those raised in the Western tradition. Races so dissimilar as the white and the Asiatic, he declared, could not exist together. One or the other must survive. "This is," he said, "a law of nature."[53]

During the session several bills were introduced in the House or the Senate calling for an absolute ban on all Chinese immigration, not just on the immigration of laborers. Some called as well for all Chinese present in the United States to be photographed and given certificates of residence.[54] The hope, said the report accompanying one of the measures, was that if it were passed, "gradually, by voluntary departures, death from sickness, accident, or old age, this race may be eliminated from this country, and the white race fill their places without inconvenience to our own people or to the Chinese, and thus a desirable change be happily and peacefully accomplished."[55] These measures were apparently found to be too drastic and could not win sufficient support to be moved through Congress, but the measure that ultimately did pass and win presidential approval was radical enough.

The Geary Act, as it came to be known, in honor of the California Congressman who was one of its chief sponsors, began by continuing for another ten years all laws then in force affecting Chinese immigration.[56] It then went on to create what was in effect America's first internal passport system. It imposed on each Chinese laborer residing in the United States the duty to apply within a year of the act's passage for a certificate of residence. Thereafter, if found without a certificate, he was to be presumed to be in this country unlawfully and was to be subject to immediate arrest. If arrested he was to be brought promptly before a judge and ordered deported unless he could show by the testimony of a white witness that he had been unable to obtain his certificate by reasons of sickness or accident.[57] (This was also, it is surely significant to remark, the first and only time that a federal statute sought to put a racial limitation on the right to testify in federal court.) The statute introduced other innovations as well. It forbade bail to Chinese who were refused permission to land and who applied for habeas writs in federal courts.[58] And, for the first time it made illicit residence in the United States a federal crime, punishable by a year's imprisonment at hard labor.[59] The act purported to affect only laborers, but in truth it cast a pall over the right of residence of all Chinese, for in effect it created a legal presumption that every Chinese person was here unlawfully and threw on him or her the burden of proving the contrary.[60] Its true spirit and purpose were reflected in its caption: "An Act to Prohibit the Coming of Chinese Persons Into the United States."[61]

The Chinese legation in Washington had followed the congressional deliberations on a new exclusion law closely and with considerable dismay. This dismay it communicated on several occasions to the U.S. Department of State. Commenting in April on one of the bills then under consideration, Minister Tsui Kuo-yin wrote to Secretary Blaine that it violated every single one of the articles of the 1880 treaty between the United States and China. He expressed special revulsion for its requirement that all Chinese be photographed. This was not required of any other aliens and was deeply humiliating.[62] When the Geary Act at length passed the Congress, he again remonstrated with Blaine, declaring that the measure's certificate requirement had reduced his compatriots to the status of, as he put it, Australian "ticket-of-leave" men. (A ticket of leave, in British penological parlance, was a license given to a convict permitting him to work outside of prison before the term of his imprisonment ended.)[63] A few months later in a letter he said he was writing at the request of the foreign office and in response to numerous petitions received from Chinese residents of the United States, he described the statute quite simply as "a violation of every principle of justice, equity, reason and fair dealing between two friendly powers" and urged in the strongest terms that the department do what it could to see that the law be repealed.[64]

THE CHINESE IN AMERICA REACT TO THE GEARY ACT

These reactions to the Geary Act were muted compared to those that came eventually from the main institution of Chinese America, the Chinese Six Companies. On September 9 the Six Companies issued a proclamation denouncing the measure and urging resistance to it. Copies of the proclamation were posted all over the Chinese quarter of San Francisco and attracted a great deal of attention. The act, it said, was detrimental to the interests of all Chinese. "We must organize and subscribe money to hire lawyers to defend ourselves." Thomas Riordan, it said, had already been engaged for that purpose, but further legal action was contemplated, and to finance it every Chinese in the United States was asked to make a contribution of $1.[65] No Chinese should register, the proclamation said. If a person was arrested for refusing to register, the proclamation assured that person of the Six Companies' support. However, if a person registered and got into trouble, he or she could not count on any assistance. "The United States does not treat the Chinese right because it compels no other nation to do such things, and no other nation in the world treats Chinese like the United States does," the proclamation concluded.[66] If there was any doubt that the Six Companies was here calling for massive civil disobedience to the Geary Act, that doubt was removed a few days later. Replying to a written inquiry from John Quinn, the collector of internal revenue in San Francisco, as to whether they were advising the Chinese not to register, the *hui-kuan* presidents wrote back that that was precisely what they were doing. They claimed they had consulted with their attorneys and had been told that the law was unconstitutional. And in response to a suggestion by Quinn that the Six Companies could be held criminally liable for urging Chinese to violate the law, the presidents replied, "[O]ur attention has not been called to any law which makes it a crime for us to advise our fellow-subjects that they have a right to disregard a law which is in violation of the constitution."[67]

A second proclamation, this one with a translation in Chinese of the Geary Act, was issued by the *hui-kuan* presidents on September 19. It gave full vent to the feelings of humiliation and anger that most Chinese must have felt upon learning of the statute's requirements.[68] It was directed "to all Chinese in the United States" and is worth quoting in full:

> [The Geary Act] is an unjust law and no Chinese should obey it. The law degrades the Chinese and if obeyed will put them lower than the meanest of people. It is a cruel law. It is a bad law. Read it and see how cruel the law is to our people. See how mean and contemptible it wants to make the Chinese. We do not want the Chinese to obey it. We do not believe the Chinese will obey it. In making the law the United States has violated the treaties. They have disregarded our rights and paid no attention to their promises, and made a law to suit themselves, no matter how unjust to us. No Chi-

> nese can read this law without a feeling of disgust. Many whites say the law is not right. Let us stand together. We hope all will work with us and then we can and will break this infamous law.[69]

At the same time, the secretary of the Six Companies announced at a public meeting covered by the Caucasian press that the Six Companies expected to raise $100,000 with which to hire eastern lawyers ("the best that money can hire," was the way he put it) to challenge the Geary Act in the courts. He promised that the *hui-kuan* would take care of anyone who was arrested for refusing to comply with the act's terms.[70]

The day after publication of this, their second, proclamation, the *hui-kuan* presidents made public an appeal they were sending directly to the imperial Chinese government. "Believing that our Government is in ignorance of the manner in which its treaties with the United States are being violated," it read, "and the indignities being heaped upon the Chinese people by the Government of the United States, we, the six companies of the United States, do now appeal to you for relief in behalf of your children in this country."[71] The document's opening words suggest that the *hui-kuan* leaders were not fully satisfied with the way in which the consulate or, for that matter, the legation in Washington was representing the interests of Chinese immigrants in the United States. (During the 1890 congressional hearings Consul Bee testified that the San Francisco consulate and the Six Companies were often at odds with one another.)[72] However, one can find evidence elsewhere that the consulate, for its part, was not entirely pleased with the actions of the Six Companies. While certainly sharing the outrage felt by all Chinese at the insult that the Geary Act represented, the consulate may have thought the call for outright defiance too brash. A consular official interviewed by a San Francisco reporter shortly after publication of the first proclamation, for example, seemed to want to take pains to distance himself from it. He said that it was entirely the work of the Six Companies and that the consulate had had nothing to do with it. The official did, however, assure the reporter that the Six Companies had not decided precipitously to issue the proclamation but rather had deliberated for a long time before reaching that decision.[73]

It is interesting to note that while these events were transpiring on the West Coast, the Chinese in the New York City area, now the center of a moderately-sized Chinese population, were themselves reacting with considerable vigor to the passage of the Geary Act.[74] The *New York Times* reported on August 21 that the Chinese of Brooklyn, some six hundred in number, were very agitated about the legislation and had decided to engage the services of a prominent local attorney to inform them on their legal rights.[75] And on September 22 a newly formed organization, calling itself The Chinese Equal Rights League, organized a mass meeting at the Cooper Union to protest the passage of the law. Over one thousand, including many Caucasians, attended the gathering, where they heard speaker after speaker denounce the measure for its unfairness and injustice. The meeting concluded with the adoption of a resolution condemning it as unconstitutional.[76] The Equal Rights League in due course issued a denunciation of the Geary Act and an appeal to the people of the United States under the title "The New and Monstrous Anti-Chinese Bill." One of its more eloquent passages read:

> We feel keenly the disgrace unjustly and maliciously heaped upon us by a cruel Congress. That for the purpose of prohibiting Chinese immigration more than one hundred thousand honest and respectable Chinese residents should be made to wear the badge of disgrace as ticket-of-leave men in your penitentiaries; that they should be tagged and branded as a whole lot of cattle for the slaughter; that they should be seen upon your streets with tearful eyes and heavy hearts, objects of scorn and public ridicule.[77]

FONG YUE TING V. THE UNITED STATES

Yung Wing, a man whose name we have mentioned before,[78] was a Cantonese of rather extraordinary background. He had graduated from Yale College in 1854 and in 1872 had led the Manchu Empire's first educational mission to the United States. When China established its first legation in Washington in 1878, it chose him as its second-ranking officer. He served in the legation for several years then left, became a naturalized U.S. citizen and settled in the United States. He continued, however, to maintain contact with the legation and to interest himself in the plight of his Cantonese compatriots in the United States.[79] In mid-December 1892 Yung wrote to the Reverend E. R. Donohue of Pittsburgh outlining the plans he had learned the Chinese had for attacking the Geary Act. The strategy which he saw taking shape was a three-pronged one. First, the constitutionality of the act would be tested in court. The well-known constitutional lawyers Joseph Choate and Charles Seward would have charge of the case he said, and all Chinese living in the United States would be assessed $1 to support the litigation. Second, the Oriental Club of New York (he may have meant the Chinese Equal Rights League referred to above) would organize mass meetings and would see to it that Congress was flooded with petitions. Finally, he said, the Chinese government would cease protecting American merchants and missionaries in China and would end all commercial intercourse between the two nations.[80]

Yung's predictions proved only partially accurate. In January 1893 Wong Chin Foo and Tom Yuen, the president and vice president, respectively, of the Chinese Equal Rights League did appear before the Foreign Affairs Committee of the House of Representatives to denounce the Geary Act in the strongest terms, and Congress did receive a fair number of petitions protesting the treatment of the Chinese.[81] The Chinese foreign office made menacing noises about retaliating against the United States for Congress's treatment of the Chinese but took no drastic action; nor is there any record of further mass meetings beyond the one that was organized in the immediate aftermath of the act's passage. The litigation strategy, however, did take shape more or less as Yung had forecast.

By mid-March of 1893, approximately two months before the Geary Act's penal provisions were to go into effect, the Six Companies reported that their appeal to their countrymen had been successful in raising some $60,000 in litigation support funds, and they began preparations to test the act's constitutionality. In this connection they sent their attorney, Thomas Riordan, to the East Coast for the purpose of assembling a team of lawyers. In New York he engaged James C. Carter, Joseph Choate, another leading figure of the New York and American bars, and Maxwell Evarts, the son of the eminent New York attorney and former Senator and Secretary of State, William Maxwell Evarts. (Both Maxwell Evarts and Choate were affiliated with the same New York firm.)[82] In Washington he recruited for good measure the well-known constitutional lawyer, J. Hubley Ashton. The *New York Times*, which reported these events, described these men as having been "employed as assistant counsel," but it must have been using this term loosely since it could not have failed to be clear to all concerned that the East Coast lawyers would be playing the primary and Riordan the supporting role in the lawsuit.[83] At these meetings counsel agreed on the litigation strategy they would pursue. As they saw it, arrangements would be made for the arrest of several Chinese on May 6, the day after the registration period expired. Writs of habeas corpus would quickly be sued out in the lower federal courts and a decision obtained. The matter would then be ready for review by the Supreme Court. The proceedings, it was also agreed, would be brought in New York City rather than in San Francisco.[84]

On March 13, 1893, Minister Tsui informed Secretary of State Gresham that the Chinese planned to challenge the constitutionality of the Geary Act and asked for his cooperation in assuring that the matter was decided at an early date by the U.S. Supreme Court. The Chinese residents of the United States, he wrote, were looking to that tribunal to vindicate their rights, strengthened in that belief by the fact that James C. Carter had already prepared a written opinion for them, assuring them that the act was not a valid exercise of legislative power. Certain time constraints were now coming into play, he noted. The act's penal provisions were to go into effect May 6 while the Supreme Court's term was scheduled to end May 15. He thought that the Chinese would be in a position to argue their case by May 12 if the Court would consent to hear it. He asked that the U.S. attorney general join counsel for the Chinese in a request that the Court hear argument no later than that date. He also asked that enforcement of the act be suspended, that is, that no arrests take place under it, until the law's validity or invalidity was established by the Supreme Court.[85] A week later Gresham wrote Tsui informing him that the attorney general had agreed that once the test case was brought he would concur in any motion made by counsel for the Chinese to advance the matter on the Court's calendar. The Secretary did not respond to the request that enforcement of the act be suspended until the high court had spoken. One suspects it was a deliberate omission.[86]

The Six Companies' heads issued a circular at the end of the month, giving the Chinese community more details of their plans for challenging the Geary Act in court. "We have employed five attorneys to go to Washington to fight this unjust law," they declared. The Chinese minister, they said, had already consulted with the U.S. government to arrange for the bringing of an early test case. Negotiations were also afoot to suspend operation of the act until the U.S. Supreme Court had had time to hear and decide the case. They thought these negotiations would be successful and that therefore no one need fear being arrested for not having a certificate of residence. They again urged Chinese not to comply with the act's registration requirements and again guaranteed their assistance to any Chinese who was arrested for failing to register. The companies expressed complete confidence that the Court would find the Geary Act unconstitutional. All authorities agreed on this, they said. Besides issuing the circular, the *hui-kuan* leaders published a notice with essentially the same contents in the San Francisco Chinese-language newspaper, the *Oriental*.[87]

On May 6, 1893, the day the Geary Act's penal provisions went into effect, counsel for the Chinese, just as planned, launched their attack on the measure's constitutionality. Once set in motion the process moved forward rapidly. By prearrangement, it appears, with federal authorities, three Chinese, selected in advance by the Six Companies' lawyers, were arrested by the U.S. marshal for the southern district of New York on the charge of being Chinese laborers without certificates of residence. Two of the men were brought immediately before the district court judge and were ordered deported. Within hours, and before the third man could be brought to district court, counsel petitioned for habeas writs on their behalf in the U.S. Circuit Court for Southern District of New York. Two of the habeas petitions, those filed on behalf of the Chinese laborers Fong Yue Ting and Wong Quan, made substantially the same allegations and raised substantially the same questions. These men, claiming to be permanent residents of the United States, admitted that they had deliberately refused to register under the Geary Act. The third petition, filed on behalf of the laborer Lee Joe, alleged a slightly different set of facts and was designed to raise a somewhat different issue. Lee Joe had applied to the collector of internal revenue for a certificate of residence on April 11 and had produced two Chinese witnesses to prove the necessary facts entitling him to receive one. The collector, however, had refused to hear the Chinese testimony and had insisted on white witnesses. When brought before the district court on May 6 he offered his own testimony and that of another Chinese to prove that he was without the certificate by reason of an unavoidable cause, the cause being the refusal of the collector to give him one. He then sought by his own testimony and that of the same Chinese witness to prove the fact of his residence in the United States at the time of the law's passage. The court had received this testimony into evidence but had nonetheless ruled against him. All three habeas petitions alleged that Section 6 of the Geary Act, the registration provision, was unconstitutional. The cases were all heard on May 6, and in each the court dismissed the writs and ordered the petitioners remanded to the custody of the federal marshal.[88] The cases were now in a posture to be appealed to the Supreme Court.

On May 8, 1892, Thomas Riordan filed a notice of appeal, and a scant two days later the Supreme Court convened in special session to hear oral argument in the three cases, now consolidated for review. In oral argument and in two lengthy briefs filed with the court more or less contemporaneously (the briefs had obviously been long in preparation) counsel for the Chinese, Joseph Choate at the head, sought to make the same points. They seemed first and foremost interested in preventing the Court from assimilating the case at bar to the *Chinese Exclusion Case* or extending any further the principles that case stood for. In that case, it will be recalled, Field, speaking for a unanimous Court, had held that Congress had unfettered power to deal with aliens seeking to enter the United States. When it dealt with these classes of persons, said Field, it was unconstrained by the Constitution. It is true that the case had technically only to do with Congress's power over aliens beyond the nation's borders. But the opinion was susceptible to the interpretation that the principle Field was talking about applied to aliens in general, that is to say that Congress had virtually unconstrained power to deal with aliens whether within or without its borders. Under this view of things the registration scheme set up by Congress under Section 6 of the act would easily pass muster. If Congress could do virtually anything it wanted with aliens in its midst, including expel them from its shores, surely it could force them to apply for certificates of residence.

Choate and his colleague on the brief, Maxwell Evarts, dealt with this issue somewhat obliquely. They argued that Congress could not have been asserting such a broad prerogative when it enacted Section 6 because, among other reasons, the body must have understood that it was beyond its constitutional power to do so. Chinese resident aliens, the attorneys argued, stood in contemplation of the Constitution practically on a par with U.S. citizens. They were, by virtue of their long residence in the United States, "denizens," that is to say in a position midway between that of citizens and transient aliens. Under the Constitution, Congress had only such powers as it had been expressly delegated or that it had by necessary implication. But just as Congress could not claim any express or implied power to banish citizens, except possibly as a punishment for crime, it could not claim any power to banish resident aliens.[89]

If, rather than being seen as a conditional exercise of a claimed right to expel resident aliens, the Geary Act were seen as a scheme for identifying Chinese who had a right to be here, the question then arose whether that scheme was constitutional. The Six Companies' lawyers argued that it was not. The registration system provided for under Section 6 of the act violated several constitutional provisions. It violated the Fifth Amendment prohibition against the taking of property or liberty without due process of law inasmuch as it set up a procedure for determining the legality of one's presence that was fundamentally unfair. It vested complete, final authority to determine entitlement to a certificate in a customs official and allowed for no challenge of that decision in court. A Chinese laborer, it was pointed out, could not complain to a court of law that the collector of customs had demanded a bribe in exchange for a certificate. It was also infirm on due process grounds in that it insisted on the testimony of one white witness when a Chinese who did not have a certificate of residence because of circumstances beyond his control was brought before a judge for deportation. The scheme violated the Fourth Amendment inasmuch as it provided for the arrest of alleged violators without the necessity of an oath before a neutral magistrate or a showing of probable cause. The lawyers attacked Section 4 of the act as well. It was infirm on both Fifth and Sixth Amendment grounds, they contended, because even though it made imprisonment at hard labor the penalty for illegal residence, it had no provision for grand jury indictment and denied the accused the right to a jury trial. Finally, it was alleged, the punishment provided for under the act for not having a certificate, a punishment described in the briefs as "transportation for life," was cruel and unusual, totally out of proportion to the offense committed, and therefore violated the Eighth Amendment.[90]

THE SUPREME COURT DECISION

On May 15, 1893, five days after oral argument in the case, the Supreme Court handed down its decision. By a vote of 6–3 the Court had decided to do exactly what counsel for the Chinese had hoped it would not do. "The general principles of public law which lie at the foundation of these cases are clearly established by previous judgments of this court," Justice Horace Gray said in his opening remarks.[91] The *Chinese Exclusion Case,* the justice noted, stood for the proposition that the power to exclude foreigners was an attribute of national sovereignty and was not limited in any way by the Constitution. It was a short distance, he thought, from this proposition to the next. "The right of a nation to expel or deport foreigners, who have not been naturalized or taken any steps towards becoming citizens of the country," he declared, "rests upon the same grounds, and is as absolute and unqualified as the right to prohibit and prevent their entrance into the country."[92] Under this conception of the matter the Geary Act was easy to sustain. If Congress had the unqualified right to expel Chinese aliens or to permit them to remain in the country, as it chose, it clearly had the power to provide for a system of registration and identification.[93] The Court again affirmed that Chinese aliens had acquired no rights under any of the treaties or federal laws previously enacted that were assertible against the Congress. Such rights of residence as Chinese laborers had they had "at the license, permission and sufferance of Congress," to be withdrawn, as Gray put it, at that body's will.[94] In one brief paragraph the Court disposed of the allegations that the act's deportation provisions ran afoul of particular guarantees in the Bill of Rights. The procedures provided for under the act were not in any true sense criminal proceedings, said the Court, and the deportation that these proceedings might result in could not truly be seen as punishment. It was rather but a method of enforcing the return to his own country of an alien who had failed to live up to the conditions of his continued residence.

Seen in this light, the provisions in the Bill of Rights securing individuals the right to trial by jury, protecting them against unreasonable searches and seizures, forbidding cruel and unusual punishments, or assuring them that they should not be deprived of life, liberty, or property without due process of law had no application.[95]

As to the claim of the petitioner Lee Joe, the laborer who had applied for but been refused his certificate, Justice Gray thought it not surprising that the collector of internal revenue should have declined to find the fact of residence upon testimony that would be insufficient to establish that fact at a hearing before a judge. In any event the petitioner had had a second chance, at the deportation hearing in district court, to establish his right to a certificate and had there failed or been unwilling to produce, per the statute's requirements, a credible white witness who could support his claim.[96]

Chief Justice Fuller, Justice David Brewer and, somewhat surprisingly Justice Field, strongly dissented from the majority opinion. For Brewer, the nephew, incidentally, of Stephen Field, the salient fact was that the Chinese petitioners had each lived in the United States since the 1870s, as long a period, he noted, as some of the members of Congress who had passed the Geary Act. Counsel for the Chinese was right to call them "denizens," he said.[97] Resident aliens, while here, were under the complete protection of the Constitution. They were entitled, as a matter of right (not sufferance) to all the safeguards of life, liberty, and property declared in the Bill of Rights.[98] They were not, as the majority would have it, subject to the absolute power of Congress. He vehemently rejected the notion propounded by the majority that Congress had such untrammeled power to deal with resident aliens that it could summarily expel them if it pleased. "The expulsion of a race may be within the inherent powers of a despotism," he observed, but it had no application in the United States.[99]

Brewer entertained no doubt that deportation, involving as it did forcible removal from friends, family, and property was punishment ("cruel and severe" punishment he called it), and punishment implied "the due and orderly procedure of a trial as recognized by the common law."[100] But the scheme provided for under the act fell short of these requirements. It made the liberty of the individual Chinese laborer subject, in the first instance, to the arbitrary and unregulated discretion of an administrative official. (The principles enunciated by the Court in *Yick Wo v. Hopkins* seemed to him here to be applicable.) If found without a certificate, a Chinese was then to be taken before a judge for a deportation hearing. But, contrary to the provisions of the Sixth Amendment, it was not specified that the court be in the district where he resided. Moreover, the accused was not given the right to have compulsory process to obtain witnesses in his favor. Finally, there was no mention in the statute of the right to trial by jury.[101] Brewer thought the act a great betrayal of constitutional principles and did not hide his contempt for the men who had enacted it. "In view of this enactment of the highest legislative body of the foremost Christian nation," he asked sarcastically at the end, "may not the thoughtful Chinese disciple of Confucius fairly ask, Why do they send missionaries here?"[102]

Justice Field, author of the opinion that had affirmed Congress's authority to exclude aliens, even resident aliens, from the shores of the United States, now distanced himself from the view that such authority extended to aliens living within the nation's borders. Exclusion and expulsion were to be radically distinguished, he insisted. Field, like Brewer, labeled as altogether extraordinary the doctrine contended for by the majority that Congress was at total liberty to provide for the removal of aliens living in the United States. He quoted extensively from James Madison's commentaries on the Alien Act of 1798—an act which Field noted had expired after two years and which had been ever since the object of universal condemnation—to show that the father of the Constitution believed that the measure, providing as it did for the summary removal of aliens belonging to friendly nations and guilty of no serious crime, was beyond the power of Congress to enact.[103] Field said he did not doubt that Congress had the authority to require Chinese laborers to procure certificates of identification, but he found unconstitutional the procedures Congress had adopted for enforcing this requirement. Like Brewer, he believed that Chinese laborers were entitled to all the guarantees of the Bill of Rights, and he agreed with the petitioners' lawyers that the Geary Act's procedures fell afoul of several of those guarantees. First he described the penalty provided by the act for nonregistration as "beyond all reason in its severity," strongly implying by those words, though he did not explicitly say so, that it violated the Eighth Amendment prohibition against cruel and unusual punishments. (Field implied that this might not have been a problem had the penalty been a fine rather than deportation.)[104] Since the penalty was of an infamous character it could only be imposed after grand jury indictment, trial, and conviction. None of these procedures were provided for under the act. The act also permitted the arrests of persons without oath, affirmation, or warrant and thus violated the Fourth Amendment.[105]

Further Federal Legislation on Chinese Immigration

THE EXTENSION OF THE PERIOD OF REGISTRATION

In the wake of the decision in *Fong Yue Ting* federal officials laid plans to move against Chinese who had failed to register for the Geary Act with a view to deporting them from the country. As the weeks passed more and more reports of impending legal actions reached the ears of Chinese diplomatic officials in San Francisco and in Washington. The legation received an alarming telegram on September 6 from the consul general in San Francisco reporting that a federal judge in southern California had ordered that the deportation of Chinese should proceed even though Congress had not specifically appropriated funds for that purpose and that the authorities in Los Angeles and San Francisco planned to apply for large numbers of arrest warrants the next day. The consul general pointed out that the Chinese had acted in good faith in failing to register, having been informed by eminent constitutional counsel that the act was void. He asked the minister to seek relief from the executive and legislative branches of the national government.[106] The request was duly conveyed to the Department of State.

Acting, it appears, in response to these concerns, the House Committee on Foreign Affairs on October 4 reported favorably on a bill for extending the time for registration under the Geary Act by six months. In recommending passage, the committee referred specifically to the advice that the attorneys Choate, Carter, and Ashton had given the Chinese, and though it commented that the Chinese had been misled, nonetheless concluded that considerations of justice and fairness dictated that they should have additional time. Considerations of finance entered into the calculations as well. Deporting all of the unregistered Chinese would have cost a small fortune.[107]

If the committee was gracious or semi-gracious with the one hand it was harsh with the other. It recommended that a broad definition of the term "laborer" be included in the act. The term was to be understood to apply to the skilled and the unskilled, including Chinese peddlers and those employed in mining, fishing, and the laundry business. Interestingly, the committee also recommended that the words "one credible white witness" in the provision having to do with the applications of those with lost or stolen certificates be changed to "one credible witness other than Chinese."[108] The bill underwent one major change after it left committee. A definition of "merchant" was added, the term being defined as "a person engaged in buying and selling merchandise, at a fixed place of business, which business is conducted in his name, and who . . . does not engage in the performance of any manual labor, except such as is necessary in the conduct of his business as such merchant." The same provision specified that when persons claiming to be merchants sought to enter the country they were to establish their merchant status by the testimony of "two witnesses other than Chinese." The measure as so modified went into effect as an amendment to the Geary Act on November 3, 1893.[109] Approximately nine months later Congress passed another law with even more negative consequences for the Chinese.

LEM MOON SING V. THE UNITED STATES

On March 3, 1891, President Harrison had signed into law a major new piece of federal immigration legislation. Enacted during the second session of the Fifty-first Congress, the measure was designed to supplement and strengthen previously enacted legislation on the subject. Among its most important provisions was one creating a new federal office, that of superintendent of immigration, within the Treasury Department (the title was changed to commissioner general in 1895) and another creating a new class of federal officials charged with the specific responsibility of enforcing federal immigration laws. (Previous to this time the immigration laws were enforced by general federal agents, such as collectors of customs or port officers, or by state officials.) These officials—"inspection officers" they were called under the new law—were given the authority to determine the right of aliens to land, and the law provided that their decisions should be final, subject only to administrative appeal to the superintendent of immigration and thereafter to the secretary of the treasury.[110] The 1891 act did not purport to deal with the subject of Chinese immigration, still seen as a separate and distinct area of federal immigration policy, and the enforcement of the Chinese exclusion legislation was left in the hands of the collector of customs and his staff of Chinese inspectors. But in August 1894 Congress made clear that it wished immigration officials to have the same authority in administering the Chinese exclusion laws that they had in administering the 1891 act. It added the following language to a law appropriating funds for the enforcement of the Chinese Exclusion Act:

> In every case where an alien is excluded from admission into the United States under any law or treaty now existing or hereafter made, the decision of the appropriate immigration or customs officers, if adverse to the admission of such alien, shall be final, unless reversed on appeal to the Secretary of the Treasury.[111]

In 1892 a Japanese national, denied entry into the United States by immigration officials in San Francisco, had challenged their authority in the federal circuit court. The court, however, refused to hear the case and remanded her to custody, holding that under the 1891 act the decisions of federal immigration officials were unreviewable by the federal judiciary. The matter went up to the U.S. Supreme Court on appeal, where the Court affirmed the lower court decision. It held in the case of *Nishimura Ekiu v. United States* that given Congress's plenary power over immigration matters, it could, if it wished, vest in executive officials the right to determine who should be able to enter the country, and if it did no court could attempt to re-examine or controvert their decisions.[112] *Nishimura Ekiu* was not conclusive of all questions concerning the power of immigration officers. The appellant in the case was a nonresident alien who was seeking to enter the United States for the first time, and there was language in the opinion suggesting that the principle of total administrative discretion announced in the case conceivably might not apply to aliens who claimed to be domiciled in the country.[113] This question was of special concern to Chinese merchants living in the United States since many of them for personal or business reasons were in the habit of making frequent trips abroad, and all too many of them had had unpleasant experiences with immigration officers upon trying to re-enter the country. A Chinese merchant would force the high court justices to address this issue in 1894.

Lem Moon Sing, a member of the San Francisco firm of Kee Sang Tong & Co., wholesale and retail druggists, returned to the city in November 1894 after a nine-month visit to China. He applied to the collector of customs for permission to land, and pursuant to the exact terms of the 1893 act, he presented the collector with the testimony of two white witnesses to the effect that he had been a merchant in San Francisco for at least a year prior to his departure from the United States. The collector, however, refused to allow him to land. His sole ground seems to have been the fact that Lem Moon Sing's name did not appear in the name of the firm with which he was connected. This raised an interesting point.

In refusing Lem Moon Sing permission to land, the collector was but implementing the policies of his superiors in Washington. On April 6, 1894, Attorney General Richard Olney had rendered an opinion that Chinese seeking to return to the United States as merchants did not bring themselves under the 1893 statutory definition of the term unless their names appeared in the names of the firms of which they claimed to be members. Two weeks later, on the basis of this opinion the secretary of the treasury had informed the collectors of customs at various ports, including San Francisco, that no Chinese who had left the United States after November 3, 1893 (the effective date of the 1893 act) was to be permitted to return unless his name appeared in the name of a mercantile firm.[114] However, on May 21, 1894, the Ninth Circuit Court of Appeals had ruled that a person's name did *not* have to appear in a firm's name for that person to be classified as a merchant. The law's terms were met, said the court, if a person's name appeared in its articles of partnership or incorporation.[115] The collector, it seems, did not feel this ruling was binding on him.

On March 5, 1895, Lim Lung, one of Lem Moon Sing's partners in the business, applied to the federal district court in San Francisco for a writ of habeas corpus on his behalf. The court, however, refused to issue the writ because, it said, the application showed on its face that Lem Moon Sing was being detained by the collector of the port under the authority vested in him by the act of August 18, 1894. The court was therefore without jurisdiction to hear the case. The same day a notice of appeal to the U.S. Supreme Court was filed by Thomas Riordan, the petitioner's attorney.[116]

Riordan and Evarts argued the appeal in the Supreme Court. They had two main points to press. They contended that the appellant did not come within the terms of the 1894 act or that if he did the act's vesting of final decision-making power over his right of entry in administrative officials was unconstitutional. There were in fact several lower court decisions involving domiciled Italians denied admission under the 1891 act holding that the final authority vested by that act in immigration officers applied only to "alien immigrants," by which the courts meant aliens seeking to enter the United States for the first time.[117] As the headnote to one of these opinions put it, "One who is a resident of the United States, though of foreign birth and not naturalized, and who is returning from a visit to the country of his birth is not an alien immigrant within the meaning of the laws regulating immigration."[118] The statute in question, these cases held, confided a limited jurisdiction to immigration officials, and courts upon a habeas petition were always free to inquire into the question whether these officials had exceeded that jurisdiction in denying entry to someone seeking to get into the United States.

Evarts and Riordan sought to assimilate their client's case to that of the litigants in those decisions. The 1894 law, they said, gave immigration officers authority over aliens excluded from admission to the United States under any law or treaty. But Lem Moon Sing didn't fit that description. There was nothing in the record to controvert his claim that he was a domiciled merchant and as such therefore perfectly free to enter the country. Immigration officials, therefore, did not have the authority to rule finally on his admissibility.[119] If the 1894 act was seen as applying to Lem Moon Sing, Evarts and Riordan contended it was unconstitutional.

They conceded Congress's right to vest final decision-making power in administrative officers when it came to aliens seeking to enter the country for the first time. But, they argued, it violated the due process clause of the Fifth Amendment to give these officials such authority in the case of foreigners who had acquired domicile in the United States. Resident aliens stood in the same constitutional position as citizens and it was arbitrary and oppressive and violative of American notions of due process to deprive them of the right to court review over decisions so deeply affecting their liberty and property interests.[120]

The argument of the Chinese attorneys was competent and forceful enough, but they must have known that theirs was an uphill battle given the direction in which the Court's immigration jurisprudence had been moving for the past several years. In a decision handed down on May 27, 1895, the Court, with a lone dissent from Justice Brewer, held that the statute of 1894 applied to Chinese aliens who claimed domicile in the United States and that it was fully constitutional. "The present case," said Justice Harlan, "is, in principle covered by the former adjudications of this court."[121] He then went on to discuss the *Chinese Exclusion Case*, *Nishimura Ekiu*, and *Fong Yue Ting*, quoting copiously from the three opinions. Congress's power over foreigners was plenary, whether it was a matter of expelling or excluding them, and it could exercise this power in whatever way it saw fit. It could entrust the determination of initial entry of foreigners to immigration officials; it could likewise entrust to these same officials the determination of the foreigner's right to return. To hold otherwise, said Harlan, would bring into the Court the case of every alien who claimed the right to come into the country but was prevented from doing so by executive officers, which in turn would defeat the very scheme that Congress had put in place.[122] While resident in the country the alien's rights were as fully protected by the supreme law of the land as a native's, Harlan wrote. On leaving the country, however, the alien became subject to the will of "the political department of the government," the judicial department having no further jurisdiction in the matter.[123] Harlan noted that the Court was not ruling on the merits of Lem Moon Sing's claim that he was domiciled in the United States and had the legal right to return to the country, but the opinion made clear that even if this was true the federal courts had no authority to disturb a contrary determination made by immigration officials. Theirs was the right of final determination.[124]

It will be recalled that as early as 1884 in the case of *Jung Ah Lung* the U.S. attorney in San Francisco had argued before the federal district court that customs officials had the final authority to determine the right of

Chinese aliens to land and that these decisions were not reviewable in court. But Judge Hoffman had rejected this claim out of hand, insisting that until he heard to the contrary from the Congress he would assume that Chinese were entitled to use the writ of habeas corpus to challenge such decisions.[125] The Supreme Court was now leaving no doubt that it believed the Congress had spoken. Henceforth the freedom of movement to and from the country of all Chinese, whether new immigrants of the exempt classes or returning merchants, was to be committed to the hands of the federal immigration bureaucracy, a bureaucracy that most Chinese were deeply suspicious of. Chinese who left the country now did so at their peril. There would be no possibility of recourse to the courts for the rectification of errors or injustices committed by executive officials. The Constitution, a train of decisions had now made crystal clear, did indeed stop at the water's edge.[126]

With *Lem Moon Sing* we conclude our discussion of the immigration decisions of the federal courts. The most important questions concerning national power over the Chinese (and other aliens, for that matter) had now been answered and answered for the most part adversely to the Chinese.[127] The Chinese continued to litigate cases, many cases indeed, in subsequent years, and their efforts did not go for naught. In the years immediately following *Lem Moon Sing* they were able to win two victories of some significance. In *Wong Wing v. United States*,[128] for example, a case that arose in Michigan and that was decided in 1896, the Supreme Court held that those portions of the Geary Act which provided for the punishment at hard labor of any Chinese found illegally within the United States, such punishment to be inflicted without the necessity of a jury trial, were unconstitutional. Persons subject to such punishment were, the Court said, entitled under the Fifth and Sixth Amendments to a grand jury indictment and a jury trial. And in 1898, in *Wong Kim Ark v. United States*,[129] the Court at length affirmed the lower court decision in *Look Tin Sing* that, under the Fourteenth Amendment, birth in the United States conferred citizenship.[130] To conclude this book we return to San Francisco, the great hub and heart of the anti-Chinese movement, and to two episodes that occurred in the city in the century's last decade. They illustrate the depths to which racial antagonism was capable of sinking and the kind of legislative excesses it was capable of leading to and may perhaps be seen as constituting something of a coda to this long and sorry tale.

IV

CENTURY'S END

Last Episodes of Sinophobia

9 Challenging Residential Segregation

The Case of In re Lee Sing

It was the misfortune of the Chinese that they chose to settle in the center of San Francisco, in an area cheek by jowl with what would become the city's central business district. Their location made them a particular focus of Caucasian attention. Inevitably the Chinese district became crowded and parts of it quite unsanitary (what poor district of a great nineteenth-century city did not fit this description?),[1] but one may be reasonably sure that these conditions would not have caused nearly so much comment among whites had the Chinese district not been located in the city center and had it not been inhabited by a despised racial group.

Complaints from Caucasians about the alleged overcrowdedness and unsanitary conditions in the Chinese quarter and appeals to do something about it date from the beginnings of the immigration. As early as 1854, for example, the San Francisco *Herald* printed an editorial criticizing the state of the Chinese quarter and expressing the wish that the Chinese could be relocated to another less desirable part of the city.[2] We discussed in chapter 3 the board of health's abortive attempt in 1880 to declare Chinatown a nuisance and remove the Chinese population from it and the passage the same year of the state law, enacted pursuant to Article XIX of the 1879 state constitution, authorizing cities to cause the removal of the Chinese without their limits or to set aside prescribed portions for their residence. This law, we noted, was thought by many to have been voided by implication by the 1880 federal circuit court decisions in *Ah Chong* and *In re Parrott*. Nonetheless, the law remained on the books and at least twice during the 1880s municipalities came close to implementing its provisions. In May of 1880, for example, the small Sierra foothill town of Nevada City passed an ordinance calling for the removal of its Chinese and only relented from enforcing it when it was informed by the Chinese consulate that any attempt to enforce it would be resisted in the courts. And in early 1886 a similar ordinance was only narrowly defeated by the Sacramento Board of Trustees.[3]

Passage of the Bingham Ordinance

What led the San Francisco Board of Supervisors in early 1890, after years of refusing to take action, finally to cast caution to the winds and attempt to implement the Chinese removal provisions of state law remains something of a mystery. One certainly cannot point to any single catalyst. Anti-Chinese agitation was ever-present, but it was no more intense at this time than at many others during the late nineteenth century. Concern about Chinatown's strategic geographic position was certainly high, but no higher than it had been five years earlier, in 1885. In that year a special committee of the board had issued a report on the Chinese quarter that was almost hysterical in tone. It described the area as variously "a moral cancer on the city" and "a Mongolian vampire sapping [San Francisco's] vitals" and suggested that urgent action was needed to scatter the Chinese, not only out of Chinatown but out of the state of California altogether. The authors of the report included a detailed map of Chinatown, highlighting the uses to which every parcel of property in the area was being put and showing in the most graphic way its proximity to the San Francisco business district. (One newspaper commented that the map revealed that the Chinese occupied the best part of the most desirable business district in San Francisco and were gradually encroaching upon what remained.)[4] Perhaps all one can say is that something had caused Caucasian frustrations and fears to reach the breaking point.

On February 3, 1890, Supervisor Henry Bingham introduced in the board a resolution providing that after the expiration of sixty days from the date of passage it should be unlawful for any Chinese person to locate, reside, or carry on business anywhere in San Francisco except in an area bounded by Kentucky, First, I, Seventh, and Railroad Avenues. As noted earlier, this area had by previous legislation been set aside for slaughterhouses, tallow factories, hog factories and other businesses thought to be prejudicial to the public health or comfort. The sponsor argued for quick passage of the ordinance but agreed that it should first go to the Judiciary Committee for consideration.[5]

There was much support out-of-doors for Supervisor Bingham's resolution. The central committee of the Democratic party endorsed the measure at a special meeting called for the purpose. "We have in our midst hordes of Chinese who have located in the heart of our city and there erected one of the most pernicious plague spots ever known in the history of civilization," the resolution read. It alluded to the growing importance of that part of the city from a commercial standpoint and the steady push of the Chinese population outward beyond the borders of Chinatown.[6] A similar theme was struck by the *Evening Bulletin.* It described Chinatown as a blight athwart the northern portion of the city, cutting off some of the fairest residential areas of town from the commercial center. Moreover, it was a "cancer" that was gradually spreading outward "toward the old aristocratic quarters . . . perilously near Nob Hill and . . . threatening the old select regions of Powell and Mason streets." With the removal of the Chinese would come a healthy expansion of manufacturing establishments, of commerce and of living quarters for whites.[7]

The fiercely Sinophobic Hearst paper, the *Examiner,* argued that Chinatown was a "social, moral, industrial, sanitary, and business curse" and only wondered why it had taken so long to act on the state constitutional provisions. In explanation for the delay, the editors did acknowledge that in previous instances the courts had nullified anti-Chinese measures passed by the city and implied that this ordinance too might face rough going if challenged, but its attitude seemed to be to encourage the supervisors to pass their measure and then dare the courts to nullify it. There was after all little to lose by the effort and potentially much to gain. "The glorious future that would lie before this city with Chinatown removed is surely worth an effort to attain it," the paper editorialized.[8]

The Judiciary Committee of the board of supervisors met on February 4 and decided to report favorably on the proposed ordinance but voted also to refer it to the city and county attorney for his opinion. The city attorney furnished his opinion a week later. Totally abandoning the position previously taken by his predecessors, he now thought the order perfectly within the power of the board to enact. Limiting himself to the narrow question of whether the municipality had been specifically granted power to do what it proposed to do and citing the pertinent provisions of the state constitution and state law, he declared, "If those laws do not delegate power to the Board of Supervisors to take such action as contemplated by the proposed order, then it is difficult to understand what language or law would be sufficient to delegate such power."[9] At its regular meeting of February 17 the San Francisco Board of Supervisors voted unanimously to pass the measure to print. A final vote of approval was taken March 3, and the ordinance received the mayor's endorsement March 10.

First Arrests under the Ordinance and the Initiation of Litigation

The Bingham ordinance went into effect May 10, but the city authorities decided to proceed in a cautious and orderly fashion in implementing it.

A plan was worked out, it appears, with the consent of the Chinese consulate, under which a single Chinese would be arrested for violating the law and then that arrest would serve as a vehicle for getting a quick court test of the ordinance's validity. Until that determination was reached, the understanding was, no other Chinese would be harassed or molested in any way.[10] The chief of police and prosecuting attorney accordingly on May 12 had a sergeant of the Chinatown squad swear out a complaint against a prominent Chinese merchant residing in the district and had the man arrested and committed to the city prison to await trial. No sooner had the man been arrested than did Consul Frederick Bee appear with a writ of habeas corpus issued by Judge Hoffman of the federal district court, returnable that very afternoon. In short order the prisoner was turned over to the United States marshal, admitted to bail (set at $2,000), and the matter was set for hearing on July 14.[11]

These well-laid plans, as it turned out, were sabotaged by none other than Supervisor Bingham himself, who had decided to take the matter into his own hands. On May 20 accompanied by his own lawyer he went to the local police court, and had the court issue some seventy-five warrants essentially in blank for the arrest of alleged Chinese violators of the law (since he did not know their real names he gave them fictitious ones such as "Jack Pot," "One Lung," etc.). These he placed in the hands of the chief of police. A squad of police, in the company of the supervisor and a goodly contingent of the local press, then descended on the Globe Hotel, a major residential hotel in Chinatown, where they randomly arrested twenty Chinese, not without a certain amount of brutality. A father was forcibly pried away from a sick child, for example, and at first the queues of the Chinese prisoners were tied together to prevent them from escaping. They were later untied and the prisoners were marched off, two in the custody of each police officer. One of the Chinese prisoners voiced his protest. "Wha' fo' we here?" the *Morning Call* reported him as saying, "No mo tleaty us. No constituton? Chinaman not good as 'Melican man: no mo', eh?"[12]

A Pointed Diplomatic Exchange

The *Daily Alta,* San Francisco's leading Republican journal and an outspoken antagonist of the Democratic-controlled board of supervisors, had, from the moment the Bingham ordinance was introduced, dealt with it as something that was not to be taken seriously. It was to the paper nothing more than grandstanding on Bingham's part. (According to the *Alta* when the ordinance was passed, the public looked upon it as "a bit of humor.") And it treated the first arrests made under the law in the same vein, comparing the Bingham-led raid on Chinatown to Don Quixote's tilt at the windmills.[13]

The diplomatic representatives of the imperial Chinese government certainly did not see the matter in the same light. The Chinese consulate reacted to the arrests with indignation. Consul Bee described them as "a high-handed outrage" and warned the city that the Chinese government would bring civil suits for damages on behalf of each arrested Chinese. The city of San Francisco, he predicted, would be held strictly liable in damages.[14] More important, the arrests set off a major diplomatic brouhaha at the ambassadorial level in Washington.

On May 23, 1890, three days after the first arrests were made under the Bingham ordinance, an official of the Chinese legation in Washington, Pung Kwang-yu, wrote a strongly-worded letter to Secretary of State Blaine, informing him that he had received news of the first arrests under the San Francisco ordinance. He complained bitterly of "the enormity of the outrage which is sought to be inflicted upon my countrymen" and demanded that the federal government (it is clear from the context that he meant the executive branch) intervene immediately and forthrightly to stop it. This, in his view, was mandated under Article 3 of the 1880 treaty between the United States and China, which provided: "If Chinese laborers, or Chinese of any other class, now either permanently or temporarily residing in the territory of the United States, meet with ill treatment at the hands of any other persons, the Government of the United States will exert all its power to devise measures for their protection and to secure to them the same rights, privileges, immunities and exemptions as may be enjoyed by the citizens or subjects of the most favored nation, and to which they are entitled by treaty."

Blaine quickly acknowledged receipt of Pung's letter, but he denied that the executive branch was under any obligation to act under Article 3 of the treaty. He pointed out that the U.S. Constitution made treaties the supreme law of the land and that the judicial power of the United States extended to all cases that arose under treaties. Blaine noted that the Chinese who had been arrested could apply to the courts for release from imprisonment and a determination of the legality of the San Francisco ordinance, and implied that this was sufficient compliance with the treaty. He did inform the official that he had forwarded a copy of his letter to the attorney general for his consideration.[15]

Pung replied that he thought something more was called for under the circumstances than pointing out that the courts of the United States were open to Chinese subjects. They always had been, he noted. He rehearsed at some length the negotiations that had led to the 1880 treaty, emphasizing that it was the United States that had insisted China surrender certain treaty rights that it had previously had with regard to immigration and that the Chinese government had surrendered these rights with the understanding that Chinese subjects remaining in the United States should receive some *special and additional* protection from the federal government. Pung wrote with more than a trace of sarcasm: "It would hardly have been considered by the Imperial Government as a sufficient inducement to enter into the new treaty to be assured that, when the authorities of the great and powerful city of San Francisco should seize upon the Chinese subjects in that city and drag them from their long-established homes and business, the Federal Government would do nothing more than point them to the courts, where they would have the poor privilege of carrying on a long and expensive litigation against a powerful corporation in a community where they were treated as a despised and outcast race."[16] Blaine, however, persisted in a narrow and literal interpretation of the treaty language, contending that it meant that the federal government was bound to take new steps only where existing measures or remedies were found to be inadequate, and there had been as yet, he insisted, no such showing. The Chinese had an ample and immediate remedy in the courts. He had, he noted, received a reply from the attorney general confirming him in this view and informing him as well that in the attorney general's opinion the San Francisco ordinance violated both the treaty and the Fourteenth Amendment to the federal Constitution. Blaine reminded Pung that in more than one instance federal courts had vindicated the supremacy of federal treaties over the positive law of the state of California.[17] What Blaine said was literally true but, one suspects, not terribly comforting to the Chinese. It seems clear that what the minister was looking for was some concrete manifestation of solidarity from the high organs of the national government, an intervention in court by the U.S. attorney on the scene, for example, or even a statement from some prominent federal official. He was to get none of these.

The consulate in San Francisco had in the meantime already taken decisive steps of its own. Within hours of the arrests, Consul Bee filed in the federal Circuit Court for the Northern District of California a petition for a writ of habeas corpus on behalf of the twenty Chinese arrested in the Bingham-led raid on Chinatown. The petition alleged that the ordinance under which they had been arrested was unconstitutional and void inasmuch as it abridged rights, privileges, and immunities granted the Chinese under the federal Constitution, statute, and treaty and constituted a rank discrimination against them as opposed to other ethnic groups.[18] In the afternoon the prisoners were brought before Judge Hoffman, now sitting in the capacity of an acting circuit judge, released on bail, and had their cases consolidated with that of the single merchant whose case was already pending.[19]

The hearing on the Chinese habeas cases had originally been scheduled for July 14, but the city moved successfully to have the matter postponed several weeks. It then filed an extended amendment to its original return to the habeas petition, in which it sought to set forth at some length its justification for the ordinance under challenge. The pleading deserves some brief discussion inasmuch as it represents undoubtedly one of the more appalling statements of racial bigotry in Western legal history. Among its allegations: that the Chinese were as a race criminal, vicious, and immoral; that they were all incorrigible perjurers; that they abandoned their sick in the street to die; that their occupation of property anywhere decreased the value of surrounding property; that their presence in any number anywhere was offensive to the senses and dangerous to the morals of other races; and that these racial and national characteristics could only be made tolerable if they were removed from the center of town to a remote area where they would have less contact with other races. (To its credit the court eventually ordered most of these allegations concerning the racial propensities of the Chinese stricken from the record.)[20] The case of *Lee Sing* came on for oral argument August 18 before Circuit Judge Lorenzo Sawyer.

The attorney for the Chinese, Thomas Riordan, argued to the bench that the San Francisco ordinance constituted the broadest and most scandalous discrimination imaginable against the Chinese. He pointed out that it compelled all Chinese, and not just those living in Chinatown, to move into the new district or leave the city. Some 30 percent of the city's Chinese lived outside of the Chinese quarter, he claimed. The ordinance if implemented would cause enormous financial damage to Chinese merchants, he averred. They carried on business in San Francisco to the amount of $15 million a year and would doubtless lose much of it if required to move. According to one newspaper's account, Riordan cited several of Sawyer's own opinions in support of his position, which the paper did not say. The city, for its part, claimed the ordinance was a measure of self-defense. Counsel analogized it to an immigration law excluding paupers, lepers, and known criminals from landing on a nation's shores. Chinatown, he said, was "an ulcer in the very heart of a prosperous city." During oral argument Sawyer betrayed considerable irritation with the ordinance and with the city's attempt to defend it. He noted, echoing Riordan's point, that it painted with the broadest brush imaginable, being directed at a whole community irrespective of class or business. And he curtly rejected an offer by counsel for the city to present evidence on the extent of vice and crime in Chinatown. It was a well-known fact, said the judge, that there were ten times as many Caucasian prostitutes in the city as there were Chinese.[21]

Judge Sawyer's Opinion

Sawyer read his opinion in open court on August 25. It was terse, to the point, and, though it did not mention the body by name, fairly dripping with sarcasm for the board of supervisors. Three provisions of positive law were applicable to the case, the Fourteenth Amendment to the Constitution, with its guarantees to all persons of the equal protection of the laws and due process of law; Article 6 of the Burlingame Treaty with China, which assured that Chinese subjects visiting or residing in the United States should have the same "privileges, immunities, and exemptions" as were enjoyed by the citizens or subjects of the most favored nation; and Section 1977 of the Revised Statutes of the United States, which provided:

> All persons within the jurisdiction of the United States shall have the same right in every state and territory to make and enforce contracts, to sue, be parties, give evidence, and to the full and equal benefit of all laws and proceedings for the security of persons and property as is enjoyed by white citizens, and shall be subject to like punishment, pains, penalties, taxes, licenses, and exactions of every kind, and to no other.

That the ordinance discriminated against the Chinese, in violation of each of these should, he said, be completely apparent to any intelligent person whether lawyer or layman.[22] The ordinance was not aimed at any particular vice or immoral occupation or practice but was rather designed, as he put it, "to forcibly drive out a whole community of twenty-odd thousand people, old and young, male and female, citizens of the United States, born on the soil, and foreigners of the Chinese race, moral and immoral, good, bad, and indifferent, and without respect to circumstances or conditions, from a whole section of the city which they have inhabited, and in which they have carried on all kinds of business appropriate to a city, mercantile, manufacturing and otherwise, for more than 40 years."[23] Upon no groups other than the Chinese were such disabilities imposed, he noted.

Besides discriminating against the Chinese and operating unequally between the Chinese and other groups, the ordinance amounted as well to an arbitrary deprivation of property. Forced to leave their customary places of abode and relegated to a single section of the city, the Chinese would be completely at the mercy of the landowners in that vicinity. "They would," as Sawyer put it, "be compelled to take any lands, upon any terms . . . or get outside the city and county of San Francisco."[24]

The question of the ordinance's invalidity, he thought, was not even worthy of extended discussion. Aiming another barb at Supervisor Bingham and his colleagues, he wrote: "To any reasonably intelligent and well-balanced mind, discussion or argument would be wholly unnecessary and superfluous. To those minds, which are so constituted, that the invalidity of this ordinance is not apparent upon inspection . . . discussion or argument would be useless."[25] He concluded with a citation to the long line of federal decisions vindicating Chinese rights against hostile state action that had by then accumulated, among them his own in *In re Ah Fong*, the Chinese fishing rights case, and *In re Tie Loy*, the Stockton laundry case, and that of the United States Supreme Court in *Yick Wo v. Hopkins*.[26]

The *Examiner* reported that a large number of Chinese were present in Judge Sawyer's courtroom when he read his opinion and that it gave them general satisfaction. The paper's editors said the decision was exactly what was to be expected from Judge Sawyer, "Mandarin Sawyer" as it now dubbed him. "To Judge Sawyer's mind discussion or argument on any question affecting the Chinese is wholly unnecessary. The only thing needed is a glimpse of the almond eye."[27] The city, for its part, does not appear to have given any thought to appealing the decision. Thus ended the first attempt by an American municipality to segregate its inhabitants on the basis of race.

Benno Schmidt, in his major study of race relations and the law in the late nineteenth and early twentieth centuries, argues that residential segregation is "racism's ultimate expression,"[28] and it is certainly impossible to imagine any stronger expression of Caucasian antipathy toward the Chinese race than the state constitutional provision, the state statute, and the local ordinance that have been the subject of this discussion. They are perversely eloquent testimony to the depth of anti-Chinese feeling present in the populace. The very extremity of the state law provisions, calling as they did for the forcible uprooting of thousands of people from their homes and residences, doubtless made them suspect from the beginning even in the minds of their sponsors. This is no doubt the explanation for the reluctance of California towns and cities to act on them. That there was a will to act cannot be doubted. As noted earlier, at least one California municipality did enact a removal statute and several others came close to doing so. One must also not forget that in the years immediately preceding the enactment of the San Francisco ordinance marauding bands forcibly drove Chinese inhabitants out of any number of communities in the western states.[29] Had the decision concerning the San Francisco law come down the other way, it would unquestionably have led to the enactment and the implementation of similar measures in other California municipalities. The circuit court decision ended once and for all any thought San Francisco (or any other city) might have had of using the obnoxious provision of the California Constitution as the basis for creating a permanent racial ghetto within its borders. As we shall see in the next chapter, however, it did not prevent officials in San Francisco ten years later from again seeking to physically isolate the Chinese.

Postscript on Residential Segregation

It is somewhat odd, given subsequent events, that *Lee Sing*, with its ringing condemnation of racial ghettoization, did not have a greater impact upon constitutional history. Attempts to achieve residential segregation of blacks and whites by law did not begin until the early twentieth century. In 1910 the city of Baltimore enacted a residential segregation ordinance. Several other cities in border and southern states followed suit in subsequent years. The typical form these ordinances took was to forbid blacks from buying property on blocks where the majority of occupants were white and vice versa.[30] Though nominally less extreme (most did not disturb the rights of existing property owners), these measures in final analysis had much in common with the San Francisco law. They were at the same time both an expression of deep-seated racial hostility and of fear about the alleged depreciating effect on property values of the presence of nonwhite populations. They also had the same object. Like the San Francisco law they were calculated, albeit in more indirect fashion, to ghettoize a minority racial group in less desirable living areas. The laws were challenged initially in state courts and, unlike other types of Jim Crow laws, met there a mixed reception. The Maryland Supreme Court, for example, struck down the Baltimore ordinance and the Georgia court, at least initially, nullified a similar ordinance passed by Atlanta.

Eventually the NAACP, alarmed by the spread of this kind of legislation, determined to seek a definitive test of de jure residential segregation in the federal courts. The vehicle chosen was a challenge to a segregation ordinance passed by the city of Louisville, Kentucky. The United States Supreme Court in 1917, in *Buchanan v. Warley*,[31] ruled unanimously that the Louisville law and all similar measures violated the rights of blacks to be free of racial discrimination in the purchase and sale of property and the property rights of whites as well as blacks. Though *Lee Sing* was in fact the only federal precedent on the subject of residential segregation by race, it played a very small role in the argument or decision of any of these cases. Counsel for the plaintiff-in-error challenging the law in *Buchanan* cited the case in support of his argument that the Louisville law was unconstitutional. The NAACP's Moorfield Storey mentioned it as well in his brief.[32] Neither discussed it extensively, however, and it is not mentioned at all in the decision by Justice Day.

10 Medicine, Race, and the Law

The Bubonic Plague Outbreak of 1900

During the night of March 6, 1900, the body of a middle-aged Chinese man was discovered in the basement of a Chinatown hotel, with badly swollen lymph nodes in the groin. The physician who first noticed this reported the fact to A. P. O'Brien, health officer of San Francisco, who in turn asked Dr. Wilfred H. Kellogg, bacteriologist of the city board of health, to do a microscopic examination of tissue from the nodes in question. Kellogg detected bacilli under the microscope that he strongly suspected were those of bubonic plague and reported this fact immediately to O'Brien and to John Williamson, president of the San Francisco Board of Health. The discovery of a suspected case of plague in a large city would under any circumstances be an alarming development. This was particularly so in the year 1900.

Bubonic Plague

Plague is a disease caused by the bacterium now called *Yersinia pestis.* It can manifest itself in any of a number of forms, but historically the most important form of the disease has undoubtedly been bubonic plague, a terrifying malady with classic clinical symptoms. A patient infected with the bubonic plague microorganism initially experiences a sudden onset of fever, chills, weakness, and severe headache. Soon the lymph nodes of the groin, neck, and armpits, the parts of the body in which the plague bacteria first proliferate, swell dramatically, at times reaching the size of an orange in the groin area. The patient suffers excruciating pain, and barring effective intervention, almost invariably succumbs to the disease in a matter of three to five days.[1] If caught early enough, the disease may now be effectively treated with antibiotics, but this is a very recent therapeutic development.

Plague is primarily a rodent disease, with humans acting as incidental hosts. The disease is spread from rat to rat and, when rats are not available in sufficient number, from rat to human beings through the bite of infected rodent fleas. Plague, at least in its bubonic form, is not directly communicable from one human being to another. If, however, the bubonic infections should invade the lungs, another potentially very contagious form of the disease, pneumonic plague, may develop. Pneumonic plague is spread through the coughing of those ill with the disease to persons in close proximity. Though one's intuitions might lead to the opposite conclusion, the development of pneumonic epidemics out of bubonic outbreaks has been the exception rather than the rule. Bubonic plague has in fact been described as "one of the least infectious of epidemic diseases."[2] In 1900, it is worthy of note, the distinction between bubonic and pneumonic plague was not understood.

Bubonic plague has probably been endemic in many population centers throughout recorded history, but on several occasions the disease has flared into a pandemic involving large geographical areas of the world and vast numbers of victims. The most notable of those was of course the Black Death of the fourteenth century. The most recent pandemic of plague originated in southern China in the last decade of the nineteenth century, and by 1894 it had invaded with force the cities of Canton and Hong Kong. From southern China it spread rapidly to India, Egypt, South Africa, parts of France, Britain, and Australia. By the end of December 1899 a dozen cases had been reported in the Hawaiian islands, concentrated almost exclusively in the Chinese section of Honolulu.

In 1894 two scientists, Alexander Yersin and Shibasuburo Kitasato, had independently identified the short, ovoid bacillus responsible for causing the disease. There remained, however, a considerable misconception about the ailment's mode of transmission. In 1900, physicians and sanitary authorities around the world were generally convinced that bubonic plague was transmitted from person to person through disease germs that had been emitted by human or rodent plague victims and that were to be found lurking in the soil, in the air, or in food products. There was an understanding that rats played some sort of role in plague transmission but virtually no understanding of the role played by the rat flea.[3]

The Decision to Quarantine Chinatown

Having conferred about Kellogg's discovery, O'Brien and Williamson decided to take immediate and rather drastic action. The chief of police was summoned and told that the health authorities wished to impose a total blockade on Chinatown. Thoroughly in agreement with the decision, he dispatched a force of thirty-two officers to the Chinese quarter with orders to first see to it that all Caucasians who could be found were removed from the affected area and then to cordon it off. The orders were quickly carried out, and by the morning of March 7, Chinatown had been effectively sealed off from the rest of the city.[4]

The custom of segregating from the community persons afflicted with diseases thought to be communicable dates back to biblical times at least and was practiced on a grand scale during the Black Death of the fourteenth century when, for example, plague sufferers in many cities were strictly confined to their houses. During that century, too, the Republic of Venice introduced the practice of requiring ships arriving from places where epidemics were in progress to wait offshore for a period of days before disembarking passengers or goods. The practice was adopted by numerous other governments, and the waiting period was eventually extended by many to forty days. Hence the name "quarantine" (from the Italian word for forty, *quarantina*).[5] The first federal quarantine law was passed in the United States in 1796,[6] and by the end of the nineteenth century all U.S. ports, including San Francisco,[7] had established quarantine regulations of their own, providing for the inspection of incoming vessels and the quarantining of those suspected of carrying contagiously ill passengers.

The quarantine decided upon by San Francisco health officials the night of March 6, 1900, was of a drastically different character, however, and, though not totally unprecedented in the history of public health in the western world, it was highly unusual. It applied not to individual ships or houses but to a whole district of a great city. Moreover, it had been adopted in response to the discovery of a single case of plague. From the perspective of modern public health we can see that such a measure could be of virtually no use in preventing the spread of bubonic plague. (As one authority put it in the context of describing earlier efforts to seal borders as a means of keeping bubonic plague at bay, "plague rats know no frontiers.")[8] Even under medical assumptions accepted at the time, the decision had a deep illogic about it, as would be forcefully pointed out by some later in the health crisis when another similar decision was taken. But the decision becomes quite understandable if one considers the then prevailing public health orthodoxy concerning Chinatown and the Chinese. As was noted in the last chapter, the district had over the years been consistently portrayed as a hub of dread diseases of all sorts.

The report of the discovery of a single suspected case of bubonic plague did not provoke any general alarm in the city. As to the measure decided upon by the health authorities, opinion differed. In general it can be said the quarantine decision met with approval, albeit of a rather tepid sort, in the Caucasian community. The consensus seemed to be that officials at worst were erring on the side of overcaution and were hardly to be faulted for that stance given the serious nature of the disease.[9] There were some notable exceptions to this rule, however. The San Francisco *Chronicle*, at the time the city's leading Republican daily, saw the whole incident as little more than an attempt by the health authorities, all Democrats, to secure higher budgetary appropriations for the board of health and, it hinted, to line their own pockets. It pooh-poohed claims of a plague outbreak and warned of the great harm that idle talk of this sort could cause San Francisco. "No greater calamity can befall a city," the paper editorialized, "than the visitation of a plague. Even the suspicion of one is sufficient to terrify the community, paralyze commerce, turn away strangers and prevent even the visits of neighbors and friends."[10] Having taken this position at the outset of the health crisis the *Chronicle* was to maintain it unaltered until the very end. The whole thing was in its view (and the view was reflected in editorial and report alike) never more than a concoction of local and federal health officials for nefarious ulterior purposes.

Reaction in the Chinese community to the quarantine decision was swift and bitter. A leading San Francisco Chinese-language daily, *Chung Sai Yat Po*, under a headline reading "Blockade is a Violation of the Law," editorialized, "According to the epidemic prevention laws a yellow flag should be planted in front of an epidemic-afflicted house, or the house should be encircled by tapes to warn people off. But never have we heard of blocking the whole town."[11] Merchants were heard to complain about the enormous financial losses they would suffer if cut off from intercourse with the rest of the city.[12] Crowds quickly gathered in Chinatown and in particular at the offices of the Chinese Six Companies to murmur their displeasure.[13]

The Six Companies in 1900, one must hasten to add, did not occupy the same position of unchallenged prominence and power that it did, let us say, in 1880. Nor was its leadership as confident and decisive as it once had been. One can detect a significant erosion in its authority within the Chinese-American community during the last decade of the nineteenth century that was due to a variety of reasons. It had lost considerable credibility due to its failure to overturn the registration provisions of the Geary Act, despite its assurances that it would. Then too it was coming to be seen by many as too narrowly tied to the merchant classes; by some as too closely allied with the regime in power in China. It was, nonetheless, still the first organization to which the Chinese, en masse, would turn for assistance when threatened with hostile action by the Caucasian world.

No statement was forthcoming from the Six Companies, but the Chinese consul general was quick to issue one. "I think the Chinese have been most unfairly treated, and if something is not done to modify the blockade I will try to obtain relief for the Chinese," he said on March 7. And he added, "It is wrong to close an extensive section like Chinatown simply upon the suspicion that a man might have died of the plague."[14] He clarified the next day what sort of relief he had in mind when he told the local press that, after consultation with counsel, he had decided to apply at once to the federal courts for an injunction to dissolve the blockade of Chinatown. Reflecting what was doubtless the dominant sentiment in the community he declared, "It is not right to single out the Chinese and treat them in this way."[15] At the same time he directed the Six Companies to assist in supervising the cleansing and disinfecting of all residences and places of business in Chinatown.[16]

Involvement of the Federal Health Officials

On the morning of March 7 board of health bacteriologist Kellogg took tissue from the suspected plague victim's lymph gland to the federal quarantine station on Angel Island in San Francisco Bay, which had an excellent bacteriological laboratory.[17] The physician in charge of the federal quarantine station and the man to whom Kellogg submitted his tissue sample was Dr. Joseph J. Kinyoun of the U.S. Marine Hospital Service, lineal ancestor of the U.S. Public Health Service. Following the standard diagnostic procedure he inoculated several laboratory animals with cells from the tissue sample with a view to observing their reaction.

Kinyoun reported directly to the supervising surgeon general of the Marine Hospital Service, Walter Wyman. Wyman had joined the service in 1876 and became its head in 1891. He was by all accounts a knowledgeable scientist and capable administrator.[18] He had taken a special interest in the worldwide plague pandemic and, in fact, in January 1900 had published a monograph on the subject.[19] Inasmuch as Wyman's views would come to play a preponderant role in shaping the San Francisco anti-plague campaign, the piece deserves careful analysis.

Medical science in 1900 could look back on its immediate past as a period of extraordinary accomplishment. The era had also witnessed, among other things, the invention of anesthesia, the development of effective techniques of antisepsis, the discovery of the pathogenic organisms responsible for a host of diseases (as noted above the bacillus responsible for plague was discovered in 1894), and finally quantum improvements in public health technology.[20] These accomplishments filled some in the medical community with a cocksure optimism verging on hubris that could distort one's vision and indeed thoroughly blind one to some fairly obvious realities. Wyman's monograph breathes this spirit. Bubonic plague, Wyman wrote, "furnishes a striking illustration of the scientific advance of modern medicine. It was not until 1894 that positive knowledge of its true nature became known. Now its cause, method of propagation, and the means to prevent its spread are matters of scientific certainty." Plague, like that other great epidemic disease, cholera, had been robbed of its terrors by the advances of modern science, he declared.[21] Having said this he then went on to faithfully echo the regnant and erroneous international consensus concerning plague's mode of transmission. "The methods by which the [plague] bacilli enter the body are three in number," he assured his readers, "by inoculation, . . . by respiration, and by introduction into the stomach."[22] An individual could, he explained, contract the disease through contact with a wound or abrasion, with infected soil, by inhaling the dust from infected houses, or by imbibing infected fluids or eating infected food. Implicit in Wyman's account of plague transmission was the notion that plague germs got into the dust or the air through the sputum, excretions, or exhalations of those infected with the disease. He went on to opine that the disease, like other contagious diseases, cholera, for example, or yellow fever, was favored in its propagation by the presence of filth or other unsanitary conditions in living quarters.[23] He also associated himself with the view that Asians, particularly the inhabitants of China and India, might be peculiarly susceptible to the disease because they were fed only on rice and other grains low in protein.[24] With respect to the long-recognized role of rats as harbingers of plague epidemics Wyman explained that rats had their snouts about an inch above the floors of houses and were thus more apt than humans to inhale plague-infested dust.[25] Wyman, like most others, believed that rats could serve as transmitters of plague germs, but through their excreta, rather than through the fleas they harbored.

The main measures Wyman recommended for preventing the spread of plague infection in the unlikely event that it should gain a foothold in North America were house-to-house inspection, the thorough cleansing and disinfection of infected or suspected houses, the removal of the sick to hospitals and the well to "refuge camps" (he did not elaborate on this measure), and the waging of an active campaign against rats and vermin. Finally, he waxed enthusiastic about a recently developed vaccine called Haffkine's prophylactic and an equally new serum developed by Yersin for the treatment of the disease and strongly recommended that sanitary officials consider their use.[26]

Wyman's confidence about medicine's ability to deal with bubonic plague was apparently not undermined, if he thought of it at all, by the recent British experience in India, where the best efforts of the health authorities, using methods similar to those he advocated, had failed dismally to check the disease's progress.[27]

Surgeon General Wyman had become aware almost immediately of the discovery of the suspected plague case both through local newspaper reports and through information supplied by surgeon James Gassaway, the Marine Hospital Service's medical officer in San Francisco[28] (given his own special interest in the malady, one may imagine how his curiosity must have been piqued by the development), and lost no time in plunging into the fray. He first directed his adjutant to offer full assistance to local authorities and then made his own views known as to what course of action ought to be followed. On March 8 he sent a wire, urging that, should plague in fact prove to be present in Chinatown, the following recommendations be conveyed posthaste to the local health authorities: that Chinatown be thoroughly disinfected, using sulfur rather than formaldehyde as the disinfecting agent, that anyone known to have been exposed to plague be treated with Yersin's therapeutic serum and, most significantly, that all other residents of Chinatown be inoculated with Haffkine's prophylactic vaccine.[29] At the same time he directed that supplies of the serum and vaccine be sent immediately to San Francisco by express mail.[30] Wyman's readiness to be of assistance was gratefully acknowledged by local health authorities.

The End of the First Quarantine

Laboratory animals inoculated with tissue containing the plague bacillus will normally develop symptoms of the disease in fairly rapid order. When, therefore, Kinyoun's animals had not yet developed symptoms by March 9, some began to waver in their analysis of what was transpiring. Dr. Kellogg, for example, now said that he was not so certain of his original diagnosis.[31] In the meantime restlessness and discontent could be seen to be increasing daily in Chinatown. The city's newspapers, the *Chronicle* in the forefront were showing signs of skepticism about the board's handling of affairs, and then of course there was the announced threat of Chinese legal action. Perhaps for all of these reasons the board of health, just as suddenly as it had decided to impose the quarantine on Chinatown, decided suddenly on March 9 to end it. Health Officer O'Brien told the press, "We raised the blockade because the general clamor had become too great to ignore and we desired to injure no more people than was absolutely necessary."[32] O'Brien noted that the time in which the inoculated laboratory animals might develop the disease had technically not yet expired but thought that, given all the circumstances, the board's rescission of its original decision was not imprudent. The *Chronicle*, evidencing little concern for the affected Chinese but much for the reputation of San Francisco, scored the board for its handling of the entire affair. "It has been telegraphed to the ends of the earth," the paper editorialized, "that San Francisco is an infected city."[33] But Democratic Mayor James Phelan, went out of his way to defend the decision to quarantine and dismissed out of hand Chinese complaints about unfairness. "I desire to say," he declared, "that they are fortunate, with the unclean habits of their coolies and their filthy hovels, to be permitted to remain within the corporate limits of any American city. In an economic sense their presence has been, and is, a great injury to the working classes, and in a sanitary sense, they are a constant menace to the public health."[34]

Health Officer O'Brien's caveat about the time that still needed to elapse before Kinyoun's laboratory animals could be declared free of the disease proved prophetic, for on March 11 three of the inoculated laboratory animals died, and both pathological and bacteriological examinations by Kinyoun's laboratory established beyond question that the cause of death was bubonic plague. Kinyoun invited members of the board of health to visit his Angel Island facility to confirm for themselves his own diagnosis.[35] Having satisfied themselves that Kinyoun's diagnosis was correct, the board convened on the night of March 11 and again the next day to determine what measures ought to be taken. For a brief moment it toyed with the idea of reimposing a quarantine on Chinatown, but when the board was informed that the mere mention of the possibility of a new blockade was causing many Chinese to flee the quarter[36] it relented and decided on a less drastic course of action. It called for a force of volunteers to undertake a house-to-house inspection of all of Chinatown, with a view to thoroughly cleansing and disinfecting the area and isolating any additional suspected plague cases.[37] It is significant to note that lawyers representing both the Chinese Six Companies and the Chinese consulate were present at the board of health meetings. They pledged their cooperation. (It will be remembered that the consul had already asked the Six Companies to supervise a general cleanup of the area.) The attorney for the Six Companies, former Judge D. J. Murphy, said that the organization could supply people to assist in the inspection of Chinatown. "The only thing I ask," he added, "is that you treat those people kindly."[38] John Bennett, the attorney representing the consul general, declared the consulate's equal willingness to cooperate and noted that it had already posted notices requesting the Chinese to summon white physicians in cases of severe illness.[39] The next day, as a token of their good faith, the Six Companies and the Chinese consulate posted joint proclamations throughout Chinatown urging all inhabitants to cooperate with board of health officials in their efforts.[40]

The board-ordered inspection and disinfection of Chinatown were dismissed by the *Chronicle* as but further proof of the incompetency of the city's governors. It continued to insist that there was neither plague nor danger of plague in San Francisco and that to say otherwise was to do irreparable harm to the city's commerce.[41] Other papers echoed the same theme, but the *Examiner* roundly rebuked its fellow journals for criticizing the board and commended it for its decision.[42]

Implementation of the board of health's decrees got underway slowly but picked up pace as the month wore on. The specific actions undertaken by city police, health officials and those who had volunteered to assist them included: a house-to-house inspection of Chinatown residences, the fumigation of dwellings and sewers with sulfur dioxide, the washing of walls and ceilings with a solution of lye or bichloride of mercury, and the spreading of chloride of lime on the districts streets. In addition a great deal of dry refuse was removed from houses and burned. The Chinese were reported to be cooperating fully with the authorities.[43] These measures were aimed primarily at killing plague germs, which, as noted above, were believed to be lurking about in the soil, on the interior surfaces of rooms, in the possessions of the sick, and in the air.[44] They were similar to the sorts of measures public health authorities would have undertaken to combat an epidemic of smallpox, scarlet fever, diphtheria or some other classic infectious disease and duplicated almost exactly the actions taken by the Municipal Council of Bombay three years earlier when plague broke out in that city.[45] In retrospect we can see that they would have been of little or no use in combating an incipient outbreak of bubonic plague.[46]

The Discovery of New Cases and the Decision to Inoculate the Chinese and Japanese

An alarming product of the inspection of Chinatown was the discovery by the middle of the month of an additional three suspected plague cases. This provoked an angry response from San Francisco Board of Health President Williamson. He declared his belief that the Chinese quarter of the city was "infested" with the disease and that the Chinese were concealing cases.[47] He pledged that every house in Chinatown would be searched and that the whole area would be, as he put it, "drenched" with disinfectants.[48] In addition he wrote to the president of the California State Board of Health, W. P. Matthews, requesting him to direct health authorities in the state's interior to keep a close watch on Chinese settlements in their vicinity and to be especially vigilant about Chinese who might recently have arrived from San Francisco.[49]

The discovery of the three new suspected plague cases was reported by the Associated Press wire service, and its dispatch appeared in several East Coast newspapers. The outcry in certain quarters of the city about the damage that these reports were doing to San Francisco prompted Mayor Phelan to send an urgent telegram on March 26 to the mayors of fifty eastern cities. "Eastern newspapers just received refer to a sporadic case [*sic*] of bubonic plague in San Francisco. The board of health reported Chinatown has been inspected and disinfected. No other case has appeared. All persons now freely visit the district as usual. On account of the vigilance and efficiency of our health department and Federal quarantine there is no further danger. Please give this to your local press as an act of justice to San Francisco."[50]

Phelan's assertion that only one case of plague had been detected in Chinatown was technically correct since the diagnosis of the other three cases had yet to be definitively confirmed. But in fact the local and federal health authorities had little doubt about them as Williamson's statement, quoted above, clearly showed. One catches in the anguished tone of Phelan's telegram something of the cold fear that must have seized him at the thought of what might happen to the city's trade and commerce should other parts of the country become convinced that San Francisco was in the grips of a full-blown epidemic of bubonic plague. It was a fear shared by many of the city's political and business leaders,[51] and Phelan doubtless would have come under pressure to do more to allay concerns outside had not events, or more accurately, the lack of events come to his rescue. Days and then weeks passed without any new reports of plague in Chinatown, and by mid-April the subject had quite faded from the public mind. The board of health's cleansing and disinfecting efforts did continue and were even extended to comprehend part of the city's Italian district, which closely adjoined Chinatown. On April 24 yet another suspicious death occurred in Chinatown, but the news caused little stir. One has the sense of general, if slightly uneasy, consensus among health officials that things were now under control and that the worst of the episode was over.

This air of confidence, if it can be so described, was rudely shattered several weeks later when in the short space of three days, May 11, 12, and 13, four deaths occurred in Chinatown that seemed in all probability due to plague. While local authorities pondered what to do about this new and untoward turn of events, Surgeon General Wyman, who had been kept abreast of developments by his officers on the scene, surgeons Gassaway and Kinyoun,[52] decided that the time had come for the federal government to thrust itself more forcefully into the events that were transpiring. Indeed the time had come for the Marine Hospital Service to seize the initiative and assume control of the plague-control campaign. On May 15 he dispatched the following telegram to quarantine officer Kinyoun.

> Chinese Minister has agreed to wire Consul General, San Francisco, to use his influence to have the Chinese comply cheerfully with necessary measures and consult with you as representative of the United States Government. Confer with Consul General. Have about twenty thousand Haffkine on hand; will be sent to-morrow. If Gassaway has any get it. Suggest advisability of following measures: One man in supreme charge; subordinates in charge of division. Cordon of suspected area; guard ferries and R.R. stations with reference to Chinese only; house to house inspection with Haffkine inoculation; Chinatown to be restricted; pest house in Chinatown, using some substantial building; suspects from plague houses to be removed to a suspect house in Chinatown, if you deem necessary to Angel Island; a disinfecting corpse; destruction of rats; inspection of R.R. and outside territory.[53]

If still a trifle vague on some details, the telegram's message was in its main point quite clear. As the chief means of combating the plague outbreak Wyman had decided on the mass inoculation of San Francisco's Chinese population with Haffkine's prophylactic vaccine.[54] And the plan would have an element of coercion to it.

Haffkine's Prophylactic Vaccine

The vaccine with which federal and local health authorities were proposing to inoculate the Chinese inhabitants of San Francisco consisted of a killed broth culture of the plague bacillus. It had been introduced to the world only three years earlier, in 1897 by Waldemar Haffkine, a renowned Swiss bacteriologist, who had been trained in Paris at the Pasteur Institute. Haffkine had found himself in India when the plague epidemic broke out in that country and had been commissioned by the Indian Home Department to conduct research on methods of dealing with the disease. After a few short months he announced that he had available and ready for use an effective vaccine against the plague. In short order something resembling a controlled experiment with the vaccine was attempted in a Bombay prison (Bombay was one of the worst affected Indian cities), where half of the inmates volunteered to be inoculated. The results seemed encouraging to Haffkine and his fellow researchers, and a laboratory was soon founded for the mass production of the vaccine. Needless to say, Haffkine's announcement aroused enormous interest around the world, especially in those countries where plague had taken root, and thousands of doses were sent out from Haffkine's laboratory in the next few years.[55]

The vaccine was highly toxic, and its administration was frequently accompanied by localized pain and swelling, headache, and high fever. Reactions were occasionally quite severe and could render an individual prostrate for many days. There were occasionally even reports of death. (In a Punjab village, for example, fourteen people died after they were inoculated with a contaminated batch of the vaccine.)[56] Under the best of circumstances an inoculated person would be incapacitated for a day or two. For these reasons it proved difficult, not only in those early years but even later when improved versions of the vaccine were developed, to persuade people to submit to inoculation. (Adding to the difficulty was the fact that inoculated individuals occasionally still caught the disease.)[57] Nonetheless, in the period between the development of the vaccine and the close of the nineteenth century many thousands did agree to be inoculated, the overwhelming majority in those parts of India where plague seemed to be raging out of control.[58]

It is almost impossible to assess today with any degree of certainty how effective Haffkine's early solution might have been as an anti-plague preventive. Some data suggests it was efficacious although the statistical evidence that most impressed the world, namely that offered by Indian authorities, is now viewed with some skepticism.[59] Plague immunology, it turns out, has from the very beginning been a controversial subject. Indeed as recently as 1983 a leading authority on plague, despite decades of improvement in the technology of producing Haffkine's vaccine, of experimentation with laboratory animals, and of observation of human subjects, could write, "The efficacy of killed vaccines in preventing human plague has been claimed but never proven in a randomized field trial."[60] One thing can be said with certainty: in May of 1900 Haffkine's prophylactic was understood by most scientific contemporaries to be still an experimental drug.

Events Immediately Following the Wyman Telegram of May 15

For what transpired in the immediate wake of Surgeon General Wyman's May 15 telegram we must rely entirely upon the recollections of surgeon

Kinyoun, contained in a letter that he wrote to his chief on June 11.[61] According to this letter, immediately upon the receipt of the telegram (whether on May 15 or 16 is not clear) he met with the Chinese consul general, Ho Yow, and his attorney, John Bennett. At this meeting, he relates, he fully discussed the plague situation with them and secured their agreement that "the most reasonable solution of the question was to advise all the Chinese residents living in the infected area" to submit to inoculation with the Haffkine vaccine.[62] On the same day, he further relates, he attended a conference with, significantly, representatives of the San Francisco Merchants Association and the local board of health, at which conference Bennett also was present. According to Kinyoun, it was the general impression among those present at the meeting "that the Chinese *and Japanese* [emphasis added] would gladly avail themselves of inoculation in order to obviate the necessity of enforcing more severe measures." He records that he expressed skepticism at this prediction, suggesting that compulsory inoculation, while it could not then be considered, "was the only recourse."[63] The following day (at Bennett's suggestion, according to Kinyoun) yet another meeting was held, this one involving, in addition to the consul general, the board of health, and representatives of the Merchants Association, a large number of Chinese from the Six Companies. Kinyoun was not present at this meeting, but his deputy surgeon Gassaway was. The meeting's main upshot was a reaffirmation by the Chinese leaders of their commitment to recommend to the Chinese population that it submit to inoculation. "It was understood by the board as well as others that there would be no opposition by the Chinese to accepting vaccination," Kinyoun writes.[64]

One should read Kinyoun's narrative with some measure of reserve. It was written almost a month after the events, at a time when federal health policies had suffered several reversals and when Kinyoun had every reason to paint his actions a month earlier in as rosy a hue as possible. The letter has the strong air of an apologia about it. That said, on the bare facts it is probably correct. One may well believe that the Chinese leaders promised Kinyoun that they would recommend inoculation. One may be excused from believing, however, that they did so entirely of their own accord, having become persuaded, as it were, by Caucasian merchants and health authorities that this was the most prudent course of action from a community health standpoint. These decisions were taken in what surely must have been a pressure-cooker atmosphere. Furthermore, Kinyoun's task was not to win Chinese approval for a plan under deliberation but to secure their endorsement of a course of action already decided upon. And he had a powerful bargaining chip on his side, the threat, as he put it, of "more severe measures."[65]

On May 18 Surgeon General Wyman sent a second telegram to Kinyoun, expanding further on the steps that were to be taken to implement the proposed inoculation scheme.

> In event bumpkin [i.e. plague] becomes officially proclaimed see J. C. Stubbs third Vice President Southern Pacific or J. Kruttschmitt General Manager and request refusal sale of tickets to Chinese or Japanese without accompanying certificate from Marine Hospital officer.[66]

The May 15 dispatch had referred to the guarding of ferries and railroad stations "with reference to Chinese only." What Wyman had in mind now became much clearer. Through the cooperation of the transport companies the Chinese were going to be presented with the alternatives of being inoculated or having their freedom of movement severely restricted. Interestingly, for the first time, Wyman's concern was now extended beyond the Chinese to include San Francisco's small but growing Japanese population as well. The same evening the San Francisco Board of Health met in extraordinary session to consider the new federal proposals. Little time was lost in debating them, and in short order they were unanimously endorsed although the resolution of endorsement took a curiously general form. It said simply that it was the board's sense that bubonic plague existed in the city and county of San Francisco and that the steps already taken for the prevention of its spread should be continued "together with such additional measures as may be required."[67]

On May 19 Kinyoun informed the railroads that they should refuse passage out of San Francisco to any Chinese or Japanese who did not possess a certificate of inoculation.[68] At the same time he ordered inspectors posted at common points of exit from the city and at crossing points between California and the adjacent states of Arizona, Nevada, and Oregon.[69] Two days later the government in Washington sought to provide these decisions with a retroactive legal basis. The secretary of the treasury, at Wyman's insistence, promulgated a regulation authorizing the surgeon general, while plague existed in the United States, "to forbid the sale or donation of transportation by common carrier to Asiatics or other races particularly liable to the disease."[70] The regulation was said to be based on a federal statute passed in 1890.[71]

Reaction in the Chinese Community

Rumor that the health authorities were planning some kind of mass inoculation had begun to percolate through Chinatown as early as May 17 and, in the words of the Chinese daily *Chung Sai Yat Po,* immediately "plunged the town into disorder."[72] Spontaneously a large crowd of very agitated people gathered at the offices of the Chinese Six Companies, shouting their determination not to submit to inoculation. The merchant leaders of the association seemed at a loss as to what to do to calm the crowd until one of them took the floor and promised that a lawyer would be retained and some sort of legal action brought against the health officials. A reporter for *Chung Sai Yat Po,* apparently unable to locate the Chinese consul, took it upon himself to find the Chinese consulate's attorney, John Bennett, in order to find out exactly what was going on. Bennett sought to allay popular fears by assuring the reporter that inoculation would cause minor, temporary discomfort and would do no long-lasting harm. The reporter told Bennett that the Chinese would never submit to forced inoculation and wondered aloud why Consul Ho "was so lazy as not to lodge a protest." Bennett sought to defend Ho. The consul, he said, had been very energetic in representing Chinese interests, and it was only because of these efforts and those of some sympathetic American merchants that more draconian measures, a blockade, or even worse, the razing of the Chinese quarter to the ground, were thwarted.[73]

As word spread to more people in the community, fear, at times bordering on panic, and resentment increased. The next day large groups of people could be found milling about in the streets of Chinatown murmuring anxiously about what was in the offing. An even larger and more unruly crowd gathered at the Six Companies offices. Many could not squeeze into the association's premises and hovered around outside. Someone in the assembly pointed out (correctly as it turns out) that what was being proposed was quite different from smallpox immunization, that persons inoculated with the plague vaccine would run a fever for several days and that inoculation might be devastating to a person of frail constitution. Someone else proposed that all business establishments in Chinatown be shut down in protest, a proposal that met with great approval from those assembled.[74] Events were beginning to press in on the leaders of the Chinese community. It does not seem likely that either Consul Ho or his counterparts in the Six Companies had foreseen how deep or intense the community's opposition would be to the idea of inoculation with the plague prophylactic.

On May 18 the Chinese Six Companies and Consul General Ho sent an urgent joint cable to the Chinese minister in Washington

> Authorities insist inoculation, even by force, all Chinese object, would rather go back to China than subject. They say there is no plague at all. Please use your influence at once have authorities have officers here to facilitate matters as they intend to commence at once. If they inoculate by force there might be trouble and bloodshed and may lead to serious complications.[75]

They also dispatched the attorney Bennett and two other lawyers to inform the health board of Chinese resistance to forcible immunization. This they did, but they returned to the offices of the Six Companies late in the evening of the 18th quite empty-handed. The authorities, they said, could not be deflected from their inoculation plans, which were set to commence the next day. The Chinese could refuse to be inoculated but if they did they would not be permitted to leave the limits of the city and county of San Francisco. Having taken these actions the Six Companies informed the Chinese community that their lawyers would continue to consult with the health authorities and that the community should await the result of these consultations and of the negotiations that the Chinese minister could be expected to enter into with Federal officials in Washington. In the meantime they urged the Chinese "not to argue with the health officers" who would be coming to administer inoculation.[76]

Early in the morning of May 19, 1900, a sizable force of physicians and municipal health workers, armed with hypodermic syringes and ample supplies of Haffkine's prophylactic, descended upon Chinatown to administer the inoculation to those who would have it. Not surprisingly they found very few takers. Caucasian journalists who visited Chinatown reported that opposition to inoculation was well nigh universal. Large numbers of businesses were shut down to signify opposition to the health board's actions. Knots of Chinese gathered on street corners to denounce it. Many were frantically trying to leave Chinatown. Chinese merchants, interviewed by the press, threatened to go to court to prevent forcible inoculation. Coming quickly to the crux of the matter, they pointed out that the vaccine was "experimental" and, they declared, "they wished to protect their persons."[77] By the end of the first day the merest handful of Chinese had agreed to be inoculated.

Nothing materially changed in the next days. No mass of Chinese presented themselves for inoculation on the morning of May 20, as had been envisioned by the plan discussed a few days earlier. Someone from the health authorities conceived the idea that if health personnel publicly allowed themselves to be inoculated, the example would persuade the Chinese that they had nothing to fear from the vaccine. The example had no such effect, and opposition, if anything, stiffened as each succeeding day passed. Rumors began to circulate in Chinatown at least according to the western press that tong gangsters were threatening anyone who submitted to inoculation.[78] Despite the pleas from the Six Companies and the consul general that they reopen, most businesses continued to remain closed, and posters appeared threatening to take the life of any merchant who dared reopen.[79] A large and unruly crowd of people twice surrounded the residence of Consul Ho on May 21, demanding that he take forceful steps to prevent compulsory inoculation, and the police had to be summoned to disperse them.[80] Matters were becoming dicey indeed, and actions taken by Caucasian officials did little to ease tensions. A notice ordered posted by the board of health, for example, sought to assuage Chinese concerns by assuring the Chinese population that the government had spared no expense in preparing the medicine that was being used for vaccination and that the Chinese could avail themselves of the opportunity of being inoculated by their own doctors if they so chose. However, the notices added that it would be self-defeating for the Chinese to refuse vaccination and that if they balked long enough harsher measures would be considered.[81]

The Chinese Seek the Assistance of the Courts

In spite of the general suspicion of the vaccine that prevailed in the community a small number of Chinese had agreed to be inoculated in the first days of the campaign. One need not look far for reasons. Many Chinese either worked or had business interests beyond the borders of San Francisco or lived outside the city and worked within it. For these confinement in the city posed the threat of severe economic hardship, and this prospect was doubtless enough to cause some to suppress their concerns for bodily safety. Reports of what had happened to those Chinese who had submitted to inoculation first appeared in the press on May 22. They were not encouraging. On that date, for example, the *Record-Union* quoted the Chinese consul general as saying that many of the Chinese who had been inoculated, his own clerk among them, were deathly ill and that this was well known throughout the community.[82] The next day *Chung Sai Yat Po* published a detailed account of the sufferings endured by two Chinese who had submitted to vaccination. According to this report, entitled "Zhao and Shen's Case Is a Warning To Us," one young man named Zhao had received an injection of the vaccine in the stomach whereupon he had begun to run a fever and suffer excruciating pain. Shortly after arriving home he had lost consciousness, and his father had had to summon a physician. Another Chinese had had a similar experience. He had, said the paper, been injected at the wharf upon returning to San Francisco (from across San Francisco Bay, one may guess), had almost immediately begun to suffer pain and had gone to the offices of the Six Companies to complain. He there collapsed and seemed about to expire until a doctor, who had been called, was able to revive him. Word of his condition spread and a crowd of several hundred gathered at the Six Companies building and began to create a din.[83]

Incidents of this sort could not have helped but bring home to the Six

Companies leadership and to Consul Ho as well the need to take some more forceful initiative than had theretofore been taken if they hoped to preserve their authority in the community at large. The step that they decided to take was the sort of step that the Chinese had over the course of almost a half century become habituated to taking when they felt themselves pushed into a corner by adverse governmental action. They sought recourse and protection in the courts.

On May 24, 1900, the law firm of Reddy, Campbell, and Metson, a firm under retainer to the Six Companies, filed a bill of complaint in the United States Circuit Court for the Northern District of California on behalf of one Wong Wai, a Chinese merchant engaged in business in San Francisco. Named as defendants were J. J. Kinyoun and all of the members of the San Francisco Board of Health. The complaint averred that the defendants had adopted a resolution requiring all Chinese residents of the city to be inoculated with Haffkine's prophylactic vaccine and as a means of enforcing the order were refusing the Chinese the right to leave the city unless they submitted to inoculation.[84] The bill went on to allege that the vaccine in question was an experimental drug of high toxicity, whose efficacy had not been conclusively demonstrated, that under the best of circumstances it was of use only as a plague preventive and of no possible use where plague did not exist and that plague did not exist in San Francisco.[85] The actions of the health authorities, urged the complainant, constituted a "purely arbitrary, unreasonable, unwarranted, wrongful and oppressive interference" with his and his Chinese compatriots' personal liberty (the complaint pleaded the impracticality of joining all twenty-five thousand Chinese as complainants and asked the court to see Wong Wai as representative of a class of complainants) and with his and their right to "pursue a lawful business."[86] Furthermore, inasmuch as the authorities' actions were only directed against the Chinese, they constituted a denial of "the equal protection of the laws," guaranteed the Chinese by the Constitution of the United States, by law and by treaty.[87] The complaint asked the court to issue a "provisional injunction" (to be made permanent on final hearing), enjoining the defendants and all persons acting in their behalf from continuing to deprive the Chinese of "their right to freely pass from [the] city and county of San Francisco to other parts of the State of California."[88]

Accompanying the complaint were affidavits from several Chinese merchants to the effect that they carried on mercantile business throughout the state and, having from time to time to travel beyond the borders of San Francisco, had sought on May 23 to go to Oakland across San Francisco Bay but had been prevented from doing so by agents of the defendants because they could not produce certificates of inoculation.[89]

The request for a "provisional injunction" was the equivalent of a request for a "temporary restraining order," an ex parte decree that would have halted straightaway, pending a hearing on the merits of the Chinese case, any further implementation of the inoculation plan.[90] Circuit Judge William Morrow, who heard this request, refused to issue the sought after provisional injunction but did direct the defendants to appear in his court the next day to show cause why an injunction should not issue.[91]

The hearing which convened in the circuit court on May 25 before Circuit Judge Morrow and District Judges Thomas Hawley and John DeHaven brought out a large crowd, including many prominent members of the Chinese and Japanese communities.[92] Spokesmen for the Chinese cause were James Maguire, a former judge appearing on behalf of the Chinese Six Companies, John E. Bennett appearing for the Chinese consulate, and Samuel Shortridge, another distinguished local counsel, later to be a U.S. Senator from California, brought into the case by the San Francisco affiliate of the Chinese Empire Reform Association (Pao Huanghui), an organization founded in 1899 in Canada by the prominent Cantonese activist, K'ang Yu-wei, and dedicated to promoting radical political reform in China.[93] One reporter present at the hearing was moved to comment, "The Chinese are represented by an array of legal talent seldom, if ever before, seen in the local courts."[94] On the other side was the United States attorney for the Northern District of California, Frank L. Coombs, representing quarantine officer Kinyoun and Assistant District Attorney Charles Weller representing the other defendants.

For reasons that are not entirely clear (perhaps simply lack of time) no responsive pleadings were filed by either the San Francisco district attorney's office or the U.S. attorney. In lieu thereof the district attorney submitted a copy of the board of health resolution of May 18 declaring its sense that plague existed in the city, and the U.S. attorney produced Wyman's telegram to Kinyoun of May 21 directing him to inform the transport companies that they should not issue tickets to Asiatics. No objection being made, these documents were accepted by the court as the defendants' return to the Order to Show Cause.[95] And it was left to the defendants in oral argument to develop their theory of their case.

In argument[96] before the court the attorneys for the Chinese elaborated on the averments in their bill of complaint. They stressed the toxic and experimental character of the Haffkine vaccine, noted its possible ill effects if administered to anyone who might have been exposed to plague, denied that the health authorities had made a case that there was a plague epidemic or that Asians were peculiarly susceptible to the disease, and urged that in singling out the Chinese for inoculation or confinement in the city they were acting arbitrarily and denying to the Chinese the equal treatment that was guaranteed them by both treaty and the fundamental law. In support of their argument as to the arbitrary character of the authorities' actions they noted that the Chinese (and other Asians) were permitted to roam wherever they pleased within the city of San Francisco, hardly a logical decision if the Chinese were thought to be a threat to the general health. They made some new points as well, Maguire arguing that the board of health did not have the authority *sua sponte* and absent authorization by the board of supervisors to order measures so far-reaching and extreme. Bennett argued that the federal authorities were acting ultra vires when they sought to restrict the *intrastate* movement of persons and that, further, the Wyman telegram furnished no authorization for Kinyoun to act as he did.

The chief spokesman for the government side was U.S. Attorney Coombs. His strategy, it appears, was first to establish that plague did exist in the city and then to argue that in health emergencies of this sort the authorities should be given almost unlimited berth in fashioning remedial measures. The court, however, ordered him to address himself only to the allegations of arbitrariness and unjust discrimination raised by the Chinese. To this Coombs could only make the bald assertion, without any offer of proof, that it was well known that Asiatics were peculiarly susceptible to the disease and that this was more than ample justification for the measures being taken. "If the Federal authorities cannot regulate against a class of people in which this disease is most likely to occur, then Congress had no right to pass the exclusion act,"[97] he declared.

The State of Public Health Law in 1900

In challenging the health measures, counsel for the Chinese were embarking on something of an uphill battle. Public health legislation of one sort or another dated back to time immemorial and boards of health had by 1900 become familiar governmental institutions,[98] and by that date a body of public health jurisprudence had begun to emerge. There was not a plethora of case authority but what did exist confirmed that the state's power to make regulations to protect the public health was at the core of the so-called police power; and the cases also suggested that both the legislature and the administrative agencies such as local boards of health were invested with wide discretion in determining the content of health regulations. The issue of the limits of health authorities' powers had been raised with some frequency in the last decade of the nineteenth century in connection with measures that made smallpox vaccination a condition of school attendance, and here the overwhelming weight of authority was that such measures, even though they involved severe restraints on the individual, were legitimate exercises of the police power. One of the first courts to say so, in fact, was the California Supreme Court, which in 1890 had rejected a challenge to an 1889 law providing for the vaccination of all children attending the public schools and for the exclusion of the unvaccinated.[99] Of course smallpox vaccination could hardly be called experimental. It went back over a century and was thought by virtually the whole of the medical establishment to be an effective disease preventive. Furthermore, the courts had not given governmental officials carte blanche in designing public health measures nor had they said that such measures simply because they had been duly adopted were insulated from court scrutiny. Those tribunals that had sustained compulsory smallpox vaccination, for example, had usually made clear that such measures, like all other exercises of the police power that restrained individual liberty, needed justification and could be blocked if they smacked of arbitrariness or did not seem warranted by the facts.[100]

Judge Morrow's Decision

The man in whose hands the decision in the *Wong Wai* case chiefly lay, Judge Morrow, had been a federal judge since 1891. Before that he had served three terms as a Republican member of the House of Representatives. While still involved in partisan politics he had hardly distinguished himself by any special solicitude for the Chinese, describing them in one of his speeches as a class "destitute of moral qualities" and once referring to the Chinese Six Companies as the ultimate power enforcing the servitude of the Chinese masses.[101] While on the bench he had heard a number of Chinese exclusion cases and in general had sided with the government, construing the terms of the exclusion legislation strictly so as to defeat Chinese claims.[102] But he had also ruled (in a decision that foreshadowed in some ways the position ultimately taken by the U.S. Supreme Court) that the 1894 act, giving immigration officials final authority to make exclusion decisions, did not apply to persons claiming the right to enter the country on grounds of citizenship. These he said were subject to court review via habeas proceedings.[103] On May 28, Judge Morrow, speaking for a unanimous court, handed down an opinion, completely vindicating the Chinese claims.

He had questions first about the authority of the board of health to act as it was acting. The alleged basis for its action was the resolution of May 18, but the legislative authority of the board seemed rather narrowly circumscribed by the city charter. It had authority to "enforce all ordinances, rules and regulations which may be adopted by the supervisors for the carrying out and enforcement of a good sanitary condition in the city, and for the protection of the public health." It also had the limited authority to draft and submit to the supervisors for approval such ordinances, rules, and regulations as it might deem necessary to promote the public health. But nowhere did the charter appear to give it the authority to legislate on its own initiative. Then too the extremely vague quality of the resolution in question did not escape Morrow's notice. "The resolution of the board of health furnished to the court fails to disclose the method it has adopted [for promoting the public health] under the conditions it has declared to exist."[104] For Morrow, however, there was no need to dwell on the question of whether the board had adequate authority to do what it was doing. Its actions, whether or not authorized, were from a constitutional viewpoint clearly infirm. (The court, it should be noted, also questioned the authority of Kinyoun, noting that there had been no presidential finding that plague existed in San Francisco as the 1890 statute seemed to require and, more important, that Wyman's telegram said nothing about compulsory inoculation.)[105]

The court recognized that public authorities were often presented with unexpected emergencies affecting the public health and should have wide discretion in devising means of dealing with them, but it noted that these means could not be arbitrary. And that was the problem with the measures adopted by the health authorities. They were, wrote Morrow cutting to the pith of the matter, "not based upon any established distinction in the conditions that are supposed to attend this plague, or the persons exposed to its contagion" but were instead "boldly directed against the Asiatic or Mongolian race as a class, without regard to the previous condition, habits, exposure to disease, or residence of the individual." Asians were supposed to be more liable to contracting the disease than others, but when he had asked defendants' counsel to substantiate this claim in oral argument they had not been able to do so.[106]

Morrow took note of those features of the authorities' actions that would have rendered them suspect even had they not been directed exclusively against a racial minority. He observed, for instance, that while those subject to the order were being forbidden to leave the city without inoculation, no limits were placed on their freedom of movement within the city.[107] The surgeon general had himself cautioned public health officials that Haffkine's vaccine was strictly a preventive drug and that it should not be administered to anyone who might have been exposed to infection, its administration to such persons being highly dangerous. Yet everyone subject to the order, it appeared, irrespective of possible previous exposure to the disease, was being required to submit to inoculation.[108]

It was, however, the racially discriminatory character of the health officials' actions to which Morrow felt compelled to return, and it was this that condemned them decisively in his eyes. It was this feature of the inoculation campaign that put it in clear violation of the equal protection clause of the Fourteenth Amendment, which guaranteed that Asians, absent some compelling reason, should be subject to the same restrictions and conditions for the benefit of the public health as the members of other ethnic groups.[109]

On the same day the decision was handed down U.S. Attorney Coombs sent a telegram to his superior, tersely noting its terms and rationale. "The matter," he said, "was argued and well considered on its merits."[110] A few days later he wired again, this time striking something of a more defensive tone, contending that the outcome had come as a surprise to all and that it might have been different had the court not refused his offer to demonstrate that plague did exist in San Francisco. He did not, however, suggest that the decision be appealed, nor did he think there was any reason for further involvement by the federal quarantine officer. "The local Board of Health has now taken hold of the matter and I think it can safely be left to its authority," he declared.[111]

Local Authorities Consider a New Strategy

By the time Coombs sent his second telegram the San Francisco Board of Health was busy implementing a new plan for containing the bubonic plague outbreak. Its actions seem to have been prompted by an ultimatum it had received from the California State Board of Health.

The state board, charged with protecting the health of the state as a whole, had, as events unfolded in San Francisco during the spring, become increasingly apprehensive about the possible spread of bubonic plague to other California communities. It grew equally concerned as the weeks passed about the increasing attention being given to the San Francisco situation by the out-of-state news media and by the actions being taken in reaction to the news by some out-of-state health authorities.[112] At its May 21 meeting in San Francisco, for example, the state board had heard reports that New Orleans was refusing to permit Chinese, Japanese, or poor whites from San Francisco to travel there and was refusing to receive certain classes of freight. More important, it was told that the health officer of Texas was quarantining at the border against all passengers and freight destined to Texas points from San Francisco. The board's response was to send notice to health authorities across the country, acknowledging that a limited number of plague cases had previously been discovered in San Francisco (all of them "Chinese found dead in their unsanitary quarters") but informing them that there were no longer any cases to be found and that the San Francisco health authorities were implementing every precaution to see that they did not recur. The board ordered a special telegram sent to the Texas health officer, urging him to remove the quarantine on goods and persons from California or at least modify it to apply to Chinese only.[113]

Within hours of Morrow's decision the state board convened in special session in San Francisco. In attendance were a number of invited guests including federal and local health officials, officers of the railroads, and a fair cross section of the San Francisco mercantile community. At the outset one board member introduced a resolution urging the counties contiguous to the city and county of San Francisco to close their gates to the entry of Chinese or Japanese from the city. No one bothered to reflect on how such a racially partial ban on travel between counties would comport with the sense or spirit of Judge Morrow's decision, but several businessmen were quick to point out how counterproductive the passage of such a resolution could be from a commercial standpoint. The freight manager of Southern Pacific said, in view of the free intercourse between Orientals and Caucasians within the city ("they wash our clothes; they are in the houses as servants"), that he did not see how the resolution could be limited to Orientals alone. It would have to apply to everyone, and that would amount to a statement that plague was epidemic in San Francisco and a declaration of the city of a self-imposed quarantine. The vice president of the railroad endorsed this view, predicting that the measure would cause other states to follow the example of Texas and "bar their ports to the products of this state." Both urged the board to exercise the utmost care and prudence in whatever it decided because whatever decision it took held the potential of affecting the entire industrial economy of California.

The first trial balloon having been quickly punctured, those present at the meeting seemed at a loss as to what steps to recommend and the discussion for a time meandered aimlessly. The logjam was finally broken by a suggestion offered by Dr. W. F. Blunt, the health officer of Texas. Blunt had been sent to California on a mission of investigation, had been in the city now for several days, and had been invited to come and observe the board's proceedings. He rose to say that he had been surprised to observe during his visit to the city the extent to which whites and Chinese freely intermingled. He thought it would make much more sense from a public health standpoint if the Chinese were strictly confined to one district and no intercourse with them permitted. "Put on a strong quarantine on Chinatown, allow no citizen to go in or out," he declared, and he would, after the elapse of thirty days, advise lifting Texas' blockade of California goods. The suggestion met with immediate, enthusiastic approval from most present, one merchant even volunteering to finance a volunteer "pickax" brigade to keep the Chinese in Chinatown should the local constabulary prove unequal to the task; and the members of the San Francisco Board of Health who were present were instructed that they should proceed forthwith to have Chinatown quarantined.[114]

The same day the San Francisco Board of Health met to consider the state board's request. A large number of the city's merchants were present at this meeting as well, and many lent their strong support to the state board proposal. One member voiced an objection to the proposal, claiming that it amounted to a ban on travel based on race and as such was in conflict with the *Wong Wai* decision. A merchant interposed (disingenuously?) that this was not the case inasmuch as Judge Morrow's decision forbade legislation aimed at a particular racial group ("class legislation") whereas the state board proposal was aimed only at a particular urban district. One obstacle that the *Wong Wai* decision did put in the way of any board action, all agreed, was its ruling that the board needed the sanction of the board of supervisors before implementing measures of this sort, and so a resolution was moved and approved to ask the board of supervisors for authority to quarantine Chinatown.[115] The supervisors' decision, if there was ever any doubt about it, became a foregone conclusion when a California State Board of Health representative told them that if they did not quarantine Chinatown the state would order the whole city quarantined. The resolution that was passed authorized the board of health to "quarantine persons, houses, places and districts within the city and county when in its judgment it is deemed necessary to prevent the spreading of contagious or infectious diseases."[116]

When the city board of health, now armed with full power by the San Francisco supervisors, reconvened on May 29, it heard further arguments in support of the Chinatown quarantine. A spokesman for the fruit canning industry contended that even though there was no proven plague epidemic and few alleged cases had been discovered, many outside the city and state were convinced that the disease did exist and something needed to be done to allay those kinds of concerns. Moreover, there was the state board's threat to quarantine the entire city if proper precautions were not taken. Dr. Kinyoun, who either had not heard or did not heed the U.S. attorney's advice that federal officials stay aloof from the matter, also spoke. Chinatown would always be a focus of plague infection, he said, and ought to be cordoned off from the rest of the city. This should be followed by a systematic inspection of the district with the removal of confirmed plague cases to a hospital and suspicious cases to a detention center. He also called for the systematic destruction of rats which he said served as a vehicle for disseminating contagion, the first time that this had been brought to the fore as a means of combating the plague. The board then passed a resolution quarantining the district of San Francisco bounded by Kearny, Broadway, Stockton, and California streets. When the chief of police pointed out that there were a handful of whites living in the proposed district, it was resolved to leave it to the discretion of the health officers and the chief of police to modify the lines of quarantine to take this into account.[117] To cap matters off and eliminate all doubts as to authorization, the board of supervisors on May 31 passed an ordinance ratifying the health board resolution and reconfirming its authority to implement a quarantine of the designated district.[118]

The Second Quarantine of Chinatown

The chief of police did not wait long to implement the board's resolution. A force of 159 police was detailed in three watches to enforce the decree.[119] Fifty-three were sent immediately to the district to guard all points of ingress and egress.[120] A newspaper reporter noticed that there were a few buildings fronting on the borders of the quarantine district that were occupied by Caucasian residents or business establishments. These were left out of the quarantine district although when the buildings had entrances these were guarded. "By a careful discrimination in fixing the line of embargo," he commented, "not one Caucasian doing business on the outer rim of the alleged infected district was affected."[121] This anomaly would later not go unnoticed by the Chinese or their attorneys. Shortly after the quarantine was put in force, Mayor Phelan gave a statement to the Associated Press to the effect that nine dead bodies showing evidence of plague had been removed from Chinatown in the past two months but that there was no evidence of infection in the city proper. As a result quarantine measures had been adopted "in order to protect outside territory from even the remotest possibility of contagion." They were, he stressed, "merely precautionary."[122]

In the immediate aftermath of the board action, Samuel Shortridge told a reporter for the San Francisco *Examiner* that legal action was probable. "The passage of the order was done in such a hasty manner that it may be vulnerable," he said. And he pointed out what the likely area of vulnerability was. The city authorities seemed to be under the impression that the only infirmity in their previous health measure (the one invalidated in the *Wong Wai* case) was the lack of supervisorial sanction for the health officials' action. But, as Shortridge commented, that was only part of the problem. There was the larger question of the substantive reasonableness of this new interference with the personal liberty of the Chinese residents of San Francisco. "That was the basis of Judge Morrow's decision in the other case, he noted, "and although the court indicated the Board of Supervisors as the proper body to make regulations of this sort, it does not follow that its acts are not subject to review by the courts."[123]

The statement issued the next day by the Chinese Six Companies was more cautious than Shortridge's. It in fact began with a pledge not to take precipitate legal action and requested that if bubonic plague in fact existed (something it did not concede) no expense be spared to stamp it out. It requested that the sanitary measures that the health authorities had been pursuing for some time be continued and promised Chinese cooperation. It did, however, pose the interesting question why, if there was a belief that a contagious disease, bubonic plague, existed in Chinatown, nothing was being done to protect the Chinese living in the district from infection. Why, for example, were the authorities not quarantining the individual buildings in which suspected plague cases had been found but rather allowing the residents of these places to mingle freely with the other inhabitants of the district. The statement included a plea that the city begin to think about how it intended to feed and care for the thousands of Chinese now effectively incarcerated in Chinatown, many cut off from all means of earning their livelihood.[124] Consul General Ho, who issued a statement the same day, was quite blunt in arguing that the city was under an obligation to care for the Chinese community at public expense,[125] a view that Judge Maguire, another legal counselor to the Six Companies echoed. "It has been held by some of the highest courts that persons in quarantine are in the same position as public prisoners and . . . [are] therefore . . . properly a charge on the public Treasury."[126]

Caucasian reaction to the new board action was mixed and, initially at least, followed along partisan lines. The editorial writers of the *Chronicle* saw everything through party-political lenses. To them this was but another instance of incompetence on the part of Mayor Phelan, his allies on the board of supervisors and the political hacks they had appointed to serve on the board of health.[127] The *Chronicle* never relented in its insistence that there was no plague in the city and that to suggest otherwise constituted high treason against the reputation and economic interests of San Francisco. The Hearst-owned *Examiner*, however, which had from the beginning been generally supportive of official action, continued in its support. To it the latest measures adopted by the board of health were well calculated both to deal with the situation in Chinatown, to protect the health of other San Franciscans, and to allay the concerns of those outside the city's borders.[128] If the measures were going to cause serious hardship to the Chinese, the paper could muster up little in the way of sympathy for them. The Chinese, after all, so reasoned the paper, were "unwelcome guests of the city" and had brought the plague into it, thereby bringing these measures on themselves. It did not think that they were deserving of any special consideration on the part of other San Franciscans.[129]

The reaction of the San Francisco *Call* to the second quarantine of Chinatown is instructive. The *Call* was as bitterly partisan a paper as the *Chronicle* and all along had faithfully echoed its sister journal's editorial stance that the plague was a concoction of either venal or incompetent health officials. Its first reaction to the quarantine decision of May 29 was to ridicule it, insisting yet again that plague allegations were "fake and a fraud."[130] In order, one may presume, to lend the support of science to this position, the paper brought out to San Francisco at the end of May one Dr. George Schrady, a New York physician with (at least in the paper's opinion) something resembling a national medical reputation. When Schrady said shortly after his arrival in San Francisco that local health officials had not been able to show him a single living case of plague, the *Call* trumpeted this loudly in a full front-page headline that read: "Board of Health Confesses to a Famous Expert Who Crossed the Continent that there is No Bubonic Plague in this City."[131] It was put into a highly embarrassing position the next day, however, when Schrady had been invited to witness the autopsy on a corpse found in Chinatown and that the autopsy had confirmed the presence of plague germs in the tissue of the deceased. The *Call* was now forced to do some backing and filling.

It duly printed Schrady's comments, but, seeking to put the best face on them, it also stressed that the New York doctor did not consider his experience any cause for alarm. He in fact had gone out of his way to assure the city's white residents, the paper noted, that they need not be concerned about contracting the disease so long as they kept their premises clean and the city continued its sanitation of the Chinese quarter.[132] In subsequent days' issues of the paper, Schrady stated more fully his own view of the matter. He reported that he was convinced that there had been sporadic cases of bubonic plague in San Francisco but that these presented no threat to the general population and in no sense constituted an epidemic ("One swallow does not make a summer, and one case of plague does not make an epidemic.") The authorities he thought were taking proper steps, including the quarantining of Chinatown, to contain the disease, and he thought that these measures were entirely to the benefit of the city's Chinese population. "The Chinese should consider that this movement is for their good," he wrote in one article that appeared in Chinese translation on the same page. "[T]he white man is a friend to the Oriental, in spite of what is said to the contrary." He thought the quarantine of California goods that had been imposed by the state of Texas entirely unwarranted and thought, finally, that one benefit of the entire episode was to alert San Francisco to the generally unclean condition of Chinatown and the need to do something about it.[133]

These were views that the *Call* could live with, without suffering too much embarrassment about its previous editorial posture. Yes, the paper said, there may have been sporadic cases of plague, but no, these did not constitute an epidemic. "If there was the slightest fear that San Francisco was to become the sufferer of an epidemic of the dread disease the apprehension has passed away," it wrote.[134] It agreed with Schrady that one benefit of the whole affair was to alert the city to the pressing necessity to do something about Chinatown, and it did not mince words about what it thought needed to be done. The sort of acerbic rhetoric it was in the habit of directing at the city fathers it now aimed at the Chinese community.

> In no city in the civilized world is there a slum more foul or more menacing than that which now threatens us with the Asiatic plague. Chinatown occupies the very heart of San Francisco. . . . So long as it stands so long will there be a menace of the appearance in San Francisco of every form of disease, plague and pestilence which Asiatic filth and vice generate. The only way to get rid of that menace is to eradicate Chinatown from the city. . . . Clear the foul spot from San Francisco and give the debris to the flames.[135]

Mass Removal of the Chinese and Razing of Chinatown Considered

The *Call*'s was not the only voice now being heard in favor of using the torch to combat the plague, a measure, of course, which would have driven the plague-infested rats that probably were at the origin of Chinatown's cases to other parts of the city, thereby assuring the widest possible dissemination of the disease. Indeed, it might almost be said that something of a consensus was beginning to emerge on the subject in the lay and scientific communities alike. Schrady himself had referred to this possibility on two separate occasions. In his May 30 report for the *Call* he had said that every infected house in Chinatown should be emptied of its inhabitants and either thoroughly disinfected or burned to the ground.[136]

More significantly, in an interview which he gave the same day to *Chung Sai Yat Po* he had, while not advocating such a step, spoken of the eventual possibility of having to raze the entire quarter. He thought it would be a fairly simple matter to evacuate the Chinese from the district, rebuild a new Chinatown on the ashes of the old, and compensate everyone for any property lost. And he cautioned the Chinese against taking such a measure amiss should it eventually prove necessary. A decision to burn Chinatown, he assured his interlocutor, should be seen as betokening love and concern rather than hatred for the Chinese.[137] The bluntest comment (and it was quickly picked up and publicized by the Chinese-language press) had come from D. D. Crowley, a member of the California State Board of Health. "I would advocate," he had said, "the complete destruction of Chinatown by fire as the best and safest method of stamping out the plague," and he had pointed with approval to the example of what had happened in December of the previous year in Honolulu, where a so-called "sanitary fire" designed to burn down the residence of a plague victim had gone out of control and destroyed the whole of Honolulu's Chinatown.[138]

A reporter who toured Chinatown the day after the imposition of the quarantine commented that it had the look of a besieged city. The area was surrounded by armed guards, and within it, he wrote, "business has been suspended, stores are closed, doors barred and the Asiatics gather on the street corners, excitedly gesticulating while they discuss the embargo placed upon them, much as inhabitants of a beleaguered town might be expected to do."[139] One can be certain that the remarks of Schrady and Crowley, which appeared the next day in the Chinese press did nothing to alleviate this sense of beleaguerment. A more immediate concern of the inhabitants, however, was the sheer question of sustenance. A large number of Chinese worked outside the district and the blockade cut them off from their means of livelihood. Of more importance, the district as a whole was cut off from its sources of food supply, and the effects of this severance began quickly to manifest themselves. On May 31, for example, Consul Ho told the press that there was a sense of general, serious food shortage in the district and that the prices of the foodstuffs that were available were being bid up rapidly. He described the matter of provisioning Chinatown as one of great urgency and implored the city authorities to take speedy, decisive action to deal with it. If they did not, he held out the prospect of legal action.[140]

The cooperation that Ho asked for was not forthcoming. The board of health did meet on May 31 to discuss the ongoing plague situation, and at the behest of attorneys for the Six Companies, who were present, did take up the question of provisioning Chinatown. It agreed in principle with the Chinese representatives that the city was duty-bound to care for the blockaded residents of the district, but it refused to say what concrete steps it might take in order to deal with the matter. As if to add insult to this rebuff, it took a series of actions that, together, could have only had the effect of exacerbating Chinese anxiety. It ordered that an autopsy be performed on the occasion of any death in the Chinese quarter. The Six Companies, on the request of its lawyers, was given permission to designate a physician to be present. The board ordered as well the inspection and, if necessary, fumigation of all Chinese laundries, wherever situated in the city, on the grounds that they might be harboring refugees from Chinatown. Finally, it approved a resolution asking the Mayor to enlist the aid of the federal government in securing sites outside the city that could be used as detention centers, it having been shown, the resolution said, that such centers were "well adapted to circumscribe and limit the injurious results of contagious and infectious diseases." They should be able to accommodate up to seven thousand persons. Possible sites mentioned were Mission Rock, a small, barren island about a half mile offshore claimed by both the United States and a private proprietor, the California Dry Dock Company, and occupied completely at the time by the proprietor's warehouses and wharves, and Angel Island, a much larger federal preserve in the middle of San Francisco Bay.[141]

The idea of setting up facilities outside San Francisco where suspected plague victims could be detained had originated with Kinyoun. In mid-May he had broached with the Army's representative in San Francisco the idea of using a portion of Angel Island as a camp in case a large number of plague suspects were discovered. (The army's response was that authorization for such use would have to come from the highest levels of the War Department.)[142] Kinyoun, who had something of an apocalyptic turn of mind, may indeed have been genuinely concerned about the limited plague outbreak turning into a major epidemic. It seems more likely, however, given what would shortly transpire, that he saw the camp not as a place to harbor plague suspects but as a place to detain the mass of the Chinese population, pending the razing and rebuilding of the district, an idea for which, we know, he had a great deal of sympathy. In any event, the idea first achieved general public currency when the board of health endorsed it at its May 31 meeting, and one of its first effects was to send an immediate large shudder through the Chinese community. *Chung Sai Yat Po*, for example, which reported the board's decision in its June 1 edition, interpreted the board's resolution as saying in effect that the whole of Chinatown should be evacuated. Not surprisingly, too, it coupled its report of the proposal with a reminder of the cries then being heard for the razing of Chinatown. Without exactly saying so, it seemed to be intimating that the one action was but a natural preliminary to the other.[143]

Contretemps Involving Chinese-employed Physicians

In response to the health board decision that it should be permitted to have one of its own doctors present at autopsies conducted in Chinatown, the Six Companies designated three local physicians whom it had retained for this purpose.[144] Shortly thereafter the Chinese Empire Reform Association sought to secure the same privilege for a physician in its employ.[145] It was exceedingly rare at this time to find a Chinese organization other than the Six Companies seeking to negotiate directly with Caucasian authorities on a matter of community concern. Its independent action may have betokened a certain suspicion of the Six Companies, seen, perhaps, by virtue of its working relationship with the consul general's office, to be too closely connected with the Chinese government of the day.[146]

The Empire Reform Association's petition for independent representation at autopsies was summarily dismissed. Indeed, the next day the permission granted the Six Companies was revoked, this due to a serious indiscretion committed by one of its physicians. This man, a bacteriologist named Ernest Pillsbury, had on June 2, without securing advance approval from the health authorities, ordered two other physicians to remove the lymph glands of a Chinese who had died under suspicious circumstances. Upon analyzing the tissue he announced in the face of much contradictory evidence that the deceased had died of syphilis.[147] When they discovered that this had occurred, the health authorities were apoplectic. The lymph glands were recovered with little trouble, but this did not stop the board of health from accusing Pillsbury of trying to destroy evidence and of frustrating the board's ongoing investigation. In reaction it not only revoked the permission granted him and other Six Companies physicians to witness autopsies but also declared that in the future no Chinese-employed physicians would be allowed to enter the quarantine district for any purpose whatsoever.[148] There is no real evidence that Pillsbury was in fact trying to destroy the lymph glands he had ordered removed or conceal them from the authorities. He seems rather to have been interested in doing his own bacteriological examination. The fact remains that he was guilty of a serious impropriety and this did serious damage to the Chinese cause.

When after several days' waiting no action seemed forthcoming from the board of health on the request that arrangements be made for the provisioning of Chinatown, the Six Companies had its attorneys write to the board of supervisors with a request that it do something.[149] It also persuaded the consul general to ask the legation in Washington to make representations to the State Department about the worsening situation in Chinatown and the local authorities' refusal to address it.[150] One Chinese merchant, Chue Yet, an officer of the Chinese Merchant's Exchange wired Wu T'ing-fang, Chinese minister to the United States. The telegram complained of the immediate problem brought on by the board of health's quarantine decision, the fact, as Chue Yet put it, that there were now isolated in the quarantine district some eight thousand Chinese cut off from their means of support. It complained as well of the board decision no longer to permit physicians in Chinese employ to enter the quarantined area and of the great losses being sustained by Chinese merchants. Most important, however, the telegram attacked the very idea of the general quarantine of Chinatown, which it characterized as unjustified by the facts and discriminatory in operation. The quarantine, the telegram noted, applied to Chinese only and was enforced "against buildings and persons that have not been infected or exposed" to the alleged plague outbreak. The Chinese had no objection to the quarantine of buildings where alleged plague victims had died but protested against the general quarantine of the entire district. It begged the minister "to lay these matters before the proper authorities, through the proper medium, so that we may be saved from irreparable loss and granted the rights we are entitled to by law and treaty."[151]

The Quarantine Is Tightened and the Groundwork Laid for Mass Removal

At a meeting held June 4, the San Francisco Board of Health, prompted by pressure from the city's white merchants, decided on yet sterner measures incidental to the quarantine.[152] Among them: the halting of all streetcar traffic through Chinatown (streetcars had theretofore been allowed to pass through so long as they did not stop); the doubling of the police guard on the district's perimeter; and the use of barbed wire wherever feasible to seal in the area.[153] Much more important, it made an announcement that must have taken many by surprise, first and foremost the Chinese. It reported that it had already secured the consent of the California Dry Dock Company to use its docking facilities on Mission Rock and that "steps were underway" to begin sending the next day the first of the 1,500 Chinese it expected to quarter there. In the meantime, it said, discussions were proceeding apace to secure from the federal government a much larger facility on Angel Island, one that could accommodate 8,000 persons.[154] The board resolution of May 31 had been couched in terms purely of negotiations with the federal government for the use of facilities in its control suggesting a process that might take some time. What now become clear was that the board had been unwilling to await the result of these negotiations but had rather decided to enter into negotiations of its own that would secure the quick availability of a detention site. It was significant too that the board announcement of an imminent deportation was not accompanied by any finding of the sudden discovery of a large number of plague suspects in Chinatown. Given the wording of the announcement and the context in which it was issued,[155] the proposed board action could only have been seen as the first step of an operation aimed at some sort of mass removal of the Chinese from San Francisco. And it was so interpreted by the Chinese.

The Chinese reaction to the announcement was one of indignation and defiance. Consul Ho undoubtedly spoke for the whole community when he told a reporter:

> The feeling among the Chinese is such that they would prefer to risk their lives rather than be compelled to remain in the power of the American physicians for an indefinite period.[156]

As if to underscore this comment, the Six Companies, hardly a radical organization, announced itself the next day that any attempt by the board of health to remove the Chinese from Chinatown would be resisted, if necessary, by force.[157]

However, another means of resistance was available. Notwithstanding the Six Companies' pledge in the immediate aftermath of the imposition of the blockade not to take precipitate legal action, the possibility of having to resort to litigation was from the very outset never very far from the minds of the Chinese leadership. Indeed, the evidence would suggest that they began to lay their litigation plans very soon after the blockade began. They held them in abeyance for some time while they sought to sort out exactly what was happening and on the thought perhaps that some sort of compromise might yet be worked out with city health officials, but the course of events, in particular the worsening living conditions in Chinatown, was limiting more and more their freedom of action.[158] The established leadership must have felt some additional concern when the competitor organization, the Chinese Empire Reform Association, announced on June 3 that it intended itself to go to court shortly to force the authorities to justify their actions.[159] The board of health announcement of June 4 eliminated all room for maneuver, and the next day the Chinese Six Companies, this time joined by the Empire Reform Association, repaired again to the courtroom of Judge Morrow.

The Chinese Return to Federal Court

A bill in equity was filed on June 5 in the United States Circuit Court for the Northern District of California on behalf of Jew Ho, a grocer with a place of business within the limits of the quarantine district. He complained of an interference with his personal liberty and with his right to carry on his business.[160] Like the earlier litigant Wong Wai, he stated that he was bringing suit not only on his own behalf but also on behalf of the upwards of ten thousand Chinese who resided in the quarantine district, it being impractical to join them all as complainants.[161] The averments of the complaint, like those of Wong Wai, sought to impress the court with the arbitrariness and discriminatory character of the board of health's quarantine resolution, first and foremost the discriminatory character.

The resolution purported to be general in its terms and to impose the same restrictions upon everyone within the quarantine district, but, said the complainant, it was in fact enforced only against the Chinese and not against persons of other races.[162] Drawing the court's attention to the perimeter of the quarantine district, it sought to show how on virtually every side of the quadrangle instances could be found where Caucasian residences and businesses that lay within the district were not being subjected to quarantine. A particularly telling allegation concerned the block of Stockton Street on which Jew Ho lived and conducted his business. There, according to the complaint, every other address was occupied by a Caucasian residence or business and the record showed a perfectly saw-toothed pattern of enforcement—every Caucasian address free of restrictions, every Chinese address subjected to them.[163] The enforcement of the quarantine in the manner described, the complainant concluded, deprived the Chinese residents of the quarantined district of the equal protection of the laws and their rights and privileges under U.S. law and treaty.[164]

The complaint also spoke in some detail to the allegedly arbitrary character of the quarantine. It first denied that bubonic plague existed or ever had existed in Chinatown, in which case, of course, the imposition of a quarantine was self-evidently arbitrary.[165] In the alternative, it was submitted, if plague did exist in Chinatown, the board's chosen method of dealing with it was arbitrary and capricious and posed serious threats to the health of the Chinese population. In the first place the board was quarantining whole blocks of Chinatown on which it had never claimed to have found any cases of plague. More important, by failing to isolate houses where plague had occurred or individuals who were suspected of having had contact with plague victims and, at the same time, by refusing to permit the Chinese to leave Chinatown, the board was exposing the residents of that district to an enhanced danger of infection.[166]

The complaint also faulted the board for failing to provide the indigent Chinese with food and for refusing to permit physicians in the employ of the Chinese to enter the district for the purpose of caring for the sick.[167] It called attention as well to the proposed imminent evacuation of Chinatown. The defendants, it was said, were in the process of surrounding Chinatown with "a high and substantial fence of posts, beams and . . . lumber." (In the wake of the board's resolution that the perimeter of Chinatown should be secured with barbed wire, the authorities had gone one step further and begun to erect a high wooden wall around the district.) They were threatening, it went on, to maintain this barrier unless and until the Chinese should consent to their removal "to an island in the Bay . . . there to remain during the pleasure of the defendants."[168]

The real purpose behind all of the measures described in the complaint, it was claimed, was not to prevent the spread of plague but rather to prevent the California State Board of Health and health authorities outside of California, themselves acting on unfounded and exaggerated rumors, from levying a quarantine against the city and "for the further purpose of wrongfully, unlawfully and tyrannically oppressing, annoying, harassing and injuring" the Chinese.[169]

The complaint concluded with a prayer for a permanent injunction forbidding the defendants from maintaining any quarantine except one limited to such stores, residences, and other buildings as might be found upon proper investigation to be infected with the germs of contagious diseases and to persons found to have been "distinctly exposed to the danger of infection."[170]

Contemporaneous with their filing of their bill of complaint the attorneys for the Chinese obtained from Judge Morrow an Order to Show Cause directing the defendants to appear in his courtroom on June 7 to answer to the request for an injunction and a Temporary Restraining Order enjoining the defendants from preventing the physicians in the Chinese employ, so long as they complied with health board rules, from entering Chinatown to examine or attend to the sick. Copies of the complaint and orders were served by the U.S. marshal on each member of the board while it sat in session that afternoon.[171] Two days later, counsel for the San Francisco Board of Health, clearly not ready to respond on such short notice to the detailed allegations in the *Jew Ho* complaint, appeared in court to ask for a continuance. The request was granted, the matter being put over until June 13, on the condition that no action be taken to remove the Chinese to Mission Rock.[172]

In sharp contrast to its curiously lackadaisical procedure in *Wong Wai*, when it had not seen fit to submit any responsive pleading, relying by way of response instead on certain official documents, the board on June 12 filed a lengthy and detailed answer to Jew Ho's complaint, denying or avoiding every material allegation in it. The attorneys for the board, mindful no doubt of the problems it had encountered on this score in connection with its mandatory immunization plan, spent a considerable amount of time first laying out in exhaustive detail the authority upon which the board had proceeded in implementing its quarantine plan. And here there was no problem in showing supervisorial sanction for every step the health authorities had taken.[173] Having eliminated this as any possible grounds of objection, they proceeded to the merits of the measures that had been adopted. They were, counsel argued, nondiscriminatory and perfectly reasonable in the light of all the circumstances.

The defendants denied flatly that the board was singling out the Chinese for discriminatory treatment. The board's quarantine rules and regulations, they said, were being "enforced equally and similarly against all persons whatever [within the quarantine district] without distinction of race, age, sex or nationality."[174] As to the alleged nonenforcement of the quarantine against Caucasians on the district's perimeter, the defendants either denied that this was happening or claimed that the Caucasians in question lived outside the affected area.[175] Quarantine, was, the defendants declared, a perfectly reasonable way of dealing with an incipient epidemic of bubonic plague. Its purpose was to prevent "promiscuous communication" between persons within the district where the outbreak was occurring, who were exposed to the danger of contagion, and persons outside the district who were free from such danger.[176] And how had the health authorities determined the precise boundaries of the district where the outbreak was occurring, the district that should be sealed off from the rest of the city? The answer to the question, to the defendants at any rate, was fairly self-evident. Every victim of the bubonic plague to date, the defendants noted, had been Chinese. Every case of the disease that had been detected so far had been discovered in that part of San Francisco in which the Chinese clustered, a part of the city with well-recognized borders.[177] The defendants went on to deny that they were refusing to supply food to the hungry or that they were preventing physicians from entering the district to treat patients.[178] They conceded that they were erecting a high, wooden barrier around Chinatown but denied that there was anything unusual about this or that they were using the barrier as a bargaining chip to force the Chinese to relocate out of Chinatown to an island in the bay or anywhere else.[179] They denied finally that either their orders or their actions deprived any Chinese residents of the quarantine district of the equal protection of the laws or of their rights under law and treaty.[180] The issue was now nicely joined, and the matter was in a good posture for address in oral argument.

Oral argument was held before two of the three judges who had heard the *Wong Wai* case, Morrow and DeHaven, and consumed two days, June 13 and 14. Counsel for the defendants raised several new points. He argued that the court had no authority to inquire into the regularity, legality, or reasonableness of the legislative acts in question. The city had made it clear in its return to the order to show cause that a duly constituted department of the city government had adopted steps which it deemed necessary to deal with a public health emergency. Under well-established precedent, that department was the exclusive judge of the reasonableness of these measures. A federal court, he argued, was without jurisdiction to make inquiry of its own. In support of this proposition he submitted a series of cases in which federal courts had denied themselves the right to inquire into state or local police power measures. In the alternative, citing another line of cases including the 1887 decision of the U.S. Supreme Court in *Mugler v. Kansas*,[181] he argued that, even if it could examine police power measures, its standard should be one of almost total deference to the will of the legislative body.[182]

A good deal of the debate revolved around the allegedly discriminatory way in which the quarantine was being implemented. At one point an attorney for the Six Companies, J. C. Campbell, invited the judges to tour the borders of the quarantine district to see for themselves how white residents were being given favorable treatment. The city, while continuing to deny that there was any pattern of discrimination, did concede that along the street that constituted the western boundary of the district certain houses were not being subjected to restrictions and for no apparent reason. It asked for leave to redraw the quarantine boundaries to correct this mistake.[183]

The attorneys for the Chinese presented to the court some eighteen affidavits from licensed San Francisco physicians, three describing themselves as being under retainer to the Six Companies. These attacked the basis for the board of health's diagnosis of plague, or, if it could be assumed that plague existed, the methods the board had chosen to deal with the disease. Some, it must be acknowledged, bespoke medical competence of a low order. One, for example, insisted that the microbe that had been isolated in postmortem examinations was the bacillus that causes blood poisoning and not the plague bacillus. (Throughout this episode the Chinese do not seem to have been nearly as well served by their physicians as by their lawyers.) Others raised the plausible question why, if a highly infectious disease existed in Chinatown, so few victims had succumbed to it.[184] The attorneys for the Chinese were able to add to the affidavits of their physicians a statement from a most unlikely ally, the governor of the state, Henry T. Gage. On May 31 Secretary of State John Hay had asked Gage to look into a complaint about the quarantine of Chinatown that he (Hay) had just received from the Chinese minister.[185] Gage traveled to San Francisco to conduct an investigation of his own and on June 13 wired back a report to Hay. Gage had never in his career manifested any particular concern or solicitude for the Chinese, but he was eager to quash the rumor then being "broadcast over the world," as he put it, "of the existence of the dreadful plague in the great and healthful city of San Francisco." He could not find any proof, he said, "that the plague alleged to be here is either infectious or contagious." Certain individuals who had been repeatedly exposed to the disease without taking any precautions, had failed to contract it, including members of the family of plague victims and coinhabitants of the same building. He firmly believed, he declared, that the bubonic plague did not exist or if it did, then the measures being undertaken were unreasonable and discriminatory.[186]

The Ruling in Jew Ho

The court did not wait long to answer the questions put to it. Stressing the exigent nature of the circumstances that had given rise to the case, Judge Morrow decided to defer the preparation of a written opinion, and on June 15 he summoned the parties and the public to hear his opinion in open court.

After rehearsing the contentions and countercontentions of the parties, Morrow proceeded to address the defendants' claim that the court did not have the jurisdiction to look into the regularity or legality of the defendants' acts. His response was that the complainants were aliens and were invoking his court's jurisdiction not only on the ground of their specific Fourteenth Amendment equal protection claim but also on the ground of diversity of citizenship. When a federal court's jurisdiction was invoked on diversity grounds, he pointed out, it had authority to determine all claims raised in the case, whether of a federal or state character, and, just as if it were a state court, might inquire into "*all matters* [emphasis added] relating to the legality of the restraint imposed upon the complainant."[187]

The court next addressed the argument that once a state or municipality invoked "the general police power" in justification of a measure its determination was final and the courts were precluded from looking beyond that justification. Morrow, echoing a line of argument he had broached but not pushed very far in *Wong Wai*, was able to adduce any number of opinions, state and federal, showing that the police power, while broad was not unlimited, and that it was the proper province of courts, either as a matter of federal or state constitutional law or both, to determine whether governments had stepped beyond the limits established by law. He cited, for example, the 1894 U.S. Supreme Court opinion in *Lawton v. Steele*,[188] where the court had conceded that a large measure of discretion was vested in the legislature in determining what it ought to do to protect the public safety but at the same time had said that a legislature's determination as to whether its exercise of the police power was proper was not final or conclusive but was, under the due process clause of the Fourteenth Amendment, "subject to the supervision of the courts." He cited as well *Mugler*, offered by defense counsel in support of its view, and noted that while *Mugler* did give wide berth to the police power it also said there were "limits beyond which legislation cannot rightfully go."[189] He brought in finally a range of state court opinions—including a California decision nullifying, apparently on both federal and state constitutional grounds, a local health and safety regulation—all of which were in accord that in any measures affecting the property or liberty interests of the citizen the legislature must at least be prepared to show that its exercise of the police power bore some relation to the facts and was not arbitrary or capricious.[190]

Having established that the law "as established in the various states of the Union, as well as by the supreme court of the United States"[191] permitted him to inquire into the reasonableness of the quarantine of Chinatown, he went on to show why he found the measure unreasonable and therefore invalid. The classical purpose of a quarantine, with respect to infectious and contagious diseases, he noted, was to prevent the spread of disease among the inhabitants of localities. It accomplished this goal by restricting to their houses persons afflicted with the disease or those with whom they had come in contact, thereby reducing the opportunities for the disease to transmit itself from one person to another. But this quarantine had been thrown around an entire section of the city, comprising twelve square blocks and over ten thousand residents. By confining these ten thousand within a limited area and at the same time failing to restrict the movement of the residents of the buildings where the disease was thought to have appeared, the health authorities had in fact increased the danger that these persons would become infected with and spread the disease. "Every facility has been offered by this species of quarantine," he declared, "to enlarge [the disease's] sphere and increase its danger and its destructive force."[192]

The arbitrary character of the quarantine was, in Morrow's eyes, alone enough to condemn it. One presumes that had the board of health singled out *any* area of the city for such treatment its actions would have been vulnerable on this ground. But this quarantine had the additional defect of being racially discriminatory, the fact, as Morrow put it, that it "discriminates against the Chinese population of this city, and in favor of the people of other races."[193] Sufficient proof of this for Morrow could be found in the artful way in which the authorities had drawn the boundaries of the quarantine district so as deliberately to exclude residences on the periphery occupied by Caucasians. This, said Morrow, was "in effect, a discrimination" and of a kind that had been "frequently called to the attention of the federal courts where matters of this character have arisen with respect to the Chinese."[194] *Yick Wo v. Hopkins,* he thought, was relevant to the case at bar. Here, as in that case, according to Morrow, the law was administered "with an evil eye and an unequal hand"[195] and that under the principle established by the Supreme Court in *Yick Wo* was violative of the equal protection clause of the Fourteenth Amendment.[196]

The court ordered counsel to prepare an injunction ordering the general quarantine of Chinatown lifted although it made clear that it would permit the board of health to maintain a quarantine around such places as it believed were infected with contagious diseases. In the event such a quarantine should be imposed, Morrow ordered, a physician selected by the Chinese Six Companies should have the right to attend persons suspected of being afflicted with the disease and the privilege likewise of attending any autopsies that might be made although Morrow recognized that the health authorities had the right to place reasonable limitations on the privilege. And, aware no doubt of problems that had arisen in the past, he cautioned those who exercised the privilege not to abuse it.[197] Morrow remarked finally that if at any time an emergency should arise requiring a modification of his order he would be prepared to issue one.[198]

Within hours the San Francisco Board of Health convened in special session to act on Judge Morrow's decree. It passed a resolution officially lifting the quarantine of Chinatown and directed the chief of police to remove his forces cordoning off the district. It resolved as well that the physicians for the Chinese should be allowed to attend patients and witness autopsies. Finally, it directed that the general cleaning of Chinatown and fumigation of the district's sewers be continued.[199] There must have been more than a little resentment among the board members. For the second time in less than a month they had seen their well-considered plans for dealing with the plague stymied by the intervention of the federal judiciary. At a second meeting of the board held later in the day a Honolulu physician in attendance commented that only the burning to the ground of the Chinese district had put an end to the plague in his city.[200] One suspects that more than a few members of the board, hearing this remark, must have thought how welcome the occurrence of just such an accident would be in San Francisco.

One reporter, who witnessed the end of the quarantine of Chinatown, compared it to the lifting of a siege. "The Board of Health's inspectors broke their encampment in Portsmouth Square," he wrote, "folded their tents and retreated in good order." At the same time "a horde of Chinese poured through the lines like the advance guard of a relief column."[201] In short order the district was again presenting to the world the picture of lively, bustling commercial activity that it had presented before the imposition of quarantine. "No more sullen crowds gather on the street corners to excitedly discuss the iniquities of the white man," the same reporter commented.[202]

Epilogue

Plague continued to smolder during the months following the *Wong Wai* and *Jew Ho* decisions, taking on average one victim every ten to fourteen days, almost all of them Chinese (it took its first Caucasian victim on August 11, 1900).[203] In January 1901 the secretary of the treasury sent a team of eminent scientists to San Francisco to make a definitive determination as to the existence or nonexistence of the disease. It received full cooperation from city authorities and from the Chinese Six Companies, which assisted the scientists in gaining access to the sick and the dead in the Chinese quarter,[204] but only the most minimal support from the governor, who manifested throughout the deepest suspicion towards it. The men were in the city for two weeks and during that time conducted autopsies on the bodies of thirteen dead Chinese. It confirmed that six of them had in fact died of bubonic plague.[205] In the wake of the team's report national, local, and state officials, the last group grudgingly, agreed on the principal points of a public health offensive aimed at eradicating plague from Chinatown. It was but an intensive version of what had gone before, with emphasis placed on the cleansing and fumigation of houses and the disinfection of personal effects. These measures, completed in June, had no impact on the disease, which continued to take victims at about the same rate it had in the past. In November 1902 the San Francisco Board of Health for the first time employed three men to begin to trap rats in Chinatown, but these efforts do not seem to have been pursued very systematically or very vigorously. In early February 1904, federal, city, and state health authorities adopted a resolution urging the rat-proofing of buildings in Chinatown, and a campaign of rat-proofing got underway. But the disease, it would turn out, had already about run its course. On February 29, it claimed its last human victim. The final tally of the epidemic of bubonic plague in San Francisco: 121 cases and 113 deaths, all but a handful Chinese.

Some three years after the conclusion of the first outbreak a second outbreak of bubonic plague began in San Francisco. It would last approximately a year and a half, would produce 160 cases of the disease and 78 deaths. Virtually all of the victims were Caucasians.[206] During this second outbreak, unlike the first, the principal efforts of the health authorities were directed at the trapping and extermination of rats.[207] No thought appears to have been given by anyone to quarantine or the use of the Haffkine prophylactic vaccine as anti-plague measures.

Conclusion

With the *Wong Wai* and *Jew Ho* decisions we bring this book to a close. These were certainly not the last cases in which the Chinese were involved. The Chinese remained committed to using the courts to protect their rights. In California, and increasingly elsewhere in the nation,[1] they continued to bring cases aimed at modifying official policies or practices. These had mainly to do with the administration of the exclusion laws.[2] A few reached the Supreme Court of the United States and established important constitutional principles. One worthy of special mention is *Chin Yow v. United States*,[3] a 1908 case originating in San Francisco and argued in the high court by Maxwell Evarts, the man who had represented the Chinese in *Fong Yue Ting* and several other cases. There the Court held that a Chinese person (or anyone else for that matter) claiming citizenship but denied entry into the United States by immigration officers could use the writ of habeas corpus to challenge the fairness of the hearing that had led to his or her exclusion and that the court issuing the writ could decide the claim on the merits if it determined that the hearing had not been fair. Here then was a small breach in the seemingly impermeable wall of administrative discretion that *Ju Toy* and other cases had established.[4] The *Wong Wai* and *Jew Ho* cases, however, seem to have been the last great confrontations in the courts between the Chinese and Caucasian officialdom. They round out a distinct episode in American legal history and therefore are an appropriate place at which to end our discussion. To recapitulate, then, its main points and to elaborate further on several of them.

At a comparatively early date in the Chinese immigration to California a consensus formed among the majority of the Caucasian population and its political leaders that the Chinese were unwelcome immigrants and that their presence was to be discouraged. New immigrants were to be discouraged from coming; those already here were to be given every incentive to leave. A desire to accomplish these purposes drove and distorted lawmaking in the state (and other western states as well) for a half century and more. Initially the state sought to ban Chinese immigration outright. When it became clear that no court, even one sharing the general population's antipathy for the Chinese, would accept such an intrusion on federal prerogatives and when the federal government could not be persuaded to act, California turned to another strategy, the passage of legislation designed to make the life of the Chinese in the state as onerous as possible.

The enactment of "stringent laws," a state legislative committee had said as early as 1858, was one way of ridding the state of Chinese. And under this rubric a program of action began shortly to unfold. Acting at times impulsively, at others after careful deliberation, the state and its municipalities passed measure after measure designed to afflict the Chinese and make their life in California unpleasant. Some measures discriminated against the Chinese overtly, subjecting them to discriminatory taxation, forbidding them from working for corporations, for example, or from fishing in the state's waters; others vested enormous discretion in officials, and perforce allowed enormous discretion to discriminate. Still others sought to exploit real or perceived flaws in Chinese living habits. As a committee of the San Francisco Board of Supervisors had put it in an 1885 report: "The fact that the race is one that cannot readily throw off its habits and customs, the facts that these habits and customs are so widely at variance with our own, makes the enforcement of our laws and obedience to our laws necessarily obnoxious and revolting to the Chinese; and the more rigidly this enforcement is insisted upon and carried out the less endurable will existence be to them, the less attractive will life be to them in California. Fewer will come and fewer will remain."[5] The Chinese may well have had living habits that needed to be curbed in the interests of promoting the public health and safety, but the police power measures here described, as one utterance after the other made clear, were motivated first and foremost by a desire to harass the Chinese, only secondarily by a desire to promote the public health and safety. (It was to say the least a curious way for a governmental authority to go about forming its public policy.) Eventually, of course, when these schemes proved unavailing or less efficacious than hoped, California, with the support of other western states, appealed to the national government for assistance. This appeal ultimately succeeded. But the enactment of federal laws restricting Chinese immigration did not prevent the state and its municipalities from continuing to follow the practices just described, to help the federal process along so to speak.

The Chinese, as this work has shown, understood perfectly well the ways in which they were being singled out for invidious treatment, resented this fact as deeply as any Caucasian immigrant group might have, and resisted it at every turn, principally in the courts. In her classic monograph on China's legal system, *Legal Institutions in Manchu China*, the sociologist Sybille van der Sprenkel comments on how totally foreign to traditional Chinese ways was the idea of public-spirited litigation aimed at challenging official policy. But she goes on to note that Chinese merchants were very quick to appreciate the protections and advantages that the western system of law offered once they came into contact with it.[6] Something like this was the case with the Chinese in America. They came quite early to understand how the courts could be used to frustrate the Sinophobic impulses of the Caucasian majority, and they learned to repair to them when their interests were threatened. (This regular recourse to the courts is in one sense of course decisive refutation of the charge so often leveled against the nineteenth-century Chinese immigrants that they were incapable of understanding American institutions or adapting to them.) In American courts, for a time at least, they compiled a remarkable record of success, a record that can be explained by reference to a number of factors.

First, they had the resources to bring their claims before the courts. The Chinese community was not a wealthy one, but it was not impoverished either. Most members were gainfully employed. There was a relatively prosperous merchant class, made up in the main of small entrepreneurs. These men could often afford to litigate claims on their own. Much more important, it was a highly organized community, consisting of associations both voluntary (e.g., the Tung Hing Tong) and ascriptive (e.g., the *hui-kuan*). When members of these associations pooled resources, as they were wont to do, a considerable war chest could result. The laundry litigation and the challenge to the Geary Act are cases in point. Finally, after 1878 at any rate, the Chinese had their consulate. The consulate, as this work has made clear, showed itself to be vigorous in protecting Chinese rights and contributed financially to some of the litigation. Using their resources the Chinese were able to employ competent counsel to represent them. They may indeed even have been able to offer a premium, thereby further increasing their chances of procuring effective representation.

Able counsel would of course have availed the Chinese little had not the legal climate in which they pressed their claims been favorable. It was in several respects. The United States, whatever its faults, was a country devoted to the rule of law. Embodied in federal law and treaty were provisions with which the state and local ordinances were either in tension or rather patently in conflict, and it would have been very hard for any court to ignore these conflicts. The Sixth Article of the Burlingame Treaty of 1868 guaranteed to the Chinese the same privileges and rights as those accorded to the citizens or subjects of the most favored nation, a guarantee that was reconfirmed in the treaty revision agreed to in 1880. Laws that treated the Chinese differently from other aliens were prima facie suspect under these provisions. Then there was the Civil Rights Act of 1870. Section 16 of that act, as noted, was enacted for the specific purpose of shielding the Chinese against hostile action by the states, a fact widely appreciated in the West at the time of its passage and in subsequent years. Counsel for the Chinese repeatedly pleaded both legal provisions in attacking legislation. Finally, and most important, there was the Fourteenth Amendment itself. The Chinese were recognized as coming under the protection of this great constitutional provision quite early in the day and thereafter invoked its due process and equal protection provisions repeatedly in their lawsuits.

The legal climate was favorable in another more specific respect. It undoubtedly helped the Chinese that the hostile official action about which they were complaining was in so many instances aimed at harming them in their economic interests. But the Fourteenth Amendment was thought by many, Stephen Field at the head, to have embodied in the positive law the old Jacksonian principle that no one should be arbitrarily disadvantaged by government in the pursuit of economic advantage. Indeed a large part of the post-Civil War judiciary was committed body and soul to this view. And discrimination based on group membership was an instance of arbitrary interference with this right. As the Supreme Court was to put it in the 1915 case of *Truax v. Raich* (another case involving aliens and the right to work): "[T]he right to work for a living in the common occupations of the community is of the very essence of the personal freedom and opportunity that it was the purpose of the [Fourteenth] Amendment to secure. . . . If this could be refused solely upon the ground of race or nationality, the prohibition of the denial of the equal protection of the laws would be a barren form of words."[7] Jacksonian constitutionalism gave the Chinese, if I may borrow words used by Benno Schmidt in connection with another set of cases, "a doctrinal structure that could . . . confront racist ideology and judicial deference to state's rights with a powerful counterweight."[8] These points are developed in greater detail in the discussion of the California laundry laws in chapter 4.

But it was not just economic discrimination that bothered the judges.

They accepted as well *at some level* the more general principle that one of the responsibilities of courts in a constitutional democracy was to protect minority groups, including racial minorities, against majoritarian excesses of any kind. The principle was not as fully developed as was the concept of economic discrimination. It was not always consistently applied. But it is clearly detectable in the decisions. The principle of equal protection of the laws, said Field in *Ho Ah Kow*, forbade "hostile and discriminating legislation by a state against persons of any class, sect, creed, or nation, in whatever form it may be expressed." And in the case we hear him thundering against what he saw as the gratuitous cruelty of the queue-cutting ordinance. Cruel and unusual punishment he called it, comparable to punishing Jewish prisoners by forcing them to eat a diet of pork. Lorenzo Sawyer thought the city ordinance under review in *Lee Sing* null and void not because of its economic effects but because of its sheer inhumanity, calculated as it was to "forcibly drive out a whole community of twenty-odd thousand people, old and young, male and female, citizens of the United States, born on the soil, and foreigners of the Chinese race, moral and immoral, good, bad, and indifferent" from an area of the city they had inhabited for well-nigh half a century. The principle relied on by Judge Morrow in *Wong Wai* and *Jew Ho* certainly transcended economic considerations. It was that race or ethnicity could not be the principal basis for imposing radical and draconian health restrictions. These decisions in their broad reach and general application seem to me to presage the contemporary jurisprudence of equal protection for minority races. I differ then from the view expressed by the late Robert Cover that it was only in 1938, with the U.S. Supreme Court decision in *United States v. Carolene Products*, that racial minorities became a special object of judicial protection.[9] In an important sense the nineteenth-century Chinese were a special object of judicial solicitude, and the judges saw themselves as discharging the function of protecting a beleaguered minority against invidious majority mistreatment, whatever form it might take.[10]

If the Chinese were the beneficiaries of late nineteenth-century notions of equality in their struggles with the state of California and its municipalities, they were victims of classic notions of national sovereignty in their struggles with the federal government over the various exclusion laws. When confronted head on with the question, as it was in the *Chinese Exclusion Case*, the Supreme Court decided that the power to exclude foreigners was an incident of sovereignty belonging to the political branches of the general government and that the judicial department was to have little or nothing to say about its exercise. One might say that here in a way the Chinese were victims of their own successes. The Chinese had themselves been instrumental in establishing the principle that the states were utterly without power to regulate foreign commerce, including immigration, and that the Constitution had placed "the whole of it" as the court was wont to say, in the Congress. Having reached that conclusion, it was a short step for the court to rule that "the whole of it" meant that Congress, in exercising its power over foreign immigration, was as immune from interference from the courts as it was from the states.

The most the Chinese realistically might have hoped for in their exclusion act battles was some mitigation in the severity of the legislation. And it initially seemed as if they might get that. In the first test case the Chinese brought under the exclusion legislation, the *Case of the Chinese Cabin Waiter* (1882), Justice Field had said: "The wisdom of [the law's] enactment will be better vindicated by a construction less repellent to our sense of justice and right" and "Laws are to be construed so as to prevent an unjust result." This same sentiment was echoed by other judges. Eventually, however, this was lost sight of, and the judges become quite hard-nosed about interpreting the law. This very harsh construction might have been as much tied up with the exclusionary nationalism that was then coming to dominate American immigration policy in general as it did with hostility toward Chinese immigration in particular.[11] But even here we see the Chinese vigorously contesting federal action and occasionally managing to work some mitigation in the law's severity.

By 1900, the year of *Wong Wai* and *Jew Ho*, the Chinese population in California had dwindled to about 60 percent of what it had been at the high point in the immigration. It would decline much further as the century progressed. The exclusion legislation was having its intended effect, and there were signs that the Chinese were no longer preoccupying the mind of Caucasian California as once they had.[12] (The fact that the plague episode on the whole received such subdued newspaper coverage is some evidence of this fact. Had the incident occurred in the 1880s, it is safe to guess that the story would have continually occupied the front pages.) But if the Chinese were beginning to recede from Caucasian consciousness, another group of Asian immigrants was simultaneously rising to take their place. A trickle of Japanese immigration to the state had started in the early 1880s, but its pace picked up substantially in the first decades of the twentieth century. The Japanese came mainly as farmers. In much the same manner as the first Chinese miners, who specialized in working abandoned or borderline mining claims, the Japanese settled on marginal rural lands and by dint of hard work and the application of their knowledge of intensive farming techniques turned them to productive use. As their success grew they became the target of increasing Caucasian resentment. The state government, showing that history occasionally does repeat itself, responded to the Japanese in exactly the same way it had to the Chinese. It sought to discourage a Japanese presence through the enactment of onerous domestic legislation, this time legislation affecting the ownership of agricultural land. In 1913 the state legislature passed a law limiting ownership of such lands by persons ineligible to citizenship, that is, Chinese and Japanese, to three-year leaseholds. Other more stringent measures soon followed. As it had with regard to Chinese immigration, the state also sought the succor of the federal government.

In 1920 the California State Board of Control, an administrative agency in the executive department, prepared for Governor William D. Stephens a comprehensive report on persons of Asian descent then living in the state. The report was entitled *California and the Oriental,* but it focused primarily on the Japanese. The report was forwarded to the U.S. secretary of state with an accompanying letter from the governor. The letter was full of the traditional rhetoric of the yellow peril. In it he described California as "an outpost on the western edge of Occidental civilization" threatened again by the teeming millions of the Orient. Noting how effective federal exclusion legislation had eventually proven to be in stemming the tide of Chinese immigration, he called for passage by Congress of a Japanese exclusion act.[13] This one, he said, like the Geary Act, should provide for the exclusion of all Japanese save certain selected classes. Like that act also it should require all Japanese lawfully within the U.S. to procure certificates of registration and to carry them as a condition of continued residence. This, said the governor, was the only way effectively to remedy the problem of Japanese immigration.[14] Congress never enacted a registration system for the Japanese, but in 1924 it passed and President Coolidge signed a very restrictive immigration act which, among other things, forbade any further Japanese immigration to the United States.[15]

List of Abbreviations

art.	article
C.C.D. Cal.	Circuit Court (old federal), California
Cal.	California Reports
Cal. Civ. Proc. Code	California Code of Civil Procedure
Cal. Legis.	California Legislature
Cal. Stat.	Statutes of California
ch.	chapter
Cong. Res.	Congressional Resolution
Cong.	Congress
D. Cal.	U.S. District Court, California
F.	Federal Reporter
F. Cas.	Federal Cases
H.R.	House bill
H.R. Exec. Doc.	House of Representatives Executive Document
Or.	Oregon
S.	Senate bill
Sess.	Session
slip op.	slip opinion
Stat.	United States Statutes at Large
U.S.	United States Reports 1875–date
(Wall.)	United States Reports (Wallace) 1863–74
(How.)	United States Reports (Howard) 1843–60
(Pet.)	United States Reports (Peters) 1828–42
(Wheat.)	United States Reports (Wheaton) 1816–27

Notes

INTRODUCTION

1. See, e.g., Lucille Eaves, *A History of California Labor Legislation* (Berkeley, California: The University Press, 1910); Elmer Sandmeyer, *The Anti-Chinese Movement in California* (1939; reprint, Urbana: University of Illinois Press, 1973); Stuart Miller, *The Unwelcome Immigrant: The American Image of the Chinese 1785–1882* (Berkeley: University of California Press, 1969); Alexander Saxton, *The Indispensable Enemy: The Anti-Chinese Movement in California* (Berkeley: University of California Press, 1971). Sandmeyer's monograph, originally published in 1939, remains the best overview of the evolution of official policy toward the Chinese in California.

2. Roger Daniels, "Westerners from the East: Oriental Immigrants Reappraised," *Pacific Historical Review* 35 (1966): 373, 375. Anyone doing work on the history of anti-Orientalism in California must acknowledge the seminal character of the work of Roger Daniels. See, e.g., *The Politics of Prejudice: The Anti-Japanese Movement and the Struggle for Japanese Exclusion* (Berkeley: University of California Press, 1962).

3. See Gunther Barth, *Bitter Strength: A History of the Chinese in the United States, 1850–1870* (Cambridge: Harvard University Press, 1964); K. Y. Zo, "Chinese Emigration into the United States, 1850–1880" (Ph.D. dissertation, Columbia University, 1971).

4. Barth, *Bitter Strength*, passim. This work contains much useful information on the social structure of early Chinese America but is, in my judgment, badly off the mark on this point.

5. Chew Heong v. United States, 112 U.S. 536, 567 (1884) (Field, J., dissenting). The case that gave him occasion to make this remark was a Chinese challenge to the implementation of one of the federal exclusion laws.

6. Barth, *Bitter Strength*, pp. 179–80. He acknowledges that there were instances of resistance to mistreatment but sees these merely as efforts on the part of individuals to attain their own personal goals.

7. Sandmeyer, *The Anti-Chinese Movement*, p. 24, quoting Robert Glass Cle-

land, *A History of California: The American Period* (New York: The Macmillan Co., 1922), p. 416.

8. Linda C. A. Przybyszewski, "Judge Lorenzo Sawyer and the Chinese Civil Rights Decisions in the Ninth Circuit," *Western Legal History* 1 (1988): 23–56; Lucy Salyer, "Captives of Law: Judicial Enforcement of the Chinese Exclusion Laws, 1891–1905," *Journal of American History* 76 (1989): 91–117. The topic is also dealt with in the final chapter of Christian Fritz's fine recent biography of California's first federal judge, *Federal Justice in California: The Court of Ogden Hoffman, 1851–1891* (Lincoln, Neb.: University of Nebraska Press, 1991). See also the articles by professors Wunder and Mooney cited in note 12, below.

9. See, e.g., Sandmeyer, *The Anti-Chinese Movement*; Miller, *The Unwelcome Immigrant*; Saxton, *The Indispensable Enemy*. A number of factors no doubt account for the rise and persistence of Sinophobia in California though I, for my part, would put racial demagoguery at the top of the list. It was a constant feature of the political landscape. Economics too played its part. It is well known that bad economic times magnify and intensify racial antagonisms, and bad times there were aplenty during this period.

10. Sucheng Chan, *This Bittersweet Soil: The Chinese in California Agriculture, 1860–1910* (Berkeley: University of California Press, 1986); see also the many fine scholarly contributions collected in Sucheng Chan, ed., *Entry Denied: Exclusion and the Chinese Community in America, 1882–1943* (Philadelphia: Temple University Press, 1991); Sandy Lydon, *Chinese Gold: The Chinese in the Monterey Bay Region* (Capitola: Capitola Books, 1985). See, e.g., Him Mark Lai, "China Politics and the U.S. Chinese Communities," in Emma Gee, ed., *Counterpoint: Perspectives on Asian America* (Los Angeles: UCLA Asian American Studies Center, 1976), pp. 152–59, and "Historical Development of the Chinese Consolidated Benevolent Association/*Huiguan* System," in *Chinese America: History and Perspectives* (San Francisco: Chinese Historical Society of America, 1987).

11. Hudson N. Janisch, "The Chinese, the Courts and the Constitution: A Study of the Legal Issues Raised by Chinese Immigration to the United States, 1850–1902" (J.S.D. dissertation, University of Chicago, 1971).

12. See, e.g., John R. Wunder, "The Chinese and the Courts in the Pacific Northwest: Justice Denied?" *Pacific Historical Review* 52 (1983): 191–211, and Ralph James Mooney, "Matthew Deady and the Federal Judicial Response to Racism in the Early West," *Oregon Law Review* 63 (1984): 561–637.

CHAPTER ONE

1. Theodore Hittell, *History of California* (San Francisco: N. J. Stone, 1898), 4:98–99.

2. Ibid.

3. Gunther Barth, *Bitter Strength: A History of the Chinese in the United States, 1850–1870* (Cambridge: Harvard University Press, 1964), p. 136.

4. San Francisco *Herald*, May 16, 1852, p. 2, col. 1. They would do so again at several junctures in the future.

5. Hittell, *History of California* 4:99.

6. Assembly Committee on Mines and Mining Interests, *Report,* Cal. Assembly, 3d Sess., Appendix to the Journal of the Assembly (1852), p. 829.

7. Ibid., p. 830. Though the report concentrated on Chinese immigrants, it also viewed with alarm the presence of those it described as "Mexican and South American peons." Ibid., p. 835.

8. Ibid., p. 831. In March 1852 Senator George Tingley had in fact introduced a bill that would have allowed for enforcement through the criminal law of long-term labor contracts made in China. S. 63, 1852 Cal. Legis., 3d Sess., California State Archives, Sacramento. Since the bill would have established a system of effective indentured servitude, it got nowhere in the legislature. It did, however, provide ammunition to anti-Chinese agitators for many years to come. Though in the early years of the immigration there were a few instances of Chinese coming to this country under contracts of labor for terms of years, the overwhelming majority of Chinese do not seem to have come under an obligation to work for any particular employer. Many, to be sure, had had their passage to California financed by lenders in China, and repayment of these debts was enforced in various ways by the institutions of Chinese society in the United States. It should be noted that it is extremely difficult, given the very fragmentary evidence that is available, to put together a complete picture of how Chinese immigration to the West Coast was facilitated.

9. In 1850, the California legislature had enacted a law, aimed not only at the Chinese but at all foreigners, that required all who were not native-born citizens of the United States or who had not acquired citizenship by the Treaty of Guadalupe Hidalgo, to pay a fee of $20 per month for the privilege of working in the state's mines. Act of Apr. 13, 1850, ch. 97, §§ 1, 5, 1850 Cal. Stat. 221, 221–22. Although the constitutionality of the measure had been upheld in a California Supreme Court decision, People v. Naglee, 1 Cal. 232 (1850), it had proved impossible to enforce and was soon repealed. Act of Mar. 14, 1851, ch. 108, 1851 Cal. Stat. 424.

10. Assembly Committee on Mines and Mining Interests, *Report,* Cal. Assembly, 3d Sess., Appendix to the Journal of the Assembly (1852), p. 834.

11. It was the first of several such messages to come from Bigler and the first in a long series of anti-Chinese pronouncements that were to emanate from the state capital over the course of the nineteenth century.

12. "Governor's Special Message," *Daily Alta California,* Apr. 25, 1852, p. 2, col. 2.

13. Ibid. Elsewhere in the message, Bigler noted that he had no hard information about the terms of these contracts and as much as admitted that he was reporting rumors.

14. A decade later, in 1862, Congress enacted a law prohibiting the importation of "coolie" labor. Act of Feb. 19, 1862, ch. 27, 12 Stat. 340. Bigler recognized that much of what he was advocating came close to encroaching on the federal government's exclusive jurisdiction over foreign commerce; but he argued for the program's constitutionality and, in any case, strongly hinted that this was not the time to be indulging constitutional scruples. "Governor's Special Message," *Daily Alta California,* Apr. 25, 1852, p. 2, col. 2.

15. "Governor's Special Message," *Daily Alta California,* Apr. 25, 1852, p. 2, col. 2.

16. Every element of the legislative program Bigler outlined was eventually enacted into law by the California legislature.

17. "The Chinese Immigration," *Daily Alta California*, Apr. 26, 1852, p. 2, col. 1.

18. Ibid. According to Hittell, Bigler's attack upon the Chinese was considered very offensive and uncalled for by "some of the most intelligent and liberal-minded classes of the community." Hittell, *History of California* 4:108.

19. Little is known about Asing (sometimes spelled Assing) except that he was a man of substantial power and influence in the early Chinese community in San Francisco and was perceived by the white population as a leader and a spokesman. He is portrayed in Gunther Barth's monograph as a somewhat shadowy figure who exercised tight and autocratic control over his countrymen and whose rule was widely resented. Barth, *Bitter Strength*, pp. 83–85. Whatever the truth of these charges, Asing's rejoinder to Bigler was cogent, eloquent, and more than a little feisty.

20. Asing, "To His Excellency Gov. Bigler," *Daily Alta California*, May 5, 1852, p. 2, col. 2.

21. Ibid. Although it had not been settled by authoritative judicial decision at the time, it was almost universally believed that the Chinese could not avail themselves of the federal naturalization laws to become U.S. citizens. Their belief was based on language in the federal naturalization laws. For a full discussion of the question of Chinese naturalization rights, see ch. 2.

22. Asing, "To His Excellency Gov. Bigler." Apparently other Chinese responded to Bigler, and they drew favorable comment. "[T]hey evinced a decided superiority to [Bigler] not only in temper but also in logic." Hittell, *History of California* 4:108, citing F. Soule, J. Gihon, J. Nisbet, *The Annals of San Francisco* (New York: Appleton, 1855), p. 381.

23. Act of May 4, 1852, ch. 37, 1852 Cal. Stat. 84, *repealed by* Act of Mar. 30, 1853, ch. 44, 1853 Cal. Stat. 62.

24. Act of May 4, 1852, ch. 37, §§ 6, 9, 1852 Cal. Stat. 84, 85.

25. Ibid., § 10, 1852 Cal. Stat. 84, 86.

26. Ibid., § 8, 1852 Cal. Stat. 84, 85. This last provision was to lead to severe abuses and to have deadly consequences for the Chinese since these deputies had a tendency to exact the fee in a rather violent manner. *Report of the Joint Select Committee Relative to the Chinese Population of the State of California*, Cal. Legis., 13th Sess., Appendix to the Journals (1862) [hereafter *Joint Select Committee Report*], p. 7.

27. Act of May 3, 1852, ch. 36, 1852 Cal. Stat. 78, *amended by* Act of Apr. 2, 1853, ch. 51, 1853 Cal. Stat. 71.

28. Ibid. §§ 1–3 (§ 1 as amended, 1853 Cal. Stat. 71–72). In New York v. Miln, 36 U.S. (11 Pet.) 102 (1837), the United States Supreme Court had upheld a New York law requiring shipmasters to report foreign passenger identification.

29. Act of May 3, 1852, ch. 36, §§ 1, 5, 1852 Cal. Stat. 78, 80 (§ 1 as amended, 1853 Cal. Stat. 71–72). The tax was to remain in effect until 1872, when it was declared unconstitutional by the California Supreme Court. State v. S. S. Constitution, 42 Cal. 578, 590 (1872).

30. Lucille Eaves, *A History of California Labor Legislation* (Berkeley: The University Press, 1910), p. 112.

31. Eaves comments "[The Chinese] had learned at this early date the advantages of employing an able lawyer to present their side of the situation." Ibid., p. 108.

32. See H. B. Morse, *The Gilds of China* (London, New York: Longmans, Green, 1909), p. 45. Morse calls them "provincial clubs."

33. In 1882 a more formal organization with better defined powers and a presidency that rotated among the constituent district associations was formed. The most complete account of the origins and complex organizational history of the district associations and of the coordinating council, the Chinese Six Companies, is to be found in Him Mark Lai, "Historical Development of the Chinese Consolidated Benevolent Association/*Huiguan* System," in *Chinese America: History and Perspectives* (San Francisco: Chinese Historical Society of America, 1987), pp. 13–51. See also Shih-shan Henry Tsai, *China and the Overseas Chinese in the United States, 1868–1911* (Fayetteville, Ark.: University of Arkansas Press, 1983), pp. 31–38; A. W. Loomis, "The Chinese Six Companies," *Overland Monthly* (September 1868): 221–27; William Speer, *The Oldest and the Newest Empire: China and the United States* (Hartford, Conn.: S. S. Scranton & Co., 1870), pp. 558–65; and William Hoy, *The Chinese Six Companies* (San Francisco: The Chinese Consolidated Benevolent Association, 1942).

34. However, it needs to be said that the Chinese community, at least in its urban parts, was a distinctly mercantile community. One scholar has estimated that between 1870 and 1900 some 40 percent of the Chinese living in San Francisco and Sacramento were merchants while another 5 to 12 percent were artisans and professionals. See Sucheng Chan, *This Bittersweet Soil: The Chinese in California Agriculture, 1860–1910* (Berkeley: University of California Press, 1986), p. 404.

35. Assembly Committee on Mines and Mining Interests, *Report on the Chinese Population*, Doc. No. 28, Cal. Assembly, 4th Sess., Appendix to the Journal of the Assembly (1853) [hereafter *Report on the Chinese Population*], p. 9.

36. It happens that we know something about the background and later career of one of these men. Tong K. Achick, who represented the Yeong Wo district association and who acted as the whole delegation's interpreter, was born in Canton and attended the Morrison Educational Society elementary school in Macao. Among his classmates were Yung Wing, who would later become the first Chinese to graduate from an American college (Yale), and Lee Kan, later the editor of the *Oriental*, a Chinese newspaper published in San Francisco. Achick returned to China in the 1860s and died there in 1897. Him Mark Lai, "A Short History of the Jop Sen Tong," unpublished paper.

37. *Report on the Chinese Population*, pp. 7–10.

38. Ibid., p. 10.

39. Ibid., p. 9.

40. Ibid.

41. Ibid., p. 10.

42. Ibid. In its separate and accompanying report on proposed legislation, the committee spoke of a desire "to allure to our shores the vast accumulations of Asiatic capital which are the result of ages of labor and economy." Assembly Committee on Mines and Mining Interests, *Report on the Proposed Legislation*,

Doc. No. 28, Cal. Assembly, 4th Sess., Appendix to the Journal of the Assembly (1853) [hereafter *Report on the Proposed Legislation*], p. 6.

43. The report spoke of the peculiar influences which tended to keep the Chinese at home. Ibid., p. 5.

44. Ibid. "The superior energy of the Caucasian will always conquer the sullen industry of the Mongol."

45. Ibid.

46. Ibid., p. 3.

47. Act of Mar. 30, 1853, ch. 44, § 6, 1853 Cal. Stat. 62, 63.

48. *Golden Hills News*, May 27, 1854.

49. Act of May 13, 1854, ch. 49, 1854 Cal. Stat. 55.

50. Cal. Cong. Res. of May 13, 1854, 1854 Cal. Stat. 230 (Redding).

51. Assembly Select Committee on Foreign Miners, *Majority Report on Assembly Bills Nos. 206, 207 and 208*, Doc. No. 19, Cal. Assembly, 6th Sess., Appendix to the Journal of the Assembly (1855).

52. Act of Apr. 30, 1855, ch. 174, 1855 Cal. Stat. 216 (amending 1853 Cal. Stat. 62), *repealed by* Act of Apr. 16, 1856, ch. 119, § 1, 1856 Cal. Stat. 141.

53. Act of Apr. 28, 1855, ch. 153, 1855 Cal. Stat. 194. A minority of the senate select committee recommended imposing the tax on the Chinese "upon their landing in the country [because] it will be difficult if not impossible for them to pay it." Senate Select Committee, *Minority Report on Resolutions of Miners' Convention of Shasta County*, Doc. No. 16, Cal. Senate, 6th Sess., Appendix to the Journal of the Senate (1855), p. 5. The minority thought that by making it nearly impossible for additional Chinese to immigrate to California those already in the state would be induced to leave. The Chinese were already complaining about the legislature's oppressive acts, the report noted.

54. The United States Supreme Court in The Passenger Cases, 48 U.S. (7 How.) 282 (1849), had struck down a state law imposing a tax on alien passengers arriving from foreign ports. Eight separate opinions were written, however, and the exact basis of the decision was none too clear.

55. Cal. Cong. Res. of May 13, 1854, 1854 Cal. Stat. 230 (Redding).

56. As bleak as the session proved to be for the Chinese, it is interesting to note that two of the Chinese district associations, the Sze Yup and Ning Yeung Companies, were able to secure passage of a special bill permitting them to own, buy, and sell real property and enter into contracts in their own names. Act of Apr. 30, 1855, ch. 159, 1855 Cal. Stat. 202. The measure was necessary because neither organization was incorporated.

57. See *Report of the Assembly Committee on Mines and Mining Interests to Whom Was Referred the Memorial of Citizens of San Francisco*, Cal. Assembly, 7th Sess., Appendix to the Journal of the Assembly (1856), p. 5.

58. Ibid., p. 3.

59. There was simply no way that the shipping companies could pass on such a steep tax—$10 more than the full cost of passage from China—to their Chinese passengers.

60. 7 Cal. 169 (1857).

61. *Report of the Committee on Federal Relations on Assembly Bill No. 402*, April 19, 1858, California State Archives, Sacramento.

62. 1858 Cal. Stat. 295. It was captioned: "An Act to Prevent the Further Immigration of Chinese or Mongolians to this State."

63. See argument of counsel, Lin Sing v. Washburn, 20 Cal. 534, 538 (1862).

64. According to figures compiled in 1856 by the state controller, the state had received $429,434 in license fees through the end of 1855. El Dorado County, one of the most important mining counties, had received $102,426 during a three-year period from 1853 to 1855. Senate Committee on Mines and Mining Interests, *Majority Report,* Cal. Senate, 7th Sess., Appendix to the Journal of the Senate (1856), p. 6. These were very large sums of money for the time and often accounted for more than 10 percent of government revenues. See, e.g., Controller of the State, *Statement of Receipts,* 1855 Annual Report, Doc. No. 2, Cal. Senate, 7th Sess., Item A. Appendix to the Journal of the Senate (1856).

65. Reverend Speer's attitude toward the Chinese and his knowledge of their history and culture are clearly evidenced in Speer, *The Oldest and the Newest Empire.* For information on Speer generally, see Michael L. Stahler, "William Speer: Champion of California's Chinese, 1852–57," *Journal of Presbyterian History* 48 (1970): 113ff.

66. Interestingly, in the first issue of Speer's bilingual newspaper, the *Oriental* (*Tung-ngai san-luk*), he made the prophetic suggestion that the Chinese, industrious and experienced in the building of large projects, would be an excellent source of labor for the construction of the proposed Trans-Pacific Railway. "Laborers for the Pacific Railroad," *Oriental,* Jan. 4, 1855, p. 2, col. 1.

67. Unfortunately, no critical biography of Speer exists.

68. William Speer, *An Humble Plea Addressed to the Legislature of California in Behalf of the Immigrants from the Empire of China to This State* (1856).

69. Ibid., pp. 32–33.

70. Ibid., p. 32. Speer also argued for reducing the passenger tax from $50 to $5.

71. Ibid., p. 5.

72. See reports of the Senate and Assembly Committees on Mines and Mining Interests, Cal. Assembly, 7th Sess., Appendix to the Journal of the Assembly (1856). One had to read the assembly report *very* carefully to see that this was the recommendation.

73. In the period 1850–70, the mood of the legislature was mercurial. In some sessions nary a voice was heard on behalf of the Chinese. In others, a fair number of legislators spoke on their behalf.

74. Senate Committee on Mines and Mining Interests, *Report,* Cal. Senate, 7th Sess., Appendix to the Journal of the Senate (1856), p. 3. The thoughts if not the language of the report resonated perfectly with the pamphlet prepared by Speer.

75. Ibid., p. 4.

76. Assembly Committee on Mines and Mining Interests, *Report,* Cal. Assembly, 7th Sess., Appendix to the Journal of the Assembly (1856), p. 13.

77. Ibid., p. 3.

78. Ibid., p. 13.

79. Ibid., p. 9.

80. Act of Apr. 19, 1856, ch. 119, 1856 Cal. Stat. 141 (amending 1853 Cal. Stat. 62).

81. Indictment, p. 1, People v. Hall case file, California State Archives, Sacramento.

82. Trial Transcript, p. 1, People v. Hall case file. George Brown, ed., *Reminis-*

cences of Senator William M. Stewart of Nevada (New York: Neale Publishing Co., 1908), p. 78.

83. Act of Apr. 16, 1850, ch. 99, § 14, 1850 Cal. Stat. 229, 230. A parallel but not identical provision applied to testimony in civil cases. Civil Practice Act of 1851, ch. 5, § 394(3), 1851 Cal. Stat. 51, 114.

84. *Hall*, 4 Cal. 399 (1854).

85. Ibid., p. 400.

86. Ibid., pp. 400–401.

87. Ibid.

88. Ibid., pp. 403–4.

89. Ibid., p. 404.

90. Ibid., pp. 404–5.

91. In 1859 the California Supreme Court extended the ban on Chinese testimony against whites to civil cases. Speer v. See Yup Co., 13 Cal. 73 (1859). The Speer in the case was one James Speer, who, so far as is known, was unrelated to the Reverend William Speer.

92. Lai Chun-chuen to John Bigler, January 1855, *Remarks of the Chinese Merchants of San Francisco on Governor Bigler's Message*, trans. W. Speer, p. 5, Bancroft Library, University of California, Berkeley. The letter, prepared on behalf of the Chinese Merchants' Exchange of San Francisco and widely circulated in the Chinese merchant community, offered a point-by-point refutation of the charges made against the Chinese by the governor.

93. Ibid.

94. Ibid.

95. Ibid. The letter was translated into English by Reverend Speer and circulated as a pamphlet in the state capital. Y. Oy, H. M. Lai, and P. Choy, eds., *A History of the Sam Yup Benevolent Association in the United States* (San Francisco, 1975), p. 16.

96. Senate Select Committee, *Minority Report on Resolutions of Miners' Convention of Shasta County*, Doc. No. 16, Cal. Senate, 6th Sess., Appendix to the Journal of the Senate (1855), p. 7.

97. "Chinese Testimony," *Oriental*, Jan. 18, 1855, p. 3, col. 1.

98. Three years later, when lamenting the assembly's defeat of a bill that would have reversed the *Hall* result, the San Francisco *Evening Bulletin* commented, "We regret this action, based as it is entirely upon prejudice, and can only express our conviction that the period will ultimately arrive when it will be clear to all that the law as it stands is mischievous and prejudicial in the highest degree to the public interests." "Admissibility of Chinese and Negro Testimony," *Evening Bulletin*, Apr. 10, 1857, p. 2, col. 1.

99. Act of Mar. 18, 1863, ch. 70, 1863 Cal. Stat. 69, *repealed by omission from codification* Cal. Penal Code § 1321 (1872). The 1863 codification omitted the proscription on black testimony.

100. Act of Mar. 16, 1863, ch. 68, 1863 Cal. Stat. 60, *repealed by omission from codification* Cal. Civ. Proc. Code §§ 8, 1880 (1872).

101. See Christian Fritz, *Federal Justice in California: The Court of Ogden Hoffman, 1851–1891* (Lincoln, Neb.: University of Nebraska Press, 1991), p. 211.

102. William Speer, *Answer to Objections to Chinese Testimony and Appeal for Their Protection by Our Laws* (1857), p. 1, Bancroft Library, University of California, Berkeley. The pamphlet provided the legislators with information on

the Chinese religion and sought to show that the Chinese by virtue of their religious beliefs and ethical values were quite sensitive to the obligations of an oath. It argued that Chinese testimony was accepted by courts in other parts of the common-law world and was sanctioned by U.S. law. It endorsed a bill pending in the legislature that would have allowed judges to receive Chinese testimony if they were convinced that the witness comprehended the responsibility of an oath and the nature of the crime of perjury.

103. A. W. Loomis to Walter Lowrie, Jan. 3, 1860, Presbyterian Church in the U.S.A., Board of Foreign Missions, *Correspondence, 1852–1865,* re: California, (microfilm, San Francisco Theological Seminary Library, San Anselmo, California).

104. Ibid.

105. Ibid. Loomis added, however, that "as the case now stands, I fear they have a dim prospect."

106. A. W. Loomis to Walter Lowrie, Jan. 30, 1860.

107. Ibid. Unfortunately, the judge's identity remains a mystery. We know only that he was "an elder in Dr. Anderson's church."

108. Ibid. The terms called for payment of expenses and a fee contingent upon the lawyer's success.

109. No external evidence on the question exists either.

110. 19 Cal. 106 (1861). The term "Ah" is a diminutive used by the Cantonese with given names to address each other in familiar speech. As the reader will notice, the term appears frequently in the names of cases involving Chinese litigants. How the custom arose of designating Chinese litigants by their familiar names rather than by their full family names in official court records is unclear.

111. Act of May 17, 1861, §§ 90, 93, 1861 Cal. Stat. 447.

112. *Ah Pong,* p. 107.

113. Ibid.

114. Ibid., p. 108.

115. 19 Cal. 491 (1861).

116. Ibid.

117. *Ah Hee,* pp. 494–96. Section 17 provided: "Foreigners who are or who may hereafter become *bona fide* residents of this state, shall enjoy the same rights in respect to the possession, enjoyment and inheritance of property as native born citizens."

118. Ibid., pp. 496–97. Plaintiff in this case had leased the land from the owner.

119. The court accepted the argument quoting Article I, Section 17 of the California Constitution, but erroneously cited it as Section 7. Ah Hee v. Crippen case file, slip op. 1–2 (Mariposa County Dist. Ct., Mar. 18, 1861) (on file with the *California Law Review*). The court added in dictum, "I Suppose the Legislature did not intend the foreign Miners license law to apply to foreigners working mines on private lands."

120. Ah Hee v. Crippen case file (Mariposa County Dist. Ct., Mar. 23, 1861) (order granting plaintiff relief requested), California State Archives, Sacramento.

121. *Ah Hee,* pp. 497–98. The holding in *Ah Hee* was confirmed three years later in another case involving the refusal of a Chinese miner to pay the Foreign Miners' License Tax. Ah Yew v. Choate, 24 Cal. 562, 566 (1864).

122. If the surviving court records of one California mining county are at all

typical, individual Chinese in the mining districts made wide use of the courts during this time period. The Index to Civil and Criminal Actions for Nevada County contains numerous references to civil cases involving Chinese litigants, and the Niles Searls Historical Library, located in Nevada City, the county seat, contains the actual case files of some two dozen civil cases involving Chinese litigants decided by the county court between 1860 and 1874. Among them are: a successful action for conversion brought in 1868 by Chinese merchants against two Caucasians alleged to have forcibly removed goods from their store (Lung Lee & Co. v. John Perkinpine and Terry Lyons, No. 3180 [14th Dist. Ct., Nevada Co.]); a successful defense by eighteen Chinese gold miners in the same year of a trespass claim brought against them by a Caucasian landowner (Dunstone v. Ah Jack et al., No. 3161 [14th Dist. Ct., Nevada Co.]); and an action to foreclose a mechanics lien, also successful, brought in 1873 by a Chinese firm that had supplied laborers to do railroad grading and that had not been paid (Hong Hi v. J. B. Logan and Star Quartz Mining Co., No. 3795 [14th Dist. Ct., Nevada Co.]). It is interesting to note that under the terms of the contract the defendants agreed to pay the Chinese workers $1.75 per day, a high wage for the time, and to supply them with food and lodging as well. The amounts were paid to the Hong Hi firm with the understanding that it was responsible for paying the Chinese workers their wages. We of course do not know how much of a cut the Hong Hi firm took before it paid the laborers. I am grateful to Professor Sucheng Chan for calling my attention to these records.

123. The legislature took for granted that the merchants were the leaders of the community.

124. *Report of the Joint Select Committee Relative to the Chinese Population of the State of California*, Appendix to the Journals, 13th Sess., Cal. Legis. (1862) [hereafter *Joint Select Committee Report*].

125. *Report on the Proposed Legislation* (1853), p. 5.

126. Ibid., p. 3.

127. Ibid., p. 6.

128. Ibid., pp. 4–6, 10. The report contains a fair dose of what can perhaps best be described as Manifest Destiny and white man's burden rhetoric. "To develop [California's] latent resources, and vitalize all her powers, we need sound, liberal, far-seeing Legislators; men who can mould and harness *all* inferior races to work out and realize our grand and glorious destiny," the report declared. Ibid., p. 6 (emphasis in original).

129. Ibid.

130. Ibid., pp. 10–11.

131. Treaty of Tientsin, June 18, 1858, 12 Stat. 1023. Although a generally unremarkable document, the Treaty of Tientsin did make some general declarations of peace and the observance of basic human rights between the United States and China. In Article I, for example, the treaty provides that the two peoples "shall not insult or oppress each other for any trifling cause," Ibid., art. I, 12 Stat. 1023. The Joint Select Committee believed it was this provision, plus a provision in Article XXVIII, that some California statutes violated. *Joint Select Committee Report*, pp. 10–11. Article XXVIII expressly prohibited "extortion of illegal fees." Treaty of Tientsin, art. XXVIII, 12 Stat. 1023, 1029.

132. *Joint Select Committee Report*, p. 4. The committee noted, for example,

that the Chinese companies had furnished it a list of eighty-eight Chinese who had been murdered by whites, including eleven by collectors of the Foreign Miners' License Tax. Only two of the murderers had been brought to justice. The actual numbers were probably much higher in the committee's view. "It is a well known fact," the committee declared, "that there has been a wholesale system of wrong and outrage practiced upon the Chinese population of this State, which would disgrace the most barbarous nation upon earth." Ibid., p. 7.

133. Ibid., p. 4.

134. Ibid., pp. 11–12.

135. In his inaugural address, Stanford had called for the use of all legitimate means to discourage "the settlement among us of [this] inferior race." Elmer Sandmeyer, *The Anti-Chinese Movement in California* (1939; reprint, Urbana: University of Illinois Press, 1973), pp. 43–44.

136. Act of Apr. 26, 1862, ch. 339, 1862 Cal. Stat. 462.

137. The legislature's own committee had expressed the strong opinion that there was "no system of slavery or coolieism amongst the Chinese in this State." *Joint Select Committee Report*, p. 4.

138. Act of Apr. 26, 1862, ch. 339, 1862 Cal. Stat. 462.

139. Lin Sing is so described in the *Daily Alta California*, Sept. 25, 1862, p. 2, col. 1.

140. 20 Cal. 534 (1862).

141. See Petition for Rehearing, p. 3, Lin Sing v. Washburn case file, California State Archives, Sacramento.

142. Counsel for appellant in *Lin Sing* sounded these themes in argument on appeal. See *Lin Sing*, pp. 548–49.

143. *Daily Alta California*, Sept. 25, 1862, p. 2, col. 1.

144. See A. W. Loomis to Walter Lowrie Feb. 28, 1862, (microfilm, San Francisco Theological Seminary Library, San Anselmo, California). Loomis was quite concerned that the actions of the legislature would adversely affect Protestant missionary work among the Chinese. He commented to Lowrie on April 14: "The Chinese know full well that legislators are chosen by the people, and they think that the people should be governed by the principles of their religion, and they suppose that Christianity is the religion of America and this being the case they see no reason for exchanging Confucius for Christ."

145. Sacramento *Record-Union*, June 6, 1862, p. 3, col. 2.

146. Pixley was later to become a leader of the anti-Chinese movement and his utterances on the Chinese question throughout his career were to be distinguished by the basest demagoguery.

147. *Lin Sing*, p. 555.

148. Ibid., p. 554.

149. 25 U.S. (12 Wheat.) 419 (1827).

150. 48 U.S. (7 How.) 282 (1849).

151. *Brown*, p. 436.

152. Ibid., p. 444.

153. *Lin Sing*, pp. 576–77.

154. Ibid., p. 577.

155. Ibid., p. 578.

156. Ibid., pp. 582ff.

157. 1 Cal. 232 (1850).

158. 27 Cal. 638 (1865).

159. Ibid. Four years later Sawyer would be named the Pacific Coast's first federal circuit judge. He would go on to hear many important Chinese civil rights cases over the next few decades.

160. *Awa*, pp. 638–39.

161. See, e.g., *Daily Alta California*, Feb. 2, 1865 (6 Bancroft Scraps 27, Bancroft Library, University of California, Berkeley); *Daily Alta California*, Apr. 10, 1866, p. 2, col. 1. Interestingly, in this editorial the paper expressed the view (a mistaken one) that the 1866 Civil Rights Bill, which had just been passed by the Senate over President Johnson's veto, would if enacted into law give Chinese the right to testify in the state courts regardless of any limitation in state law.

162. Editorial Notes, *Daily Alta California*, Jan. 24, 1868, p. 2, col. 2.

163. The San Francisco *Stars and Stripes* commented that the legislature's failure to pass the bill was a "source of deep regret on the part of all intelligent people." Chinese Testimony, *Stars and Stripes*, Apr. 23, 1868 (6 Bancroft Scraps 67, Bancroft Library, University of California, Berkeley). The renewed Caucasian interest in Chinese grievances might have had some connection with the new importance the Chinese were coming to assume in the state's economy. In early 1865 Charles Crocker and Leland Stanford of the Central Pacific Railway, eager to push ahead with the western arm of the transcontinental railroad and unable to secure an adequate, reliable white labor force, decided to experiment with a small crew of Chinese laborers. The experiment was an enormous success, and within a year several thousand Chinese, many of them ex-miners now looking for more remunerative work in other sectors of the economy, were toiling away in the employ of the railroad on the western slopes of the Sierra Nevada.

164. For general background on Burlingame, see Frederick W. Williams, *Anson Burlingame and the First Chinese Mission to Foreign Powers* (New York: Scribner's, 1912).

165. On the genesis and progress of the Burlingame mission, see Foster Rhea Dulles, *China and America; The Story of Their Relations Since 1784* (Princeton: Princeton University Press, 1946), pp. 63–77.

166. The Burlingame Treaty, July 28, 1868, 16 Stat. 739.

167. Ibid., art. V, 16 Stat. 740.

168. In a letter written some years later, the Chinese minister in Washington described the principle of free emigration as "a doctrine strange to our traditions" and said that this provision had been inserted in the treaty at the suggestion of the United States. See Chinese minister to the U.S. Department of State, Mar. 9, 1880, in *Notes from the Chinese Legation in the United States to the Department of State, 1868–1906*, Record Group 59, microfilm, Reel 1, National Archives. The historian Michael Hunt comments that this was not the first time that the Chinese had accepted in a treaty what her legal codes forbade. Michael Hunt, *The Making of a Special Relationship: The United States and China to 1914* (N.Y.: Columbia University Press, 1983), p. 98.

169. The Burlingame Treaty, art. VI, 16 Stat. 740.

170. On July 27, 1868, Daniel Cleveland, a San Francisco attorney with contacts in the Chinese community, wrote to J. Ross Browne, then in San Francisco en route to China to replace Burlingame as U.S. envoy: "The prospect of receiving

greater protection than they have done from its [the treaty's] provisions, has given our Chinese residents much satisfaction, and greatly excited their hopes." Daniel Cleveland to J. Ross Browne, July 27, 1868, in *Diplomatic Correspondence*, H.R. Exec. Doc., 40th Cong., 3d Sess., 1:535 (1869). Browne, who knew that Cleveland was preparing a work on the Chinese in California, had asked him to share his views with the U.S. State Department. Browne to Cleveland, July 21, 1868, pp. 530–531. Cleveland in his reply, in addition to reporting Chinese interest in the pending treaty, recounted how, in the midst of preparing his letter, he had been invited to a meeting by the heads of the *hui-kuan*. (They apparently had learned that the U.S. government had asked him to submit his views on the Chinese question.) There they conveyed to him their deep sense of the wrongs that were being inflicted upon them and expressed the hope that they might "yet be freed from them and be protected in their lives and property." If protected by just legislation, they assured him, American trade with China would increase and Chinese merchants would be prepared to invest more capital in the state. Browne to Cleveland, p. 543.

171. Chinese foreign office to Anson Burlingame, dated Peking, 1868, 4th Moon, 27th Day (corresponding to either May 19 or June 17 in the western calendar) in *Notes from the Chinese Legation*, Record Group 59, microfilm, Reel 1, National Archives.

172. "Local Intelligence—Equal Protection for All," *Daily Alta California*, July 30, 1868, p. 1., col. 1.

173. Speer, *The Oldest and the Newest Empire*, p. 433.

174. Section 1 of the Fourteenth Amendment reads, in full: "All persons born or naturalized in the United States, and subject to the jurisdiction thereof, are citizens of the United States and of the State wherein they reside. No State shall make or enforce any law which shall abridge the privileges or immunities of citizens of the United States; nor shall any State deprive any person of life, liberty, or property, without due process of law; nor deny to any person within its jurisdiction the equal protection of the laws."

175. The account of Louderback's argument in this case, *People v. Cunningham*, is to be found in the *Daily Alta California*, Dec. 13 and 18, 1868, p. 1, col. 1. The substantive provisions of the Civil Rights Act of 1866, by their terms, of course, applied only to "citizens." And the Chinese victim in this case was certainly not a citizen. Louderback's clever attempt to widen the Act's coverage by invoking the broader terms of Section 2 was not terribly compelling. It is clear that this was for him a subordinate argument. His case hinged really on the Constitutional provision. It is interesting, however, that when the 1866 bill was enacted into law, at least one newspaper read it as having the effect of removing Chinese testimonial disabilities. See *Daily Alta California*, Apr. 10, 1866.

176. *Daily Alta California*, Dec. 13, 1868, p. 1, col. 1. The case in question, *People v. Washington*, raised issues under the Civil Rights Act of 1866 but did not squarely raise the Constitutional question, a fact that Louderback pointed out. See discussion of the California Supreme Court decision below.

177. *Daily Alta California*, Dec. 20, 1868, p. 2, col. 2. Interestingly, the defendant was convicted of the charge, but by what means, one cannot say.

178. 36 Cal. 658 (1869).

179. Civil Rights Act of 1866, ch. 31, § 1, 14 Stat. 27 (1865–67).

180. *Washington*, pp. 666–67.

181. Cal. Const., art. I, § 11 (1849) provided: "All laws of a general nature shall have a uniform operation."

182. *Washington*, pp. 671–72. There was some question as to whether the equal protection issue was properly before the court. As Louderback had noted in his argument before Judge Provines, the case had arisen before the amendment was ratified.

183. *Daily Alta California*, June 24, 1869, p. 2, col. 1.

184. *Daily Alta California*, Oct. 7, 1869. The decision occasioned a great deal of comment, generally favorable, in the local press (see, e.g., the San Francisco *Times*, Oct. 8, 1869, p. 2, col. 2) and elsewhere. The travel writer and social commentator, W. F. Rae, who was visiting San Francisco when the decision was rendered, greeted it with approval. See W. F. Rae, *Westward by Rail: A Journey to San Francisco and Back and a Visit to the Mormons* (London: Longmans, Green, 1871), p. 305.

185. It will be recalled that attorney Murphy had assisted Louderback in his June effort before Judge Provines.

186. *Daily Alta California*, Nov. 26, 1869, p. 1, col. 1. Conness's remarks can be found in the *Congressional Globe*, 39th Cong., 1st Sess. (1865–66), p. 2892. They are accurately quoted in the newspaper report of Murphy's argument but are not as unequivocally supportive of Murphy's point as he suggested. Conness's remarks are somewhat ambiguous. The specific question in the debate was whether language should be added to Section 1 of the Fourteenth Amendment declaring persons born in this country to be citizens of the United States. Conness thought it should be. He, interestingly, also thought that under the new language, children of Chinese born in this country would be considered U.S. citizens, and he thought this was entirely right and proper. Other parts of Conness's speech, however, suggest that he thought the concept of equal protection applied only to citizens, including those persons the new language was now declaring to be citizens. See *Congressional Globe*, pp. 2890–92.

187. Ibid. Murphy's partner, Darwin, also took part in oral argument in the case.

188. *Daily Alta California*, Dec. 8, 1869, p. 2, col. 4.

189. Ibid.

190. Recall the statute applied to "Indians and Mongolians."

191. *Daily Alta California*, Dec. 8, 1869, p. 2, col. 4.

192. See Argument of respondent, People v. Brady, 40 Cal. 198, 199–207 (1871).

193. Ibid., p. 208.

194. Ibid.

195. Ibid., p. 213.

196. Ibid., p. 209.

197. Ibid., pp. 214ff.

198. *Chronicle*, Jan. 7, 1871, p. 2, col. 1.

199. *Daily Alta California*, Jan. 7, 1871, p. 2, col. 1.

200. Ibid., Feb. 6, 1871, p. 1, col. 8.

201. It is interesting to note that Wade had evidenced sympathy for the Chinese while in the Senate. He had, for example, spoken out against that provision in Oregon's proposed constitution which excluded them from the state. See H. L.

Trefousse, *Benjamin Franklin Wade, Radical Republican from Ohio* (New York: Twayne Publishers, 1963), p. 119.

202. To this end, Fung advocated doubling the subsidy to the United States-China steamship lines.

203. See *Daily Alta California*, June 26, 1869, p. 1, col. 1. San Francisco *Times*, June 26, 1869, p. 1, col. 1; Interestingly, an account of the meeting appeared the next day on the front page of the *New York Times*, June 27, 1869, p. 1, col. 2.

204. See "Ben Wade Interviewed: His Ideas on the Chinese Problem," *Cincinnati Commercial*, July 12, 1870 (6 Bancroft Scraps 253, Bancroft Library, University of California, Berkeley).

205. *Congressional Globe*, 41st Cong., 2d Sess. (1869), p. 3.

206. Ibid., p. 301.

207. S. 365, 41st Cong., 2d Sess., *Congressional Globe* (1869–70), p. 323.

208. Ibid., p. 1536.

209. S. 810, 41st Cong., 2d Sess., *Congressional Globe* (1869), p. 3658.

210. Ibid., p. 3807. These and other relevant passages from the congressional debates are quoted in Justice Byron White's dissenting opinion in Runyon v. McCrary, 427 U.S. 160, 195–201 (1976).

211. In his autobiography, published when he was a very old man, Stewart complained about the unfairness of the Foreign Miners' License Tax and the rough way in which it was collected from the Chinese. Stewart, *Reminiscences*, p. 78.

212. Russell R. Elliott, *Servant of Power: A Political Biography of Senator William M. Stewart*, (Reno: University of Nevada Press, 1983), pp. 64–65.

213. Elliott, *Servant of Power*, passim.

214. Civil Rights Act of 1870, ch. 114, § 16, 16 Stat. 140, 144 (1869–71). The reference to Indians was excised. "Emigrating" was changed to "immigrating."

215. *Examiner*, July 1, 1870, p. 2, col. 2–3. For additional press reaction to the Stewart bill, see The Very Latest—Washington, *Daily Alta California*, May 24, 1870, p. 1, col. 6; and The Very Latest—Congressional, *Daily Alta California*, May 25, 1870, p. 1, col. 6.

216. United States v. Jackson (C.C.D. Cal. 1871), Files 572, 583, National Archives, San Francisco branch.

217. See United States v. Thomas W. Breeze (C.C.D. Cal. 1871), File 709, National Archives, San Francisco branch. See also *Evening Bulletin*, May 12, 1871, p. 3, col. 5.

218. *Evening Bulletin*, May 6, 1871, p. 3, col. 4. Section 17 of the Civil Rights Act of 1870 made it a misdemeanor for anyone acting under color of law to subject any inhabitant of the United States to a deprivation of rights guaranteed under Section 16. Act of May 31, 1870, ch. 94, § 16, 16 Stat. 140, 144. Section 1 of the Civil Rights Act of 1871, the so-called Ku Klux Klan Act, gave a civil action for damages to anyone deprived under color of law of constitutional rights. Act of Apr. 20, 1871, ch. 22, 17 Stat. 13.

219. *Evening Bulletin*, May 10, 1871, p. 3, col. 6.

220. *Evening Bulletin*, May 26, 1871, p. 3, col. 3.

221. Ibid.

222. See *Evening Bulletin*, Mar. 11, 1872, p. 2, col. 1; *Chronicle*, Mar. 13, 1872, p. 3, col. 2.

223. *Evening Bulletin*, Mar. 12, 1872, p. 3, col. 4.

224. Sections 1879 and 1880 of the Civil Code and Section 1321 of the Penal Code are the relevant sections.

225. After the legislature passed its revisions but before the new codes went into effect an interesting case came before the state supreme court. People v. McGuire, 45 Cal. 56 (1872), was an appeal of a conviction for assault with intent to commit murder. The conviction had been based principally on the testimony of the appellant's Chinese victim. The high court reversed the conviction. The trial court, it said, had acted improperly in disregarding *Brady* and admitting Chinese testimony. "*Nisi prius* [trial] courts are not at liberty to set aside or disregard the decisions of this court because it may seem to them that the decisions are unsound. Until reversed or modified by this court its decisions must be accepted by all inferior tribunals," it declared. The court declined to reconsider or review the *Brady* holding, as counsel for the state urged it to, but did note that that holding would shortly be moot in light of what the legislature had done. *McGuire*, pp. 57–58.

CHAPTER TWO

1. The statistics are taken from Sucheng Chan, *This Bittersweet Soil: The Chinese in California Agriculture, 1860–1910* (Berkeley: University of California Press, 1986), p. 43.

2. Remarkably, however, Chinese persisted in placer mining in relatively large numbers well into the 1890s. In 1870 some 45 percent of the Chinese population of the state was still located in the mining regions, but this was down from 84 percent in 1860. See Chan, *This Bittersweet Soil*, tables 1 and 2, pp. 43, 48–49.

3. On the occupational distribution of the Chinese in San Francisco at this time and generally in the second half of the nineteenth century see Ping Chiu, *Chinese Labor in California, 1850–1880: An Economic Study* (Madison, Wis.: State Historical Society of Wisconsin, 1967). See also Chan, *This Bittersweet Soil*, pp. 62–63. *The Pacific Coast Business Directory for 1871–73* (San Francisco: H. G. Langley, 1871) lists six Chinese firms in the boot and shoe manufacturing business out of a total of twenty-one in the city (p. 453) and forty-nine Chinese cigar makers out of a total of one hundred (p. 465). Interestingly a few of the cigar-making firms owned by the Chinese bear Hispanic names, e.g., Alvarez & Co., Mendez & Co.

4. See, e.g., *Evening Bulletin*, June 15, 1870, p. 2, col. 2.

5. *Evening Bulletin*, June 14, 1870, p. 1, col. 3. The alleged overcrowdedness and unsanitary condition of the Chinese district of San Francisco was a subject constantly agitated by leaders of the anti-Chinese movement throughout the period of the immigration and was often the justification put forward for legislation aimed at the Chinese. It cannot be doubted that living conditions in the Chinese quarter of San Francisco in 1870 and throughout the nineteenth century were extremely crowded. Just how crowded, both in absolute terms and in relation to other immigrant districts, is difficult to say. The health authorities of the day, on whom one must rely for information but who were among the most Sinophobic of Caucasians, kept living conditions in Chinatown under a kind of constant scrutiny and, conversely, paid comparatively little attention to living conditions elsewhere in the city. Their reports are characterized by such sensational rhetoric, racial bias, and obvious exaggeration that one simply cannot know how much

credence to put in the findings that they purport to contain. Facts and figures provided are themselves often conflicting. The health officer's report for the fiscal year ending June 30, 1870, for example, began by describing the Chinese as "a moral leper in our community," and the life of the typical inhabitant of Chinatown was described as "little better than the brute creation." In passing through the Chinese quarter, the report went on, "the most absolute squalidness and misery meets one at every turn. Vice in all its hideousness is on every hand." Board of Supervisors, *San Francisco Municipal Reports for the Fiscal Year, 1869–70*, p. 233. In the same report the health officer stated that as many as six to ten men were occupying rooms in Chinatown intended for a single occupant. A month earlier the health authorities had advised the local press that as many as *forty* Chinese were living in a single room in the district. See *Daily Alta California*, May 16, 1870, p. 1, col. 1.

It is interesting that in Jacob Riis's classic 1890 study of the New York tenements, *How the Other Half Lives* (New York: Hill & Wang, 1957), the Chinese district of the city comes off quite favorably in terms of livability and cleanliness compared to other ethnic districts. Of course this was a city on another coast with a much smaller Chinese population.

6. *Chronicle*, July 8, 1870, p. 2, col. 3.

7. In a letter to the editor of the *Chronicle*, July 13, 1870, Mooney stated that, if requested, he would resign his bank presidency and offer himself to the people of the state as their governor and protector against "Chinese barbarians." If elected, he promised to rid the state of the Chinese within three months.

8. Account of the meeting taken from *Chronicle*, July 9, 1870, p. 3, col. 3.

9. *Chronicle*, June 16, 1870, p. 3, col. 2–3.

10. *Evening Bulletin*, July 19, 1870, p. 1, col. 2.

11. *Chronicle*, July 18, 1870, p. 3, col. 3.

12. *Daily Alta California*, July 26, 1870, p. 1, col. 1.

13. Ibid.

14. *Evening Bulletin*, Dec. 13, 1870, p. 3, col. 3. The *Chronicle* reported the introduction of the ordinance under the heading, "Against Chinese Scavengers." *Chronicle*, Nov. 29, 1870, p. 3, col. 4.

15. *Chronicle*, Jan. 14, 1871, p. 3, col. 3 and Jan. 19, 1871, p. 3, col. 5. For evidence suggesting that this might have been a test case on behalf of Chinese street peddlers in general see the article in the *Daily Alta California*, Feb. 5, 1871, p. 1, col. 2.

16. *Evening Bulletin*, Jan. 31, 1871, p. 3, col. 3. *Daily Alta California*, Feb. 1, 1871, p. 1, col. 1.

17. *Daily Alta California*, Feb. 4, 1871, p. 1, col. 1.

18. *Daily Alta California*, Feb. 5, 1871, p. 1, col. 2.

19. *Daily Alta California*, Feb. 4, 1871, p. 1, col. 1.

20. *Evening Bulletin*, Feb. 4, 1871, p. 3, col. 3.

21. *Daily Alta California*, May 27, 1873, p. 1, col. 1.

22. *Herald*, Apr. 12, 1852, p. 2, col. 3.

23. For interesting speculation on what induced Chinese to enter the laundry trade in such large numbers during the nineteenth century, both as shopowners and laborers, see Paul Man Ong, "The Chinese and the Laundry Laws: The Use and Control of Urban Space," Master's thesis, University of Washington, 1975.

24. Chan, *This Bittersweet Soil*, pp. 62–63.

25. Ong, "The Chinese and the Laundry Laws," pp. 57ff. See also *Daily Alta California*, May 23, 1870, p. 1, col. 1, for report of a riot in Chinatown occasioned by a violation of the Laundrymen's Association's rules concerning the location of washhouses. The article provides considerable information as well on the functions the organization performed.

26. On the craft guilds in China see H. B. Morse, *The Gilds of China* (London, New York: Longmans, Green, 1909), pp. 9ff. Besides the laundrymen, the cigar makers, restaurateurs, clothing manufacturers, commercial fishermen, and domestic servants also had their own guilds.

27. The original laundry-licensing scheme imposed a fee of $2 per quarter for laundries using one horse-drawn vehicle, $4 per quarter for those using two, and $15 per quarter for those using more than two. See *Evening Bulletin*, July 9, 1874, p. 3, col. 6.

28. Ibid. Content of the ordinances taken from the *Evening Bulletin* article. At the same meeting when these ordinances were first discussed the supervisors passed a resolution under which they pledged neither to employ Chinese nor to purchase Chinese-made goods.

29. *Evening Bulletin*, May 27, 1873, p. 3, col. 6. The *Evening Bulletin* had this comment on the hair-cutting ordinance: "The Board of Supervisors have passed to print an ordinance requiring the cropping of the hair of every person who is serving a term in the jail under a criminal conviction. The ordinance, while it nominally makes no discrimination as to race or condition, is aimed specially at the Chinese. . . . The Chinese who offend against the [lodging house] ordinance refuse to pay the fine, but go to jail and board it out. The Supervisors, casting about for some means of relief, have hit upon the plan of cropping the hair. White criminals would care nothing about this, and the ordinance would probably never be enforced against them. The loss of a pigtail is a great calamity to the Chinese. It is his national badge of honor. If it is cut off he is maimed." *Evening Bulletin*, June 2, 1873, p. 2, col. 2.

30. Lai Yong et al., *The Chinese Question from a Chinese Standpoint*, trans. Otis Gibson, San Francisco, 1874. A copy of the statement is to be found in the California State Library, Sacramento, California. The statement was issued under the names Lai Yong, Yang Kay, A Yup, Lai Foon, Chung Leong. See also *Daily Alta California*, June 3, 1873, p. 1, col. 4.

31. *Daily Alta California*, June 7, 1873, p. 1, col. 5. The Reverend A. L. Stowe of the First Congregational Church said the laws were "of the nature of a discriminating persecution, a violation of the acts of the supreme government of the land, an outrage upon common humanity and decency." *Daily Alta California*, June 16, 1873, p. 1, col. 5.

32. The grounds advanced by Mayor Alvord for vetoing the law were almost precisely those offered by Justice Stephen Field a few years later when he struck down exactly the same sort of measure in the case of *Ho Ah Kow v. Nunan*. See p. 74, below.

33. *Daily Alta California*, June 24, 1873, p. 1, col. 5. In its story reporting the debate on the laundry license and queue ordinances, the *Evening Bulletin* referred to the measures as "the anti-Chinese ordinances" and "the ordinances discriminating against the Chinese." June 24, 1873, pp. 1, 3.

34. Otis Gibson, *The Chinese in America* (Cincinnati: Hitchcock & Walden, 1877), pp. 283–84.

35. *Daily Alta California*, Feb. 7, 1874, p. 1, col. 1.

36. See testimony of Henry Haight, *Report of the Joint Special Committee to Investigate Chinese Immigration*, Report No. 689, 44th Cong., 2d Sess., Washington, D.C.: Government Printing Office, 1877; reprint, Arno Press, 1978) [hereafter *Joint Special Committee Report*], p. 295. "The Chinese laundrymen employed me here against the laundry ordinance, which was a very disgraceful piece of legislation, in my judgment, and they were in my office somewhat in that business." Notwithstanding this connection, Haight was notably disparaging of the Chinese in his remarks before the visiting federal legislators, arguing among other things that by temperament and culture they were completely unfitted to be granted the franchise. *Joint Special Committee Report*, pp. 290ff. Haight had argued vehemently against Chinese naturalization while governor but at the same time had urged the legislature to remove the ban on Chinese testimony. H. Brett Melendy and Benjamin F. Gilbert, *The Governors of California from Peter H. Burnett to Edmund G. Brown* (Georgetown, Cal.: The Talisman Press, 1965), pp. 143–55.

37. Gibson, *The Chinese in America*, pp. 283–84. I have been unable to find any independent verification of the assertion concerning the white laundrywomen.

38. Thomas Cooley, *A Treatise on the Constitutional Limitations Which Rest upon the Legislative Power of the States of the American Union* (Boston: Little, Brown & Co., 1868) Special Legal Classics Reprint, Birmingham, Ala., The Legal Classics Library, 1987, pp. 72–84; John F. Dillon, *The Law of Municipal Corporations*, 2d ed., (New York: J. Cockroft & Co., 1873), §§ 253–63; See ch. 8, *passim*. The Massachusetts cases are: Austin v. Murray, 33 Mass. (16 Pick.) 125 (1834) (holding as unreasonable and without public health justification a law that had the effect of making it impossible for the Bishop of Boston to bury the dead in a Catholic burial ground in Charlestown); City of Boston v. Shaw, 42 Mass. (1 Met.) 130 (1840) (nullifying as unequal and unreasonable a sewer assessment scheme); and Drury v. Vannevar, 59 Mass. (5 Cush.) 442, (1850) (a case involving a promissory note, the relevance of which is unclear).

39. *Evening Bulletin*, July 9, 1874, p. 3, col. 6.

40. Ibid.

41. Order 697, ch. 8, § 9, subdiv. 19. Board of Supervisors, *San Francisco Municipal Reports for the Fiscal Year 1874–75*, p. 856.

42. The *Daily Alta* called the law "[a]n ordinance, drawn for the purpose of extracting $15 per quarter as license from Chinese laundrymen." Mar. 7, 1876, p. 1, col. 3. And, when the ordinance was passed, the *Evening Bulletin* commented, "The ordinance charging a license of $15 per quarter on laundries having no horse and wagon, and referring particularly to Chinese laundries, was finally passed." *Evening Bulletin*, Mar. 14, 1876, p. 1, col. 1.

43. The newspapers of March and April are filled with reports of anti-Chinese rallies in San Francisco and other California cities. On March 27, as a newspaper report put it, "in furtherance of the present anti-Chinese movement," the board adopted a resolution to the effect that no member of the board or public official should employ any Chinese in any capacity or knowingly use any article of Chinese manufacture. Sacramento *Record-Union*, Mar. 28, 1876, p. 2, col. 4.

44. A different newspaper from the one published in the 1850s by the Reverend Speer and called the *Oriental* (*Tung ngai san luk*).

45. *Oriental,* Mar. 18, 1876. The Chinese title of this newspaper, which published in San Francisco between 1875 and 1909, varied, but it always bore the English title "The Oriental" on its masthead. More issues of this newspaper than of any other nineteenth-century Chinese periodical survive, but even then we are talking about only a handful of numbers.

46. Sacramento *Record-Union,* Apr. 3, 1876, p. 2, col. 3. The letter was sent to the Tung Wah Hospital in Hong Kong. The *hui-kuan* leaders asked that it be posted "in all conspicuous places in Hong Kong." On or about the same date the leaders delivered a communication to the board of supervisors suggesting that the board by its resolutions was helping to stir up anti-Chinese feelings and that it accordingly would bear responsibility if those feelings issued in harm or damage to the Chinese. It suggested that the board ought to take precautions to protect the Chinese. Sacramento *Record-Union,* April 4, 1876, p. 3, col. 5.

47. *Daily Alta California,* May 3, 1876, p. 1, col. 1.

48. Ibid., citing State ex rel. v. Cin. Gas-Light and Coke Co., 18 Ohio St. 262 (1868). Judge McKee may have been reading too much into this opinion. This was a complicated case involving the regulation of a gas company by a municipality. One issue was whether the city had abused its power to regulate by deliberately setting the price of gas so low that the company would be forced to go out of business. On this issue the court, more by way of dictum than holding, said that the judiciary, while it could not inquire into the motives of the state legislature, a coordinate branch, or even of a city council if it were simply exercising normal police powers, could in other instances inquire into the motivations of local legislative bodies. *Cin. Gas-Light and Coke,* p. 302.

49. B. E. Lloyd, *Lights and Shades in San Francisco* (San Francisco: A. L. Bancroft, 1876), p. 253.

50. They did not prevent other cities, however, from embarking on the same strategy. Santa Clara, approximately a year after the *Hung Hai* decision and during a period of intense anti-Chinese agitation, enacted into law a laundry taxation scheme similar to that of San Francisco. It raised the tax on laundries in the city, all of which happened to be owned by Chinese, from $1 to $20 per quarter. The Chinese laundrymen, however, refused to submit and appealed to the courts where they obtained redress. In July 1878, in *Town of Santa Clara v. Sang Kee* a local court struck the measure down. San Jose *Herald,* July 17, 1878, p. 3, col. 2.

51. This was also the first case involving Chinese litigants to be decided by the United States Supreme Court. For that reason alone it would deserve mention in any narrative of the Chinese and the courts in the nineteenth century.

52. On Chinese prostitution see Chan, *This Bittersweet Soil,* pp. 387–91 and passim; Professor Chan estimates that there were some one thousand Chinese prostitutes in San Francisco in 1874, 8 percent of the city's total Chinese population; Chan, *This Bittersweet Soil,* pp. 62–63. See also Lucie Cheng Hirata, "Free, Indentured, Enslaved: Chinese Prostitutes in Nineteenth-Century America," in *Signs: Journal of Women in Culture and Society* 5 (1979): 3–29.

53. On the history of prostitution in San Francisco in the nineteenth century see Jacqueline Baker Barnhart, *The Fair but Frail: Prostitution in San Francisco, 1849–1900* (Reno, Nev.: University Press of Nevada, 1986). The study makes clear how thoroughly cosmopolitan the traffic was. See also the *Daily Alta California,* July 27, 1870, p. 2, col. 1–2 for an editorial complaining about the spread

of prostitution throughout San Francisco and about the failure of the authorities to do anything about it. It noted that a Chinese house of prostitution had been shut down recently because of loud public clamor but that nothing was being done about white-operated houses, which were flourishing.

54. Act of Mar. 31, 1866, ch. 505, 1866 Cal. Stat. 641–42. Section 1 of the act provided that "common repute" should serve as competent evidence of the character of the house. In 1874 the word "Chinese" was stricken from the law so that all houses of prostitution were now declared to be public nuisances. Act of Feb. 7, 1874, ch. 76, 1874 Cal. Stat. 84.

55. See A. W. Loomis, "Chinese Women in California," *Overland Monthly* 2 (April 1869): 345. Loomis is the Presbyterian minister mentioned in chapter 1. See also Gibson, *The Chinese in America*, pp. 140ff. noting that in the summer of 1873 he, along with several Chinese merchants, succeeded in having members of the Hip Yee Tong, a criminal enterprise active in prostitution, arrested and prosecuted. According to Gibson the Chinese merchants of their own accord hired the noted San Francisco trial lawyer Hall McAllister to assist in the prosecution.

56. *Memorial of the Trustees of the Chinese Six Companies to the Governor* (1868), California State Archives, Sacramento.

57. Act of Mar. 18, 1870, ch. 230, 1869–70 Cal. Stat. 330. On the same date that it enacted this statute, the California legislature passed another law making it a criminal offense to bring *any* Chinese *or* Japanese, male or female, into the state without presenting evidence that he or she was a voluntary immigrant and was of "correct habits and good character." Act of Mar. 18, 1870, ch. 231, 1869–70 Cal. Stat. 332.

58. Cal. Pol. Code § 2952, as amended.

59. According to the *Examiner* two Chinese named Ah You and Tom Poy made the application. Aug. 25, 1874, p. 3, col. 4. The *Daily Alta* described the applicant as a man named Ah Lung, who, according to the paper, trafficked in this kind of business. Aug. 26, 1874, p. 1, col. 3. In the trial transcript from the Fourth District Court (in Ex parte Ah Fook case file, No. 10114, California Supreme Court, California State Archives, Sacramento) the man's name is listed as Chy Lung. There was a prominent Chinese mercantile firm in San Francisco by the name of Chy Lung & Co., but it is unclear whether this firm was involved in the litigation.

60. Account of the hearing based upon articles in the *Examiner*, Aug. 26, 1874, p. 3, col. 5 and Aug. 29, 1874, p. 3, col. 3; the *Daily Alta California*, Aug. 27, 1874, p. 1, col. 1; Sacramento *Record-Union*, Aug. 27, 1874, p. 3, col. 5; and the Transcript of Hearing, Ex parte Ah Fook case file.

61. Under an Act of Congress passed February 19, 1862, entitled "An Act to prohibit the Coolie Trade by American Citizens in American Vessels," the Hong Kong consul was required to satisfy himself that all Chinese bound for the United States were voluntary immigrants. The act made it a criminal offense for any U.S. citizen or foreigner coming into the United States to have anything to do with any vessel transporting Chinese to any country there "to be disposed of, or sold, or transferred for any term of years or for any time whatever, as servants or apprentices, or to be held to service or labor." Act of Feb. 19, 1862, ch. 27, 12 Stat. 340.

62. Transcript of Fourth District Court Hearing, pp. 21–22 (Ah Fook case file, California State Archives, Sacramento).

63. An editorial in the *Chronicle* congratulated the Pacific Mail Steamship Company on the recent growth of its trade with China, noting that a year ago the company had been almost insolvent. *Chronicle*, Sept. 16, 1874, p. 2, col. 2.

64. *Chronicle*, Aug. 29, 1874, p. 1, col. 1.

65. Ex parte Ah Fook, 49 Cal. 402 (1874).

66. In 1867 federal courts were for the first time given authority to grant writs of habeas corpus to persons in state custody, whether before or after trial, when the persons alleged they were restrained of their liberty in violation of the Constitution or any treaty or law of the United States. Act of Feb. 5, 1867, ch. 27, 14 Stat. 385, § 1. Previously they had had no such authority. This represented of course an enormous expansion of federal judicial power vis-a-vis the states. On the significance of the 1867 act see W. Wiecek, "The Reconstruction of Federal Judicial Power," 13 American Journal of Legal History 333 (1969).

67. Account of oral argument based on articles in *Morning Call*, Sept. 18, 1874, p. 1, col. 7 and *Chronicle*, Sept. 19, 1874, p. 3, col. 4.

68. 83 U.S. (16 Wall.) 36 (1873).

69. In charging the federal grand jury in San Francisco in 1873, Field had said concerning the Chinese question: "If public policy requires that the Chinese should be excluded from our shores, let the General Government so provide . . . but until it does so . . . they have a perfect right to immigrate to this country, and whilst here, they are entitled, equally with all others, to the full protection of our laws." Quoted in *Daily Alta California*, June 10, 1873, p. 1, col. 4.

70. *Slaughter-House Cases*, pp. 109–10.

71. *Morning Call*, Sept. 18, 1874, p. 1, col. 7. This and the other newspaper accounts have Field making remarks that indicate a belief that the Fourteenth Amendment had nationalized the Bill of Rights. Thus he said that before the passage of that amendment a state could have established Islam as a state religion or abolished freedom of the press whereas such actions were now prohibited by the amendment which placed all the great rights of the citizen under the protection of the national government.

72. In re Ah Fong, 1 F. Cas. 213, 216–17 (1874).

73. Ibid., p. 217.

74. Ibid.

75. Ibid.

76. Ibid., p. 218.

77. Ibid.

78. Ibid.

79. Justice Swayne, who like Field, had supported the butchers' claims in the *Slaughter-House Cases* had said almost as much in his own dissent in that case. Swayne was the first justice to call attention to the fact that the framers of the Fourteenth Amendment had dropped the term "citizen" and substituted "person" in Section 1's due process and equal protection clauses. He thought the butchers' claims as valid under the latter two clauses as it was under the privileges and immunities clause. Indeed he seemed to conflate the three provisions, seeing all as designed to do the same thing, that is throw national protection against state interference around the civil rights of all. "The equal protection of the laws," he wrote, "places all upon a footing of legal equality and gives the same protection to all for the preservation of life, liberty, and property, and the pursuit of happi-

ness." *Slaughter-House Cases*, 83 U.S. (16 Wall.) 36, 127 (1873), citing, among other cases, *Corfield v. Coryell*. Field's dissent in the cases rested entirely on his interpretation of the amendment's privileges and immunities clause.

80. *Ah Fong*, p. 218.

81. *Chronicle*, Sept. 22, 1874, p. 1, col. 2. See also *Morning Call*, Sept. 22, 1874, p. 1, col. 8.

82. *Morning Call*, Sept. 22, 1874, p. 1, col. 8.

83. This is the so-called Page Act, ch. 141, 18 Stat. pt. 3, 477–478. The law, quite long and complex, covered other matters besides prostitution. It seems quite clearly to have been drafted with Field's circuit court opinion in mind.

84. 92 U.S. 259 (1875).

85. Chy Lung v. Freeman, 92 U.S. 275, 279–80 (1875).

86. See *Ah Fong*, p. 216; *Chy Lung*, p. 280.

87. *Chy Lung*, p. 280.

88. The transcript of testimony as well as the committee's findings of fact and recommendations are to be found in Special Committee on Chinese Immigration, *Chinese Immigration; Its Social, Moral, and Political Effect, Report to the California State Senate*, Appendix to the Journals, Cal. Legis., 22d Sess., vol. 3, Sacramento, 1878 [hereafter *California State Senate Committee Report*].

89. The year 1876 saw the introduction in Congress by western legislators of several bills aimed at stopping or reducing Chinese immigration. A joint resolution was introduced in the House for example (H.R. 29) urging that existing treaties with China be modified so as to prevent any further Chinese immigration. Senator Aaron Sargent of California introduced several measures, among them a resolution (S. 829) that would have limited the number of Chinese passengers on any one ship traveling to the United States to ten. None of these severe measures were passed, and the creation of the joint committee may have been seen as a sop to western representatives.

90. As noted in chapter 1, many motives, including genuine humanitarianism and aversion toward racial discrimination, appear to have been at work in the support that some members of the Protestant clergy gave the Chinese. There may also have been something of a religious animus to the support as well. Many of the leaders of the anti-Chinese movement were Irish-Catholic. The mainstream American Protestant churches were fiercely anti-Catholic through most of the nineteenth century. On alliances forged by white Protestants with people of color against the urban, Catholic working class during the pre-Civil War period see the examples discussed in Robert J. Cottroll, "Law, Politics and Race in Urban America: Towards a New Synthesis," *Rutgers Law Journal* 17 (1986): 483, 505ff. The fiercely anti-Catholic Know-Nothing party in Massachusetts, for example, supported school integration.

91. *Joint Special Committee Report*, p. vi.

92. Ibid., p. viii.

93. See testimony of Frederick A. Bee before Joint Congressional Committee to Report on Chinese Immigration, H.R. Rep. No. 4048, 51st Cong., 2d Sess., p. 374 (1891). (This second congressional investigation of Chinese immigration, conducted on the Pacific Coast in 1890, is not to be confused with the one now under discussion.) See also unpublished biographical sketch of Frederick Bee prepared by the historian H. H. Bancroft, Bancroft Library, University of California,

Berkeley (hereafter *Bancroft Sketch*), and a biographical profile that appeared in *The Bay of San Francisco, The Metropolis of the Pacific Coast and Its Suburban Cities* (Chicago: Lewis Publishing Company, 1892), 2:491–93.

94. *Joint Special Committee Report*, p. 901. It is regrettable that the only information available on these two men is what can be culled from scattered, short press notices, from biographical sketches in popular compilations, and, in Bee's case, from a brief unpublished biographical profile prepared by the historian H. H. Bancroft.

95. *Sketches of Leading and Representative Men of San Francisco*, 1875, p. 1003. Obituary, *Morning Call*, May 1, 1884, supp. p. 1, col. 4.

96. *Morning Call*, May 27, 1892, p. 8, col. 3. See also *The Bay of San Francisco*, pp. 491–93; *Bancroft Sketch*.

97. *Joint Special Committee Report*, pp. 50, 902.

98. These sentiments are apparent in the following excerpt from a pamphlet on the Chinese that Brooks published the year following the committee deliberations:

> The charges against this people which are supported by evidence would in other lands be esteemed virtues; their undying love for native land, their devotion to their religious faith, their veneration for their parents and ancestors, their love and affection for their families, their generous contribution to their support and happiness, their untiring industry, their uncomplaining patience, their courageous venturing to the most distant lands where honest wages may be earned, their frugality, proud independence, resistance to oppression and partial laws, these are the charges proved against them. If they cannot assimilate with us, can it be because these qualities are foreign to *our* nature?
>
> Benjamin Brooks, *The Chinese in California*, 1877, pp. 21–22.

99. Statute of Apr. 3, 1876, Cal. Legis., 21st Sess., ch. 496, p. 759. The *Daily Alta California* reported passage of the bill in the State Assembly under the headline "After the Chinese." *Daily Alta*, Mar. 12, 1876, p. 1, col. 5. The *Chronicle* pointed to the bill, as well as a state exhumation law then under consideration, as an example of the kind of laws the state could use, failing federal help, to ward off Chinese immigration. Eastern newspapers, it commented, would not understand how such measures would discourage immigration, but all Californians understood it perfectly well. *Chronicle*, Mar. 19, 1876, p. 4, col. 3.

100. *Evening Bulletin*, Apr. 18, 1876, p. 1, col. 1.

101. Sacramento *Record-Union*, Apr. 4, 1876, p. 3, col. 5. The *Evening Bulletin* later in the month described the measure as "Mr. Gibbs' resolution providing for the cutting of Chinamen's hair." Apr. 18, 1876, p. 1, col. 1.

102. The law read, in relevant part: "Each and every male prisoner incarcerated or imprisoned in the county jail of this city and county, under and pursuant to a judgment or conviction had by any court having jurisdiction of criminal cases in this city and county, shall, immediately upon their arrival at said county jail, under and pursuant to a judgment or sentence as aforesaid, have the hair of their head cut or clipped to a uniform length of one inch from the scalp thereof." *Joint Special Committee Report*, app. D, p. 1166.

103. There were 213 arrests made in May and 219 in June of 1873. Board of Supervisors, *San Francisco Municipal Reports for the Fiscal Year 1872–73*, p. 154.

104. The San Francisco police made 92 arrests in April 1876 for violation of the lodging house law. Board of Supervisors, *San Francisco Municipal Reports for the Fiscal Year 1875–76*, p. 232.

105. See report of successful appeal by the owner of the Globe Hotel, a Chinatown residential hotel, of a conviction under the ordinance. The exact grounds of the court decision are unclear from the report. *Evening Bulletin*, Sept. 9, 1873, p. 3, col. 3.

106. A San Francisco police officer who had been involved in making some 1,100 arrests under the cubic air ordinance told the Joint Special Committee in October that he knew of no instance of whites being arrested under the ordinance. See statement of Officer James Rogers, *Joint Special Committee Report*, pp. 234–35.

107. *Evening Bulletin*, June 22, 1876, p. 3, col. 3. As will be noticed, there is a discrepancy in the newspaper's account. If one adds up the tenants of the individual rooms, one reaches a total of 59 rather than 56. There is also an account of the raid in the bilingual newspaper, the *Chinese Record*, Sept. 27, 1878, p. 1, col. 1.

108. *Evening Bulletin*, June 22, 1876, p. 3, col. 3.

109. See letter of April 5, 1875, to the mayor of San Francisco and letter of April 1, 1876, to the San Francisco chief of police, reproduced in *Joint Special Committee Report*, pp. 46–47.

110. Reproduced in *Joint Special Committee Report*, p. 39.

111. *Oriental*, Apr. 29, 1876. Interestingly, the previous week's issue of the paper, April 22, 1876, contains a letter to the paper urging it to persuade the Chinese Six Companies to hire lawyers to combat discriminatory rules. It is not clear whether the writer had particularly in mind the cubic air law or the city's queue law then under consideration.

112. *Oriental*, May 13, 1876.

113. Statistics on arrests are to be found in the chief of police's annual report to the Board of Supervisors, *San Francisco Municipal Reports for Fiscal Years, 1875–76 and 1876–77*, at, respectively, pp. 237 and 358.

114. Sacramento *Bee*, June 22, 1876, p. 2, col. 2.

115. *Chronicle*, Aug. 25, 1876, p. 3, col. 8.

116. Ibid., Sept. 16, 1876, p. 3, col. 6.

117. *Joint Special Committee Report*, pp. 47, 62.

118. Benjamin Brooks, *Brief of the Legislation and Adjudication Touching the Chinese Question, Referred to the Joint Committee of Both Houses of Congress* (San Francisco: Women's Cooperative Printing Union, 1877), p. 77.

119. The *Chinese Record* did print an interesting piece on April 16, suggesting that the federal courts should be looked to as the main means of protecting the Chinese against unjust and unequal enactments such as the queue-cutting and lodging house laws. *Chinese Record*, April 16, 1877.

120. The *Chronicle* reported that the Six Companies had raised $5,000 to mount this court challenge. The petitioner is referred to by both names—Ah Wing and Chin Ah Win—in the court documents. *Chronicle*, Feb. 28, 1878, p. 2, col. 4.

121. The complaint is to be found in No. 1880, Record Group 21, Old Circuit Court, Civil Cases, National Archives, San Francisco Branch.

122. The wording of Section 1979 of the Revised Statutes differed slightly from Section 1 of the Civil Rights Act of 1871. Section 1 of the 1871 act (17 Stat. 13) spoke only of the deprivation of rights secured by the Constitution. Section 1979 added "laws" to the formulation. Section 1979 is the lineal ancestor of Title 42, Section 1983, that provision of the United States Code which is today the basis for almost all constitutional challenges by individuals to the actions of state and local officials.

123. *Chronicle,* Mar. 5, 1878, p. 2, col. 3. Ah Wing had been sentenced to a five-day county jail term by the police judges court on March 1.

124. This account of the proceedings based on reports appearing in the *Examiner,* Apr. 16, 1878, p. 3, col. 4; *Morning Call,* Apr. 16, 1878, p. 1, col. 7; *Daily Alta California,* Apr. 16, 1878, p. 1, col. 2; *Chronicle,* Apr. 16, 1878, p. 1, col. 1.

125. See *Daily Alta California,* Apr. 16, 1878, p. 1., col. 2; *Morning Call,* Apr. 16, 1878, p. 1, col. 7. It is not clear whether Hoffman insisted that the police secure a warrant before acting.

126. *Morning Call,* Apr. 16, 1878, p. 1, col. 7. Ogden Hoffman was appointed as the first judge of the federal court for the northern district of California in 1851 and presided over that court for the next forty years. On Hoffman's career generally, see Christian G. Fritz, *Federal Justice in California: The Court of Ogden Hoffman, 1851–1891* (Lincoln, Neb.: University of Nebraska Press, 1991).

127. *Morning Call,* Apr. 18, 1878, p. 2, col. 1; Sacramento *Record-Union,* Apr. 18, 1878, p. 2. col. 4; *Chronicle,* Apr. 19, 1878, p. 3, col. 4.

128. *Chronicle,* Apr. 19, 1878, p. 3, col. 4.

129. Act of Mar. 26, 1790, ch. 3, 1 Stat. 103.

130. See James Kent, *Commentaries on American Law,* 3d ed., (Boston: Little, Brown & Co., 1836). This passage had been cited by Chief Justice Murray in the 1854 California case, *People v. Hall,* p. 403.

131. Act of July 14, 1870, ch. 254, § 7, 16 Stat. 254, 256.

132. Revised Statutes of the United States of 1875, § 2165. A separate section of the Revised Statutes, Section 2169, confirmed the naturalization privilege to persons of African descent.

133. Revised Statutes of the United States of 1875, § 2169.

134. Act of Feb. 18, 1875, ch. 80, 18 Stat., pt. 3, 316, 318.

135. According to Benjamin Brooks eight Chinese filed applications, five in the circuit court and three in the district court. See Brooks, *Brief of the Legislation,* p. 96.

136. See *Daily Alta California,* Jan. 5, 1876, p. 2, cols. 1–2. Under the then existing naturalization law one had to wait two years after filing a declaration of intention before filing final papers. See also Brooks, *Brief of the Legislation,* p. 96.

137. H.R. 1303, 44th Cong. 1st Sess.

138. *Evening Bulletin,* Dec. 30, 1875, p. 3, col. 5; *Examiner,* Dec. 30, 1875, p. 3, col. 4.

139. Testimony of Hong Chung, Inspector of the Sam Yup company, *California State Senate Committee Report,* p. 179. In the *Examiner* article of Dec. 30, 1875, one of the two Chinese applicants is identified as Hong Chung.

140. Minute Book, Mar. 26, 1878, United States District Court, December Term, (microfilm, National Archives, San Francisco Branch, Series T-717, Reel 79). See also reports in *Examiner*, Apr. 23, 1878, p. 3, col. 6; *Daily Alta California*, Apr. 23, 1878, p. 1, col. 2.

141. See *Daily Alta California*, Apr. 23, 1878, p. 1, col. 2; In re Ah Yup, 1 F. Cas. 223 (C.C.D. Cal. 1878) (No. 104).

142. *Evening Bulletin*, Apr. 22, 1878, p. 3, col. 3.

143. Ibid.

144. *Ah Yup*, p. 157.

145. The research on this point seems to have been previously done by a state court magistrate, Judge Morrison of the Fourth District Court. See *Evening Bulletin*, Apr. 22, 1878, p. 3, col. 3; Horace Davis Scraps, vol. 2, p. 22, Bancroft Library, University of California, Berkeley.

146. *Ah Yup*, p. 158.

147. *Ah Yup*, p. 159. Section 2165, the basic naturalization provision, would have been the more logical place to put the words.

148. Clipping in Horace Davis Scraps, vol. 2, p. 23, in Bancroft Library, University of California, Berkeley. The date of the *Chronicle* story is illegible.

149. If any doubt remained on the question after Sawyer's decision it was settled in 1882 with the enactment by Congress of the first Chinese Exclusion Act. That act explicitly forbade any court, state or federal, from admitting Chinese to citizenship. Act of May 6, 1882, ch. 126, § 14, 22 Stat. 58. Chinese aliens were not made eligible for naturalization until 1943.

150. Case files of Lee Ah Quang, No. 1907; Joe Ah Jim, No. 1908; Long Ah, No. 1871.

151. Clipping in Horace Davis Scraps, vol. 2, p. 24, Bancroft Library, University of California, Berkeley. Name and exact date of the newspaper are illegible.

152. Complaint, Ho Ah Kow v. Nunan, 12 F. Cas. (C.C.D. Cal. 1879) (No. 6546). The complaint did take certain liberties with history, it must be said. It spoke of the wearing of the queue as an ancient and honorable custom among the Chinese and said that, according to the religious faith of the Chinese, its loss was attended by suffering after death. In fact, the wearing of the queue had been forced on male Chinese in the 1640s by the Manchu conquerors of China as a token of acceptance of Manchu rule. And indeed in the late nineteenth century the wearing of the queue became a symbol of shame to Chinese nationalists, some of whom made a point of cutting theirs off. See J. Spence, *The Gate of Heavenly Peace: The Chinese and Their Revolution, 1895–1980* (New York: Penguin Books, 1982), p. 97. Notwithstanding the somewhat demeaning origins of the custom of wearing the queue, the complaint was certainly correct in stating that the average Chinese would have experienced deep hurt and humiliation in having his queue cut off against his will by a Caucasian.

153. The constitutional claim seems to have been first made in a brief submitted by Attorney McElrath in support of a demurrer to defendant's answer.

154. See Brief by B. S. Brooks on Demurrer to Defendant's Answer, Ho Ah Kow case file. The brief submitted by the lead counsel for Ho Ah Kow, J. E. McElrath, is missing from the court file, but its contents in broad outline can be deduced from other documents in the file and from the opinion of the court.

155. Minute Book, Oct. 1, 1878, Circuit Court, July Term, National Archives, San Francisco Branch.

156. The *Chronicle* reported that four such suits had been filed the previous day and that fifteen other Chinese were preparing to file shortly. Sept. 20, 1878, p. 2, col. 2.

157. See *Evening Post*, Sept. 20, 1878, p. 2, col. 2; *Chronicle*, Sept. 20, 1878, p. 2, col. 2.

158. Ho Ah Kow v. Nunan, 12 F. Cas. 252 (C.C.D. Cal. 1879) (No. 6546).

159. Ibid, p. 255.

160. Ibid.

161. Ibid., p. 256.

162. Ibid.

163. Ibid.

164. Ibid. Inasmuch as this case looms large in the account, this is probably as appropriate a point as any to offer some reflections on the views concerning *Ho Ah Kow* and other Chinese civil rights cases propounded by Howard Jay Graham in chapter 3 of his classic study of the Fourteenth Amendment, *Everyman's Constitution: Historical Essays on the Fourteenth Amendment, the "Conspiracy Theory," and American Constitutionalism* (Madison: State Historical Society of Wisconsin, 1968).

Graham's thesis is that the foundations of twentieth-century substantive due process jurisprudence were laid in a series of dissenting opinions authored by Supreme Court Justice Stephen Field in the 1870s and in a series of rulings concerning the Chinese made by Field in his capacity as circuit justice and by other federal magistrates in the Ninth Judicial Circuit in the 1870s and 1880s. According to Graham it was the Paris Commune of 1870 that turned Field, previously a moderately restrained judge, into a conservative judicial activist, anxious to use the judicial power to protect property (corporate property in particular) and contract rights against populist legislation. The vehicle he saw for doing this was the first section of the Fourteenth Amendment. Field first set forth his view of the meaning of that provision in the *Slaughter-House Cases*, arguing in dissent that the privileges and immunities clause barred certain kinds of legislation infringing on economic liberty. He then proceeded to incorporate these views in *Ah Fong* and in *Ho Ah Kow*, emphasizing in both cases that the equal protection clause applied to "persons" as opposed to citizens (thereby making it possible for corporations eventually to invoke its terms) and in the latter that it implied accessibility to the courts for the enforcement of contracts. He thereby set the stage, in Graham's estimation, for later court recognition of the principle that corporations were constitutional persons and therefore eligible to invoke the protections of the Fourteenth Amendment and of the principle of liberty of contract. See, in particular, Graham, *Everyman's Constitution*, pp. 143ff.

Judicial motivation is a slippery subject to get a handle on and judges' motives are often complex, but I do not think that what drove Field's decision making was a desire to protect wealth and property per se. He seems to have been driven much more by a distaste for particularistic legislation favoring certain individuals and groups at the expense of others or for laws such as the San Francisco queue ordinance which struck him as gratuitously cruel. (Field's intense hatred for partial or special legislation is explored in Charles McCurdy, "Justice Field and the Jurisprudence of Government-Business Relations," *Journal of American History* 61 (1975): 970–1005.) He certainly was a strong-willed (some might say a head-strong) justice who was utterly convinced of the rightness of his Fourteenth Amendment views. He doubtless too was anxious to chip away in any way he could at the view of that amendment that had won out in *Slaughter-House*. He may well have seen his decisions in the two cases as aiding that project. But there seems to me nothing forced or tendentious in his assertion of the general principle that the Fourteenth Amendment's equal protection clause applied to noncitizen Chinese as well as to citizens. Indeed, it would have been exceedingly strange had he taken the opposite view. To do so would have required him to argue that the amendment's drafters had no particular purpose in mind when they used the obviously more comprehensive term "person" as opposed to the narrow one "citizen" in the amendment's due process and equal protection clauses. Furthermore, Section 16 of the 1870 Civil Rights Act, which was generally understood to have been passed in implementation of the amendment, also used the term "person" instead of "citizen," and there was direct evidence that the terminology had been deliberately chosen in order to protect Chinese aliens.

Nor does it seem to me that there was anything contrived about his including in *Ho Ah Kow*, in the list of civil freedoms secured by the equal protection clause, the right to make contracts and have them enforced on the same basis as others (Field "pressing for judicial recognition of the concept of freedom of contract" is the way Graham describes it, p. 145). The right to enter into contracts and have those agreements enforced was universally recognized as one of the most basic civil freedoms. The inability to make and enforce contracts was indeed seen as one of the fundamental characteristics of slavery. It is inconceivable that an amendment designed to secure equal civil freedom for all would not have been seen as protecting it. Direct evidence that the amendment did embrace this civil freedom is provided again by the Civil Rights Act of 1870, which, as noted above, was seen as implementing the amendment and which Field goes on to quote in the very next paragraph of the opinion. The right to make and enforce contracts on an equal basis is prominent among the rights there mentioned as being secured to all persons within the jurisdiction of the United States. (Field's list in *Ho Ah Kow* of civil rights secured by the Fourteenth Amendment corresponds exactly to the list of rights set forth in the 1870 statute.) There is nothing in *Ho Ah Kow* to suggest that Field was trying to make any special argument in support of freedom of contract in the sense it came to attain in later years, that is, freedom from state regulation of contractual terms and conditions.

165. *Chronicle*, July 8, 1879, p. 2, col. 2.

166. *Examiner*, July 8, 1879, p. 2, col. 1.

167. *Morning Call*, July 10, 1879, p. 2, col. 1.

168. Sacramento *Record-Union*, July 9, 1879, p. 2, col. 3.

169. Writing for the majority in the *Slaughter-House Cases*, the first cases to construe the Fourteenth Amendment, Justice Miller had said he doubted whether any action of a state not directed by way of discrimination against Negroes would ever be held to come within the purview of that amendment's equal protection clause. "It is so clearly a provision for that race and that emergency," he had said, "that a strong case would be necessary for its application to any other." But elsewhere in the opinion he had allowed as how it might have greater reach than

that. "We do not say that no one else but the negro can share in this protection. Both the language and spirit of these articles are to have their fair and just weight in any question of construction. . . . And so if . . . rights are assailed by the States which properly and necessarily fall within the protection of these articles, that protection will apply, though the party interested may not be of African descent." 83 U.S. (16 Wall.) 36, 72, 81 (1873). On *Ho Ah Kow's* significance see also Aviam Soifer, "On Being Overly Discrete and Insular: Involuntary Groups and the Anglo-American Judicial Tradition," *Washington and Lee Law Review* 48 (1991): 381, 413–15.

CHAPTER THREE

1. Carl Brent Swisher, *Motivation and Political Technique in the California Constitutional Convention, 1878–79* (New York: Da Capo Press, 1969), p. 17.
2. Elmer Sandmeyer, *The Anti-Chinese Movement in California* (Urbana: University of Illinois Press, 1973), p. 65.
3. Swisher, *Motivation and Political Technique*, pp. 10–11.
4. *Daily Alta California*, Nov. 4, 1877, p. 1, col. 1.
5. Sandmeyer, *The Anti-Chinese Movement*, p. 66.
6. Of the 152 delegates selected, 52 belonged to the Workingmen's party, 10 were Republicans, and 9 were Democrats. *Chronicle*, Sept. 18, 1878, p. 1, col. 2.
7. *Debates and Proceedings of the Constitutional Convention of the State of California* (Sacramento, 1880–81) 1:637.
8. Swisher, *Motivation and Political Technique*, p. 86.
9. *Debates and Proceedings* 1:628.
10. The San Francisco *Morning Call*, a vehemently anti-Chinese newspaper, itself noted the conflict between the immigration provisions and federal law. Nov. 2, 1878, p. 2, col. 2.
11. *Evening Bulletin*, Feb. 21, 1879, p. 1, col. 4.
12. California Constitution of 1879, art. XIX, § 4.
13. As noted in chapter 1, Article I, Section 17 of the Constitution of 1849 had simply read: "Foreigners who are, or who may hereafter become bona fide residents of this State, shall enjoy the same rights in respect to the possession, enjoyment and inheritance of property as native born citizens."
14. Swisher, *Motivation and Political Technique*, pp. 100ff.
15. Sacramento *Record-Union*, Dec. 21, 1878, p. 4, col. 1.
16. *Morning Call*, July 9, 1879, p. 2, col. 2.
17. Act of Feb. 13, 1880, ch. 10, 1880 Cal. Stat. 6.
18. See, for example, *Evening Bulletin*, Feb. 12, 1880, p. 3, col. 6; *Daily Alta California*, Feb. 13, 1880, p. 4, col. 1; *Evening Post*, Feb. 10, 1880, p. 2, col. 1.
19. *Evening Post*, Feb. 14, 1880, p. 8, col. 2.
20. See, for example, *Daily Alta California*, Feb. 21, 1880, p. 1, col. 4.
21. In the same report the *Alta* noted that a Workingmen's party representative had told a rally the previous evening that anyone who dared test the corporations bill's constitutionality stood in danger of losing his head.
22. On the history of mercury production in California see H. H. Bancroft, *History of California, 1860–1890* (San Francisco: The History Company, 1890) 8:656ff.
23. *Daily Alta California*, Feb. 19, 1880, p. 1, col. 5.

24. The text of the complaint is to be found in the Application for Writ of Habeas Corpus, In re Tiburcio Parrott case file, No. 2275, Record Group 21, Old Circuit Court, Civil Cases, National Archives, San Francisco Branch.

25. Ibid.

26. The Lake County *Bee* reported that Sulphur Bank had discharged all of its Chinese employees. Feb. 26, 1880, p. 3, col. 2.

27. Sawyer had commented to his friend Oregon District Judge Matthew Deady when the corporations bill was passed that he expected to have it before his court in short order. Sawyer to Deady, Feb. 15, 1880, Deady Papers, Oregon Historical Society, Portland.

28. *Chronicle*, Mar. 7, 1880, p. 7, col. 1.

29. Bee would remain on the staff of the San Francisco Consulate until his death in 1892. On the establishment of the first permanent Chinese diplomatic mission in the United States see Shih-shan Henry Tsai, *China and the Overseas Chinese in the United States, 1868–1911* (Fayetteville, Ark.: University of Arkansas Press, 1983), pp. 38–43; and Michael Hunt, *The Making of a Special Relationship: The United States and China to 1914* (New York: Columbia University Press, 1983), pp. 98–99.

30. And indeed it would remain unclear. A member of the Chinese diplomatic mission had told a local reporter in July that the Chinese hoped that the consulate to be established in the city would supersede the authority of the Six Companies "and tend to a better control of the Chinese here." *Evening Post*, July 27, 1878, p. 8, col. 1. If that in fact was the intention of the Chinese foreign office, it was one that was never realized. The Six Companies continued to exist as an independent entity and to exercise considerable power in the Chinese community for the duration of the nineteenth century.

31. Meanwhile, the Chinese legation in Washington was taking forceful action of its own. On March 9, 1880, Yung Wing, second in command at the legation and a graduate of Yale, wrote an urgent letter to Secretary of State William Evarts, complaining about the danger that the Chinese in California were being exposed to by reason of the actions of public bodies in that state. He called attention in particular to the recently enacted corporations bill, a statute which he claimed threatened the Chinese with starvation and which was, in his view, in direct conflict with Article VI of the Burlingame Treaty. *Notes from the Chinese Legation in the United States to the Department of State, 1868–1906*, microfilm, Reel 1, Record Group 59, National Archives.

32. *Daily Alta California*, Feb. 22, 1880, p. 1, col. 2; *Chronicle*, Feb. 24, 1880, p. 2, col. 6. In 1870 the health officer of San Francisco had characterized the Chinese as "moral lepers," whose manner of life could be counted upon to breed disease wherever they resided. He also expressed the fear that, dwelling as they did in the center of the city, any communicable disease that developed in Chinatown might spread rapidly to the whole community. Health officer's report, in Board of Supervisors, *San Francisco Municipal Reports for the Fiscal Year Ending June 30, 1870*, p. 233. The available health statistics disclose that, if anything, the Chinese were less prone to disease than their Caucasian counterparts. See health officer's report, passim. In fact in the midst of his denunciation of the depravity of the Chinese, the health officer was prompted to observe, "It is indeed wonderful that they have so far escaped every phase of disease." Ibid., p. 233.

33. *Chronicle*, Feb. 24, 1880, p. 2, col. 6.

34. *Examiner*, Feb. 24, 1880, p. 3, col. 4.
35. *Chronicle*, Mar. 1, 1880, p. 3, col. 5. Lake pointed out that in the first place, judicial proceedings were necessary to abate nuisances and that in the second, government officials could not, on the basis of a visit to certain premises in a large urban district condemn the whole district as a nuisance.
36. Dartmouth College v. Woodward, 17 U.S. (4 Wheat.) 518 (1819).
37. *Daily Alta California*, Mar. 7, 1880, p. 1, col. 2.
38. *Chronicle*, Mar. 7, 1880, p. 7, col. 1.
39. 100 U.S. 303 (1880).
40. Account of oral argument taken from *Daily Alta California*, Mar. 7, 1880, p. 1, col. 2; *Chronicle*, Mar. 7, 1880, p. 7, cols. 1–3.
41. Ibid.
42. In re Tiburcio Parrott, 1 F. 481, 486 (C.C.D. Cal. 1880).
43. Ibid., p. 491.
44. Ibid., p. 493.
45. Ibid., p. 497.
46. Ibid., p. 495.
47. Ibid., p. 514.
48. Ibid., p. 516.
49. The term "privileges and immunities" appears in two different places in the Constitution—Article IV, Section 2 and Section 1 of the Fourteenth Amendment. By this time, as Sawyer correctly pointed out, there was general agreement on the meaning of the term as used in Article IV, Section 2. It referred there to rights deemed fundamental and the provision meant that with respect to the exercise of such rights a state could not discriminate in favor of its own and against out-of-state citizens. (Whatever fundamental rights it accorded its own citizens it had to accord to the citizens of other states sojourning or residing within its borders.) The principal dispute in the *Slaughter-House Cases* was over the meaning of the term as used in Section 1 of the Fourteenth Amendment ("No State shall make or enforce any law which shall abridge the privileges or immunities of citizens of the United States.") Justices Field, Bradley, and Swayne argued that the purpose there was to protect citizens against infringements on their fundamental rights *by their own state governments*. The majority of the court thought otherwise, maintaining that the term here referred to a narrower set of rights, appertaining to national, as opposed to state, citizenship.
50. *Parrott*, pp. 504–7. Sawyer noted that the previous year the federal circuit court in Oregon had expressed the same view of the Burlingame Treaty. In Baker v. Portland, 2 F. Cas. 472 (C.C.D. Or. 1879) (No. 777), Judge Deady, Sawyer's close friend, had argued that Article VI of the Burlingame Treaty gave the Chinese the right to follow any occupation or employment that was open to citizens or subjects of other foreign powers. Deady, in fact, had taken this position as early as 1876. See Chapman v. Toy Long, 5 F. Cas. 497 (C.C.D. Or. 1876) (No. 2610). For an illuminating discussion of Deady's Chinese decisions see Ralph J. Mooney, "Matthew Deady and the Federal Judicial Response to Racism in the Early West," *Oregon Law Review* 63 (1984): 561–637.
51. *Parrott*, p. 509.
52. Ibid., p. 512.
53. Ibid., p. 513. It also appeared to Sawyer that the California statute might

violate the due process clause of the amendment inasmuch as the right to labor was a person's property and to deprive that person of this right was to take away both property and liberty without due process within the meaning of that clause. *Parrott*, p. 510, citing Field, Bradley, and Swayne in *The Slaughter-House Cases*. But Sawyer did not stress this line of argument. The overwhelming bulk of this part of his opinion sounded in equal protection analysis.

54. *Parrott*, p. 520.

55. *Parrott*, pp. 520–21.

56. *Daily Alta California*, May 24, 1880, p. 1, col. 3. In 1868 Congress abolished the right of the Supreme Court to review habeas corpus decisions of lower courts. Act of Mar. 27, 1868, ch. 34, § 2, 15 Stat. 44. Seventeen years later it restored the right to hear such appeals. Act of Mar. 3, 1885, ch. 253, 23 Stat. 437.

57. *Record-Union*, Mar. 23, 1880, p. 2, col. 3.

58. *Examiner*, Mar. 23, 1880, p. 2, col. 2.

59. *Daily Alta California*, Feb. 14, 1880, p. 1, col. 4.

60. Act of Apr. 3, 1880, ch. 66, 1880 Cal. Stat. 114–15.

61. Act of Apr. 12, 1880, ch. 102, 1880 Cal. Stat. 192.

62. Act of Apr. 23, 1880, ch. 226, 1880 Cal. Stat. 388–89.

63. *Daily Alta California*, Feb. 11, 1880, p. 4, col. 1.

64. *Evening Bulletin*, Feb. 13, 1880, p. 3, col. 8.

65. *Evening Bulletin*, Mar. 9, 1880, p. 4, cols. 1–2.

66. *Evening Bulletin*, Feb. 12, 1880, p. 3, col. 6. During debate on the measure the representative from Sonoma complained that the bill would harm the wine producers in his district, most of whom kept their books of account in French or German. He moved to amend the bill so that it would apply only to aliens ineligible to citizenship. Interestingly, the bill foreshadowed almost exactly a measure that would be enacted in the next century by the territorial legislature of the Philippines. That measure, aimed at Chinese businesses, forbade the keeping of books of account in any language other than English, Spanish, or Tagalog. It was struck down by the Supreme Court in Yu Cong Eng v. Trinidad, 271 U.S. 500 (1926).

67. Sacramento *Record-Union*, Feb. 25, 1880, p. 2, col. 3.

68. See *Chronicle*, July 14, 1988, for a report concerning the discovery of what appear to be the remains of a Chinese fishing village in San Francisco dating from about 1850. For an excellent discussion of the Chinese fishermen of the Monterey Bay area see Sandy Lydon, *Chinese Gold: The Chinese in the Monterey Bay Region* (Capitola: Capitola Books, 1985), pp. 29ff.

69. See Sucheng Chan, *This Bittersweet Soil: The Chinese in California Agriculture, 1860–1910* (Berkeley: University of California Press, 1986), table 5, pp. 68–69.

70. The sheriff of Santa Cruz County arrested three Monterey Bay Chinese fishermen around the same time. See Lydon, *Chinese Gold*, p. 53.

71. Petition for Writ of Habeas Corpus, In re Wong Hoy case file, No. 2300, Record Group 21, Old Circuit Court, Civil Cases, National Archives, San Francisco Branch. On the consulate's involvement see *Chronicle*, May 28, 1880, p. 4, col. 2.

It is probable that the Chinese fishermen would have themselves mounted a challenge to the law had the consulate not acted on their behalf. In early 1876 the Chinese fishermen's guild, after consultation with the Six Companies, had hired counsel to represent them in a complaint brought before the state Harbor Commission by a group of Italian fishermen. The Italians claimed that the Chinese were using too fine a mesh net and were thereby destroying valuable breeding stock. The Chinese denied that this was their general custom. See reports in *Chronicle*, Dec. 30, 1875, p. 4, col. 1; *Oriental* (*T'ang fan kung pao*) Jan. 15, 1876, Feb. 26, 1876.

72. Petition for Writ of Habeas Corpus, In re Wong Hoy.

73. 94 U.S. 391 (1876).

74. In re Ah Chong, 2 F. 733, 735–6 (C.C.D. Cal. 1880).

75. Ibid., p. 736.

76. Ibid.

77. Ibid., p. 737.

78. Section 16 of the Civil Rights Act of 1870, from which Section 1977 of the Revised Statutes of the United States of 1875 derived, did in its second sentence contain a provision placing all aliens on the same plane with respect to taxes and charges levied by a state.

79. *Ah Chong*, pp. 739–40. Some three quarters of a century later the U.S. Supreme Court would be asked to rule on the constitutionality of another, similarly worded California statute, this one aimed at Japanese residents of the state. In Takahashi v. Fish and Game Comm., 334 U.S. 410 (1948) the question was whether a California law that permitted all except "aliens ineligible to citizenship" (at this time a description comprehending only Japanese) to obtain commercial fishing licenses ran afoul of the equal protection clause. The Court held that it did. Justice Black, who wrote the majority opinion, declined to bottom his decision on the racial animus that obviously lay behind the law. Murphy, who wrote a concurring opinion, had no such hesitation. Murphy's discussion of the twentieth-century California statute is in fact remarkably similar to Sawyer's discussion of the 1880 act. See *Takahashi*, pp. 422ff.

80. San Francisco *Report*, June 2, 1880.

81. *Evening Bulletin*, Mar. 9, 1878, p. 3, col. 5. In 1876 the state assembly had come close to passing a bill requiring the governor's permission before bodies could be disinterred. That one of its primary purposes was to deter Chinese immigration is clear from the debates. One assemblyman declared during the debates that when the Chinese found out that their remains could only be returned with the consent of the governor they would not want to come. Sacramento *Record-Union*, Mar. 30, 1876, p. 1, cols. 3–4.

82. Ibid. One San Francisco newspaper reported the debate under the headline "Taxing the Chinaman's Hope of Heaven." *Evening Bulletin*, Mar. 9, 1878, p. 3, col. 5.

83. Act of Apr. 1, 1878, ch. 673, 1877–78 Cal. Stat. 1050–51.

84. During the constitutional convention an amendment to the new constitution was proposed under which it would be a criminal offense to send "to any foreign country the bones or remains of any alien after the person has been interred for a period of two months or more." It was referred to the Committee on the Chinese, but no further action appears to have been taken on it. *Debates and Proceedings*, 1:140.

85. See *Daily Alta California*, Oct. 3, 1879, p. 1, col. 6.

86. Procedural history taken from In re Wong Yung Quy case file, No. 2187,

Record Group 21, Old Circuit Court, Civil Cases, National Archives, San Francisco Branch; and from the opinion itself, In re Wong Yung Quy, 2 F. 624 (C.C.D. Cal. 1880).

87. In re Wong Yung Quy, 47 F. 717 (C.C.D. Cal. 1880).

88. In re Wong Yung Quy, 2 F. 624 (C.C.D. Cal. 1880), p. 632.

89. Ibid., p. 629. Judge Sawyer's handling of the Chinese civil rights cases of the early 1880s is ably discussed in Linda C. A. Przybyszewski, "Judge Lorenzo Sawyer and the Chinese Civil Rights Decisions in the Ninth Circuit," *Western Legal History* 1 (1988): 23–56.

CHAPTER FOUR

1. Some 2,100 in the city of San Francisco, for example. Sucheng Chan, *This Bittersweet Soil: The Chinese in California Agriculture, 1860–1910* (Berkeley: University of California Press, 1986), p. 69.

2. See ch. 2, pp. 50–54.

3. See testimony of John Durkee, U.S. Senate, *Joint Special Committee Report*, pp. 997–1000. He said, however, that the Chinatown fires were seldom serious.

4. Testimony of Henry Bigelow, *Joint Special Committee Report*, pp. 969–74.

5. The fire marshal's report to the Board of Fire Underwriters of San Francisco for the year July 1, 1875 to June 30, 1876 lists 255 fires as occurring in the city during this period, 8 of these in Chinese washhouses. Of these 8 fires, 6 were distinctly minor, with losses ranging from $5 to $85. In two the losses were more serious, $800 and $2,040, respectively. *Twelfth Annual Report of Fire Marshal Durkee to the Board of Fire Underwriters of San Francisco from July 1, 1875 to June 30, 1876*, San Francisco, 1876, pp. 12–15. The comparable statistics for 1876–77 are 304 fires, 8 in Chinese washhouses. All save one of these were minor with damage amounting to no more than $50. The one serious blaze caused $500 damage. *Thirteenth Annual Report of Fire Marshal Durkee to the Board of Fire Underwriters of San Francisco from July 1, 1876 to June 30, 1877*, San Francisco, 1877, pp. 12–15.

6. *Joint Special Committee Report*, pp. 970, 973.

7. Ibid., p. 972.

8. Testimony of William Dye, *Joint Special Committee Report*, pp. 660–66. The quotation is at p. 661.

9. See reports of the riots in the *Morning Call*, July 24, 1877, p. 3. Several Chinese residents who sustained property losses during the disturbances filed suit against the city for failure to furnish them adequate protection and succeeded in recovering damages. See Board of Supervisors, *San Francisco Municipal Reports for the Fiscal Year Ending June 30, 1879*, pp. 704, 706–7. It is interesting that the damage judgments followed jury trials.

10. *Evening Post*, Sept. 25, 1877, p. 1, cols. 1–3; Sept. 27, 1877, p. 1, cols. 1–2; Oct. 2, 1877, p. 1, cols. 1–2.

11. *Evening Post*, Sept. 25, 1877, p. 2, col. 2.

12. Ibid., p. 1, col. 1.

13. Ibid., p. 1, col. 1.

14. *Daily Alta California*, Feb. 6, 1880, p. 1, col. 2.

15. *Evening Post,* Feb. 10, 1880, p. 1, col. 2.

16. *Evening Bulletin,* Feb. 16, 1880, p. 1, col. 3.

17. San Francisco Board of Supervisors, Order No. 1559, approved Feb. 24, 1880, § 1. The text of the ordinance can be found in *In re White,* 6 West Coast Reporter 644 (1885) [hereafter Order No. 1559].

In March 1888 the board of supervisors passed an ordinance forbidding the use of metal doors in any public building. The purpose of the ordinance was, according to its caption, "to compel the removal of serious obstacles from buildings which prevent ingress and egress of officers and members of the fire department in extinguishing fires." Order No. 1954, approved Mar. 6, 1888, *General Orders of the Board of Supervisors Providing Regulations for the Government of the City and County of San Francisco* (1890), p. 227.

18. San Francisco Board of Supervisors, Order No. 1569, approved May 26, 1880, § 1. The full text of the ordinance appears in Alfred Clarke, "Report of Alfred Clarke in the Laundry Order Litigation," Board of Supervisors, *Municipal Reports for the Year Ending June 30, 1885* [hereafter Alfred Clarke Report], p. 69.

19. The hanging of clothes indoors had been a contributing cause to the February 5 fire at the Chinese laundry.

20. The same may be said, I think, of the seven other ordinances affecting the maintenance or operation of laundries that the supervisors would proceed to enact over the course of the next four years. (No other industry or line of work would receive more legislative attention from the city fathers during this period.)

21. The board did not always feel such compunctions about displaying its anti-Chinese sympathies in the text of its laws. Two months after passing the second laundry law, it passed an ordinance banning the use in the paving or repairing of San Francisco streets, sidewalks or sewers of any material "of Chinese importation or of Chinese production, manufacture or preparation." Order No. 504, approved July 28, 1880, *General Orders of the Board of Supervisors,* San Francisco, 1890, p. 70.

22. On the origins of the Tung Hing Tong (Chinese laundrymen's guild) see ch. 2, pp. 47–48.

23. *Chronicle,* July 1, 1880, p. 4, col. 4. The newspaper article appeared under the headline "Testing the Laundry Ordinance."

24. The decision is reported in the *Chronicle,* Aug. 25, 1880, p. 1, col. 1. It is not clear whether the police court nullified the law or simply declared that it could only be made to operate prospectively.

25. For evidence of the Tung Hing Tong's sponsorship of this case see Authorities and Argument for Defendant and Respondent, p. 3, United States Supreme Court Records and Briefs, Yick Wo v. Hopkins, 118 U.S. 356 (1886).

26. The substantive provisions of the February 17 and May 24, 1880 ordinances were included as Sections 67, 68, and 69 in a comprehensive police power measure covering so-called "offensive trades, occupations and nuisances" enacted by the board of supervisors in July 1880. Order No. 1587, *General Orders of the Board of Supervisors,* San Francisco, 1890, pp. 44–45.

27. *Chronicle,* May 8, 1881, p. 5, col. 7.

28. See pp. 51–54.

29. Petition for Writ of Habeas Corpus, p. 10, Ex parte Quong Woo case file, No. 2866, Record Group 21, Old Circuit Court, Civil Cases, National Archives, San Francisco Branch.

30. *Evening Post,* May 16, 1882, p. 1, col. 4.
31. Ibid.
32. See, e.g., *Evening Post,* May 15, 1882, p. 3, col. 4.
33. *Evening Post,* May 15, 1882, p. 3, col. 4. The newspaper ran its story under the headline "Chinese Laundries: The Order Providing that None of Them Shall Be Located Inside of Larkin or Ninth Streets." According to the paper there were numerous complaints from white citizens that Chinese laundries depreciated the value of property in their neighborhoods.
34. See reports in *Evening Post,* July 21, 1882, p. 1, col. 3; *Chronicle,* July 25, 1882, p. 3, col. 4; *Chronicle,* Aug. 1, 1882, p. 2, col. 4. See also Petition for Writ of Habeas Corpus, pp. 23–24, Ex parte Quong Woo case file.
35. *Evening Post,* July 21, 1882, p. 2, col. 1. See also *Daily Alta California,* July 20, 1882, p. 1, col. 3.
36. Petition for Habeas Corpus, Ex parte Quong Woo case file.
37. Ex parte Quong Woo, 13 F. 229, 231 (C.C.D. Cal. 1882).
38. Ibid., p. 233.
39. Ibid.
40. Ibid., p. 232. Field cited the California case Ex parte Frank, 52 Cal. 606 (1878), as authority on the point. In that case the California Supreme Court had struck down a San Francisco ordinance imposing differential license fees upon the sellers of goods depending upon whether the goods were within or without the city at the time of sale. The ordinance was probably aimed at protecting local merchants against sellers from out of state who sold using samples.
41. *Quong Woo,* p. 232.
42. Field took note of the recent congressional act restricting Chinese immigration (Act of May 6, 1882, ch. 126, 22 Stat. 58) but pointed out that that legislation had not affected the petitioner's right to remain in the United States or to pursue a business. *Quong Woo,* p. 233.
43. *Quong Woo,* p. 233.
44. Ibid., p. 231.
45. The only other San Francisco businesses forbidden to operate at night at the time seem to have been dance halls and shooting galleries. These were not, however, prohibited from operating on Sundays. *General Orders of the Board of Supervisors,* San Francisco, 1890, pp. 33, 196.
46. *Report,* Oct. 21, 1882, p. 2.
47. That at least according to the allegation of the laundrymen's attorney. *Evening Post,* Jan. 19, 1886, p. 2, col. 6.
48. Petition for Writ of Habeas Corpus, p. 14, Ex parte Tom Tong case file, No. 2953, Record Group 21, Old Circuit Court, Civil Cases, National Archives, San Francisco Branch.
49. Petition for Writ of Habeas Corpus, Ex parte Tom Tong. Account of oral argument, *Evening Post,* Jan. 29, 1883, p. 3, col. 7. Among the averments in the petition was an allegation that the "Board of Supervisors will not grant, nor will any of the officers in said ordinance specified grant to your Petitioner any of the authorizations mentioned in said ordinance." And the petition describes the laundryman as being "unable to procure the authorizations" mentioned in the ordinance. Petition, p. 14.
50. Since the judges were not able to agree on a decision, there is no published circuit court report in this case. Sawyer recalled his views on the substan-

tive questions raised in In re Wo Lee, 26 F. 471, 472–73 (C.C.D. Cal. 1886).

51. Revised Statutes of the United States of 1875, §§ 650–53, 693.

52. Ex parte Tom Tong, 108 U.S. 556 (1883). During the pendency of this case in the Supreme Court the laundrymen applied for a writ of habeas corpus in that tribunal itself. But the Court refused to entertain the application on the grounds that with certain well-known exceptions it could not issue habeas writs as an original matter. Ex parte Hung Hang, 108 U.S. 552 (1883).

53. See Alfred Clarke Report, p. 72.

54. For full text of the ordinance see *Report,* June 18, 1883, p. 2, col. 5.

55. The opinion was handed down on Nov. 2, 1883. See Alfred Clarke Report, p. 70.

56. *In re Woo Yeck,* 12 Pacific Coast Law Journal 382 (1883). The court was unmoved by the city's contention that the ordinance was enacted because of the noise attending the washing and ironing of clothes. If that were so, said the court, then the city would have full warrant to limit the hours during which printing presses could operate or any other manufactures for that matter. Ibid., pp. 383–84. Given the close similarity in the spelling and the fact that there was no agreed upon convention for romanizing Chinese names, there is a strong possibility that the Chinese laundry involved in this case was the same Chinese laundry that three years later would be involved in the U.S. Supreme Court case of *Yick Wo v. Hopkins,* discussed in detail below.

57. Alfred Clarke Report, p. 73. *Chronicle,* Feb. 9, 1884, p. 4, col. 2.

58. Ex parte Moynier, 65 Cal. 33 (1884).

59. Account of the procedural history taken from Alfred Clarke Report, pp. 73–74. See also Soon Hing v. Crowley case file, No. 3275, Old Circuit Court, Civil Cases, National Archives, San Francisco Branch.

60. This account of the procedural history of these two cases is based largely upon the Alfred Clarke Report, pp. 74ff.

61. 113 U.S. 27 (1885).

62. 113 U.S. 703 (1885).

63. *Barbier,* pp. 30–32.

64. Ibid., p. 31. "Class legislation" was a term of art widely used in constitutional discussion at the time. It referred to laws that subjected individuals from a certain class or locality to peculiar rules or burdens not imposed on others similarly situated. Other terms used to connote the same thing were "unequal legislation" and "partial legislation." All terms referred to the arbitrary dispensation of legislative favors. See Thomas Cooley, *A Treatise on the Constitutional Limitations Which Rest upon the Legislative Power of the States of the American Union* (Boston: Little, Brown & Co., 1868) Special Legal Classics Reprint, Birmingham, Ala., The Legal Classics Library, 1987, pp. 389ff.

Despite this passage's broad phraseology, Field's conception of equal protection was, even by the standards of the time, a narrow one. The guarantee of the equal protection of the laws did not, he was emphatic, encompass the right to be free of racial discrimination in jury selection. Compare his dissents in Strauder v. West Virginia, 100 U.S. 303 (1880) and Virginia v. Rives, 100 U.S. 313 (1880) with the majority opinions in those cases. These cases involved blacks, but in Neal v. Delaware, 103 U.S. 370, 407–8 (1881) he made clear that under no conceivable conception of equal protection that he entertained could Chinese complain about being barred from serving on juries or being tried before juries from which their compatriots had been barred. The right to serve on juries or to hold political office in a state was, according to Field, a "political" as opposed to a civil right and was entirely within the discretion of the states to administer.

65. Though the subject can hardly be described as free of controversy, there is a considerable body of scholarly opinion now that says that Field and his fellow dissenters in that case more accurately reflected the intentions of the framers of the Fourteenth Amendment than did the majority. Considerable evidence exists that many members of the Thirty-ninth Congress did intend to nationalize fundamental civil rights and place them under federal protection. It is clear too that for many members among the most important of these rights were the rights to acquire property and to pursue economic interests free of invidious and partial treatment by the state. See William Nelson, *The Fourteenth Amendment: From Political Principle to Judicial Doctrine* (Cambridge: Harvard University Press, 1988); Earl Maltz, *Civil Rights, the Constitution and Congress, 1863–1869* (Lawrence, Kans.: University of Kansas Press, 1990); James Kettner, *The Development of American Citizenship, 1608–1870* (Chapel Hill, N.C.: University of North Carolina Press, 1978), pp. 346–49.

What is not clear, however, is whether the framers of the Fourteenth Amendment saw themselves as extending to aliens as well as citizens protection for the same fundamental rights mentioned above. Indeed, it is not clear whether they even considered the question. Debate on Section 1 of the Fourteenth Amendment revolved mainly around the meaning of its privileges and immunities clause ("No State shall make or enforce any law which shall abridge the privileges or immunities of citizens of the United States"). The equal protection and due process clauses, which refer to the rights of "persons" rather than "citizens," were added to the amendment at the very end of the debates and very little was said about them. It is interesting to note that Senator Jacob Howard, commenting on these provisions in the Senate, did say that their great object was to do away with "all class legislation in the States" and "with the injustice of subjecting one caste of persons to a code not applicable to another." See Charles Fairman, *Reconstruction and Reunion, 1864–1888* (New York: Macmillan, 1971), p. 1295.

66. The Court was in effect adopting the view of Section 1 of the Fourteenth Amendment that Justice Swayne had expressed in the *Slaughter-House Cases*, namely that all clauses in the section—privileges and immunities, due process, equal protection—were designed to accomplish the same thing. See The Slaughter-House Cases, 83 U.S. (16 Wall.) 36, 124ff.

67. *Soon Hing*, p. 709.

68. Ibid., p. 710.

69. Ibid., p. 711.

70. People v. Ah Ling, *Chronicle*, May 8, 1881, p. 5, col. 7.

71. Petitioner's Brief, In re E. White case file, California Supreme Court, State Archives, Sacramento (No. 21350).

72. *In re White*, 6 West Coast Reporter 644 (1885). The opinion can also be found in Alfred Clarke Report, p. 83.

73. See Alfred Clarke Report. Clarke commented later that "few jurists were better qualified than he to understand the questions involved." Alfred Clarke Report, p. 70.

74. *Ex parte E. White*. San Francisco Superior Court decision. The full opinion can be found in Alfred Clarke Report, pp. 83–86.

75. Alfred Clarke Report, p. 70.
76. Petitioner's Brief, pp. 5–6, In re White case file.
77. Affidavit for Rule to Show Cause, p. 9, In re White case file.
78. Ibid., p. 6.
79. Ibid., pp. 7–8.
80. Both items, the Order to Show Cause and the Stipulation, are to be found in In re White case file.
81. It is interesting to note that E. White, twice prosecuted for operating wooden laundries without supervisorial permission, had no difficulty securing that permission when he sought it. See Authorities and Argument for Defendant and Respondent, p. 26, case file, Yick Wo v. Hopkins (118 U.S. 356), U.S. Supreme Court Records and Briefs.
82. *In re White, On Habeas Corpus.*
83. The petitions were filed by Van Schaick, attorney for the Tung Hing Tong. I have been able to document the filing of some 197 petitions in the period between June 21 and August 1, 1885. See the *Examiner,* June 21, 1885, p. 5, col. 3; July 7, 1885, p. 3, col. 3; July 30, 1885, p. 3, col. 5; Aug. 1, 1885, p. 2, col. 5.
84. Some are convinced that Yick Wo is a fictitious business name and not that of a person. See *New York Times,* Dec. 14, 1981, p. 14, col. 3. This is quite possible. Indeed it is quite possible that many of the other names that appear in the other laundry cases discussed in this chapter are fictitious business rather than personal names. Since the very fragmentary evidence that is available is not absolutely dispositive on the question, however, I have, as noted in the introduction, adopted the convention of treating all Chinese names that appear in the cases as if they were the names of individuals.
85. In the Matter of Yick Wo on Habeas Corpus, 68 Cal. 294, 296 (1885). See also Transcript of Record, pp. 28–29, Yick Wo v. Hopkins; Transcript of Record, pp. 18, 22, Wo Lee v. Hopkins, case file Yick Wo v. Hopkins, Wo Lee v. Hopkins, U.S. Supreme Court Records and Briefs.
86. Newspaper reports are quite unilluminating on the supervisors' reasons for denying permission. See article in the *Examiner,* July 23, 1883, p. 3, col. 2, reporting that the License Committee of the board of supervisors had met the previous day and recommended that thirty Chinese applicants be refused permission to operate. It reads simply: "In relation to Chinese laundries, the committee reported thirty had been examined and found to be dangerous, and it was deemed necessary to withhold license from that number. These buildings are all constructed of wood, which accounts for the danger." Some two hundred Chinese laundries would eventually apply for and be refused permission to operate during this period. See Admissions of Respondent, In the Matter of Yick Wo on Habeas Corpus, California Supreme Court, State Archives, Sacramento (No. 20126).
87. In his Petition for a Writ of Habeas Corpus before the California Supreme Court, Yick Wo alleged that some 150 Chinese had been arrested. Petition for Writ, para. VI, Yick Wo v. Hopkins case file. *Examiner,* Aug. 26, 1885, p. 3, col. 6 reported that as of that date sixty Chinese laundry owners had been convicted under the ordinance.
88. The *Examiner* reported on August 26 that counsel for the Chinese laundrymen had deliberately chosen the Yick Wo case "with special reference to rais-

ing every possible objection under the Chinese treaty, the Fourteenth Amendment, the Civil Rights bill and the Constitutions of the United States and this State." Aug. 26, 1885, p. 3, col. 6. For further evidence that the case was carefully chosen by counsel for the Chinese laundrymen as one that would raise in the most vigorous fashion all of the points that he wanted raised, see Authorities and Argument for Defendant and Respondent, p. 9, Yick Wo v. Hopkins.

89. Yick Wo had been convicted of violating Section 1 of Order 1569 and Section 68 of Order 1587, the former passed May 26, the latter July 28, 1880. The two provisions were in substance and effect the same.

90. Petition for Writ of Habeas Corpus, para. IX, Transcript of Record, U.S. Supreme Court Records and Briefs, p. 7. There is no copy of the petition in the California Supreme Court case file, but its contents are reproduced in the Transcript of Record filed in the U.S. Supreme Court case.

91. Petition, para. V, Transcript, p. 3.

92. Petition, para. VI, Transcript, p. 5.

93. Petition, para. VII, Transcript, p. 6.

94. Petition, paras. VI, VII, Transcript, pp. 5–6.

95. Petition, para. IX, Transcript, p. 8.

96. Points and Authorities for Respondent, In the Matter of Yick Wo on Habeas Corpus, California Supreme Court, State Archives, Sacramento (No. 20126). Accompanying this document and incorporated by reference in it is a reply brief filed by the city in the original police court action against the petitioner. In that document the petitioner (there the defendant) is designated Yick Wo Chang.

97. The brief is not to be found in the state supreme court case file, but excerpts from it appear in the written argument filed by Clarke in the U.S. Supreme Court in Argument and Authorities for Defendant and Respondent, pp. 10–20, 21–26, 97–103, Yick Wo v. Hopkins [hereafter Clarke, U.S. Supreme Court Brief, Yick Wo v. Hopkins].

98. Admissions of Respondent, p. 3, In the Matter of Yick Wo on Habeas Corpus case file. The admissions can also be found in Clarke, U.S. Supreme Court Brief, Yick Wo v. Hopkins, pp. 10–11.

99. Clarke, U.S. Supreme Court Brief, Yick Wo v. Hopkins, p. 12.

100. In the Matter of Yick Wo on Habeas Corpus case file, California Supreme Court, State Archives, Sacramento (No. 20126).

101. Clarke, U.S. Supreme Court Brief, Yick Wo v. Hopkins, pp. 13–14.

102. Ibid., pp. 13, 14, 99.

103. Clarke, U.S. Supreme Court Brief, Yick Wo v. Hopkins, pp. 99–100. It will be recalled that Yick Wo had received a fire certificate from the Board of Fire Wardens. These certificates confirmed, among other things, that the laundry owner's "stoves, washing and *drying apparatus*" [emphasis added] had been inspected by the board and that it had determined that their use presented no fire danger to surrounding property. A copy of a standard San Francisco fire certificate is to be found in Petition for Writ of Habeas Corpus, In re Wo Lee case file, No. 3947, Record Group 21, Old Circuit Court, Civil Cases, National Archives, San Francisco Branch. Clarke suggested that the reason Yick Wo had received a fire certificate was that when he was inspected he did not have a scaffold on his roof. Clarke, U.S. Supreme Court Brief, Yick Wo v. Hopkins, p. 97. Clarke submitted no evidence to support this allegation.

104. Clarke, U.S. Supreme Court Brief, Yick Wo v. Hopkins, p. 20.

105. Ibid., p. 13. Like Section 1, which forbade the operation of a laundry in a wooden building without supervisorial permission, Section 2 of Order 1569 forbade the use of scaffolding without supervisorial permission. Clarke filed with the California Supreme Court seven photographs of Chinese laundries, including a photo of the Yick Wo establishment, all showing scaffolds on the roof.

There is no evidence as to whether the Chinese who applied for permission to operate in wooden buildings also sought permission to use scaffolding. According to Clarke's brief in the California Supreme Court none of the eighty-odd Caucasian laundries had scaffolds on the roof. Clarke, U.S. Supreme Court Brief, Yick Wo v. Hopkins, p. 13.

106. Ibid., p. 99. See also pp. 17ff.

107. Ibid., p. 100.

108. Ibid., pp. 15–16.

109. The case was submitted on written briefs. There was no oral argument.

110. In the Matter of Yick Wo on Habeas Corpus, 68 Cal. 294 (1885).

111. Ibid., pp. 304–5.

112. Ibid., p. 305.

113. Ibid., pp. 305–6.

114. Sometime between the filing of the petition for habeas corpus and the rendering of the California Supreme Court opinion the Tung Hing Tong attorneys, Van Schaick and Smoot, had associated Hall McAllister into the case. (McAllister's name appears on none of the pleadings or legal documents in the state supreme court case file, but in the published opinion of the California court he is listed as one of the three counsel of record.) The chief of police of the city of San Francisco claimed that the Chinese laundrymen had accumulated a war chest of $20,000 to fight the laundry litigation. If true, this may account for the presence of such an array of high-powered counsel in the case. See the *Morning Call*, Jan. 12, 1886, p. 5, col. 1.

115. Yick Wo v. Crowley, 26 F. 207 (C.C.D. Cal. 1886). Section 720 of the Revised Statutes of the United States of 1875 provided: "The writ of injunction shall not be granted by any court of the United States to stay proceedings in any court of a state, except in cases where such injunction may be authorized by any law relating to proceedings in bankruptcy." Case law had limited the provision to proceedings *first commenced* in state court, permitting federal courts to act when they had first obtained jurisdiction over the parties and subject-matter.

116. An account of the oral argument can be found in *Morning Call*, Jan. 19, 1886, p. 7, cols. 4–5., In re Wo Lee case file, No. 3947, Record Group 21, National Archives, San Francisco branch.

117. In re Wo Lee, 26 F. 471, 473 (C.C.D. Cal. 1886).

118. 49 Md. 217 (1878).

119. *Wo Lee*, p. 472.

120. Ibid., pp. 473–74, 475. When Sawyer spoke of the "notorious public and municipal history of the times," he may have been referring not to the background Sinophobia that was always present in California but to the extraordinary movement then gathering force in the state to expel the Chinese from California's cities. The day before Sawyer rendered his decision, for example, Sacramento had narrowly defeated an ordinance requiring the expulsion of the Chinese. *Morning Call*, Jan. 20, 1886, p. 3, col. 5.

121. *Wo Lee*, pp. 474–75.
122. Ibid., p. 476.
123. Ibid., pp. 476–77.
124. See In re Quong Woo, 13 F. 229, 231 (1882).
125. Argument of Plaintiff-in-Error and Appellant, p. 3, case file, Yick Wo v. Hopkins, 118 U.S. 356, U.S. Supreme Court Records and Briefs [hereafter McAllister U.S. Supreme Court Brief].
126. Ibid., p. 2.
127. Ibid. The lawyers for Yick Wo and Wo Lee took some liberties in restating the admissions, declaring for example that the city had admitted that eighty Caucasians had applied for permits and all but one had been approved. The city's admission said simply that "all the petitions of those who were not Chinese with one exception . . . were granted." It mentioned no particular number. Admissions of Respondent, p. 3, In the Matter of Yick Wo on Habeas Corpus case file.
128. McAllister U.S. Supreme Court Brief, p. 8.
129. Ibid., pp. 10–11. Ex parte Virginia, 100 U.S. 339 (1880) and Neal v. Delaware, 103 U.S. 370 (1881) involved racial discrimination in jury selection by state officials. Field had of course rejected a Chinese challenge to a San Francisco laundry law in *Soon Hing* but had clearly intimated that discriminatory enforcement of a neutral law would be unconstitutional.
130. McAllister U.S. Supreme Court Brief, p. 13.
131. Clarke U.S. Supreme Court Brief, pp. 20, 105.
132. Ibid., pp. 20, 27, 41. I have not been able to find any news reports of any prosecution of Caucasian laundrymen during this period.
133. Clarke, U.S. Supreme Court Brief, *Yick Wo v. Hopkins*, pp. 37–38.
134. Ibid., p. 20. During the winter of 1885–86 anti-Chinese rioting convulsed many rural areas of California. Many Chinese may have fled to San Francisco to escape it, but the city was hardly putting out the welcome mat for them. The anti-Chinese riots of the period are discussed in chapter 7.
135. *Yick Wo*, pp. 367–68.
136. Ibid., p. 369. This was the first instance in which the Supreme Court explicitly affirmed that the due process and equal protection clauses of the Fourteenth Amendment applied to noncitizens. As noted earlier, Field had first asserted this in the 1874 case of *In re Ah Fong* and had reasserted it again in *Ho Ah Kow*. The Court also noted that the Chinese were assured of the equal protection of the laws by treaty and by Section 1977 of the Revised Statutes.
137. *Yick Wo*, pp. 366–67.
138. Ibid., p. 368. Matthews rejected the notion that the discretion vested by the San Francisco ordinance was no different from the discretion almost universally lodged by municipal law in public bodies to determine who should be permitted to sell alcoholic beverages. (It will be recalled that Clarke, in his brief, had sought to analogize the San Francisco ordinance to these kinds of laws and had cited several cases affirming the constitutionality of such legislation.) He characterized such authorization as a privilege rather than a right, noted that in these legislative schemes the grant of the authorization depended on the applicant showing that he was a [morally] fit person, and that the assessment of such fitness called for the exercise of a discretion of a judicial nature. Ibid., p. 368.
139. Ibid., p. 370.
140. Ibid., pp. 372–73.

141. Ibid., p. 374.

142. Ibid.

143. Ibid., pp. 373–74. One of the cases cited in support of this principle was Neal v. Delaware, 103 U.S. 370 (1881), a very complex opinion authored by Justice Harlan, which held, among other things, that a showing that no black citizen had ever been summoned to serve as a juror in the state of Delaware, even though blacks constituted one seventh of the population, constituted a prima facie case of denial by state officers of "that equality of protection which has been secured by the Constitution and laws of the United States." *Neal*, p. 397.

144. The city repeated the admissions it had made in the Yick Wo state court litigation in the Wo Lee federal circuit court litigation. See Transcript of Record, pp. 17–18, Wo Lee v. Hopkins.

145. It is interesting to note that Clarke made no mention of scaffolding as the reason Chinese laundrymen had been denied permits in the brief he submitted to the police judges court in the original state court proceeding against Yick Wo. See case file, In the Matter of Yick Wo on Habeas Corpus, California Supreme Court, State Archives, Sacramento (No. 20126).

146. According to the 1885 edition of the *San Francisco Business Directory* there were some seventy non-Chinese laundry establishments in operation in San Francisco at the time. From the look of the list a good number seem to have been sole proprietorships run by Caucasian women. *Directory*, pp. 238–39.

147. At several points in its Supreme Court argument the city had suggested that the purpose of its enforcement activities against the Chinese laundrymen was not to force them to remove their scaffolds or to otherwise improve their fire safety but to induce them to move into brick or stone buildings. See Clarke U.S. Supreme Court Brief, pp. 20, 101, 107.

148. *Evening Bulletin*, May 12, 1886, p. 2, col. 1.

149. *Morning Call*, May 11, 1886, p. 8, col. 1.

150. See *Daily Alta California*, May 11, 1886, p. 5, col. 3; *Evening Bulletin*, May 11, 1886, p. 3, cols. 3–4.

151. Order No. 1930, approved Oct. 17, 1887, *General Orders of the Board of Supervisors*, San Francisco, 1890, pp. 215–17.

152. The rioting and the Supreme Court case that grew out of it are discussed in chapter 7.

153. *Evening Mail*, Feb. 13, 1885, p. 2, cols. 1–2; Feb. 21, 1885, p. 2, col. 1.

154. Ibid., Feb. 21, 1885, p. 2, cols. 1–2.

155. Ibid., Feb. 25, 1885, p. 3, col. 5.

156. Ibid., Sept. 22, 1885, p. 2, col. 2.

157. Ibid., Oct. 5, 1885, p. 2, cols. 1–2.

158. Ibid., Oct. 15, 1885, p. 3, col. 2. At a large anti-Chinese rally held in Stockton around this time another member of the city council saw the enactment of such legislation as supplementing the anti-Chinese exclusion laws that had been passed by the Congress. "The Federal Government," he said, "is the government to see that they do not further come; the local government is the government to see that we make it devilishly uncomfortable while they are here." Ibid., Oct. 23, 1885, p. 3, col. 1. Something of the same philosophy is to be found in a report issued by a special committee of the San Francisco Board of Supervisors in July of the same year. Noting that the federal Exclusion Acts had not been as effective as

planned in keeping the Chinese out, the committee suggested that one additional way of discouraging a Chinese presence in the city would be to enforce vigorously all local and state laws. The Chinese would be unable to comply and would leave. Vigorous enforcement of the law, the committee said, "can hardly fail to drive them from among us." *Examiner*, July 21, 1885, p. 2, col. 4.

159. *Evening Mail*, Oct. 27, 1885, p. 3, col. 2.

160. Ibid., Nov. 24, 1885, p. 3, col. 1. It is unclear which laundry decision he was referring to.

161. Ibid., Dec. 15, 1885, p. 3, cols. 2–3. At approximately this same time the cities of San Jose and Oakland enacted laundry laws of their own, both patterned after the 1880 San Francisco ordinances. San Jose's was sponsored and pushed through to enactment by the city's Anti-Coolie League. See San Jose *Mercury*, Nov. 20, 1885, p. 3, col. 4; Nov. 25, 1885, p. 3, col. 2; Council Minutes, Common Council of San Jose, Nov. 2, 1885, in City Clerk's Office, San Jose, California. The sponsor of the Oakland measure avowed that he saw it as part and parcel of the statewide movement then at high tide to expel the Chinese. "The sentiment of opposition to the Chinese and to use all legal means to expel them from the cities should be generally expressed at this time when Congress is about to take action and everywhere on the coast an anti-Chinese sentiment is shown," he said in urging immediate passage. Two months after the ordinance's enactment, a local paper reported that all of Oakland's Chinese laundrymen were under arrest. The same issue also reported that the men had raised $1,000 to pay an attorney to defend those held in custody. *Morning Call*, Jan. 19, 1886, p. 6, col. 4; Mar. 17, 1886, p. 3, col. 5. The latter article noted: "The Chinese are kept constantly informed of the latest news. A Chinaman in a store on Washington near Eighth translates from the morning newspapers the news concerning the anti-Chinese agitation and writes a synopsis of it in Chinese. A sheet containing this news is sent to the nearest store kept by Chinese. A copy is made and posted upon a window. The sheet is then sent to the next store where another copy is made and posted."

162. *Evening Mail*, Jan. 21, 1886, p. 3, col. 3. On January 27 the paper reported that the law firm of Terry, Campbell, and Bennett had been retained "by twenty-two Chinamen and two white clients to break the ordinance." Ibid., Jan. 27, 1886, p. 3, col. 4.

163. *Evening Mail*, Jan. 27, 1886, p. 3, col. 4.

164. Petition for Writ of Habeas Corpus, p. 9, In re Tie Loy case file, No. 3956, Record Group 21, Old Circuit Court, Civil Cases, National Archives, San Francisco Branch.

165. According to the report of the decision, Alfred Clarke was on the brief for the city of Stockton along with the city attorney.

166. In re Tie Loy, 26 F. 611, 612 (C.C.D. Cal. 1886).

167. Ibid., p. 613.

168. Ibid.

169. Ibid., p. 615.

170. Ibid., pp. 612–13. Laws similar to the Stockton ordinance—measures, that is to say, designed to force Chinese laundries out of the central parts of the cities—were enacted by the city of Modesto and the small town of Napa in the wine-growing region at about this time. (Modesto's ordinance actually preceded

Stockton's by several months.) Both were subjected to court tests. The California Supreme Court sustained the Modesto law in In re Hang Kie, 69 Cal. 149 (1886), an opinion handed down the month following Sawyer's *Tie Loy* decision. The Napa ordinance was nullified by Judge Sawyer's circuit court in April 1887. In re Sam Kee, 31 F. 680 (C.C.N.D. Cal. 1887). Thomas Riordan, counsel for the Tung Hing Tong in the San Francisco cases, represented the Napa laundrymen. His involvement raises the possibility that the litigation may have had the financial support of the San Francisco guild.

171. Carl N. Degler, *Out of Our Past: The Forces That Shaped Modern America* (New York: Harper & Row, 1970), pp. 147–48.

172. Eric Foner, *Free Soil, Free Labor, Free Men: The Ideology of the Republican Party before the Civil War* (New York: Oxford University Press, 1970), p. 300.

173. Degler, *Out of Our Past*, p. 148.

174. On the Jacksonian roots of Stephen Field's jurisprudence see Charles McCurdy, "Justice Field and the Jurisprudence of Government-Business Relations: Some Parameters of Laissez Faire Constitutionalism," *Journal of American History* 61 (1975): 970–1005. On how a common ethos shared by a group of judges can drive decision making, see Robert McCloskey, *The American Supreme Court* (Chicago: University of Chicago Press, 1960), p. 208. McCloskey discusses how a widely shared commitment to racial equality among judges appointed to the federal bench after 1937 explains the venturesomeness of the judges on questions of race discrimination.

175. It was important, of course, that the judges uniformly refused to see laundries classed alongside slaughterhouses and other offensive trades as nuisances. The business of washing and ironing clothes for hire was to the magistrates a classic example of one of the ordinary trades. The San Francisco Police Court judge, Thomas Freelon, called the business of laundering a "useful and necessary sanitary pursuit." To Sawyer it was much the same. Justice Field declared San Francisco's characterization of laundries as inherently dangerous to the public safety or against good morals as "miserable pretense."

176. But note the reference to equal protection in *Soon Kung*.

177. The process of broadening the reach of the Fourteenth Amendment may have begun earlier. Just three years after *Slaughter-House* the Court, without recorded dissent, declared that the due process clause of the Fourteenth Amendment secured the individual "from the arbitrary exercise of the powers of government, unrestrained by the established principles of private rights and distributive justice." United States v. Cruikshank, 92 U.S. 542, 554 (1876).

178. The leading interpreter of Stephen Field's jurisprudence sees the decision as holding in no uncertain terms that the core principles of Field's *Slaughter-House* dissent were the law of the land. McCurdy, "Justice Field and the Jurisprudence of Government-Business Relations," p. 978.

CHAPTER FIVE

1. Act of Apr. 28, 1860, ch. 329, 1860 Cal. Stat. 321–22.
2. Act of Mar. 24, 1866, ch. 342, 1866 Cal. Stat. 398.
3. Act of Apr. 14, 1870, ch. 556, 1869–70 Cal. Stat. 839.
4. 59 Mass. (5 Cush.) 198 (1850).

5. Ward v. Flood, 48 Cal. 36, 52–56 (1874).

6. Ibid., pp. 51, 57.

7. *Amendments to the Codes of California*, 1873–74, p. 97.

8. For a consistently interesting and illuminating discussion of Chinese efforts to gain access to public education, including an account of the episode chronicled in this chapter see Victor Low, *The Unimpressible Race: A Century of Educational Struggle by the Chinese in San Francisco* (San Francisco: East West Publishing Co., 1982). The information on the Presbyterian mission is taken from Low, p. 13.

9. Ibid., p. 14.

10. A school census taken in 1874 reported that there were 2,131 Chinese children under seventeen years of age in the state, 1,286 of whom lived in San Francisco. Ibid., p. 49.

11. *Amendments to the Codes of California*, 1873–74, p. 97.

12. *Record-Union*, Mar. 30, 1875, p. 3, col. 4. The previous month, seven Chinese, describing themselves as laborers, successfully petitioned the board for permission to use a public schoolroom in the evenings for purposes of English-language instruction. They told the board they would supply their own teacher. *Record-Union*, Feb. 23, 1875, p. 3, col. 3.

13. As quoted in the *New York Times*, Apr. 12, 1875, p. 8, col. 4.

14. *Chinese Record* (English-language version), Feb. 12, 1877, p. 1, cols. 5–6.

15. *Daily Alta California*, Aug. 22, 1877, p. 1, col. 5.

16. *Morning Call*, Mar. 7, 1878, p. 2, col. 3.

17. Journal of the Assembly, Mar. 22, 1878, 22d Sess., p. 672. *Daily Alta California*, Mar. 24, 1878, p. 1, col. 4. The submission of the original petition is nowhere noted in the official assembly journal.

18. Act of Apr. 7, 1880, ch. 80, 1880 Cal. Stat. 142–43, 152.

19. Affidavit of Joseph Tape, pp. 2–3, 6, Transcript on Appeal, Tape v. Hurley, California Supreme Court, State Archives, Sacramento (No. 9916).

20. *Evening Bulletin*, Sept. 16, 1884, p. 1, col. 6. According to the *Bulletin* there were then some 1,250 Chinese children of school age in the city.

21. *Evening Bulletin*, Oct. 22, 1884, p. 1, col. 5.

22. *Chronicle*, Oct. 11, 1884, p. 2, col. 3.; *Evening Bulletin*, Oct. 22, 1884, p. 1, col. 5.

23. Lorenzo Sawyer to Matthew Deady, Oct. 13, 1884, Deady Papers, Oregon Historical Society Library, Portland.

24. See accounts in *Evening Bulletin*, Oct. 22, 1884, p. 1, col. 5; *Daily Alta California*, Oct. 22, 1884, p. 1, col. 5. The accounts differ slightly, the *Alta* reporting that only one member voted against the resolution; the *Bulletin* reported three negative votes.

25. Affidavit of Joseph Tape, pp. 4–5, Tape v. Hurley.

26. Transcript on Appeal, pp. 13–14, Tape v. Hurley. The defendants also made some technical, procedural objections, alleging, for example, that the suit should have been brought against the board of education as a corporate entity and not against the named individuals.

27. This account of the decision is a composite taken from the *Chronicle*, Jan. 10, 1885, p. 2, col. 3; *Morning Call*, Jan. 10, 1885, p. 3, col. 6; *Evening Bulletin*, Jan. 10, 1885, p. 2, col. 3.

28. *Daily Alta California*, Jan. 11, 1885, p. 1, col. 5.

29. *Examiner,* Jan. 15, 1885, p. 2, col. 6; *Evening Bulletin,* Jan. 15, 1885, p. 1, col. 5.

30. Respondent's Brief, pp. 15–16, Tape v. Hurley.

31. Ibid., pp. 28–29. Elsewhere in the brief, and in connection with another point, Gibson had pointed out that Japanese children were attending public schools in San Francisco. Ibid., p. 27.

32. Ibid., pp. 35–36.

33. Respondent's Points and Authorities, p. 39, Tape v. Hurley.

34. Tape v. Hurley, 66 Cal. 473 (1885).

35. *Evening Bulletin,* Mar. 19, 1885, p. 1, col. 5.

36. Act of Mar. 12, 1885, ch. 97, 1885 Cal. Stat. 99–100.

37. See Board of Supervisors, *San Francisco Municipal Reports for the Year Ending June 30, 1886,* p. 632; *San Francisco Municipal Reports for the Year Ending June 30, 1887,* p. 458.

38. Wong Him v. Callahan, 119 F. 381 (C.C.N.D. Cal. 1902). The San Francisco school authorities did not even bother to defend against the lawsuit.

39. The law permitting school districts to segregate Chinese children (its terms were later changed to include Japanese children as well) was not repealed until 1947. Ch. 737, 1947 Cal. Stat. 1792 1.

40. *Daily Alta California,* Apr. 16, 1885, p. 1, col. 3. Quoted in Low, *The Unimpressible Race,* Appendix D.

CHAPTER SIX

1. *Congressional Globe,* 40th Cong., 2d Sess. (1867–68), pp. 837–38. Cited in Edward P. Hutchinson, *Legislative History of American Immigration Policy, 1798–1965* (Philadelphia: University of Pennsylvania Press, 1981), p. 53.

2. "Memorial of the Senate of California to the Congress of the United States, August 13, 1877," 22d Sess., Cal. Legis., Appendix to the Journals of the Senate and Assembly, vol. 3, pp. 8–9.

3. H. R. 2433, 45th Cong., 3d Sess. (1879).

4. Secretary of State W. M. Evarts, Minute of a Conversation with the Chinese Minister, Feb. 18, 1879, in *Notes from the Chinese Legation in the United States to the Department of State, 1868–1906,* microfilm, Reel 1, National Archives.

5. *Congressional Record,* 45th Cong., 3d Sess. (1879), p. 2275.

6. Hutchinson, *Legislative History,* p. 74.

7. Treaty of Immigration Between the United States and China, Nov. 17, 1880, 22 Stat. 826.

8. Ibid., art. III.

9. The president characterized the twenty-year suspension of immigration as unreasonably long and violative of the spirit, if not the letter, of the 1880 agreement. The system of personal registration and passports he described as undemocratic and hostile to the spirit of American institutions. *Congressional Record,* 47th Cong., 1st Sess. (1882), pp. 2551–52. The Chinese legation in Washington had itself taken strong exception to this provision while the measure was under deliberation. See Memorandum of Apr. 1, 1882, *Notes from the Chinese Legation.*

10. Congress may at this time have been having second thoughts about the policy of open immigration in general. Later in the same session it enacted the first general federal immigration law. Captioned "An Act to Regulate Immigration," it imposed a tax of fifty cents on all immigrants arriving in U.S. ports and barred the landing of persons convicted of crime, the mentally ill, and those likely to become a public charge. Act of Aug. 3, 1882, ch. 376, 22 Stat. 214.

11. Act of May 6, 1882, ch. 126, 22 Stat. 58, § 1. The act made clear that the term "skilled" laborers included those engaged in mining. Ibid., § 15.

12. Ibid., §§ 3, 4.

13. Ibid., § 6.

14. Ibid., § 14.

15. *Daily Alta California,* May 9, 1882, p. 2, col. 1.

16. *Morning Call,* May 4, 1882, p. 2, col. 1.

17. *Chronicle,* May 9, 1882, p. 2, col. 2.

18. *Evening Post,* Apr. 22, 1882, p. 4, cols. 1–2. At the very time that California was doing all in its power to persuade the federal government to cut off the flow of Chinese immigrants into the state, it was exerting itself mightily to promote European immigration. See, e.g., the article in the *Evening Post* reporting with great satisfaction the arrival of approximately three hundred immigrants the previous week. One can find numerous articles like this in the press during the decade of the 1880s. Jan. 29, 1883, p. 1, col. 2.

19. This chronology of events is taken from Note from the Chinese legation in Washington to the Secretary of State, June 8, 1882, in *Notes from the Chinese Legation* and In re Leong Yick Dew, 19 F. 490 (C.C.D. Cal. 1884).

20. *Morning Call,* Aug. 19, 1882, p. 1, col. 7. An open letter from a Chinese diplomat that appeared several months later in a New York City Chinese-language newspaper may shed some light on the consulate's participation in this and later Exclusion Act cases. In that letter, addressed to all Chinese living in the United States, the Chinese consul in New York, Ming Ou-yang, said that since coming to this country he had seen the Chinese "being humiliated and crushed" and that it was essential for the Chinese to continue to employ lawyers to represent them in important cases if they wished adequately to protect themselves. *Chinese American,* Mar. 31, 1883. In 1885 Ming would be appointed consul general at San Francisco. Shih-shan Henry Tsai, *China and the Overseas Chinese in the United States, 1868–1911* (Fayetteville, Ark.: University of Arkansas Press, 1983), p. 71.

21. Petition for Habeas Corpus, In re Ah Tie, No. 2876, Record Group 21, Old Circuit Court, Civil Cases, Common Law Series, National Archives, Pacific Sierra Branch [hereafter Ah Tie case file].

22. Return to Writ, Ah Tie case file.

23. Field had handed down the decision in *In re Quong Woo* on August 7.

24. *Evening Bulletin,* Aug. 21, 1882, p. 2, col. 2; *Daily Alta California,* Aug. 22, 1882, p. 1, col. 3.

25. Case of the Chinese Cabin Waiter, 13 F. 286, 288–89 (C.C.D. Cal. 1882).

26. Ibid., p. 289.

27. Case of the Chinese Laborers on Shipboard (*In re Ah Tie* and others), 13 F. 291, 292–93 (C.C.D. Cal. 1882).

28. Ibid., p. 294.

29. In re Low Yam Chow, The Case of the Chinese Merchant, 13 F. 605, 613 (C.C.D. Cal. 1882).

30. Ibid., pp. 606–9.

31. Ibid., p. 610.

32. Ibid., p. 611.

33. Ibid., p. 617. Some months later Judge Deady of the U.S. District Court in Oregon reached the same conclusion that Field and Hoffman had on the applicability of Section 6 to Chinese other than laborers who did not reside in China. In re Ho King, 14 F. 724 (D. Or. 1883). This case raised as an initial matter the question of whether the term "laborer" in the 1882 act encompassed a Chinese actor or theatrical performer. Judge Deady held that it did not.

34. *Morning Call,* Oct. 13, 1882, p. 2, col. 1.

35. United States v. Douglas, 17 F. 634 (C.C.D. Mass. 1883).

36. See, for example, *Daily Alta California,* Aug. 23, 1883, p. 2, col. 1.

37. See account in the *Examiner,* Sept. 8, 1883, p. 3, col. 4.

38. In re Ah Lung, the Chinese Laborer from Hong Kong, 18 F. 28, 32 (C.C.D. Cal. 1883).

39. Ibid., pp. 31–32.

40. Ibid., p. 32.

41. See the *Evening Bulletin,* Sept. 6, 1883, p. 2, col. 4; *Chronicle,* Sept. 25, 1883, p. 4, col. 2.

42. *Examiner,* Sept. 8, 1883, p. 3, col. 4.

43. *Chronicle,* Oct. 23, 1883, p. 8, col. 5. Bee told a joint congressional committee in 1891 that the Chinese consulate had for some time had a contract with Riordan under which he was obliged to represent Chinese who had been refused the right to land and whose cases the consulate considered both meritorious and significant. Bee made clear that consular officials determined which cases were to be brought and that they did not support everyone's right to land. Riordan was paid a flat yearly salary for his efforts according to Bee and had to take on whatever cases the consulate asked him to and to pursue them up to the Supreme Court if necessary, but he was also free to take on cases independently, which Bee said he did. See H. R. 4048, 51st Cong., 2d Sess., *Congressional Record,* pp. 384–85, 404–5. It is clear from the newspaper reports that Riordan was not the only attorney the consulate used although he may have been the only one under a retainer like the one just described.

44. *Evening Bulletin,* Oct. 23, 1883, p. 3, col. 4.

45. *Evening Bulletin,* Oct. 29, 1883, p. 3, col. 8.

46. Account of the hearings taken from *Evening Bulletin,* Oct. 29, 1883, p. 3, col. 8; *Daily Alta California,* Oct. 30, 1883, p. 1, col. 4.

47. In re Chin Ah On and others, 18 F. 506 (D. Cal. 1883).

48. Ibid., p. 507.

49. Circuit Judge Sawyer ordered two other Chinese aboard the *Rio* released from custody on the grounds of former residence without issuing an opinion on the subject. See *Chronicle,* Oct. 24, 1883, p. 1, col. 1.

50. See In re Chow Goo Pooi, 25 F. 77, 82 (D. Cal. 1884) and In re Tung Yeong, 19 F. 184 (C.C.D. Cal. 1884).

51. See In re Tung Yeong, 19 F. 184, 186–87 (1884).

52. Testifying in 1891, Consul Bee said the press had greatly exaggerated the

consulate's involvement in the many Chinese habeas corpus cases that had been brought in the federal courts during the previous decade. Most of these, he said, were brought independent of the consulate and involved lawyers who had no connection with it. There were about six lawyers, he said, who were involved in this business on a regular basis. He speculated that the litigants either paid these lawyers out of their own purses or got assistance from their clans ashore. H. R. 4048, 51st Cong., 2d Sess., *Congressional Record*, pp. 398–99. For very informative commentary by an attorney involved in the bringing of habeas corpus cases by individual Chinese during the mid-1880s, on how these cases were initiated and pursued, and on what on average they might have cost the litigants, see *Daily Alta California*, Aug. 26, 1885, p. 1, cols. 1–2.

53. In re Tong Ah Chee, 23 F. 441 (D. Cal. 1883).

54. 19 F. 490 (C.C.D. Cal. 1884).

55. Ibid.

56. *Daily Alta California*, Dec. 12, 1883, p. 2, col. 1.

57. Act of July 5, 1884, ch. 220, § 4, 23 Stat. 115 (1884).

58. Ibid., § 6.

59. Ibid., § 15.

60. Memo left with the Secretary of State, June 20, 1884, *Notes from the Chinese Legation*.

61. *Morning Call*, Aug. 5, 1884, p. 4, col. 2.

62. *Chronicle*, Aug. 8, 1884, p. 2, col. 4; *Evening Bulletin*, Aug. 7, 1884, p. 2, col. 3.

63. *Evening Bulletin*, Aug. 4, 1884, p. 3, col. 7.

64. *Examiner*, Aug. 5, 1884, p. 3, col. 2.

65. 21 F. 182, 183 (C.C.D. Cal. 1884).

66. Ibid., p. 186.

67. *Evening Bulletin*, Sept. 16, 1884, p. 2, col. 3.

68. *Daily Alta California*, Sept. 27, 1884, p. 1, col. 3.

69. *Morning Call*, Sept. 27, 1884, p. 3, col. 4.

70. *Evening Bulletin*, Sept. 27, 1884, p. 3, col. 5. The then existing law governing habeas appeals is to be found in Revised Statutes of the United States of 1875, Sections 650, 763, 764. On March 3, 1885, Congress amended the federal habeas corpus act to permit appeals to be taken to the Supreme Court from the decisions of the circuit courts in all cases where the petitioner alleged that he was restrained of his liberty in violation of the Constitution, laws, or treaties of the United States. Act of Mar. 3, 1885, ch. 353, 23 Stat. 437.

71. In re Cheen [Chew] Heong, 21 F. 791, 792–93 (C.C.D. Cal. 1884).

72. Ibid., p. 793.

73. Revised Statutes of the United States of 1875, § 650.

74. *Cheen Heong*, pp. 794ff.

75. *Morning Call*, Sept. 28, 1884, p. 1, col. 6.

76. 83 U.S. (16 Wall.) 36 (1873), p. 73. Account of oral argument taken from the *Evening Bulletin*, Sept. 29, 1884, p. 3, col. 5.

77. According to the opinion of Justice Field. In re Look Tin Sing, 21 F. 905, 910 (C.C.D. Cal. 1884).

78. Both Field and Judge Sawyer had adverted to this problem in the course of oral argument. The Miller dictum taken literally, of course, would have cast doubt

upon the citizenship of many thousands of residents of European descent. Pomeroy sought to deflect that concern by arguing that a distinction could be made between parents who were capable of naturalization, as the parents of all Europeans were, and the parents of those like the petitioner who were not. The Fourteenth Amendment, he argued, should be read in conjunction with the federal naturalization legislation, and the provision in question should be seen as applying only to the children of "the free Caucasian races of the world." *Evening Bulletin*, Sept. 29, 1884, p. 3, col. 5.

Though neither counsel nor the judges brought it up, the applicability of the "citizenship by birth" provision of the Fourteenth Amendment to the Chinese had in fact been discussed during the debates in the 39th Congress, with at least one Senator, a Senator from California no less, arguing that it clearly did apply to them. See chapter 1, n. 186.

79. *Look Tin Sing*, pp. 906–8.

80. Ibid., pp. 910–11.

81. See *Morning Call*, Sept. 28, 1884, p. 1, col. 6; *Evening Bulletin*, Sept. 29, 1884, pp. 1, 3, col. 5.

82. The appeal to the Supreme Court may have been partially funded by the Chinese Six Companies. The *Evening Bulletin* reported on October 8 that the Six Companies had met since Field's decision and had discussed the feasibility of retaining counsel "to press their side of the case." Oct. 8, 1884, p. 3, col. 8.

83. The Supreme Court had advanced the case on its calendar pursuant to a request from the attorney general, acting on behalf of the State Department, which wanted a quick decision from the high tribunal on the impact of the 1884 act. See Secretary of State Frelinghuysen to Tsai Kwoh-ching of the Chinese legation in Washington, Oct. 22, 1884, *Papers Relating to the Foreign Relations of the United States*, H.R. Exec. Doc., 48th Cong., 2d Sess., 1:117 (1885).

84. Chew Heong v. United States, 112 U.S. 536, 543, 550 (1884).

85. Ibid., p. 555.

86. Ibid., p. 554.

87. Ibid., p. 560.

88. Ibid., p. 561. Field did not say how he thought the treaty might apply to a Chinese laborer in the United States in November 1880 who left for a temporary absence just before the passage of the 1882 act and who sought to return, perforce without a certificate, afterwards.

89. Ibid., p. 562.

90. Ibid., p. 569.

91. Ibid., p. 568.

92. Ibid., pp. 569–71.

93. See correspondence between the Chinese legation and the Department of State, Mar. 7 through Mar. 19, 1884, in *Foreign Relations of the United States*, H.R. Exec. Doc., 48th Cong., 2d Sess., 1:106–9 (1885).

94. See correspondence between the Chinese legation and the Department of State, July-October 1884, in *Foreign Relations of the United States*, H.R. Exec. Doc., 48th Cong., 2d Sess., 1:112–18 (1885).

95. See Treasury Circular, Jan. 14, 1885, in *Foreign Relations of the United States*, H.R. Exec. Doc., 49th Cong., 1st Sess., 1:192 (1886).

96. *Evening Bulletin*, Jan. 22, 1885, p. 2, col. 4.

97. *Examiner,* Jan. 15, 1885, p. 3, col. 1. *Morning Call,* Jan. 15, 1885, supp., p. 1, col. 4. Another case involving a man seeking to land on similar facts was heard the same day and decided the same way.
98. *Evening Bulletin,* Mar. 11, 1885, p. 2, col. 5.
99. In re Ah Ping, 23 F. 329, 330 (C.C.D. Cal. 1885).
100. Ibid., p. 334.
101. 25 F. 141 (D. Cal. 1885).
102. *Evening Bulletin,* Oct. 12, 1885, p. 3, col. 7.
103. *In re Jung Ah Lung.*
104. See Transcript of Record, pp. 14ff, United States Supreme Court Records and Briefs, United States v. Jung Ah Lung case file.
105. Ibid, p. 16.
106. Ibid., pp. 17–18.
107. Ibid., pp. 19ff.
108. United States v. Jung Ah Lung, 124 U.S. 621, 628–32 (1888).
109. Ibid., pp. 634–35.
110. Ibid., pp. 635–39.
111. See In re Ah Lung, 18 F. 28 (C.C.D. Cal. 1883).
112. They must certainly have taken considerable satisfaction at the outcome of the *Look Tin Sing* litigation as well. Though this was not an exclusion act case, it certainly did have an important impact on Chinese immigration rights.

CHAPTER SEVEN

1. See Roger Daniels, ed., *Anti-Chinese Violence in North America* (New York: Arno Press, 1978). On the Los Angeles riot see William R. Locklear, "The Celestials and the Angels: A Study of the Anti-Chinese Movement In Los Angeles to 1882," in Daniels, *Anti-Chinese Violence,* reprinted from *Historical Society of Southern California Quarterly* 42 (1960): 239–56.
2. The incident was reported in the Chinese press. San Francisco *China News,* May 1, 1875.
3. In October 1883 the Chinese Six Companies offered a reward of $10 to anyone providing information that led to the arrest of persons perpetrating acts of anti-Chinese violence. A copy of the announcement appears in the San Francisco Chinese-language *Chinese Daily Evening News,* Oct. 12, 1883.
4. In the Watsonville incident the Chinese filed three lawsuits demanding a total of $205,000 in damages from the perpetrators. Ibid.
5. Paul Crane and Alfred Larson, "The Chinese Massacre," *Annals of Wyoming* 12 (1940): 47–55, in Daniels, *Anti-Chinese Violence.* See also the copious and detailed documentation of the incident prepared under auspices of the Chinese consulate in San Francisco, in *Papers Relating to the Foreign Relations of the United States,* H.R. Exec. Doc., 49th Cong., 2d Sess., 1:109–47 (1886).
6. *Oriental,* Aug. 13, 1886. The newspaper made an invidious comparison between the quick and decisive actions taken by the Chinese government in response to the anti-Western rioting in the city of Tientsin and the sluggishness with which it believed the U.S. authorities were dealing with anti-Chinese rioting in the American West.
7. See W. P. Wilcox, "Anti-Chinese Riots in Washington," *Washington His-*

torical Quarterly 20 (1929): 204–12; Jules Karlin, "The Anti-Chinese Outbreaks in Seattle," *Pacific Northwest Quarterly* 39 (1948): 103–29; and Karlin, "The Anti-Chinese Outbreak in Tacoma," *Pacific Historical Review* 23 (1954): 271–83. All reprinted in Daniels, *Anti-Chinese Violence*.

8. See, e.g., Sacramento *Record-Union*, Feb. 23, 1886, p. 1, col. 6 (reporting raid on the Chinese quarter of Oregon City, Oregon) and Mar. 7, 1886 (reporting expulsion of Chinese from Mt. Tabor, near Portland).

9. See, e.g., reports of anti-Chinese demonstrations in Truckee, California, which forced the discharge of all Chinese from employment. *Record-Union*, Jan. 18, 1886, p. 2, col. 4; *Daily Alta California*, Feb. 14, 1886, p. 5, col. 3. Accounts of mass meetings can be found in virtually every issue of the major San Francisco and Sacramento dailies from December 1885 to March 1886. On March 2, 1886, U.S. District Attorney for Oregon Lewis McArthur wrote to the attorney general in Washington, D.C.: "Large bodies of men, presumably citizens of the United States, have in nearly every town and village throughout the state organized themselves into societies whose object, as near as I can ascertain, is to expel the Chinese from our limits." Department of Justice Year File 980–84, No. 1659.

10. See *Foreign Relations of the United States*, H.R. Exec. Doc., 49th Cong., 2d Sess., 1:101–47, 158–68 (1886). See also Shih-shan Henry Tsai, *China and the Overseas Chinese in the United States, 1868–1911* (Fayetteville, Ark.: University of Arkansas Press, 1983) pp. 72–77.

11. *Foreign Relations of the United States*, H.R. Exec. Doc. No. 137, 49th Cong., 1st Sess., 1:194 (1885).

12. Ibid., Doc. No. 142, p. 196.

13. Text of the telegram can be found in *Record-Union*, Mar. 8, 1886, p. 4, col. 2.

14. *Record-Union*, Feb. 17, 1886, p. 4, col. 1.

15. Proclamation by President Grover Cleveland of Nov. 7, 1885, in *Foreign Relations of the United States*, H.R. Exec. Doc., 49th Cong., 1st Sess., 1:197–98 (1885).

16. James D. Richardson, *Messages and Papers of the Presidents, 1789–1897* (Washington, D.C.: Government Printing Office, 1898), 8:329. Three months later he sent a special message to Congress elaborating on the same theme and asking the body, as a gesture of goodwill, to make an appropriation for the payment of compensation to the victims of the Wyoming massacre. Message of Mar. 1, 1886, in Richardson, *Messages and Papers*, 8:383–86.

17. The Chinese and American positions were first set out in a diplomatic exchange concerning a riot in Denver in the fall of 1880 that took one life and destroyed a considerable amount of property. To a request from the Chinese minister that the U.S. government provide compensation for property losses and see that the guilty parties were arrested then Secretary of State William Evarts replied that the U.S. government had no responsibility to indemnify the victims and was powerless to take action against the wrongdoers. "The powers of direct intervention on the part of this Government [in the affairs of a state] are limited by the Constitution," he wrote. "Under the limitations of that instrument, the Government of the Federal Union cannot interfere in regard to the administration or execution of the municipal laws of a State of the Union." *Foreign Relations of the United States*, H.R. Exec. Doc., 47th Cong., 1st Sess., 1:319 (1881). The Chinese

minister, Ch'en Lan-pin, replied to Evarts that the case seemed different to him since it involved individuals who were present in this country under the explicit provisions of a treaty negotiated between China and the general government of the United States. "The case under consideration," he wrote, "should be a question of intercourse between China and the United States, and different from that to be dealt with under the ordinary internal administration of a State. It was with this view that I had . . . requested you to cause this case to be examined." *Foreign Relations of the United States*, H.R. Exec. Doc., 47th Cong., 1st Sess., 1:322 (1881). See also letters of Nov. 30, 1885, and Feb. 15, 1886, from Chinese Minister Cheng Tsao-ju to Secretary of State Thomas F. Bayard and Bayard's reply to Cheng of Feb. 18, 1886 in *Foreign Relations of the United States*, H.R. Exec. Doc., 49th Cong., 2d Sess., 1:101–9, 154–56, 158–59 (1886). These letters concerned Rock Springs and other disturbances of 1885–86. The Chinese minister insisted that the national government take direct and forthright measures to end what he called the reign of terror among his countrymen. "It does not become me to indicate what these measures should be. Neither is it my province to consider the internal relations of Government or the workings of the domestic laws of this country," he wrote. It just seemed to him that the national government was both empowered and obliged to do something. Letter of Feb. 15, 1886, Doc. No. 65. Bayard reaffirmed the hands-off position of his predecessor Evarts.

On the early history of U.S.-China diplomacy, see Kenneth W. Rea, ed., *Early Sino-American Relations, 1841–1912: The Collected Articles of Earl Swisher* (Boulder, Colo.: Westview Press, 1977); Delber L. McKee, *Chinese Exclusion Versus the Open Door Policy, 1900–1906* (Detroit: Wayne State University Press, 1977).

18. Washington territorial authorities, to their credit, did take rather forthright steps to deal with the anti-Chinese disturbances. The perpetrators of the Squak Valley killings were prosecuted for murder. Also, the governor of the territory declared martial law in the wake of the February riot in Seattle. For an interesting discussion of the treatment of Chinese litigants by the courts of the Pacific Northwest during this period see John R. Wunder, "The Chinese and the Courts in the Pacific Northwest: Justice Denied?" *Pacific Historical Review* 52 (1983): 191–211.

19. *Record-Union*, Feb. 19, 1886, p. 3, col. 1.

20. See the *Enterprise*, Oregon City, Oregon, Feb. 25, 1886, Mar. 4, 1886.

21. See, e.g., *Record-Union*, Feb. 23, 1886, p. 3, col. 1. He told a reporter that if he had officers to accompany him, he would take the illegally evicted Chinese back to Nicolaus.

22. Although direct evidence is lacking, it is rather difficult to believe that the two actions were not part of a coordinated strategy.

23. See Lewis L. McArthur, U.S. Attorney for Oregon, to the Attorney General of the United States, Mar. 2, 1886. Department of Justice Year File 980–84, No. 1659.

24. See In re Baldwin, File 3989, National Archives, San Francisco branch.

25. *Record-Union*, Mar. 13, 1886, p. 8, col. 1.

26. Act of Apr. 20, 1871, ch. 22, § 2, 17 Stat. 13.

27. 106 U.S. 629 (1883).

28. 109 U.S. 3 (1883).

29. Civil Rights Act of 1875, § 1, 18 Stat. 335 (pt. 3).

30. No one in the United States attorney's office had been consulted about either the filing of the complaint or the issuance of the arrest warrant. See S. G. Hilborn to Attorney General A. H. Garland, Apr. 5, 1886. Department of Justice Year File 980–84, No. 2498.

31. Best account of the argument is to be found in the *Record-Union*, Mar. 17, 1886, p. 3, cols. 2–3.

32. Ibid.

33. 62 U.S. (21 How.) 506 (1859).

34. *Record-Union*, Mar. 18, 1886, p. 2, col. 4.

35. Throughout the proceedings Hilborn seemed to be little more than a semi-cooperative bystander. The fact that from beginning to end this criminal case was under the management and control of private attorneys was never raised as an issue by counsel for the other side.

36. Various accounts of the March 18 hearing are to be found in the San Francisco *Bulletin* and *Evening Post* of that date and in the San Francisco *Morning Call*, Mar. 19, 1886, p. 3, col. 6, and the *Record-Union*, Mar. 19, 1886, p. 3, col. 6.

37. *Evening Post*, Mar. 30, 1886, p. 1, col. 2; *Morning Call*, Mar. 31, 1886, p. 3, col. 5. The inspiration for using Section 5519 came, in all probability, from events in Washington Territory. The previous November, W. H. White, United States attorney for the territory, acting entirely on his own initiative, had secured several grand jury indictments under the section against anti-Chinese rioters. (See Department of Justice Year File 980–84, Nos. 2017, 2437, 2856, 9497, 9733, 9858.) Direct evidence is lacking, but one may speculate with some confidence that White's theory in proceeding under the section rested on an important dictum in the *Civil Rights Cases*. The constitutional issue under review in those cases, it will be recalled, was almost identical to the issue in *Harris*, namely the extent to which Congress could legislate against purely private conduct. While the Court held that congressional power was quite limited when it came to the private conduct of individuals within the states, it declared that Congress had plenary power to pass legislation in every branch of municipal regulation when it came to the *territories* (109 U.S. 3, 19), and the Court in fact intimated that the legislation it was in the process of voiding insofar as it applied to the state might well pass constitutional muster as applied to the territories. (Both the legislation under review in the *Civil Rights Cases* and Section 5519 applied to the acts of individuals in any state or territory.)

It was one thing to seek to invoke the section in a federal territory, quite another to attempt to invoke it in the states where the Supreme Court had said with apparent finality it could have no application.

38. These sections had also been used in the Washington prosecutions.

39. *Morning Call*, Mar. 31, 1886, p. 3, col. 5.

40. *Evening Post*, Mar. 30, 1886, p. 1, col. 2.

41. The full text of the opinion was published in most San Francisco newspapers the next day. See, e.g., *Morning Call*, Apr. 1, 1886, p. 1, col. 1. The official report appears in In re Baldwin, 27 F. 187 (C.C.D. Cal. 1886). Citations here are to the official report.

42. *In re Baldwin*, pp. 192–93.

43. Ibid., p. 193.
44. In re Tiburcio Parrott, 1 F. 481 (C.C.D. Cal. 1880).
45. 22 Stat. 826, 827.
46. *In re Baldwin,* p. 191.
47. Ibid., p. 189.
48. 95 U.S. 80 (1877).
49. Ibid., p. 89.
50. *In re Baldwin,* p. 191.
51. Ibid., p. 194.
52. Under Section 6509 of the Revised Statutes of the United States of 1875, when, upon the trial or hearing of a criminal proceeding before a circuit court, a point occurred on which the judges were divided in opinion, the point of disagreement could be certified to the Supreme Court for authoritative decision at its next session upon motion of either the prosecution or the defense.
53. *In re Baldwin,* pp. 194–95. The "other similar cases" referred to the prosecutions then underway or under consideration in Washington and in Oregon.
54. Lorenzo Sawyer to A. H. Garland, Attorney General, Apr. 5, 1886. Department of Justice, Year File 980–84, No. 2497.
55. Ibid., No. 2559.
56. Brief on Behalf of Petitioner, p. 20, case file, Baldwin v. Franks, 120 U.S. 678, U.S. Supreme Court Records and Briefs.
57. Act of May 31, 1870, ch. 94, § 6, 16 Stat. 140, 141.
58. Brief for Respondent, pp. 15–18, case file, Baldwin v. Franks, U.S. Supreme Court Records and Briefs [hereafter Brief For Respondent].
59. Act of July 31, 1861, ch. 33, 12 Stat. 284. Re-enacted in Act of Apr. 20, 1871, ch. 22, 17 Stat. 13.
60. Brief for Respondent, pp. 18–22. At the time Deady had expressed doubts about the applicability of Section 5519 and did not instruct the grand jury on this section. See In re Impaneling and Instructing the Grand Jury, 26 F. 749 (D. Or. 1886) and the *Enterprise,* Oregon City, Oregon, Mar. 25, 1886.
61. Brief for Respondent, pp. 29–33.
62. While the case was pending yet another similar incident occurred. In August 1886 a group of one hundred men forcibly drove eighty-seven Chinese miners from Douglass Island in Alaska Territory, took them in small boats to Juneau and put them aboard small schooners, which conveyed them down the coast to a barren coastline. There they were abandoned, suffering from hunger and cold. They probably would have died had not a passenger vessel rescued them and returned them to Douglass Island. Fearful for their lives, the miners borrowed money from their employers and bought passage to San Francisco. Several months later, some of the miners submitted a formal petition to the Chinese minister in Washington, naming the ringleaders of the mob that had attacked them and detailing their monetary losses. They asked that the perpetrators be punished and that indemnification be awarded them. The Chinese minister transmitted their request to the secretary of state. *Foreign Relations of the United States,* H.R. Exec. Doc., 50th Cong., 2d Sess., 1:363–65 (1889).
63. Baldwin v. Franks, 120 U.S. 678, 683 (1887).
64. Ibid., p. 682.
65. Ibid., p. 684.

66. Ibid., p. 689, quoting Virginia Coupon Cases, 114 U.S. 269, 305 (1885).
67. *Baldwin*, p. 685.
68. 92 U.S. 214 (1875).
69. Ibid., p. 221, quoted with approval in *Baldwin*, p. 686.
70. See text at p. 183.
71. *Baldwin*, pp. 688–99.
72. Ibid., p. 685.
73. Ibid., pp. 690–92.
74. Ibid., pp. 692–94.
75. Ibid., pp. 694–98.
76. Ibid., p. 704.
77. Ibid., p. 705.
78. Ibid., p. 707.
79. As reported in the *Evening Post*, Mar. 22, 1887.
80. *Record-Union*, Mar. 9, 1887, p. 2, col. 2.
81. *Daily Alta California*, Mar. 10, 1887, p. 4, col. 2.
82. *Evening Post*, Mar. 8, 1887.
83. It is significant to note that on the very day of the Nicolaus incident, Ming Ou-yang, the consul general in San Francisco, and Consul Bee had telegraphed Governor George Stoneman of California, pleading that he take immediate action but had received a terse and completely noncommittal reply. See *Foreign Relations of the United States*, H.R. Exec. Doc., 49th Cong., 2d Sess., 1:158 (1886).
84. See Wing Hing v. Eureka, File 3948, National Archives, San Francisco branch.
85. Note left by Chinese Minister Chang Yin-huan at the Department of State, Mar. 18, 1887, in *Foreign Relations of the United States*, H.R. Exec. Doc., 50th Cong., 2d Sess., 1:368–69 (1888). The Chinese legation continued to press this line of argument—that the *Baldwin* decision had removed any doubts as to Congress's power to legislate to protect the Chinese—in subsequent communications to the State Department. In a letter dated August 16, 1887, the legation urged passage of federal legislation to protect Chinese laborers. And in a letter dated February 29, 1888, it made the interesting, specific suggestion that the word "citizen" in the first clause of Revised Statutes Section 5508 be changed to "person." See *Notes from the Chinese Legation in the United States to the Department of State, 1886–1906*, microfilm, Reel 1, National Archives.

CHAPTER EIGHT

1. Note from the Chinese foreign office to the British minister at Peking, Aug. 3, 1886, *Notes from the Chinese Legation in the United States to the Department of State, 1868–1906*, Record Group 59, microfilm, National Archives.
2. See Note left at the State Department by the Chinese minister, March 13, 1887, *Papers Relating to the Foreign Relations of the United States*, H.R. Exec. Doc., 50th Cong., 2d Sess., 1:366 (1889).
3. The diplomatic exchanges relevant to the new convention are to be found in *Foreign Relations of the United States*, H.R. Exec. Doc., 50th Cong., 2d Sess., 1:360–401 (1889). See also the very informative accounts of the negotiations in Michael Hunt, *The Making of a Special Relationship: The United States and*

China to 1914 (New York: Columbia University Press, 1983), pp. 104–6, and Shih-shan Henry Tsai, *China and the Overseas Chinese in the United States, 1868–1911* (Fayetteville, Ark.: University of Arkansas Press, 1983), pp. 81ff.

4. Hunt, *Making of a Special Relationship*, p. 105.

5. *Foreign Relations of the United States*, H.R. Exec. Doc., 50th Cong., 2d Sess., 1:354–55.

6. Act of Sept. 13, 1888, ch. 1015, 25 Stat. 476. One who spoke in support of the measure in the Senate was William Stewart of Nevada, the same man who had represented the Chinese in the *Look Tin Sing* case. Stewart had returned to Nevada in 1886 and been elected again as one of the state's representatives to the upper house. Pandering to his own state's anti-Chinese movement, then at high tide, he painted the immigration of the Chinese in the most lurid colors. Not only were the Chinese taking bread from the mouths of white laborers, said Stewart, but they were also threatening the whole of the West Coast with disease and with physical degradation. He held up the example of the Hawaiian islands as a cautionary tale.

> The Sandwich Islands, which a few years ago were the fairest portion of the earth, and held a people remarkable for their physical beauty and for their intellectual strength, although uneducated, will in a generation be depopulated, and there will not be a single native left, because when brought into contact with the Chinese they became diseased and destroyed to such an extent that in one generation more there will not be a full-blooded Sandwich Islander on the face of the earth.
>
> *Congressional Record*, 50th Congress, 1st Sess. (1888), p. 8502.

7. Thomas Bayard to W. L. Putnam, Sept. 13, 1888, quoted in C. Tansill, *The Foreign Policy of Thomas J. Bayard* (New York: Fordham University Press, 1940), p. 171.

8. Act of Oct. 1, 1888, ch. 1064, 25 Stat. 504. For background on the introduction and passage of the Scott Act see Tansill, *The Foreign Policy of Thomas J. Bayard*, pp. 166–75, and Tsai, *China and the Overseas Chinese*, pp. 90–91.

9. *Daily Alta California*, Oct. 2, 1888, p. 1, cols. 3–4; *Chronicle*, Oct. 2, 1888, p. 1, col. 4.

10. *Morning Call*, Oct. 2, 1888, p. 7, col 2. The collector of customs, however, was more skeptical. He expressed the view that as long as the Chinese were granted the right to sue out writs of habeas corpus and were allowed bail no Chinese exclusion legislation would be effective. Ibid.

11. *Morning Call*, Oct. 2, 1888, p. 7, col. 2.

12. *Daily Alta California*, Oct. 2, 1888, p. 1, col. 4.

13. *Morning Call*, Oct. 2, 1888, p. 7, col. 1.

14. *Examiner*, Oct. 3, 1888, p. 6, col. 2, citing the Customs House register. Some years later the Chinese legation put the number at twenty thousand. Note to Secretary of State Blaine, Mar. 26, 1890, *Notes from the Chinese Legation*.

15. *Morning Call*, Oct. 2, 1888, p. 1, col. 4.

16. *Daily Alta California*, Oct. 2, 1888, p. 1, col. 5; Oct. 5, 1888, p. 2, col. 2.

17. Telegram of Oct. 10, 1888, *Notes from the Chinese Legation*.

18. *Morning Call*, Oct. 12, 1888, p. 7, col. 1. Riordan may in fact have been

under joint retainer to the Six Companies and the consulate in some of the cases he handled. Suggestive of the possibility is a retainer agreement of a later date preserved in Ch'ing diplomatic records. This agreement, dating from the year 1908, was entered into between the Six Companies, the consulate, and a San Francisco attorney by the name of Oliver Stidger. Under its terms Stidger pledged to represent Chinese residing in the country and Chinese seeking to land in the defense of their constitutional, legal, and treaty rights. The contract made clear that the Six Companies and consulate had in mind cases affecting the Chinese community as a whole, although it did permit him to handle private cases involving Chinese so long as these were first cleared with the Six Companies. For his efforts Stidger was to be paid $2,400 per year in twelve equal installments. "My goal," said the attorney in a letter acknowledging his gratitude at the appointment, "is to fight for the rights of the Chinese." And he invited the *hui-kuan*, the consulate, and Chinese merchants to contact him when appropriate cases arose. Lu Feng-shih, *Hsin Tsuan Yueh-chang ta-chuan* (New Edition of Treaties, Rules, Contracts) (Shanghai, 1909–10) 60:36–37.

19. *Morning Call*, Oct. 13, 1888, p. 2, col. 3.

20. In re Chae Chan Ping, 36 F. 431, 433–36 (C.C.N.D. Cal. 1888).

21. Ibid., p. 436.

22. He spoke of the measure as being "hastily passed." Elsewhere he said it was not the function of the courts "to abrogate an unsatisfactory law by arbitrarily refusing to enforce it." Ibid., pp. 436–37.

Judge Sawyer does not appear to have derived any great pleasure from the decision he handed down in *Chae Chan Ping*, viewing the case as one in which his hands were forced. "We found ourselves compelled to shut out the Chinese who arrived after October 1," he wrote to his friend Matthew Deady of Oregon a few days afterward. But in two cases that came before his court later in the month he did not feel similarly cabined and used his discretion to promote fairness for the Chinese. The first involved three Chinese laborers, residents of Washington Territory, who had purchased passage on an American steamship in Seattle for San Francisco and arrived in the latter city after the effective date of the Exclusion Act. During its voyage the ship had touched port at Victoria, British Columbia, but the three had not gone ashore. When the ship reached San Francisco the collector refused to allow them to land on the ground that they had gone through British waters and therefore had left the United States. They promptly sued out writs of habeas corpus in Judge Sawyer's court, and the matter came on quickly for hearing. Sawyer in a one-paragraph opinion ordered them discharged from custody, holding that they had at all times been within the jurisdiction of the United States and constructively within its territory. In re Tong Wah Sick, 36 F. 440 (C.C.N.D. Cal. 1888). A week later he reached a similar result in a habeas case involving Chinese seamen returning to San Francisco from a round-trip voyage to Panama. In re Jack Sen, 36 F. 441 (C.C.N.D. Cal. 1888). Sawyer was quite irritated with the way in which federal customs officials were enforcing the new legislation and gave vent to his feelings the day after the *Tong Wah Sick* case in the same letter to Deady referred to above. "It does seem as though the executive departments [sic] were determined to make our government as odious to the rest of the world as possible," he wrote. Lorenzo Sawyer to Deady, Oct. 18, 1888, Deady Papers, Oregon Historical Society Library, Portland.

23. *Evening Bulletin*, Oct. 15, 1888, p. 3, col. 5.
24. See, e.g., the Cherokee Tobacco Case, 78 U.S. (11 Wall.) 616 (1870).
25. See discussion of the case in chapter 6.
26. The Head Money Cases, 112 U.S. 580, 599 (1884).
27. 21 U.S. (8 Wheat.) 464 (1823).
28. Brief of Hoadly, Carter, p. 20, case file, Chae Chan Ping v. United States, 130 U.S. 581, U.S. Supreme Court Records and Briefs.
29. The Sinking Fund Cases, 99 U.S. 700, 718–19 (1878). See Brief of Hoadly, Carter, pp. 38–39; Brief of Carter, pp. 4–6 for the argument, case file, Chae Chan Ping v. United States, U.S. Supreme Court Records and Briefs.
30. Brief for the United States, p. 14, case file, Chae Chan Ping v. United States, U.S. Supreme Court Records and Briefs.
31. Chinese Exclusion Case, Chae Chan Ping v. United States, 130 U.S. 581, 600–2 (1889).
32. Ibid., pp. 606, 608.
33. Ibid., p. 609. Not much has changed in the past hundred years. Under modern American immigration law the government's promise to an alien that he or she may enter the country is treated in exactly the same way. Thus even an alien holding a visa may be denied entry to the country by immigration officials, and this decision is essentially unreviewable by the courts. 8 U.S.C. § 1225(b).
34. *Chae Chan Ping*, p. 610.
35. Memorandum of July 8, 1889, *Notes from the Chinese Legation.*
36. Procedural history taken from Wan Shing v. United States, 140 U.S. 424, 424–25 (1891) and from Wan Shing case file, Records and Briefs of the United States Supreme Court.
37. *Wan Shing*, pp. 427–28.
38. Ibid., p. 428.
39. *Chronicle*, Oct. 8, 1891, p. 6, col. 6.
40. In re Lau Ow Bew, 47 F. 578 (C.C.N.D. Cal. 1891).
41. Lau Ow Bew v. United States, 47 F. 641 (9th Cir. 1891).
42. Act of Mar. 3, 1891, ch. 517, 26 Stat. 826.
43. *Lau Ow Bew*, Petitioner, 141 U.S. 583 (1891).
44. Brief of Appellants, pp. 13–18, case file, Lau Ow Bew v. United States, 144 U.S. 47, U.S. Supreme Court Records and Briefs.
45. Ibid., pp. 7–8.
46. Lau Ow Bew v. United States, 144 U.S. 47, 59–60 (1892).
47. Ibid., p. 63.
48. Ibid., pp. 62–64.
49. For the text of the resolution mandating the investigation see *Congressional Record*, 51st Cong., 1st Sess., vol. 21, pp. 2139–40. The resolution did not specifically mention Chinese immigration.
50. See House of Representatives, Select Committee on Immigration and Naturalization, Report No. 4048, *Chinese Immigration* (and accompanying transcript of the hearings), 51st Cong., 2d Sess. See, e.g., testimony in the transcript of S. J. Ruddell, pp. 252ff.; Carleton Rickards, pp. 295ff.; Charles Garter, pp. 310ff.; Ward McAllister, pp. 315ff.; T. J. Phelps, 323ff.; Stephen Houghton, pp. 342ff. Ruddell, inspector of customs in San Francisco, expressed general satisfaction with the way in which the act was being implemented but did suggest that the law

ought to be amended to deny Chinese the right to sue out writs of habeas corpus, a suggestion that the subcommittee chairman bridled at; see p. 277.

51. House of Representatives, Report No. 4048, *Chinese Immigration*, 51st Cong., 2d Sess. The Scott Act of course permanently barred the immigration of Chinese laborers, but by its terms it technically applied only to returning immigrants, that is, Chinese laborers who had once resided in the United States. The only piece of federal legislation applying to new immigrants, if one may use that term, was the original Chinese Exclusion Act of 1882.

52. During the decade that the exclusion legislation had been in effect the Chinese population in the state of California had declined by about 2,500. (It had increased by about 2,000 in the United States as a whole.) See Sucheng Chan, *This Bittersweet Soil: The Chinese in California Agriculture, 1860–1910* (Berkeley: University of California Press, 1986), p. 43. This was commented upon by Senator John Sherman of Ohio during the debates. See *Congressional Record*, 52d Cong., 1st Sess., 23:3481.

53. Ibid., p. 3478.

54. See, e.g., H.R. 6185, 52d Cong., 1st Sess., *Congressional Record*, 23:2911.

55. House of Representatives, Report No. 255, to accompany H.R. 5809, 52d Cong., 1st Sess., p. 3.

56. Act of May 5, 1892, ch. 60, 27 Stat. 25.

57. Ibid., § 6.

58. Ibid., § 5.

59. Ibid., § 4.

60. Ibid., § 3.

61. The Geary Act was not the first legislative measure to provide for the registration of resident Chinese. On March 21, 1891, the state of California had enacted a measure with provisions similar to those that would later be included in the Geary Act. It required all Chinese living in the state to register and to pay a fee of $5 to obtain a certificate of residence. It also made it unlawful for any Chinese to enter the state. Act of Mar. 20, 1891, ch. 140, 1891 Cal. Stat. 185. No attempt seems to have been made to enforce the act on any large scale after it went into effect, and it faded into the background after passage of the Geary Act. In 1894 in Ex parte Ah Cue, 101 Cal. 197, the California Supreme Court in a curt opinion nullified the measure as an attempt by a state to exercise powers that belonged exclusively to the federal government.

62. Note from Minister Tsui to Secretary Blaine, Apr. 12, 1892, *Notes from the Chinese Legation*. See also Notes of Mar. 22 and Apr. 21.

63. Ibid., Note of May 5, 1892.

64. Ibid., Note of Nov. 7, 1892.

65. Riordan, it turned out, had been in consultation with the Six Companies for some time and had assured them that in his opinion the act was unconstitutional. See *Evening Bulletin*, Sept. 10, 1892, p. 3, col. 7.

66. *Evening Bulletin*, Sept. 10, 1892, p. 3, col. 7.

67. *Morning Call*, Sept. 20, 1892 p. 1, col. 4. A Chinese consular official, commenting on these actions by the *hui-kuan* leaders, remarked that they knew that, with these actions, they had in effect thrown down the gauntlet and would have to carry the struggle through to the end. See *Morning Call*, Sept. 21, 1892, p. 1, col. 5.

68. One Chinese commented to a reporter around this time: "For some reason

you people persist in pestering the Chinamen. . . . It is not enough that we are here but you now insist on labelling us. The next thing we know the government will be hanging red lanterns on us at night." *Morning Call,* Sept. 14, 1892, p. 8, col. 2.

69. The proclamation in Chinese, along with an English translation, was reproduced in the *Morning Call,* Sept. 20, 1892, p. 8, cols. 1–2.

70. *Morning Call,* Sept. 20, 1892, p. 8, col. 3. In explanation of the suggestion in the first proclamation that the Six Companies would seek to prevent anyone who refused to pay the $1 assessment from returning to China, the secretary told the *Call* reporter that the Six Companies had no power to prevent anyone from returning to China but that it would not offer any help to anyone who cooperated with the federal authorities.

71. Quoted in the *Morning Call,* Sept. 20, 1892, p. 8, cols. 1–2.

72. House of Representatives, Report No. 4048, *Chinese Immigration,* 51st Cong., 2d Sess., p. 399.

73. *Morning Call,* Sept. 14, 1892, p. 8, col. 1.

74. Professor Chan estimates that there were about three thousand Chinese living in the New York area in 1890. Chan, *This Bittersweet Soil,* p. 46.

75. *New York Times,* Aug. 21, 1892, p. 16, col. 1.

76. *Evening Bulletin,* Sept. 23, 1892, p. 2, col. 1.

77. "The New and Monstrous Anti-Chinese Bill," Ng Poon Chew Collection, Asian American Studies Library, University of California at Berkeley.

78. As an officer of the Chinese legation in Washington he had complained to the Department of State in March 1880 about the anti-Chinese legislation then being enacted by the California state legislature. See chapter 3.

79. See Hunt, *Making of a Special Relationship,* passim.

80. *New York Times,* Dec. 17, 1892, p. 8, col. 4.

81. *Evening Bulletin,* Jan. 27, 1893, p. 3, col. 6.

82. William Evarts as Senator had authored the Evarts Act, mentioned above, which had substantially reorganized the structure of the federal courts.

83. See *New York Times,* Mar. 18, 1893, p. 1, col. 4 and Mar. 19, 1893, p. 16, col. 5.

84. See *New York Times,* Mar. 18, 1893, p. 1. col. 4.

85. Tsui Kuo-yin to Walter Gresham, Mar. 13, 1893, in *Foreign Relations of the United States,* H.R. Exec. Doc., 53d Cong., 2d Sess., 1:245–46.

86. Ibid., Gresham to Tsui, Mar. 21, 1893, pp. 246–47. Tsui noted this omission in a letter to Gresham dated April 13. Ibid., p. 248.

87. See *Oriental,* Mar. 24, 1893. (The newspaper notice included another appeal for funds.) *Morning Call,* Apr. 1, 1893, p. 8, col. 1.

88. Procedural history taken from Statement of Facts, contained in Brief of Solicitor General, Fong Yue Ting v. United States, 149 U.S. 698 (1893), U.S. Supreme Court Records and Briefs; *New York Times,* May 6, 1893, p. 11, col. 3, and *Fong Yue Ting,* pp. 699–704.

89. This summary of the argument of counsel for the Chinese is taken from the account of oral argument before the Supreme Court published in the *New York Times,* May 11, 1893, p. 11, col. 1 and from the written briefs, which are to be found in Fong Yue Ting case file, Records and Briefs of the Supreme Court (on microfilm). On this first point see, especially, Brief of Choate, pp. 13ff.

90. Ibid. See, especially, Brief of Choate, pp. 58ff, Fong Yue Ting case file.

91. *Fong Yue Ting,* pp. 704–5.
92. Ibid., p. 707. There was an unnoticed irony in this statement. The Chinese, of course, were forbidden by federal law from becoming naturalized.
93. Ibid., p. 714.
94. Ibid., pp. 723–24.
95. Ibid., p. 730.
96. Ibid., pp. 731–32.
97. Ibid., p. 734.
98. Ibid., p. 737.
99. Ibid.
100. Ibid., p. 741.
101. Ibid., pp. 741–43.
102. Ibid., p. 744.
103. Ibid., pp. 747–750.
104. Ibid., p. 759.
105. Ibid., pp. 759–60.
106. Lung Yew, the Chinese consul general, to the Chinese minister, Sept. 6, 1893, *Notes from the Chinese Legation.*
107. According to the Department of the Treasury, 13,342 Chinese had registered under the Geary Act by May 5, 1893, leaving some 93,445 Chinese unregistered. Treasury estimated that some 10 percent of these were of the exempt classes and that it would cost upwards of $6 million to deport the remaining laborers to China. House Committee on Foreign Affairs, *Report to Accompany H.R. 3687,* 53d Cong., 1st Sess., p. 2.
108. Ibid., pp. 1–2.
109. Act of Nov. 3, 1893, ch. 14, 28 Stat. 7.
110. Act of Mar. 3, 1891, ch. 551, 26 Stat. 1084, §§ 7, 8.
111. Act of Aug. 18, 1894, ch. 301, 28 Stat. 372, 390.
112. 142 U.S. 651, 660 (1892).
113. Ibid., p. 660.
114. See Attorney General Olney's opinion of Apr. 6, 1894, and the telegram from Secretary of the Treasury J. G. Carlisle to various collectors of customs, Apr. 19, 1894. Copies of these documents accompany the letter of Apr. 24, 1894, from the Chinese legation in Washington to the State Department, *Notes from the Chinese Legation.*
115. Lee Kan v. United States, 62 F. 914 (9th Cir. 1894). This was the position ultimately taken by the Supreme Court of the United States. See Tom Hong v. United States, 193 U.S. 517 (1904).
116. Facts of the case taken from the statement of facts contained in the opinion, Lem Moon Sing v. United States, 158 U.S. 538, 539–41 (1895) and from the Transcript of Record contained in the Supreme Court case file.
117. See In re Panzara, 51 F. 275 (D.C. N.Y. 1892); In re Martorelli, 63 F. 437 (C.C.S.D. N.Y. 1894); In re Maiola, 67 F. 114 (C.C.S.D. N.Y. 1895).
118. In re Panzara, at 275.
119. Brief for Appellants, at pp. 9–14, Lem Moon Sing case file, U.S. Supreme Court Records and Briefs.
120. Ibid., pp. 4–8.
121. *Lem Moon Sing,* p. 541.

122. Ibid., pp. 545–47.

123. Ibid., pp. 547–48. The Court dismissed the appellant's attempt to use *Panzara* to support his claim with the curt comment that this case had been decided in 1892 and had no applicability to cases brought under the act of 1894. *Lem Moon Sing*, p. 549.

124. Ibid., pp. 549–50.

125. See chapter 6, p. 170.

126. And, indeed, as *Fong Yue Ting* made clear, even within the water's edge it had limited application to aliens.

127. The Chinese immigration cases have the dubious distinction of having laid the foundations of modern American immigration law. It is a body of law, as one scholar has put it, "radically insulated . . . from those fundamental norms of constitutional right, administrative procedure, and judicial role that animate the rest of our legal system." Peter H. Schuck, "The Transformation of Immigration Law," *Columbia Law Review* 84 (1984): 1.

128. 163 U.S. 228 (1896).

129. 169 U.S. 649 (1898).

130. Meanwhile the Chinese government had succeeded in negotiating an amendment to the 1880 treaty, containing terms somewhat more favorable to itself and certain of its nationals living in the United States. The convention, which went into force at the end of 1894, permitted Chinese laborers who had families or property valued at $1,000 or more in this country to leave the United States with a guaranteed right of return, provided they did so within a year. It also, interestingly, while recognizing the legitimacy of the registration provisions of the Geary Act, confirmed to the Chinese government a parallel right to register American laborers living in China. Convention Between the United States and China, Mar. 17, 1894, arts. II, V, 22 Stat. 1210, 1211–12.

CHAPTER NINE

1. Frederick Bee told the congressional subcommittee that visited the West Coast in the fall of 1890 that the city of San Francisco routinely spent thousands of dollars in cleaning other parts of the city but devoted no funds to cleaning the Chinese quarter. The Chinese spent $7,000 a year of their own money for that purpose, he said. House of Representatives, Report No. 4048, *Chinese Immigration*, 51st Cong., 2d Sess., p. 374.

2. *Herald*, Aug. 22, 1854, p. 2, col. 1.

3. *Daily Report*, May 27, 1880, p. 2, col. 2; Stockton *Evening Mail*, Jan. 19, 1886, p. 2, col. 4.

4. *Daily Report*, July 25, 1885, p. 4, col. 5. The full report can be found in Board of Supervisors, *San Francisco Municipal Reports for the Fiscal Year Ending June 30, 1885*, Appendix, pp. 164–214.

5. *Examiner*, Feb. 4, 1890, p. 4, col. 5. For the ordinance designating the area for offensive trades see Order 1587, § 2, *General Orders of the Board of Supervisors*, San Francisco, 1890, p. 17.

6. *Examiner*, Feb. 9, 1890, p. 2, col. 6.

7. See the *Evening Bulletin*, Feb. 9, 1890, p. 2, cols. 1–2; Feb. 12, 1890, p. 2, cols. 1–2. The *Bulletin* noted that the Bingham ordinance provided for the re-

moval of the Chinese to a part of the city they did not own and that they would have to rely on private landowners to sell or lease to them. Therein might lie the ultimate solution to the Chinese question, thought the paper. "No treaty compels any owner to lease land to Chinese if he does not want to do so. If the Chinese cannot get any land he must go." Feb. 12, 1890, p. 9, col. 2.

8. *Examiner*, Feb. 12, 1890, p. 6, col. 2.

9. Ibid. In 1882 the then city and county attorney had informed the board that such an action in his view would be unconstitutional. *Evening Post*, May 2, 1882, p. 1, col. 1.

10. See *Daily Alta California*, May 22, 1890, p. 8, col. 3.

11. *Morning Call*, May 14, 1890, p. 8, col. 4; The chief of police told a reporter for the *Examiner* that should the ordinance be upheld "you can state for me that I will do everything in my power to carry [it] out to the full extent." He said that the city jails in an emergency could accommodate up to 600 prisoners and he intended to keep them full. *Examiner*, May 13, 1890, p. 7, col. 1.

12. *Morning Call*, May 21, 1890, p. 3, col. 5; *Examiner*, May 21, 1890, p. 4, col. 5.

13. *Daily Alta California*, May 21, 1890, p. 4, col. 3; May 22, 1890, p. 8, col. 3. The *Alta* did, however, venture to predict that the city might have to pay a "very heavy bill of damages" on account of "the ridiculous attempt on the part of the author of the Bingham ordinance to pose as a great public benefactor."

14. *Daily Alta California*, May 22, 1890, p. 8, col. 3.

15. Blaine to Pung, May 27, 1890, *Papers Relating to the Foreign Relations of the United States*, H.R. Exec. Doc., 51st Cong., 2d Sess., 1:221 (1891). Pung's letter to Blaine is to be found at pp. 219–20.

16. Pung to Blaine, June 7, 1890, pp. 221–23.

17. Blaine to Pung, June 14, 1890, pp. 223–26.

18. Petition for Writ of Habeas Corpus, In re Lee Sing et al. case file, No. 10730, Record Group 21, Old Circuit Court, Civil Cases, National Archives, San Francisco Branch.

19. *Daily Alta California*, May 22, 1890, p. 8, col. 3.

20. Amendments to Return, In re Lee Sing et al. case file.

21. *Daily Alta California*, Aug. 19, 1890, p. 8, col. 1.

22. In re Lee Sing et al., 43 F. 359 (C.C.N.D. Cal. 1890), p. 360.

23. Ibid., p. 361.

24. Ibid.

25. Ibid., pp. 361–62.

26. 118 U.S. 356 (1886).

27. *Examiner*, Aug. 26, 1890, p. 4, col. 2, p. 6, col. 1.

28. Benno Schmidt, "Principle and Prejudice: The Supreme Court and Race Relations in the Progressive Era. Part 1: The Heyday of Jim Crow," *Columbia Law Review* 82 (1982): 500.

29. See chapter 7.

30. For a history of this movement see Roger Rice, "Residential Segregation by Law, 1910–1917," *Journal of Southern History* 34 (1968): 179–99.

31. 245 U.S. 60 (1917).

32. See Brief for Plaintiff-in-Error, pp. 40–41, Brief for Appellant, p. 25, Buchanan v. Warley case file, U.S. Supreme Court Records and Briefs. The thrust

of Storey's argument was that the ultimate purpose of the Louisville law was "to establish a Ghetto for the colored people of Louisville." Brief for Appellant, p. 14.

CHAPTER TEN

1. Thomas Butler, *Plague and Other Yersinia Infections* (New York: Plenum Medical Book Co., 1983), pp. 73–79.

2. L. F. Hirst, *The Conquest of Plague: A Study of the Evolution of Epidemiology* (Oxford: Clarendon Press, 1953), p. 29.

3. Ibid., pp. 111–14. In 1897 the French researcher P. L. Simond had suggested that the rat flea was the likely plague vector, but his views met little acceptance. An Indian commission established the correctness of Simond's hypothesis beyond any doubt by experiments conducted in Bombay in 1908. Ibid., pp. 152–75.

4. *Examiner*, Mar. 7, 1900, p. 4, col. 1.

5. On the history of quarantine see George Rosen, *A History of Public Health* (New York: M. C. Publications, 1958), pp. 63–69.

6. Act of May 27, 1796, ch. 3, 1 Stat. 474.

7. *Health and Quarantine Laws for the City and Harbor of San Francisco Relating to the Public Health,* San Francisco, 1885.

8. Hirst, *The Conquest of Plague*, p. 407.

9. See, e.g., *Examiner*, Mar. 7, 1900, p. 4, col. 1. The Examiner in doggerel bemoaned the dent the absence of Chinese would put in the housework industry:

> Scorn not the humble Chinaman
> Throw not his uses down
> For, as I live, we miss him when
> He stays in Chinatown
> When happy Yip and Yellow Sin
> Quit the domestic scene
> We have to do his work ourselves
> And damn the quarantine
>
> So ere's to you, yellow Hop Sing Fong
> We're sorry that you're took
> You're a poor benighted 'eathen, but
> A first-class fancy cook.
> They say your deeds are bloody and
> Your morals are unclean
> But goodness how we miss you
> When you're held in quarantine.
>
> San Francisco *Examiner*, Mar. 9, 1900, p. 6, col. 4.

10. *Chronicle*, Mar. 8, 1900, p. 6, col. 4.

11. *Chung Sai Yat Po*, Mar. 8, 1900. I am grateful to Sucheng Chan for making available to me summaries in English of articles published by this leading Chinese daily during the plague controversy.

12. *Record-Union*, Mar. 8, 1900, p. 1, col. 7.

13. *Chung Sai Yat Po*, Mar. 8, 1900.
14. *Chronicle*, Mar. 8, 1900, p. 7, col. 5.
15. Ibid., p. 1, cols. 2–4.
16. *Examiner*, Mar. 9, 1900, p. 9, cols. 1–2.
17. *Examiner*, Mar. 8, 1900, p. 1, cols. 2–4.
18. Ralph C. Williams, *The United States Public Health Service, 1798–1950* (Washington, D.C.: Commissioned Officers Association of the United States Public Health Service, 1951), pp. 477–79.
19. Walter Wyman, "The Bubonic Plague," Treasury Department, Doc. No. 2165 (Washington, D.C.: Government Printing Office, 1900) [hereafter Wyman, "Pamphlet on Plague"]. The pamphlet was an expanded version of an article by Wyman on the same subject that appeared in the Annual Report of the Marine Hospital Service for Fiscal Year 1897.
20. On medical developments during the second half of the nineteenth century and on advances in public health see Rosen, *A History of Public Health*, passim.
21. Wyman, "Pamphlet on Plague," p. 10.
22. Ibid., p. 15.
23. Ibid., pp. 15–16.
24. Ibid., pp. 11–13.
25. Ibid., pp. 16–17.
26. Ibid., pp. 16–17; 19–24.
27. On the plague in India see Hirst, *The Conquest of Plague*, pp. 115–20, 416–17. For Wyman, and doubtless for many others, bacteriology's discovery of the plague bacillus made fully clear the way to subdue the disease. In fact, it was but the first step in a long and arduous process. The mode of plague transmission is extremely complex and controlling plague epidemics has proven to be equally complex. As one of the greatest modern authorities on bubonic plague wrote in the mid-twentieth century, "There is no ready-made stereotyped anti-plague procedure." Hirst, *The Conquest of Plague*, p. 422.
28. Gassaway to Wyman, Mar. 7, 8, 1890. The original or original copies of this telegram and most subsequent telegraphic correspondence between Marine Hospital Service personnel on the scene and the surgeon general's office in Washington referred to in this article are to be found in National Archives, Record Group 90, U.S. Public Health Service, Central File 1897–1923, No. 5608 [hereafter National Archives, Record Group 90]. Much of the telegraphic correspondence is also reproduced in *Annual Report of the Supervising Surgeon General of the Marine-Hospital Service of the United States For the Fiscal Year 1900* [hereafter *1900 Annual Report*] at pp. 530ff. The Gassaway telegrams to Wyman of March 7, 8 are to be found in *1900 Annual Report*, pp. 530–31.
29. National Archives, Record Group 90; *1900 Annual Report*, p. 531.
30. On March 14 Gassaway acknowledged to Wyman receipt of one box of "antipest serum." On March 17 he acknowledged receipt of a box of Haffkine's. National Archives, Record Group 90. On March 8 Gassaway told a reporter that three hundred bottles of "antiseptic and prophylactic serum" had been shipped. *Examiner*, Mar. 8, 1900, p. 1, cols. 2–4.
31. *Chronicle*, Mar. 10, 1900, p. 7, cols. 1–3.
32. Ibid.
33. *Chronicle*, Mar. 10, 1900, p. 6, col. 2.
34. Ibid., p. 7, cols. 2–3.

35. *Examiner,* Mar. 12, 1900, p. 2, cols. 1–3.
36. *Chronicle,* Mar. 12, 1900, p. 10, col 4.
37. Accounts of board meetings and actions taken from *Chronicle,* Mar. 13, 1900, p. 12, cols. 4–5; *Examiner,* Mar. 13, 1900, p. 7, cols. 3–5.
38. *Examiner,* Mar. 13, 1900, p. 7, cols. 3–5.
39. Ibid.
40. *Chronicle,* Mar. 13, 1900, p. 12, col. 5.
41. Ibid.
42. *Examiner,* Mar. 14, 1900, p. 6, col. 1.
43. *Examiner,* Mar. 23, 1900, p. 7, col. 3.
44. From reports in the *Examiner* and Sacramento *Record-Union* mid-March, 1900. See also, Vernon B. Link, *A History of Plague in the United States of America* (Washington, D.C.: Government Printing Office, 1955), p. 3.
45. Hirst, *The Conquest of Plague,* p. 117.
46. Even at the time the inefficacy of these kinds of measures was recognized by some. In 1898 Hankin, Simond, and other bacteriologists had pointed out that plague bacteria survived outside the body only for the shortest time, at least in tropical climates. See Hirst, *The Conquest of Plague,* p. 117. In Australia, where a true plague epidemic was raging contemporaneous with the San Francisco events, government authorities, thanks in part to the discovery by Sydney doctors of a plague bacillus in the stomachs of rat fleas, issued a circular warning plague-infested towns that cleansing and disinfecting could not stamp out the disease. They urged instead that measures be aimed at destroying rats. This was reported in the *Examiner,* May 18, 1900, p. 3, col. 7.
47. A view shared by health officer O'Brien. Throughout the epidemic Caucasian officials often expressed the belief that the leaders of the Chinese community were engaged in a conspiracy to conceal plague cases. To be sure the Chinese were very skittish about dealing with Caucasian officials, and there may have been instances where individual Chinese sought to conceal cases of sickness. But there is no credible evidence of a conspiracy among the leadership.
48. *Record-Union,* Mar. 23, 1900, p. 6. cols. 1–3.
49. *Record-Union,* Mar. 24, 1900, p. 3, col. 1.
50. *Chronicle,* Mar. 27, 1900, p. 6, col. 2.
51. Several weeks later, in mid-April, the Manufacturers and Producers Association of San Francisco adopted a resolution urging the local press to be cautious about its reports on the plague situation in San Francisco.
52. See series of telegrams from Gassaway to Wyman in National Archives, Record Group 90; *1900 Annual Report,* p. 537.
53. *1900 Annual Report,* p. 538. A copy of the telegram is also to be found in the documents submitted by the defendants in the Wong Wai v. Williamson case file, No. 12937, Record Group 21, Old Circuit Court, Civil Cases, National Archives, San Francisco Branch.
54. I have been unable to find any documents throwing light on Wyman's discussions with the Chinese minister or on what they agreed to.
55. J. Taylor, Haffkine's Plague Vaccine, The Indian Medical Research Memoirs, No. 27, 1933, pp. 3–7. For an account of Haffkine's life and work see Selman Waksman, *The Brilliant and Tragic Life of W. M. W. Haffkine, Bacteriologist* (New Brunswick, N.J.: Rutgers University Press, 1964).
56. See A. H. Moorhead, "Plague in India," *The Military Surgeon* 22, No. 3

(1980), reprinted in F. M. Todd, *Eradicating Plague from San Francisco,* Report of the Citizens' Health Committee (San Francisco: C. A. Murdock & Co., 1909), p. 279; See also J. W. Cell, "Anglo-Indian Medical Theory and the Origins of Segregation in West Africa," *American Historical Review* 91 (1986): 307, 327.

57. See K. F. Meyer et al., "Plague Immunization: Past and Present Trends," *The Journal of Infectious Diseases* 129 (1974): 513.

58. On India see J. K. Codon, *The Bombay Plague* (Bombay: The Education Society, 1900), pp. 1–50. Several hundreds of persons living in the Australian state of Victoria availed themselves of the opportunity to be inoculated with the vaccine in early 1900. See R. J. Bull, "The Practical Application of Haffkine's Plague Prophylactic in Victoria," *Intercolonial Medical Journal of Australia* 5 (1900): 148–50.

59. Hirst thinks that the vaccine probably was fairly effective. See Hirst, *The Conquest of Plague,* p. 417. Butler is much more skeptical. Butler, *Plague,* p. 199. One of the twentieth century's leading researchers on plague immunology was K. F. Meyer of the University of California. Some sense of the historical controversy concerning the efficacy of plague vaccines can be had from reading his "Plague Immunization I. Past and Present Trends," *The Journal of Infectious Diseases* 129 (1974) and "Effectiveness of Live or Killed Plague Vaccines in Man," *Bulletin of the World Health Organization* 42 (1970): 653.

60. Butler, *Plague,* p. 199.

61. All details of Kinyoun's narrative are taken from his letter to Wyman of June 11, 1900, in *1900 Annual Report,* pp. 558–61.

62. Ibid., p. 559.

63. Ibid.

64. Ibid. Gassaway's own telegraphic report of the meeting to Wyman reads: "Chinese are to be inoculated by Burlesque Physicians and will present themselves at ten o'clock on morning twentieth for that purpose. Each will be furnished certificate when inoculated. Conference very friendly. Newspapers keeping affairs quiet and no excitement among citizens." National Archives, Record Group 90. Marine Hospital Service telegrams often employed code when speaking of the plague outbreak. "Burlesque" here meant the San Francisco Board of Health.

65. It is not clear from Kinyoun's account whether the Chinese leaders fully understood the extent of what Wyman was contemplating, that is to say not just a massive, albeit voluntary, inoculation campaign, but a campaign that already had elements of coercion built into it.

66. A handwritten copy of the telegram is to be found in the Wong Wai v. Williamson case file. It is not reproduced in the *1900 Annual Report.*

67. Copy of the resolution in *Wong Wai* case file.

68. Kinyoun to Wyman, May 19, 1900, *1900 Annual Report,* p. 540, and *Record-Union,* May 20, 1900, p. 1, col. 4. The extension of the inoculation requirement to Japanese as well as Chinese seeking to leave the city caused a major diplomatic row between the State Department and Japan's diplomatic representatives in the United States. It is documented in National Archives, Record Group 90. This correspondence is especially interesting in view of the fact that certain Caucasian commentators claimed that the greater willingness of Japanese to submit to inoculation demonstrated the superiority of that nationality over the backward Chinese. See *Record-Union,* May 20, 1900, p. 1, col. 4; and May 24, 1900, p. 8, col. 1.

69. Minutes of California State Board of Health, in *Wong Wai* case file.

70. The full text of the regulation promulgated by Secretary of the Treasury L. J. Gage, and distributed as Department Circular 93 (1900) to all medical officers of the Marine Hospital Service and to state and local health authorities read as follows:

> In accordance with the provisions of the act of March 27, 1890, the following regulations, additional to existing Interstate Quarantine Regulations, are hereby promulgated to prevent the introduction of plague into any one State or Territory or the District of Columbia, from another State or Territory or the District of Columbia:
>
> 1. During the existence of plague at any point in the United States the Surgeon-General of the Marine Hospital Service is authorized to forbid the sale or donation of transportation by common carrier to Asiatics or other races particularly liable to the disease.
> 2. No common carrier shall accept for transportation any person suffering with plague or any article infected therewith, nor shall common carriers accept for transportation any class of persons who may be designated by the Surgeon-General of the Marine Hospital Service as being likely to convey the risk of plague contagion to other communities, and said common carriers shall be subject to inspection.
> 3. The body of any person who has died of plague shall not be transported except in an hermetically sealed coffin and by consent of the local health office, in addition to the local representative of the Marine Hospital Service. Wherever possible, such bodies should be cremated.

The Marine Hospital Service circular is dated May 22, 1900, but it appears that the Treasury regulation was actually issued on May 21.

71. Act of Mar. 27, 1890, ch. 51, 26 Stat. 31. The statute authorized the president, whenever it should be made to appear to his satisfaction that cholera, yellow fever, smallpox, or plague existed and threatened to spread across state or territorial lines, to cause the secretary of the treasury to promulgate such rules and regulations as would, in his judgment, be necessary to stop the spread.

72. According to Kinyoun the entire trouble was due to white physicians who went about the Chinese quarter spreading false rumors about the vaccine. Kinyoun to Wyman, *1900 Annual Report*, p. 559.

73. "What We Should Do About Inoculation," *Chung Sai Yat Po*, May 18, 1900.

74. "The Background of Vaccination," *Chung Sai Yat Po*, May 19, 1900.

75. National Archives, Record Group 90. Consul Ho sent the following separate cable to his minister: "Health officials want the Chinese to be inoculated to guard against the plague. Chinese generally unwilling. Great consternation. They say there is no plague and want to fight it out. Did all I can." Ibid. The Chinese minister passed these on to Surgeon General Wyman with a request that he wire his officers in San Francisco to "use more tact and discretion so as to avoid complications." Ibid.

76. "The Background of Vaccination," *Chung Sai Yat Po*, May 19, 1900.

77. See accounts of the first day's events in the *Record-Union*, May 20, 1900,

p. 1, col. 4. Undoubtedly another factor, besides apprehension about the vaccine's experimental character, contributing to Chinese reluctance to undergo inoculation was the lack, to their minds, of any apparent pressing necessity for such an extreme measure. To the lay mind, the Chinese included, no doubt, plague was a disease that spread like wildfire and, if it existed in San Francisco, should have been affecting dozens of victims daily. But the health authorities were talking about a relative handful of cases spread over several months. And indeed at the time the inoculation campaign began there were no existing cases under treatment. This made it difficult for the Chinese, and many Caucasians as well, to believe that plague existed at all, notwithstanding the very strong bacteriological evidence in the individual cases mentioned. On May 23, for example, *Chung Sai Yat Po* editorialized that it was "ridiculously impossible" to believe that so few people would have died over such a long period of time if a true plague epidemic existed.

78. *Chung Sai Yat Po,* May 22, 1900, p. 8, cols. 1–2.

79. "Strike Goes On," *Chung Sai Yat Po,* May 21, 1900.

80. *Record-Union,* May 22, 1900, p. 8, cols. 1–2.

81. "A Notice Given by the Wicked Health Officers," *Chung Sai Yat Po,* May 21, 1900.

82. *Record-Union,* May 22, 1900, p. 8, cols. 1–2.

83. "Zhao and Shen's Case Is a Warning to Us," *Chung Sai Yat Po,* May 23, 1900.

84. Complaint, paras. III, IV, *Wong Wai* case file. A companion case on behalf of Japanese plaintiffs was filed by the same law firm at the same time; see Obata, Negoro et al. v. Williamson, No. 12938. It seems reasonable to believe that there must have been consultation between the Chinese and Japanese communities about the bringing of these test cases. The court's decision in *Wong Wai* (described below) made it unnecessary to decide the *Obata* case.

85. Complaint, paras. V–VII, *Wong Wai* case file.

86. Ibid., para. VIII.

87. Ibid., para. XI.

88. Ibid., pp. 7–8.

89. In *Wong Wai* case file.

90. Though it was not cited in the complaint, the authority for federal judges to issue ex parte interlocutory injunctions was to be found in Section 718 of the Revised Statutes of the United States of 1875.

91. *Record-Union,* May 25, 1900, p. 8, col. 3.

92. *Chronicle,* May 26, 1900, p. 9, cols. 1–3.

93. On the Chinese Empire Reform Association see Michael Hunt, *The Making of A Special Relationship: The United States and China to 1914* (New York: Columbia University Press, 1983), pp. 251–53 and Shih-shan Henry Tsai, *China and the Overseas Chinese in the United States, 1868–1911* (Fayetteville, Ark.: University of Arkansas Press, 1983), pp. 129–30.

94. *Record-Union,* May 26, 1900, p. 7, cols. 1–2.

95. Wong Wai v. Williamson, 103 F. 1, 4 (C.C.N.D. Cal. 1900).

96. The account of the oral argument that follows is drawn from newspaper reports in the *Chronicle,* May 26, 1900, p. 9 cols. 1–3; *Examiner,* May 26, 1900, p. 2, col. 2; and *Record-Union,* May 26, 1900, p. 7, cols. 1–2.

97. *Chronicle,* May 26, 1900, p. 9, cols. 1–3. The "exclusion act" referred to was presumably the original one, passed in 1882.

98. New York City had established its metropolitan board of health in 1866. On the history of public health bodies see Rosen, *A History of Public Health.*

99. Abeel v. Clark, 84 Cal. 226 (1890). The United States Supreme Court eventually itself took the same position. See Jacobson v. Massachusetts, 197 U.S. 11 (1905).

100. See, e.g., Blue v. Beach, 56 N.E. 89 (1900).

101. W. W. Morrow, speech on "Chinese Immigration" delivered at the dinner of the Merchants Association of Boston, Dec. 29, 1886, in *Notable Speeches by Notable Speakers of the Greater West,* ed. H. Wagner (San Francisco: Whitaker & Ray Co., 1902), pp. 223–24.

102. See, e.g., In re Quan Gin, 61 F. 395 (N.D. Cal. 1894); In re Yee Lung 61 F. 641 (N.D. Cal. 1894).

103. In re Tom Yum, 64 F. 485 (N.D. Cal. 1894). "Ultimately" is the key word. In its first pass at the question the Supreme Court ruled that even when a Chinese person seeking entry claimed to be a citizen, immigration officers had the final authority to determine the person's right to enter the country and that that decision was completely unreviewable by the courts. Ju Toy v. United States, 198 U.S. 253 (1905). Three years later, however, in Chin Yow v. United States, 208 U.S. 8 (1908) the Court ruled that the writ of habeas corpus was available to review these decisions if there was a claim that the administrative hearing that led to it had been fundamentally unfair. If the habeas petitioner could show that the administrative hearing had been unfair, he or she could get a hearing on the merits of the claim before the court. Subsequent Supreme Court decisions chipped away further at the powers of immigration officers in cases involving claims of citizenship.

104. Wong Wai v. Williamson, 103 F. 1, 5 (C.C.N.D. Cal. 1900).

105. Ibid., pp. 8–9.

106. *Wong Wai,* p. 7

107. Ibid., p. 6.

108. Ibid., pp. 7–8. Wyman's original telegram of March 6, 1900, had made a distinction between Haffkine's vaccine and Yersin's serum, but no evidence was presented to the court that such a distinction was being made in the inoculation campaign then underway. The court did not note one other curious feature of the inoculation campaign. Apparently a single injection with Haffkine's vaccine was enough to obtain a certificate and free one from the supervision and control of the health authorities. However, the established medical wisdom at the time was that a single injection would confer no lasting immunity but needed to be followed by a second one if the procedure was to be efficacious.

109. Ibid., pp. 9–10. As authorities for the proposition, he cited *Ho Ah Kow* and *In re Lee Sing.*

110. Coombs to Attorney General, May 28, 1900, National Archives, Record Group 90.

111. Ibid., May 31, 1900.

112. Several out-of-state newspapers carried stories about the San Francisco plague situation. The May 27 issue of the New York *Herald* devoted the whole of page one of its sixth section and more to coverage of the worldwide plague pan-

demic. The banner headline ran "Bubonic Plague: Life's Most Awful Enemy: It Has Ravaged Continents and Decimated Populations, Finally Securing a Foothold in the United States." The story featured interviews with the prominent New York physicians Dr. George Schrady, editor of the *Medical Record* and Dr. A. H. Doty, health officer of the Port of New York. Notwithstanding the headline, neither expressed great concern about the plague reports emanating from San Francisco.

113. Minutes of the California State Board of Health meeting, May 21, 1900, can be found in the *Wong Wai* case file. See also *Record-Union,* May 22, 1900, p. 8, cols. 1–2.

114. Account of California State Board of Health meeting May 28, 1900, taken from San Francisco *Morning Call,* May 29, 1900, p. 1, cols. 2–3 and p. 2, cols. 2–3.

115. Account of San Francisco Board of Health meeting based on story appearing in *Examiner,* May 29, 1900, p. 12, col. 3.

116. *Chronicle,* May 30, 1900, p. 9, col. 5. According to the *Examiner,* a reporter for a Chinese newspaper, several Chinese merchants, and Thomas Riordan, attorney for the Six Companies and the consulate, were present at this meeting. *Examiner,* May 30, 1900, p. 3, col. 1.

117. *Morning Call,* May 30, 1900, p. 2, cols. 3–4.

118. For text of the ordinance see Jew Ho v. Williamson case file, No. 12940, Record Group 21, National Archives, San Francisco Branch.

119. *Examiner,* May 30, 1900, p. 3, cols. 1–2.

120. *Chronicle,* May 30, 1900, p. 9, col. 5.

121. Ibid.

122. *Morning Call,* May 30, 1900, p. 2, col. 4.

123. *Examiner,* May 30, 1900, p. 3, col. 3.

124. *Record-Union,* May 31, 1900, p. 8, col. 4.

125. *Examiner,* May 31, 1900, p. 3, cols. 5–6.

126. Ibid.

127. *Chronicle,* May 30, 1900, p. 9, col. 5.

128. *Examiner,* June 1, 1900, p. 6, cols. 1–2.

129. *Examiner,* June 3, 1900, p. 26, col. 1. These remarks were specifically directed at Ho's request that the city assume responsibility for provisioning Chinatown.

130. *Morning Call,* May 30, 1900, p. 6, col. 1.

131. Ibid., May 29, 1900, p. 1. *Chung Sai Yat Po* also interpreted Schrady as flatly denying that there was (or presumably ever had been) any outbreak of bubonic plague in Chinatown. See "No Evidence to Produce," May 30, 1900.

132. *Morning Call,* May 31, 1900, p. 1, cols. 1–3.

133. Ibid., June 2, 1900, p. 1.

134. Ibid., June 1, 1900, p. 2, cols. 1–2.

135. Ibid., May 31, 1900, p. 6, cols. 1–2.

136. Ibid., p. 1, cols. 1–3.

137. "Interview with the New York Doctor," *Chung Sai Yat Po,* May 31, 1900.

138. *Morning Call,* May 31, 1900, p. 1, col. 7.

139. *Examiner,* May 31, 1900, p. 3, col. 3.

140. Ibid., June 1, 1900, p. 3, col. 5.

141. See accounts of board meeting in *Examiner,* June 1, 1900, p. 3, col. 3; *Record-Union,* June 1, 1900, p. 8, col. 1. Text of the resolution in telegram from U.S. Senator George Perkins to Secretary of War Elihu Root, June 2, 1900, National Archives, Record Group 90.

142. See telegrams from Major General Shafter to Adjutant General, May 22, 1900; Kinyoun to Wyman, May 23, 1900; in National Archives, Record Group 90.

143. "Tents Are To Be Put Up," *Chung Sai Yat Po,* June 1, 1900.

144. "An Emergency Meeting to Stop Harsh Treatment," *Chung Sai Yat Po,* June 1, 1900.

145. *Chronicle,* June 2, 1900, p. 9, cols. 1–4.

146. It is difficult to gauge exactly how much hostility may have existed between the Empire Reform Association and the Six Companies. It is significant that the Reform Association used a lawyer, Samuel Shortridge, who often worked for the Six Companies. However, later in the quarantine crisis a Reform Association orator was heard accusing the Six Companies of conniving with the city authorities to maintain the quarantine. *Examiner,* June 3, 1900, p. 14, col. 5.

147. *Chronicle,* June 2, 1900, p. 9, cols. 1–4. The victim had clearly died of plague.

148. *Record-Union,* June 3, 1900, p. 5, col. 4.

149. *Chronicle,* June 2, 1900, p. 9, cols. 1–4.

150. Telegram from Consul Ho to Minister Wu T'ing-fang, June 4, 1900, attached to letter from Acting Secretary of State David Hill to the Secretary of the Treasury, June 5, 1900, National Archives, Record Group 90.

151. Telegram from Chue Yet, Chinese Merchants Exchange, to Chinese minister in Washington, June 4, 1900, attached to Hill letter cited above.

152. Both the *Examiner,* June 4, 1900, p. 3, cols. 1–2 and *Morning Call,* June 5, 1900, p. 12, col. 2, attributed the motivation for the stricter measures to pressure from merchants.

153. *Chronicle,* June 5, 1900, p. 7, cols. 3–4. See also Ibid.

154. *Morning Call,* June 5, 1900, p. 12, col. 2.

155. Scanning the pages of the June 5 *Examiner,* one would have noticed that Texas Health Officer Blount, contradicting as it were his previous promises, had stated the previous day in Texas that he would not recommend the lifting of the quarantine on California goods until the San Francisco authorities could give him assurance that Chinatown "was completely isolated and thoroughly neutralized." The only way to accomplish this, he said, was to remove all Chinese from "the infected quarter" and destroy it. *Examiner,* June 5, 1900, p. 3, cols. 6–7.

156. *Record-Union,* June 5, 1900, p. 8, col. 1.

157. *Morning Call,* June 6, 1900, p. 3, cols. 3–5.

158. On June 4 an *Examiner* journalist who had been allowed to visit the infected district reported, "Men who are accustomed to working by the day are penniless and hungry. . . . Crowds of these men roam the street sullen and desperate." He noted that the wealthier Chinese were growing daily more concerned. *Examiner,* June 5, 1900, p. 3, cols. 2–3.

159. *Chronicle,* June 4, 1900, p. 10, cols. 5–6.

160. Complaint, paras. V, XIII, *Jew Ho* case file.

161. Ibid., para. XVII.
162. The argument here was similar to that made to and accepted by the U.S. Supreme Court in Yick Wo v. Hopkins, 118 U.S. 356 (1886).
163. Complaint, para. VI, *Jew Ho* case file.
164. Ibid., para. XVI.
165. Ibid., paras. VIII, IX.
166. Ibid., para. XI.
167. Ibid., para. VII.
168. Ibid., para. XI.
169. Ibid., para. VIII.
170. Ibid., para. XVIII.
171. *Morning Call,* June 6, 1900, p. 3, cols. 3–4.
172. *Chronicle,* June 8, 1900, p. 12, col. 1.
173. Answer to Complaint, paras. III, IV, *Jew Ho* case file.
174. Ibid., para. VI.
175. Ibid.
176. Ibid., para. IV.
177. Ibid., para. X.
178. Ibid., para. VII
179. Ibid., para. XI.
180. Ibid., para. XVI.
181. 123 U.S. 623 (1887).
182. See Jew Ho v. Williamson, 103 F. 10, 16–17 (C.C.N.D. Cal. 1900).
183. *Examiner,* June 14, 1900, p. 2, cols. 3–4.
184. Affidavit of Dr. Ernest Pillsbury in *Jew Ho* case file.
185. Telegram from U.S. Secretary of State John Hay to Governor Gage, May 31, 1900, in *Appendix to the Report of the Special Health Commissioners Appointed by the Governor to Confer with the Federal Authorities at Washington Respecting the Alleged Existence of Bubonic Plague in California,* Sacramento, 1901, p. 15.
186. Telegram from Governor Gage to Secretary of State John Hay, June 13, 1900, *Appendix to the Report,* pp. 15–17. Concurring in the governor's conclusion that bubonic plague did not exist were several physicians and a number of prominent merchants and bankers.
187. *Jew Ho,* pp. 16–17.
188. 152 U.S. 133. It is interesting that in *Lawton* among examples of legitimate exercises of police power cited by the court was the compulsory vaccination of children.
189. *Jew Ho,* p. 17.
190. Ibid., pp. 18–20.
191. Ibid., p. 20.
192. Ibid., pp. 22–23.
193. Ibid., p. 23.
194. Ibid.
195. Ibid., p. 24.
196. Ibid. Having already disposed of the issue before the court Morrow went on at some length (and unwisely it would seem) to discourse upon the question of whether the plague existed at all in San Francisco. He noted that this had nothing

to do with the outcome of the case, that the medical testimony was conflicting, and that the court was not being called upon to decide the question, but, having said all of that, he could not resist voicing his own personal view that the plague had not existed and did not then exist in San Francisco. Ibid., pp. 24–26.

197. Ibid., pp. 26–27.

198. According to the report in the *Examiner,* June 16, 1900, p. 5, cols. 1–2. The remark was not in the report of the decision that appeared later in the Federal Reporter.

199. *Examiner,* June 16, 1900, p. 5, cols. 1–2.

200. Ibid.

201. Ibid.

202. Ibid.

203. Except where otherwise indicated the chronicle of events in this epilogue is taken from Link, *A History of Plague in the United States,* pp. 5–11.

204. *Report of the Government Commission on the Existence of Plague in San Francisco,* reprinted in *Occidental Medical Times* 15 (4): 102–3 (April 1901).

205. Ibid., p. 117.

206. W. M. Dickie, "Plague in California, 1900–1925," pamphlet reprinted from *Proceedings of the Conference of State and Provincial Health Authorities of North America* (1926), pp. 30–32.

207. See F. M. Todd, *Eradicating the Plague,* passim. It will be noted that, notwithstanding the focus of the authorities on the killing of rats and the rat-proofing of buildings, this plague episode claimed a large number of victims, thus illustrating how difficult a disease plague is to fight.

CONCLUSION

1. By 1900 approximately half of the Chinese in the United States were living outside of California.

2. Mainly though not exclusively. As noted earlier (see chapter 5) the Chinese community in 1902 brought an unsuccessful challenge against San Francisco's practice of segregating Chinese schoolchildren.

3. 208 U.S. 8 (1908).

4. In a case decided twelve years later, Kwock Jan Fat v. White, 253 U.S. 454 (1920), the Supreme Court, following the principles laid down in *Chin Yow,* ordered a Chinese person admitted to the United States on the grounds that federal immigration officials had disregarded evidence plainly relevant to his claim of citizenship. "It is better that many Chinese immigrants should be improperly admitted," said the Court, "than that one natural born citizen of the United States should be permanently excluded from his country."

5. Board of Supervisors, *San Francisco Municipal Reports for the Fiscal Year Ending June 30, 1885,* Appendix, p. 209.

6. Sybille van der Sprenkel, *Legal Institutions of Manchu China: A Sociological Analysis* (London: The Athlone Press, 1962), p. 78.

7. Truax v. Raich, 239 U.S. 33, 41 (1915). The words are cited with approval by Justice Harry Blackmun in his dissenting opinion in Cabell v. Chavez-Salido, 454 U.S. 447, 450 (1982).

8. Benno Schmidt, "Principle and Prejudice: The Supreme Court and Race

Relations in the Progressive Era. Part I: The Heyday of Jim Crow," *Columbia Law Review* 82 (1982): 456.

9. 304 U.S. 144 (1938); see especially footnote 4 of the opinion. Robert Cover, "The Origin of Judicial Activism in the Protection of Minorities," *Yale Law Journal* 91 (1982): 1294–95. The statement may have greater force if restricted to the Supreme Court alone, but see Benno Schmidt, "Principle and Prejudice," arguing the decisions of the White court during the progressive era represent an earlier instance of judicial solicitude for minorities.

10. In December 1884 Judge Sawyer reported with obvious pride and satisfaction to his colleague on the federal bench, Matthew Deady, that he had received a letter from a faculty member at the University of Wisconsin commending him for "maintaining the rights of the Chinese with courage and energy in opposition to a strong current of popular clamor." He commented to Deady, "I guess time will bring us out about right." Lorenzo Sawyer to Matthew Deady, Dec. 22, 1884, Matthew Deady Papers, Oregon Historical Society, Portland.

11. On the emergence of classical American immigration law in the late nineteenth century see Peter H. Schuck, "The Transformation of Immigration Law," *Columbia Law Review* 84 (1984): 1.

12. "Preoccupying" is the key word. This is in no way meant to suggest that the Chinese ceased to be victims of Caucasian discrimination. Far from it. Discrimination against the Chinese, official and unofficial, continued for many years afterward.

13. Interestingly, if somewhat contradictorily, the report declared that Chinese labor had never really been a threat to the Caucasian laboring classes. California State Board of Control, *California and the Oriental* (Sacramento: State Printing Office, 1920), p. 101.

14. *California and the Oriental*, p. 14.

15. Immigration and Nationality Act of 1924, ch. 190, 43 Stat. 153, 162, § 13(c).

Subject Index

Index of Cases

Compositor:	Maple-Vail Manufacturing Group
Text:	10/13 Aldus
Display:	Aldus
Printer:	Maple-Vail Manufacturing Group
Binder:	Maple-Vail Manufacturing Group